The
French
Quarter

From *L'Illustration*

THE WHITE LEAGUE RIOTS IN 1874

The
French
Quarter

AN INFORMAL HISTORY OF THE
NEW ORLEANS UNDERWORLD

Herbert Asbury

THUNDER'S MOUTH PRESS
NEW YORK

THE FRENCH QUARTER: AN INFORMAL HISTORY OF THE NEW ORLEANS
UNDERWORLD

Copyright © 1936, 2003 by Alfred A. Knopf, Inc.

Published by
Thunder's Mouth Press
161 William Street, 16th Floor
New York, NY 10038

Library of Congress Cataloging-in-Publication Data is available.

ISBN 1-56025-494-7

9 8 7 6 5 4 3 2 1

Printed in the United States of America
Distributed by Publishers Group West

TO HELEN

AUTHOR'S NOTE

FOR ASSISTANCE in gathering material for this book I am greatly indebted to many residents of New Orleans, among them Robert J. Usher of the Howard Library, Mrs. E. D. Friedrichs of the City Archives, Faser Wood, Robert G. Polack, J. S. W. Harmanson, Casey Jones, Albert Goldstein, Lyle Saxon, Captain Harvey O. Gregson of the Police Department, Charles J. Ferrier, George Healey, Jr., Gwen Bristow, Bruce Manning, Meigs O. Frost, and John McClure.

I am especially grateful to Roark and Mary Rose Bradford, and to James K. and Dorothy Feibleman, for many kindnesses; and to the publishers of the *Times-Picayune* for placing at my disposal the files of the *Times*, the *Picayune*, the *States*, and the *Times-Picayune*.

H. A.

Canada Lake, New York
May 1936

CONTENTS

I · NOUVELLE-ORLÉANS   3

II · IN THE DAYS OF THE DONS   47

III · DOWN THE RIVER TO DIXIE   73

IV · LE CRÉOLE S'AMUSE   114

V · THE TERROR OF THE GULF   154

VI · FILIBUSTERS   172

VII · GAMBLERS AFLOAT AND ASHORE   197

VIII · CONGO SQUARE   237

IX · VOODOO   254

X · "AN EPOCH OF DEGENERATION"   284

XI · "HELL ON EARTH"   315

XII · SOME LOOSE LADIES OF BASIN STREET   350

XIII · CRIMINALS' PARADISE   395

XIV · STORYVILLE   424

BIBLIOGRAPHY   457

INDEX   *follows page* 462

ILLUSTRATIONS

The White League Riots in 1874   Frontispiece

New Orleans in 1719   11

A Keelboat on the Mississippi   76

River Pirates   85

A Duel under the Oaks   150

Working a Sucker in a Concert-Saloon   321

A Footpad at Work   329

A Gallatin Street Dance-House   339

A Brothel-Keeper's License of 1857   356

*Our Houses of Prostitution; Their Inmates, Patrons
and Owners*   363

The Townsend Tragedy   376

The Hanging of Ford and Murphy   398

Chief of Aids Boasso and His Victim   399

Prominent Figures in the Hennessy Case   414

The Lynching of the Italians   419

*Her Throat Cut. Jules Kunemann Attemps to Murder
Abbie Reed*   427

ILLUSTRATIONS

Queen Gertie Livingston   430

The Society Column of "The Mascot," issue of January 5, 1895   440

The Society Column of "The Sunday Sun," January 31, 1904   443

Pages from the "Blue Book"   446

Some Famous Storyville Resorts   446

The Interior of Josie Arlington's Basin Street Bagnio

Advertisements from the "Blue Book"   447

The
French
Quarter

CHAPTER I

NOUVELLE-ORLÉANS

THE DEVELOPMENT of the New Orleans of legend and tradition began during the administration of the French Governor the Marquis de Vaudreuil (1743–53), with its gaudy social functions, widespread governmental corruption, and the tolerance with which lapses from the strict moral code were regarded. It continued, though slowly, throughout the domination of Louisiana by Spain, and received a considerable impetus during the three years, from 1800 to 1803, when the province was neither French flesh nor Spanish fowl, and when a general relaxing of discipline and a throwing off of restraint permitted and encouraged an influx of vagabonds and adventurers from all parts of the world. But, curiously enough, it was under the rule of the United States that New Orleans embarked upon its golden age of glamour and spectacular wickedness and attained its full stature as a city of sin and gayety unique on the North American continent.

2

IN September 1717, John Law's Company of the West, popularly known as the Mississippi Company, obtained, by royal grant, control of the French province of Louisiana, which comprised all the territory from the Illinois River to the Gulf of Mexico, and from the English settlements in the east to the dominions of Spain in the west. Into this vast area the French had penetrated only to the extent of a small settlement on the site of the present city of Mobile, another on the eastern shore of Biloxi Bay, and a third where Natchez now overlooks the Mississippi. All of these establishments had been planted between 1698 and 1716 by the Canadian explorers Pierre Le Moyne, Sieur d'Iberville, and his brother Jean Baptiste Le Moyne, Sieur de Bienville, the founder of New Orleans. Iberville also, in 1700, erected a blockhouse and a stockade on the Mississippi eighteen leagues from the sea, but this post was soon abandoned. As late as 1712, almost thirty-five years after La Salle had descended the river to the Gulf of Mexico and claimed Louisiana for France, there were in the entire province only eleven men not directly employed by the King. The total population was less than three hundred, including a garrison of a hundred and twenty-four soldiers and a few priests, twenty-eight women, and twenty-five children. There were also about fifty cows and a few pigs and chickens. Most of the men were adventurous *voyageurs* and *coureurs de bois* who had wandered into the province from Canada and Illinois, but the women, almost without exception, were deportees from the prisons and brothels of Paris, and the hardships of life in the wilderness had failed to work any changes in their manners and customs. When a worried priest suggested that sending away all immoral women would improve the general tone of the province, Lamothe Cadillac, who was Governor of Louisiana from 1713 to 1716, made this illuminating comment:

"If I send away all the loose females, there will be no women left here at all, and this would not suit the views of the King or the inclinations of the people."

The terms of the royal franchise issued to the Mississippi Company were substantially the same as those upon which the territory had been granted, in 1712, to Antoine Crozat, a French banker and financier of great wealth, who tried unsuccessfully for five years to operate Louisiana as a commercial enterprise. Law and his associates agreed to import six thousand white settlers and three thousand Negro slaves, and were to have the sole right, for twenty-five years, to exploit the province and to work the gold and silver mines and pearl fisheries with which it was supposed the country abounded. The business management of the company was vested in a board of directors, which elected Law chief director and gave him almost unlimited powers. The civil and military government of the province was to remain in the hands of the Superior Council, which during the Crozat régime consisted of the Governor or Commandant-General, the Commissaire Ordonnateur or Intendant, and two agents of the financier. The last-named officials were replaced by representatives of the Mississippi Company. With various changes and increases in membership, and delegations of authority to subsidiary and inferior tribunals, the Council continued to govern Louisiana throughout the French occupation.

Almost the only act of the company which showed any realization of the real needs of the colony was the appointment of Bienville as Governor and commander of the French forces garrisoned at the post on Biloxi Bay. Bienville had been in Louisiana for twenty years, and with his brother Iberville had played an important part in the early exploration of the territory. He had repeatedly reported to his superiors in Paris that there were no gold or silver mines in Louisiana, and that the few pearls found in the Gulf of Mexico were worthless, and had urged both Crozat and the French government to abandon the fruitless search for treasure and concentrate their energies upon the orderly development of agriculture in the rich lands of the Mississippi Valley. He particularly advocated the establishment of a town on the river bank within a few days' sail of the gulf, foreseeing the mighty volume of trade which the Mississippi was destined to carry. He predicted that such a settlement would in time become a great city of vast commercial importance.

But his recommendations were dismissed as providing too slow a method of garnering the boundless wealth which the French were certain that Louisiana held for them. Not until he was appointed Governor did Bienville have sufficient authority to carry out any of his projects. His commission arrived in the New World on February 9, 1718, and soon thereafter he led twenty-five convicts, as many carpenters, and a few *voyageurs* from the Illinois country, to a crescent-shaped bend in the river some thirty leagues from the Gulf, a site which he had noted and surveyed during a trip of exploration to the Red River in 1700. Near a fortified Indian village called Tchoutchouma, in a cypress swamp swarming with snakes and alligators, Bienville set his men to work clearing the forest and erecting sheds and barracks. He named the new settlement *Nouvelle-Orléans* in honor of the French Regent, the Duke of Orléans, that gifted scoundrel of whom his mother said that the fairies had given him every gift excepting that of making use of them. The exact date of the beginning of this work has always been a subject of dispute among Louisiana historians, and probably never will be known, although the Louisiana Historical Society, in March 1918, attempted to settle the matter by adopting a resolution declaring that New Orleans was founded between February 9 and 11, 1718. It is certain, however, that it occurred between the arrival of Bienville's commission and the first of the following June, for early in the latter month he wrote in his diary:

"We are working at New Orleans with as much zeal as the shortage of workingmen will permit. I have myself conveyed over the spot to select the place where it will be best to locate the settlement. I remained ten days to hasten the works. . . . I am grieved to see so few people engaged in a task which requires at least a hundred times the number. . . . All the ground of the site, except the borders which are drowned by floods, is very good, and everything will grow there."

Bienville sent to the directors of the Mississippi Company in Paris glowing descriptions of the salubrity of the climate at New Orleans, the fertility of the soil, and the many other advantages of the area which he had chosen for the new town. Other French officials, however, viewed the location with less optimistic eyes. The Commandant of the Natchitoches district wrote that the settlement was " situated in flat and swampy ground fit only for growing rice; river water filters through under the soil, and crayfish abound, so that tobacco and vegetables are hard to raise. There are frequent fogs, and, the land being thickly wooded and covered with cane-brakes, the air is fever-laden, and an infinity of mosquitoes cause further inconvenience in summer." The climate, and the persistent infiltration of water from the Mississippi, have always been among New Orleans' greatest drawbacks. All of the early visitors who recorded their impressions of the city complained of the penetrating cold and dampness of the winter months, and of the heat and mugginess of the summers. And neither time nor the installation of modern drainage systems have brought much relief; New Orleans is still perhaps the dampest spot on the North American continent, and certainly one of the hottest; shoes and other articles of clothing commonly mildew if left overnight on the ground floors of buildings in the old quarter of the city; it is difficult to make plaster adhere to the walls, and cellars are almost unknown. In early days water was encountered from twelve to eighteen inches below the surface of the ground, and even today it is seldom necessary to dig more than three feet to find it, except in the

7

comparatively high land of the newer parts of the city. As late as the 1840's New Orleans was known throughout the United States as the "Wet Grave," because of the difficulties encountered in burying corpses. "In digging 'the narrow house' water rises to within eighteen inches of the surface," wrote an English traveler who visited the city in 1832. "Coffins are therefore sunk three or four feet by having holes bored in them, and two black men stand on them till they fill with water, and reach the bottom of the moist tomb. Some people are particular and dislike this immersion after death; and, therefore, those who can afford it have a sort of brick oven built on the surface of the ground, at one end of which, the coffin is introduced, and the door hermetically closed, but the heat of the southern sun on this 'whited sepulchre' must bake the body inside, so that there is but a choice of disagreeables after all."[1] All burials in modern New Orleans, excepting those of Jews and the poorer classes of both whites and Negroes, are made above the ground in small ovens, or in tombs of varying degrees of beauty and elaborateness.

Bienville recorded in his diary that the average height of the land on which he proposed to erect a settlement was ten feet above sea level. Consequently it was supposed to be safe from inundation. But less than a year after the founding of the city the Mississippi overflowed its banks, and New Orleans was flooded to a depth of from six to twelve inches. Bienville immediately stopped all building construction and put the inhabitants to work digging a drainage ditch in the rear of the town and erecting a low dike along the river front, behind which shade trees were planted. Thus began the great system of levees which now protects New Orleans from the ravages of the river. During the first few years of the settlement's existence, however, there was very little to pro-

---

[1] *Transatlantic Sketches*, by Captain Sir James Edward Alexander; London, 1833; Volume II, page 30.

tect. About the middle of 1719 a French official who visited the town wrote that it contained but three houses and a store belonging to the Mississippi Company. A year later, in 1720, another official found, besides the company's buildings, a hospital, lodgings for the Governor and the director, and " about fifty soldiers, seventy clerks, hired men, and convicts drawing wages and rations from the company."

3

WHILE Bienville, handicapped by a shortage of both men and materials, was laboring desperately in Louisiana to prepare for the horde of colonists which he had been warned would presently descend upon him, John Law and his associates in Paris were starting the second phase of the Scotch adventurer's scheme. With the aid and encouragement of the French Regent, Law started a land- and stock-selling campaign which still excites the envy and admiration of financial manipulators and high-pressure salesmen. Soon all France was caught in a frenzy of speculation, the national currency was inflated for the benefit of Law's plans, and the Mississippi Bubble, that colossal fraud which was destined to drive the country to the verge of ruin, was fairly launched. Law had nothing to back his stock except his gaudy promises of immense profits from Louisiana, and colonists were required to start the flow of wealth and to create the illusion of prosperity. A Louisiana historian thus describes how they were obtained:

> " The government went boldly to the task of ransacking the jails and hospitals. Disorderly soldiers, black sheep of distinguished families, paupers, prostitutes, political suspects, friendless strangers, unsophisticated peasants straying into Paris, all were kidnapped, herded, and shipped under guard to fill the emptiness of Louisiana. To those who would emigrate

voluntarily the Company offered free land, free provisions, free transportation to the colony and from
the colony to the situation of their grants, wealth, and
eternal prosperity to them and their heirs forever; for
the soil of Louisiana was said to bear two crops a year
without cultivation, and the amiable savages were said
so to adore the white man that they would not allow
these superior beings to labor, and would themselves,
voluntarily and for mere love, assume all the burden
of that sordid necessity. Endless variations were played
upon the themes of gold and silver mines, pearl fisheries, a balmy climate that abolished disease and old
age, and a soil that had but to be tickled to give up,
almost as one wished, either the smiling harvest or the
laughing gold.

" And now the full tide of the boom began to reach
Louisiana. The emigrants, hurried out to fill seignorial
rights, began to arrive in swarms and were dumped
helplessly upon Dauphin Island. . . . Crowded, un-
sheltered and unfed, upon that barren sand heap,
the wretched emigrants sickened, grew discontented,
starved and died, yet there they had to wait until Bienville with his few boats and small force of efficient men
could parcel them out about the country. . . . Faster
than he could dispose of this mass of confusion, the
infatuated enthusiasm in France continued to unload
upon him and Louisiana. . . . To produce the human
food required by the hungry octopus, the agents of the
police scoured the kennels and alleys of Paris, and
many a shipload of wretchedness was sent to the wilderness as a sacrifice to the new god." [1]

The first colonists sent out by the Mississippi Company arrived in June 1718, a week or so after Bienville had

---

[1] *Louisiana*, by Albert Phelps; New York, 1905; pages 60–1.

returned to Biloxi Bay from his inspection of the work at New Orleans. They were about three hundred in number and came in three ships, accompanied by some five hundred soldiers and convicts. Of the settlers, one hundred and fifty-one were sent to the country around Natchez, eighty-two to the valley of the Yazoo River, and sixty-eight to New

VUE DE LA NOUVELLE ORLÉANS EN 1719.

« Les Iles ou quartiers des Bourgeois sont entourés d'eau pendant trois mois de l'année vu le débordement des eaux du fleuve depuis le 15 mars jusqu'au 15 juin. Devant la ville il y a une levée et par derrière un fossé et autres découlements. »

From a contemporary print

NEW ORLEANS IN 1719

Orleans, where they were crowded into tents and rough sheds. Most of these first inhabitants of the new town appear to have been fairly respectable, but in succeeding ship-loads vagabonds and the criminal element were vastly in the majority. Not only in New Orleans, but elsewhere in the province, there was a great shortage of unmarried women, and the men complained that they were compelled to take Indian squaws for wives or go without feminine companionship. "Send me wives for my Canadians," wrote Bienville to Paris; "they are running in the woods after Indian girls." To remedy this situation the company, in March 1721, although a royal edict had been issued pro-hibiting the transportation of vagabonds or persons of bad moral character to Louisiana, imported eighty-eight girls, most of whom had been immates of La Salpetrière, a house of correction in Paris. They were under the care of three nuns of the Gray Sisters. With them the foresighted company sent a midwife, Madame Doville, who was nicknamed *La Sans-Regret*. On April 25, 1721, Bienville wrote to Paris:

" Since the 4th of March, nineteen of them have been married off. From those who came by *Le Chameau* and *La Mutine*, ten have died. So that fifty-nine girls are still to be provided for. This will be difficult, as these girls were not well selected. . . . Whatever the vigilance exercised upon them, they could not be restrained. Among the three Directresses responsible for their conduct, two have occasioned complaints. Sister Gertrude is ill-natured, she rules sourly and capriciously, and has been guilty of a prank which cost her the respect of the girls themselves. Sister Marie has none of the talents required for such responsibilities. Sister Saint-Louis has been retained, having a very good character, but the others were sent away."

In Louisiana history, when mentioned at all, these girls are known as " correction girls," and they are carefully distinguished from the *filles à la cassette,* or casket girls, so called because they had been carefully chosen from among good middle-class families for skill in housewifely duties and excellence of character. Before the latter left France they were each given by the Mississippi Company a small chest containing two coats, two shirts and undershirts, six headdresses, and various other articles of clothing. The first of the casket girls reached New Orleans in 1728, and they continued to arrive at regular intervals until 1751. They were all lodged together, and during the day the men of the colony were permitted to see them in order that a choice might be made, but when night fell they were guarded by soldiers. Husbands were soon found for all of them, or, as a French official put it, "this merchandise was soon disposed of, so great was the want of the country." By some queer physiological mischance none of the correction girls, apparently, ever bore a child. On the other hand, the casket girls would seem to have been extraordinarily fertile, each becoming the mother of at least a hundred children, who in turn were likewise blessed with enormous families. Proof of these biological miracles is furnished by the fact that practically every native family of Louisiana is able to trace its descent in an unbroken line from one of the *filles à la cassette*.

THE history of Louisiana throughout the régime of the Mississippi Company, and especially during the first few years, is a sad record of confusion, failure, and misdirected effort and enthusiasm. The stock-jobbing directors of the company in Paris held Bienville mainly responsible for the sufferings of the colonists who were being landed in ever increasing numbers on Dauphin Island, and for the failure of exploring parties to find and bring into production the gold and silver mines and the pearl fisheries. A radical gesture of some sort was desperately needed to placate the horde of disappointed investors who were clamoring for the profits which had been promised them, and it was naturally directed against Bienville. In the summer of 1721 the company publicly announced its dissatisfaction with his administration, and sent to Louisiana a new President of the Superior Council, Duvergier, armed with powers which gave him authority over Bienville, although the latter was not officially dismissed. Duvergier was instructed to take whatever measures he might find necessary to put the affairs of the province on a sound footing, and, above all, to renew and prosecute vigorously the search for the mythical mines and pearling grounds.

The lessening of responsibility due to the arrival of Duvergier enabled Bienville to concentrate his energies upon the building of New Orleans. The new President of the Superior Council had scarcely landed and been installed in office before Bienville and the engineer Pauger, with a force of carpenters and convicts, were *en route* to the new settlement on the Mississippi. Under Bienville's supervision Pauger carefully surveyed the site, and the town was laid out in the form of a parallelogram, 4,000 feet long by 1,800 feet deep, and comprising the area now called the Vieux Carré but popularly known as the French Quarter, and bounded by the river and Canal, Esplanade, and Rampart Streets. The parallelogram was divided into sixty-six squares of 300 feet each, which in turn were subdivided into lots, each with a street frontage of 60 feet and a depth ranging from 120 to 150 feet. A square in the center of the town, fronting the river, was reserved by Bienville as a parade ground, or Place d'Armes. It is now Jackson Square, the name having been changed to honor the commander of the American forces at the Battle of New Orleans, in the War of 1812. Another square, behind the Place d'Armes, was devoted to governmental and ecclesiastical purposes. On it were erected, with the next few years, a small church, a house for the priests, another for the Corps de Garde, and a prison. This square is now the site of the St. Louis Cathedral, the Cabildo, which was the seat of the provincial government during the Spanish occupation and of municipal authority until comparatively recent years, and other religious and governmental edifices.

While Bienville was busy at New Orleans, conditions at Biloxi Bay and elsewhere throughout the province, instead of improving under Duvergier's rule, became steadily worse, and the sufferings of the colonists more intense. Having failed to discover the mines and pearl fisheries or to send the Mississippi Company the enormous profits which had been expected, Duvergier was recalled to France in less than a year. In May 1722 Bienville was restored to power. He was now able to convince the Superior Council of the necessity and practicability of a step which he had urged unsuccessfully for several years — the removal of the provincial capital from Biloxi Bay to New Orleans. By August 1722 the transfer had been completed and all the paraphernalia of government had been installed in the new settlement. But as the capital of a colony almost four times as large as the mother country, New Orleans presented a sorry spectacle. The population was considerably less than five hundred, and the town contained not more than a hundred small houses, most of them rude cabins of split cypress logs, roofed with cypress bark. Thirty of these structures, besides the church, the hospital, and three ships tied up at the wharf, were destroyed by a hurricane which struck the town on September 11, 1723 and blew with great violence for three days.

"The whole city," says Gayarré, "was surrounded by a large ditch, and fenced in with sharp stakes wedged close together. For the purposes of draining, a ditch ran along the four sides of every square in the city, and every lot in every square was also ditched all round, causing New Orleans to look very much like a microscopic caricature of Venice. Mosquitoes buzzed, and enormous frogs croaked incessantly in concert with other indescribable sounds; tall reeds, and grass of every variety, grew in the streets and in the yards, so as to interrupt all communication, and offered a safe retreat, and places of concealment to venomous reptiles, wild beasts, and malefactors, who, protected by

15

these impenetrable jungles, committed with impunity all sorts of evil deeds." [1]

The swamps and marshes in and around New Orleans not only abounded in malefic animal life, but also, if various eminent French travelers can be credited, in an almost infinite variety of extraordinary plants, whose marvelous properties were well known to, and utilized by, the Indians and a few of the more daring settlers. Among these botanical curiosities were the hair-plant, the flowers of which grew a fringe of veritable whiskers; the oil-tree, which when tapped yielded a fine grade of oil; the button-tree, which provided a never ending supply of buttons for the colonists' clothing; and the water-tree, from which, when struck with a stick, water gushed forth. But even more miraculous were a grass called *semper virens* — a drop of its juice instantly transformed water into ice; the savoyanne-root, the chewing of which made the chewer fireproof — occasionally the Indians were deeply mortified to find a captive was so full of savoyanne-root that it was impossible to burn him at the stake; and a third plant variously known as viperine, goat's-tongue, and fritter-root. This last was a sovereign cure for wounds; a little fritter-root juice dropped upon a wound healed it instantly without leaving a scar. All of these marvels, and many others, were described by F. Bossu and Perrin du Lac, the former a French naval Captain and the latter a French colonial administrator, who visited Louisiana and each wrote several books about the country. Monsieur du Lac appears to have made an especial study of the virtues of the fritter-root; he tells, for example, of an Indian, badly slashed and stabbed in battle, who ran for sixty miles chewing fritter-root and occasionally spitting on his wounds. At the end of the run the savage found himself completely healed, without even a scar to show his squaw.

---

[1] *History of Louisiana*, by Charles Gayarré; New York, 1854; Volume I, page 381.

16

Most of these plants are likewise described in the works of Baudry des Lozières, the French naturalist, to whom natural history is also indebted for one of the earliest descriptions of the man-root, or wild potato. Monsieur des Lozières was in New Orleans when some laborers, digging a ditch, unearthed specimens of this plant, and he thus set down his observations:

"These strange plants bore some resemblance to an Irish potato or white truffle, but were much larger than the largest yam. They had the perfect shape and face of a human being, with the features of the face clearly marked, a neck, shoulders, and a well-defined body. Some of the plants were small, others large; some had male, others female features. They seemed to form a regular colony or settlement, and quivered when touched, and even seemed to move away, as if they intended to defend themselves. They received at once the name of man-plant."

5

THE few years which followed the transfer of the capital to New Orleans, owing more to the energy and persistence of Bienville and succeeding governors than to any aid given them by the Mississippi Company, saw a considerable change in the physical aspect of the town. By 1727 the population had almost doubled, the streets originally laid out by the engineer Pauger had been named and new ones cut through the jungle, and some headway had been made in cutting the weeds, draining the swamps, and ridding the city of frogs, snakes, and alligators. In the early spring of that year a company of Ursuline nuns arrived in New Orleans, and one of them, Madeleine Hachard, wrote an account of the journey from France and a description of the town which was to be their new home. In the clothing of the people Sister Madeleine found " as much magnificence and refinement as in France." She thus described the town and paid her respects to the habits and customs of its inhabit-ants:

" Our town is very handsome, well constructed and regularly built, as much as I could judge on the day of our arrival; for ever since that day we have remained cloistered in our dwelling. The streets are large and straight. The houses well built, with upright joists, the interstices filled with mortar, and the exterior white-washed with lime. In the interior they are wainscoted. The roofs of the houses are covered with shingles which are cut in the shape of slates, and one must know this to believe it, for they all have the appearance and beauty of slate. The colonists are very proud of their capital. Suffice it to say, they sing here a song in the streets to the effect that this town is as fine a sight as Paris. . . . I do not, however, speak of the manners of the laity, but I am told that their habits are corrupt and scandalous. There are, however, a great number of honest people, and one does not see any of those girls who were said to have been deported on compul-sion. . . . The women here are extremely ignorant as to the means of securing their salvation, but they are very expert in the art of displaying their beauty. There is so much luxury in this town that there is no distinction among the classes so far as dress goes. The magnificence of display is equal to all. Most of them reduce themselves and their family to a hard lot of living at home on nothing but sagamité, and flaunt abroad in robes of velvet and damask, ornamented with the most costly ribbons. They paint and rouge to hide the ravages of time, and wear on their faces, as embellishment, small black patches."

The Ursulines had been sent to Louisiana under a contract made with the Mississippi Company, the official name of which had been changed to Compagnie des Indes. The order was given eight arpents of land on the New Orleans waterfront, a house, and eight Negro slaves to till the soil, and in consideration of these gifts agreed to furnish six nuns to serve as nurses in the hospital, to teach both white and Negro girls the beauties and comforts of religion, and to care for the *filles à la cassette* until husbands could be found for them. The nuns were also to attempt the reformation of the many loose women and girls of bad conduct, who were punished, as Sister Madeleine describes, "by putting them upon wooden horses and having them whipped by the regiment of soldiers that guards the town." A house for the detention of these abandoned females was built by the provincial government and turned over to the Ursulines for operation. And some such institution appears to have been sorely needed, for in less than ten years of existence New Orleans had already become notorious throughout Louisiana, and was even being spoken of in the English and Spanish settlements, as a town of loose morals. The ready-made underworld which the Mississippi Company had dumped within its borders was becoming increasingly restless; murders and robbery were of frequent occurrence, and no man's life or property was safe. A year before the arrival of the Ursulines the condition of the colony and the deplorable habits of its inhabitants were thus described by Druout de Valdeterre, commander of the French troops on Dauphin Island and at Biloxi Bay:

" The troops are without discipline and subordination, without arms and ammunition, most of the time without clothing, and they are frequently obliged to seek their food among the Indian tribes. There are no forts for their protection; no places of refuge for them in case of attack. The guns and other implements of war are buried in sand and abandoned; the warehouses are unroofed; the merchandise, goods, and provisions are damaged or completely spoiled; the company as well as the colonists are plundered without mercy and restraint; revolts and desertions among the troops are authorized and sanctioned; incendiaries who, for the purpose of pillage, commit to flames whole camps, posts, settlements, and warehouses, remain unpunished; prisoners of war are forced to become sailors in the service of the company and by culpable negligence or connivance are allowed to run away with ships loaded with merchandise; other vessels are willfully stranded or wrecked and their cargoes are lost to their owners; forgers, robbers, and murderers are sure of immunity. In short, this is a country which, to the shame of France be it said, is without religion, without justice, without discipline, without order, and without police."

Among the crimes committed during this period was a killing which, according to Gayarré, explains the origin of the lone date-palm which for almost a hundred and fifty years stood in a lot on Orleans Street between Dauphine and Bourbon Streets. The tree was known for many years as Père Antoine's date-palm, as the ground in which it was rooted was once the property of a Spanish Capuchin monk, Antonio de Sedella, who attempted to establish the Inquisition in Louisiana, was expelled from the colony by the Spanish Governor Miró, and returned a few years later to become the best-loved priest in all the history of New Orleans. Innumerable legends, all of them fantastic, arose about the tree. It was said to have sprung from the heart of a maiden who died dreaming of her lover and the happiness she had enjoyed on the palm-fringed shore of a tropical

isle; that the seed from which it grew had been blown to
New Orleans by the wind; that it had been planted by an
angel and would not bear fruit (incidentally, it never did)
until New Orleans had been cleansed of wickedness. But
the most dramatic of all the tales told of the tree, as well
as the most circumstantial, is related by Gayarré in his history of Louisiana. He describes the story as having been
told to him in 1820 by a man, then eighty years old, who
had heard it from his father:

"In the beginning of 1727, a French vessel of
war landed at New Orleans a man of haughty mien,
who wore the Turkish dress, and whose whole attendance was a single servant. He was received by the
governor with the highest distinction, and was conducted by him to a small but comfortable house with a
pretty garden, then existing at the corner of Orleans
and Dauphine Streets, and which, from the circumstance of its being so distant from other dwellings,
might have been called a rural retreat, although situated
in the limits of the city. There, the stranger, who was
understood to be a prisoner of state, lived in the greatest seclusion; and although neither he nor his attendant
could be guilty of indiscretion, because none understood their language, and although Governor Périer
severely rebuked the slightest inquiry, yet it seemed to
be the settled conviction in Louisiana, that the mysterious stranger was a brother of the Sultan, or some
great personage of the Ottoman empire, who had
fled from the anger of the vicegerent of Mohammed,
and who had taken refuge in France. The Sultan had
peremptorily demanded the fugitive, and the French
government, thinking it derogatory to its dignity to
comply with that request, but at the same time not
wishing to expose its friendly relations with the Mos-

lem monarch, and perhaps desiring, for political purposes, to keep in hostage the important guest it had in its hands, had recourse to the expedient of answering, that he had fled to Louisiana, which was so distant a country that it might be looked upon as the grave, where, as it was suggested, the fugitive might be suffered to wait in peace for actual death, without danger or offense to the Sultan. . . .

" The year 1727 was drawing to its close, when on a dark, stormy night, the howling and barking of the numerous dogs in the streets of New Orleans were observed to be fiercer than usual, and some of that class of individuals who pretend to know every thing, declared that, by the vivid flashes of the lightning, they had seen, swiftly and stealthily gliding toward the residence of the *unknown*, a body of men who wore the scowling appearance of malefactors and ministers of blood. There afterward came also a report, that a piratical-looking Turkish vessel had been hovering a few days previous in the bay of Barataria. Be it as it may, on the next morning the house of the stranger was deserted. There were no traces of mortal struggle to be seen; but in the garden, the earth had been dug, and *there* was the unmistakable indication of a recent grave. Soon, however, all doubts were removed by the finding of an inscription in Arabic characters, engraved on a marble tablet, which was subsequently sent to France. It ran thus: ' The justice of heaven is satisfied, and the date-tree shall grow on the traitor's tomb. The sublime Emperor of the faithful, the supporters of the faith, the omnipotent master and Sultan of the world, has redeemed his vow. God is great, and Mohammed is his prophet. Allah!' Some time after this event, a foreign-looking tree was seen to peep out of the spot where a corpse must have been deposited in that stormy night, when the rage of the elements yielded to the pitiless fury of man, and it thus explained in some degree this part of the inscription, 'the date-tree shall grow on the traitor's grave.' "[1]

6

THE motley rabble sent to Louisiana by the Mississippi Company had been promised a life of indolent ease, with no other labor than might be required to wrench bars of pure gold and silver from the earth and pick pearls from the waters of the Gulf of Mexico. Work was utterly abhorrent to the vast majority of the colonists, and they refused flatly to perform the labor necessary to clear the forest and bring the rich land under cultivation. Instead they spent their time drinking, fighting, and attempting to steal or otherwise acquire sufficient money to enable them to leave the province. From the beginning of the experiment in colonization, the settlers were almost constantly on the verge of actual want, and the provincial government was unable even to provide for the troops on whom the safety of the colony depended. Detachments of soldiers were quartered in the Indian villages and fed by the savages, while others were turned into the jungle and along the seashore to subsist as best they could on game and fish. On January 24, 1732 the Superior Council sent a communication to the French government urging that additional supplies be sent out. and declaring that the colonists would "absolutely starve if the India Company did not send out by every vessel an ample supply of salt meat." At the same time a French official disclosed that from 1699 to 1723 every colonist sent to Louisiana had cost the French government, Crozat, or the Mississippi Company the incredible sum of 150,000 livres annually for his maintenance.

The only solution of the problem was slave labor. As

---

[1] *History of Louisiana,* Volume I, page 387.

elsewhere on the North American continent, attempts to enslave the Indians were uniformly unsuccessful, and it was necessary to turn to Negroes. The importation of blacks was begun by Crozat in 1712, and continued by the Mississippi Company, who sold the slaves to the colonists at prices ranging from 660 to 676 livres a head, on reasonable terms. Provincial records show that on June 1, 1721, there remained in Louisiana 600 slaves and 400 white settlers who had been sent to the colony by Crozat. During the first two years of its domination of the province the Mississippi Company sent to Louisiana 7,020 persons in forty-three ships. Of this number about 2,000 had died, deserted, or returned to France. The total population in 1721, therefore, was approximately 5,000, scattered over an area of nearly one million square miles. What proportion of the inhabitants were Negroes is now unknown, although the French official La Harpe in 1724 estimated the total black population at 3,300 and that of the whites at 1,700, Louisiana historians agree that while La Harpe's total was probably correct, his figures should be reversed in estimating the proportion of black to white. Nevertheless, the presence of so many slaves formed another problem scarcely less serious than that of subsistence. All of the Negroes had been captured by slave-traders in Africa, and most of them were untamed savages from the jungles of the Congo. Stringent laws, rigidly enforced, were necessary to keep them in subjugation. Early in January 1724 Bienville and his colleagues on the Superior Council began the preparation of the famous *Code Noir*, or Black Code, which they adapted from the then existing laws of Santo Domingo, and which formed the basis of the Black Code adopted by the Louisiana Legislature after the purchase of the territory by the United States. "The harshest, the most severe penalties were provided and inflicted in case of any act on the part of slaves which tended to endanger the absolute supremacy

24

of the white race," wrote Phelps, " but within these limits the black slave was as fully protected from the tyranny, neglect, oppression or cruelty of his master as was the involuntarily bound servant or even the hired domestic of early Massachusetts." [1]

The first article of the original Black Code ordered the expulsion of all Jews from the province; and the succeeding four articles prohibited any form of worship excepting the Roman Catholic, made it imperative upon masters to impart religious instructions to their slaves, and provided for the confiscation of blacks placed under the supervision of a person not a Catholic, or found at work on Sundays or holy days. The remaining forty-nine articles dealt entirely with the conduct and government of the Negroes. In particular, the Code prohibited any mingling of the races. Concubinage with slaves, and marriages of whites and blacks, whether free or slave, was forbidden under penalty of heavy fines and other punishments. Provision was made for the manumission of slaves, which could be granted by masters over twenty-five, either while living or by testamentary act, provided permission was first obtained from the Superior Council. The final article of the Code granted to manumitted slaves " the same rights, privileges, and immunities which are enjoyed by free-born persons. It is our pleasure that their merit in having acquired their freedom shall produce in their favor, not only with regard to their persons, but also to their property, the same effects which our other subjects derive from the happy circumstance of their having been born free."

Bienville signed the Black Code in March 1724, and immediately thereafter departed for Paris, whither he had been summoned to answer charges of maladministration which had been lodged against him by jealous subordinates

---

[1] *Louisiana*, page 75. The Black Code is published in full as an appendix to the first volume of Gayarré's *History of Louisiana*.

and dissatisfied officials of the Mississippi Company. There he was relieved of all his duties and had no further connection with colonial affairs until 1731, when the Mississippi Company surrendered its charter to the French government, and Louisiana became again a royal province. The transfer of authority was completed in November of that year, and two delegates were sent out to liquidate the company's business and settle its accounts. Their report was a long recital of failure, confusion, and stupid mismanagement; on the credit side of the ledger about all that could be said of the company was that during its régime permanent settlements had been established at New Orleans and Baton Rouge. In desperation the French government turned to Bienville and reappointed him to his old post as Governor. He returned to Louisiana early in 1733, accompanied by Diron d'Artaguette, commander of the French garrison at Mobile and formerly Intendant of the province, who had been in France on an official errand.

Bienville found that during his long absence little or no progress had been made in developing the colony. The white population had remained virtually stationary, although the number of Negro slaves had increased to about two thousand. New Orleans had experienced a slight growth, with a score of new houses and other buildings erected and a few additional streets laid out. Bienville's successors had devoted themselves mainly to bickering with subordinate officials, imploring help from the Mississippi Company, and launching fruitless expeditions against the Natchez and Chickasaw Indians. The former had been on the war-path since 1730, when they attacked the French settlement at Fort Rosalie, on the site of the present city of Natchez, massacred the garrison and all the male white colonists except two, and carried off as captives one hundred white women and children and twice that number of Negro slaves. The Choctaws, influenced by the success of the Natchez foray and by the failure of successive French punitive expeditions, were wavering in their allegiance; a large faction of the tribe, led by an important chief called Red Shoe, openly urged the repudiation of all trade and military agreements made with the French and the forming of an alliance with the English. D'Artaguette, who had won many successes in the earlier wars against the Indians, asked permission of Bienville to organize a force of a hundred French soldiers, reinforced by the Choctaw warriors, against the Natchez and the Chickasaws, but Bienville refused on the ground that there were insufficient supplies of arms and provisions. Moreover, he expressed the opinion that such a small force was doomed to failure, and that a defeat would bring dishonor upon the French arms. Irritated at Bienville's attitude, d'Artaguette retired to Mobile, whereupon Bienville promptly equipped a force of thirty Frenchmen and a thousand Choctaws and sent them against the Chickasaws under the command of the Canadian Pierre Lesueur. But the Chickasaws had bribed the Choctaws, and the expedition returned to New Orleans after striking but the feeblest of blows against the fortified stronghold of the hostile Indians.

The dismal failure of Lesueur's campaign, and Bienville's weak explanation that the defeat brought no dishonor upon France because so few Frenchmen were actually engaged, did not soothe D'Artaguette's ruffled feelings. He felt that he had been slighted and that Bienville had refused him the command through jealousy. Previously he had been the Governor's staunch supporter; now he became Bienville's bitterest enemy, and neglected no opportunity to hamper and discredit him. "Thus D'Artaguette," says Gayarré, "in one of his dispatches, on the 29th of April, 1735, assures his government, that if Bienville is displeased with and complains of him, it is because he, D'Artaguette, has made known the misconduct of Bienville's protégés, or favorites, Lesueur and the Jesuit, Father Beaudoin, *who, to the great scandal of the Choctaws, seduced their women."* [1]

When Bienville again took over the reins of government in Louisiana, he found food and other supplies scarcely more plentiful than when he left in 1724. Nor was the average inhabitant any more inclined to earn his bread by the sweat of his brow. On April 23, 1733, in a dispatch to the French government from Mobile, D'Artaguette said that "our planters and mechanics are dying of hunger, and those at New Orleans are in no better condition. Some are clamorous for returning to France; others secretly run away to the Spaniards at Pensacola. The colony is on the eve of being depopulated." Less than a month later, on May 12, Bienville sent a voluminous report to Paris, covering every detail of Louisiana's history and situation, and going into such detail that he even gave the name of the first child born in the province — Claude Jousset, the son of a Canadian trader at Mobile. But Bienville also declared that the plantations were improperly organized, that the settlers lacked Negroes to do the necessary work, and that they complained bitterly of the great number of vagabonds who had been unloaded on the province by the Mississippi Company. Two years later, in 1735, Bienville was still finding fault with the character of the colonists. On April 15, 1735 he wrote:

"I neglect nothing to turn the attention of the inhabitants to agricultural pursuits, but in general they are worthless, lazy, dissolute, and most of them recoil from the labors necessary to improve the lands."

But even for the few settlers who did not fall into these categories, the year 1735 was a time of great trial and suffering. Bienville reported to Paris on August 31:

---

[1] *History of Louisiana*, Volume I, pages 462–3. The italics are Gayarré's.

" The mortality of cattle is frightful, the drought is excessive, and the heat is suffocating. Such hot weather had never been known since the foundation of the colony, and it has now lasted four months without any change. From Christmas to the Saint John the waters were very high, so that many of the levees were broken. The one which is in front of the city gave way, and we were very near abandoning our houses and taking lodgings in boats. Then the drought came, and the river went down fifteen feet — a circumstance which had never been seen before. Hence the mediocrity of our crops, our lands having been under water in the planting season."

Besides the high water and the drought and the consequent shortage of food, 1735 brought another affliction to plague the inhabitants of New Orleans — an epidemic of mad dogs, which roamed the streets and alleys in such numbers that the people were afraid to leave their houses. Business was almost at a standstill, and a score of persons were bitten. Several are said to have died of hydrophobia, although there is apparently no historical confirmation of this statement. So great a menace did the animals finally become that the Royal Commissary ordered out detachments of soldiers to hunt them down. At the same time the Superior Council passed an ordinance prohibiting the ownership of dogs by Indians and Negroes. Violators of the law were sentenced to wear the iron collar, a common punishment of the period for various offenses.

Bienville recognized the fact that growth and prosperity for New Orleans and Louisiana were impossible until the Natchez and Chickasaw Indians had been crushed, as their frequent and often successful forays not only endangered the outlying settlements, but kept the capital itself in a state of fear and unrest. In the past years the Natchez had suffered severely at the hands of the French and their allies the Choctaws, and at the beginning of 1735 it was estimated that their effectives had dwindled to fewer than two hundred warriors. But they had formed an alliance with the formidable Chickasaws, and the combined forces of the two tribes were almost always numerically superior to the weak armies that the French commander was able to send against them. The last few years of Bienville's administration were mainly devoted to warlike preparations and campaigns against the Indians. Recruits for the provincial armies were sent from France, but they must have been the scum of the French regiments, for Bienville referred to them as " pitiful blackguards " and said that they were inferior even to those who had previously been sent to help him. He wrote to the French Colonial Department in Paris:

" There are but one or two men among them whose size is above five feet, and as to the rest, they are under four feet and ten inches. With regard to their moral character, it is sufficient to state that, out of fifty-two who have lately been sent here, more than one-half have already been whipped for larceny. In a word, these useless beings are not worth the food bestowed upon them; they are burdens to the colony, and from them no efficient military service is to be expected."

With such troops as these to form the backbone of his army, Bienville launched a campaign against the Chickasaws early in 1736. The expedition was foredoomed to failure, even though Bienville had received important last-minute reinforcements — a detachment of experienced Indian-fighters from Illinois, under the command of Diron

D'Artaguette's younger brother. So badly managed was the movement that D'Artaguette's force was surprised by the Chickasaws, and all but two were either killed outright or captured and burned at the stake. When Bienville moved up with his main army to the attack his Choctaw allies began the battle before he was ready, and he was disastrously repulsed. "Bienville never recovered from the grief and humiliation of this defeat," wrote Phelps. "He was made to feel, even in the colony, that his influence had been forever lost, and the enemies who were ever ready to oppose and thwart him found material for blame in his conduct of the expedition." [1] Diron D'Artaguette in particular, holding Bienville responsible for the death of his brother, who had perished at the stake, became more than ever the Governor's enemy and sent numerous reports to Paris in which he blamed Bienville for every ill that had befallen the province. Despite his discouragement and the hopelessness of the situation, Bienville immediately began equipping another army, the command of which, to his great disappointment, was given to the Sieur de Noailles. This expedition was likewise a failure, and Noailles returned to New Orleans without having come in contact with the enemy, except in a few advance-guard skirmishes in which the French were defeated. In succeeding years other expeditions were scarcely more successful, and the menace of the Indians (the Choctaws frequently turned against the French and caused almost as much trouble as the Chickasaws) was not removed from New Orleans and the other Louisiana settlements for more than a quarter of a century.

Responsibility for the failure of Noailles's campaign was ascribed to Bienville as much as to the man who had actually commanded the troops. Unable to withstand the hatred and distrust with which he was now regarded both

---

[1] *Louisiana*, page 89.

in France and in Louisiana and realizing that his usefulness in the province was at an end, Bienville wrote to Paris
asking to be recalled. His request was granted, and as the
new head of the colony the French government appointed
Pierre Rigaut, Marquis de Vaudreuil, son of a former
Governor-General of Canada and a member of one of
France's most influential families. While awaiting the arrival of his successor, Bienville negotiated a treaty of peace
with the chiefs of the Alabama Indians, and vainly urged
the establishment of a boys' college at New Orleans. His
plea for the school was curtly dismissed by the Colonial
Department in Paris with the statement that the town was
too unimportant a settlement for such an institution. On
May 10, 1743, Bienville transferred his authority to the
Marquis de Vaudreuil and soon thereafter left the colony
forever. Forty-five of his sixty-five years had been spent
trying to conquer the Louisiana wilderness for his country,
and he had at last been beaten and overwhelmed by the
manifold stupidities of the French colonial system. Nevertheless, so diligently and persistently had he labored that
from the swampy jungle had emerged the crude beginnings
of a great city. A census taken a few months after his retirement gave New Orleans approximately 2,000 inhabitants, including 300 soldiers and 300 Negroes of both
sexes. The population of the entire province, counting 800
troops, was about 4,000 whites and 2,000 Negroes. While
this was a decrease of at least a thousand whites since 1731,
when the Company of the Indies abandoned the project
and Louisiana became a royal province, the colony as a
whole was enjoying greater prosperity than ever before.
Many of the settlers had already amassed considerable
fortunes — in New Orleans alone there were twenty-five
men whose property holdings ranged in value from 100,000
to 300,000 livres. The official report of the census specifically mentions, as the most important of this group of pros-

perous citizens, "Mr. Dubreuil, who owns five hundred Negroes, several plantations, brick-kilns, and silk-manu. factories." In a single year Dubreuil produced six thousand pounds of myrtleberry wax, which was the sole source of illumination throughout most of Louisiana. Rice, tobacco, and lumber — half a dozen saw-mills in operation near New Orleans had a combined output of fifty thousand boards a year — were the principal exports of the province, and continued to hold the lead until 1795, when Étienne de Boré, the first Mayor of New Orleans after the Louisiana Purchase, succeeded in granulating the juice of the sugar. cane, almost half a century after the plant had been intro. duced into the country by the Jesuits. Thereafter sugar played an increasingly prominent part in Louisiana commerce.

7

THE Marquis de Vaudreuil was a royal Governor in every sense of the term; he imitated as closely as possible the gay life of the French court at Versailles and beguiled the colonists with balls, elaborate state dinners, and ostentatious displays of pomp and power which must have seemed strangely incongruous in the little frontier settlement with its unpaved and unlighted streets, its long stretches of reptile-infested swamp, and its dingy, clapboarded houses. He is still recalled in New Orleans legend as "the great Marquis," and as a Louisiana historian says, "tradition through the old ladies of to-day still tells of the grandeur and elegance displayed by the Marquis, — his little Versailles of a hotel, his gracious presence, refined manners, polite speech, beautiful balls, with court dress *de rigueur,* dashing officers, and well-uniformed soldiers." [1]

One of the most celebrated of the Marquis's enter-

[1] *New Orleans, the Place and the People,* by Grace King; New York, 1896; page 79.

tainments was the first theatrical performance ever presented in the province — a tragedy called *The Indian Father,* written in blank verse by Le Blanc de Villeneuve, an officer of the garrison, and acted in the Governor's mansion early in 1753. The plot was based on an extraordinary episode which occurred in 1752. During the latter part of that year a Colapissa Indian killed a Choctaw and fled to New Orleans. The Choctaws demanded the fugitive that they might put him to death, and after vainly trying to soothe the savages with gifts, the Marquis de Vaudreuil ordered the arrest of the murderer. But the Colapissa escaped, whereupon his father called upon the Choctaws and formally offered himself as a substitute victim. The proposal was accepted, and the father was beheaded by a Choctaw chief.

Underneath the gaudy doings of the Marquis de Vaudreuil and his court, as many citizens and a few honest officials were aware, ran a vein of corruption unequaled in New Orleans until the middle of the next century, when American politicians began to plunge their greedy hands into the city's coffers. The Marquis filled important governmental posts with relatives of himself and his wife; he granted trade monoplies on condition that the holders pay him a substantial premium and a fat percentage of the profits; he confiscated and sold for his own account provisions sent to the Army, and issued to the soldiers cheaper and inferior goods; and otherwise neglected no opportunity to improve his private fortunes. He quarreled bitterly with the Intendant-Commissary, Michel de la Rouvillière, and both men dispatched long and frequent communications to the French government, each accusing the other of graft and corruption, particularly in connection with merchandise and supplies intended for the army. In a long dispatch dated June 20, 1751, the Intendant-Commissary thus summed up his charges and described the Marquis and his activities:

"No justice is to be expected from Monsieur de Vaudreuil; he is too lazy, too negligent; his wife is too malicious, too passionate, and has too strong interests in all the settlements, and in the town of New Orleans, not to prevail upon him to keep on fair, and even on servile, terms with the body of officers, and with others. . . . There is no discipline; the most indulgent toleration is granted to the soldiers, provided they drink their money at the licensed liquor-shop (*cantine*), where they are given drugs, which ruin their health; for several months there has never been less than a hundred of them at the hospital. . . . The soldiers are allowed to do what they please, provided they drink at the liquor-shop designated for them; and they carry out of it wine and spirits, which they resell to the Negroes and to the Indians. . . . It is Monsieur Belleisle, the aid-major, who has the lease and administration of the liquor-shop, and who gives for it a certain sum to the Major — others say to the Governor's lady. What is positive is that Monsieur de Vaudreuil has drawn upon the treasury for ten thousand livres of his salary as Governor, which he has given to Monsieur Belleisle, and it is with these funds that the supplies of the liquor-shop have been bought. . . . Moreover, Madame de Vaudreuil is capable of carrying on a still baser sort of trade. She deals here with everybody, and she forces merchants and other individuals to take charge of her merchandise and to sell it at the price which she fixes. She keeps in her house every sort of drugs, which are sold by her steward, and in his absence she does not scruple herself to descend to the occupation of measurement and to betake herself to the ell. The husband is not ignorant of this. He draws from it a handsome revenue, which is his sole wish and aim."

Some twelve years later, on August 15, 1763, another Louisiana official, Redon de Rassac, sent to the French Minister of Marine a long memorial in which he declared that during the régime of the Marquis de Vaudreuil the province had been handicapped by drunkenness, brawls and duels " by which half the population was destroyed," the dissolute morals of the military, and " a shameful system of plunder authorized by the Governor." Many of the Army officers openly kept mistresses, who were received at the Governor's mansion and given places above the wives of respectable colonists; and those officers who were high in the favor of the Marquis de Vaudreuil, or who adhered to his faction in his quarrels with the Intendant-Commissary, were so little subject to discipline that they went about the streets wearing only nightcap and dressing-gown.

The thieves, vagabonds, and prostitutes who had been sent to the New World by the Mississippi Company and the French government still formed, if not a majority, at least a large and disturbing minority of Louisiana's inhabitants. Under the lax rule of the Marquis de Vaudreuil they flocked into New Orleans from all parts of the province, and the capital city became more than ever the resort of the vicious and criminal elements of the population, who devoted themselves to stealing, brawling, and drinking in the many pot-houses, taverns, and gambling-dens which had made their appearance along the river front and the edges of the swamps. The area in which these dives were situated was the first recognized criminal district in New Orleans, and it was destined to spread during the next century until approximately one-third of the old city was entirely given over to vice and other forms of crime. No attempt was made to regulate the taverns and pot-houses until late in 1750, when considerable excitement was occasioned by the discovery that a great deal of the paper money in circulation in the province was counterfeit. Since the currency had been issued by the Marquis, this was a blow at his private purse, and he immediately ordered a strict investigation. All of the counterfeiters escaped, however, except a free Negro named Joseph, who was tried and convicted. As punishment he was flogged by the public executioner, branded on the shoulder with the fleur-de-lis, and transported to the West Indies to be sold into slavery.

Alarmed by the conditions which the investigation disclosed, the Marquis de Vaudreuil and the Intendant-Commissary abandoned their personal feud for the time being and jointly promulgated police regulations, in thirty articles, which became effective on February 18, 1751. These laws are historically interesting in that they mark the first attempt by the authorities of New Orleans to control vice and the sale of liquor and to check the depredations of criminals who made their headquarters in the unlicensed and unsupervised drinking-places. Particular attention was paid to tavern-keepers and others who gave shelter to runaway slaves and either taught them to steal or, if they were women, forced them into immoral lives. Said articles 10 and 11:

"All free Negroes and Negresses, living either in the purlieus of this town or in its vicinity, who may become guilty of harboring slaves, in order to seduce them and excite them to plunder their masters and lead a scandalous life, shall lose their freedom and become the slaves of the King. . . . Any Frenchman who shall be so infamous as to become guilty of the offenses described in the preceding article shall be whipped by the public executioner, and, without mercy, sentenced to end his life on the King's galleys. . . ."

Other important provisions of the new laws, summarized, follow:

No intoxicating beverages to be distributed or drunk in, or carried away from, any private house.

Six taverns to be established in New Orleans under commissions issued by the Governor.

No tavern-keeper to sell liquor to soldiers, Negroes, or Indians.

All taverns to be closed on Sundays and holidays during divine worship, and at nine o'clock every evening.

Two liquor-shops to be established for the exclusive use of the soldiers, one for the French and the other for the Swiss, to be operated by the officers in command of the respective companies.

All persons who have left their lands to settle in New Orleans must return home within eight days, or be driven from the city as people of an infamous character.[1]

In theory, these regulations were enforced by the military under the direction of the Major commanding the town; actually, they were more honored in the breach than in the observance. A few places were closed, but reopened after their owners had made the proper financial arrangements. Most of the taverns, pot-houses, gambling-dens, and other resorts forbidden by the new laws were operating full blast when the Marquis de Vaudreuil, having been appointed Governor of Canada, was succeeded in Louisiana by Louis Billouart de Kerlerec, who had already had a distinguished career as a captain in the French navy. Accompanied by his wife, his sister-in-law, and an entourage of relatives seeking the lucrative jobs held by Vaudreuil's people, Kerlerec arrived at New Orleans on February 9, 1753. On April 29, to celebrate his accession to the governorship and as a gesture to honor the Marquis de Vaudreuil, he entertained two hundred guests at an elaborate dinner, followed by a magnificent show of fireworks. The pyro-

---

[1] These regulations in full are published as an appendix to the second volume of Gayarré's *History of Louisiana*.

technic display was touched off by Madame Kerlerec and the Marquise de Vaudreuil, who released two doves which carried fire a distance of a hundred feet. While the fête was in progress, two fountains of wine flowed continuously for the common people.

This was the last of the showy functions at the executive mansion. Probably no governor of Louisiana, not even Bienville, was ever so beset with difficulties or harassed by jealous and vindictive enemies as was Kerlerec. An honest and frugal man, with the welfare of his country at heart, he was appalled by the reckless expenditure of public money, by the corruption of officials, and by the dissolute habits of the citizenry. But when he sought to correct the most obvious of the evils which afflicted the province, he was hampered at every turn by the new Intendant-Commissary, Rochemore, who was his bitter enemy from the beginning of his administration. Arrayed against him also were the adherents of the Marquis de Vaudreuil whom he had summarily dismissed from their posts, and the same clique of trouble-makers which had worked so successfully against Bienville. Dissatisfied with the failure of the provincial government to furnish gifts and reliable trade goods according to promise, the Choctaws and other Indian allies of the French were gradually being won over by the English, who had penetrated into the Ohio Valley and were even appearing in increasing numbers in the area which now forms the states of Alabama and Mississippi. Alarmed by these encroachments, and clearly discerning the cloud of war which hung over the continent and threatened the very existence of the French colonies, Kerlerec attempted to organize the defenses of the province, and particularly of New Orleans. The provincial treasury was practically exhausted, but by pledging his salary and his private credit Kerlerec at length succeeded in raising enough money to construct a palisade about the city and to strengthen the batteries at the English

Turn.[1] But when these modest works had been completed,
he was unable to muster an army sufficiently large to man
them. Most of the troops of the garrison had been sent to
Canada with the Marquis de Vaudreuil, and replacements
had not been forthcoming from France. Nor did the French
government, busy with European intrigue, pay any attention
to his appeals for men and money. To all intents and purposes, Louisiana was abandoned to its fate when the Marquis de Vaudreuil sailed for Canada.

The few soldiers who remained in the province were
the same sort as the recruits who had aroused such an outburst of indignation from Bienville more than twenty years
before. Moreover, they were for the most part commanded
by men who treated them as slaves and who put personal
gain above every consideration of honor and country. Mu-
tinies were frequent, but were put down with a gradually
increasing severity which culminated in the punishment
meted out in 1754 to the rebels of Cat Island. On this little
knob of land in the Gulf of Mexico, now called Ship Island,
was stationed a small detachment of troops under the command of an officer named Duroux, whose treatment of his
men was unbelievably harsh. The provisions issued to the
troops he confiscated and sold, and the soldiers had for food
only the few fish they could catch and what they salvaged
from the wreckage of the Gulf. Instead of performing their
military duties, they labored for long hours burning charcoal
and lime, which Duroux sold for his private profit. Duroux's
orders were enforced by a chosen few who received good

---

[1] In September 1699, when Bienville was descending the Mississippi
after his first voyage of exploration in Louisiana, he came upon an English
ship lying in midstream near the mouth of the river. The captain of the vessel
told Bienville that he was searching for a good place to make a settlement,
but Bienville informed him that the French had already explored the country
and taken possession of it. The Englishman turned his ship about and sailed
away, and Bienville called the point *Le Détour Anglais*, or English Turn, a
name which still survives.

food and treatment, and who possessed the only firearms not kept under lock and key. For the least infraction of Duroux's edicts, men were beaten and mutilated, thrown into prison to starve, or tied naked to trees in the broiling sun to be tortured to death by flies and mosquitoes. Several of the soldiers escaped and came to New Orleans to complain to the Governor, but Kerlerec, a stern believer in the military maxim that an officer is always right, sent them back to the island and horrible punishments. A few days later the soldiers rose in revolt, killed Duroux, and threw his body into the Gulf. The mutineers reached the mainland near Mobile, and in company with a party of English traders set out across the country for Georgia, but were captured by a pursuing band of Choctaws and taken to New Orleans. There they were tried and three ringleaders sentenced to death. The sentences were carried out in the Place d'Armes before an enormous crowd. Two of the doomed men were broken on the wheel, which means they were spread-eagled to a wheel-like contraption and their bones broken, one by one, with a sledge-hammer. The third was nailed alive in a coffin, and the coffin was then sawed in two.

Kerlerec's troubles in New Orleans were intensified and increased by a bitter religious controversy, known in Louisiana history as "the War of the Jesuits and the Capuchins," which raged fiercely throughout most of his administration. In 1722, when the provincial capital was transferred from Biloxi Bay to New Orleans, the French government found it "necessary to re-establish ecclesiastical divisions to avoid disputes among rival orders of missionaries. The first division, comprising the valley of the Mississippi from the Gulf to the Ohio and including the territory west of the river, was allotted to the Capuchins, whose superior was to reside in New Orleans. The second division, including the territory north of the Ohio, was given to the Jesuits, whose headquarters were among the Illinois. The third division,

lying south of the Ohio and east of the Mississippi, was put
at first under the care of the Carmelites, whose superior
was to reside at Mobile. The Church of Louisiana was still
under the general supervision of that of Canada, and each
of the three heads was a grand vicar of the Bishop of
Quebec. As the Carmelites were unable to occupy the territory assigned to them, their field of work was given to
the Capuchins, and the Jesuits were allowed to establish
missions as far south as Natchez, both east and west of
the Mississippi."

Within a few years after these allotments of territory
had been made, the Jesuits were in New Orleans, several
priests of the order having been sent to the city by the
Mississippi Company. The Jesuit Superior was given permission to reside in the city on condition that he perform
no ecclesiastical functions without the consent of the Superior of the Capuchins. This entering wedge was sufficient
for the energetic sons of the Society of Jesus. By another
year they were in full possession of a large tract of land
in the heart of the present New Orleans, given them by
Bienville, which was soon enlarged by donation and purchase. This area they cultivated, introducing the fig and the
orange into Louisiana and making experiments in the culture of indigo and sugar-cane. But they were not satisfied,
for long, to remain peaceful property-holders and tillers of
the soil. Wrote Gayarré:

"The Jesuits . . . gradually usurped many of
the functions of the Capuchins, in spite of the strenuous
opposition to the latter, and had carried their audacity
so far as to threaten to interdict their rivals altogether. The poor Capuchins, who were completely bewildered, and who were wanting in the spirit and ability
necessary to cope with such adversaries, contented
themselves with uttering loud complaints, and clamor-

ing for the help of the government. . . . This was the question which had agitated the colony for several years. . . . It was called the *War of the Jesuits and the Capuchins,* and produced much irritation at the time. It gave rise to acrimonious writings, squibs, pasquinades, and satirical songs. The women, in particular, made themselves conspicuous for the vivacity of their zeal either for one or the other." [1]

The controversy raged with increasing bitterness until 1764, when the Capuchins were victorious by reason of the famous Order of Expulsion, which banished the Jesuits from the dominions of the kingdoms of France, Spain, and Naples. All property held by the order in Louisiana was sold, bringing the then enormous sum of $180,000, most of which was confiscated by the colonial government. In 1773 the Society of Jesus was abolished by the Pope, but it was soon reorganized and within a very few years had again acquired a foothold in the province. Today the Jesuits own more property in Louisiana, and wield greater power and influence, than ever before.

8

THE Seven Years' War, which was destined to change the map of North America and end French power in the New World, began in 1755, and thereafter the position of Louisiana became increasingly perilous. Soldier and civilian refugees from the French garrisons and settlements in the north, adding to the gloom with their accounts of English victories, found the colony torn by religious and political dissension, the Indians sullen and resentful because the French had fulfilled none of their promises, and Kerlerec striving desperately but hopelessly to placate the savages and put the feeble defenses of the province in order. Scores of farmers

---

[1] *History of Louisiana,* Volume II, pages 80, 81.

had abandoned their acres and fled to the comparative safety of New Orleans, where they added to Kerlerec's troubles by clamoring for the protection and supplies which the government was obligated to furnish. But Kerlerec could do nothing for them. No help was sent or even promised by France, which had chosen to abandon her American colonies to their fate and concentrate her military efforts in Europe. For four years not a single French vessel arrived at New Orleans, and there would have been an actual shortage of food in the colony had not the English Governor of Jamaica, with more regard for his personal profit than his official honor, contrived secretly to land supplies at New Orleans by means of parlementaries, vessels which put into the port ostensibly for purposes of parley.

Meanwhile the armies of England and her colonies were everywhere victorious, and by the end of 1760 had conquered Canada and all the French posts on the upper Ohio, including Fort Duquesne, site of the present city of Pittsburgh. Of all the vast domain of France in America, nothing remained to her but Louisiana, and that unhappy province lay defenseless, at the mercy of any enemy who cared to attack it. The English conquests were confirmed in 1763 by the Treaty of Paris, whereby France ceded to England most of India and all of her American possessions lying east of the Mississippi River, and renounced all claim to Canada and Nova Scotia, or Acadia. To these grants was added a guarantee of free navigation of the Mississippi. At the same time Spain ceded to England all her territory east and southeast of the river, including Florida, and received in return Havana, which had been captured by the English fleet. By this treaty France retained possession of Louisiana and New Orleans, but actually the disposition of the province and its capital city had been decided on November 3, 1762, three months before the Treaty of Paris was signed. On that date the French monarch formally ceded to the King of Spain

" all the country known under the name of Louisiana, and also New Orleans with the island on which it is situated." But the act of cession, made under the provisions of the Family Pact to which all the Bourbon kings of Europe were signatories, was kept a close secret. Nothing was known of it in New Orleans, excepting the vaguest of rumors, until the early summer of 1764, when the French King officially notified the people of Louisiana that they were subjects of Spain. Nevertheless, Louisiana continued to be governed as a French province for almost seven years after it had actually become Spanish territory.

Kerlerec was succeeded on June 29, 1763 by Sieur d'Abadie and soon afterwards left for Paris, where he was promptly accused of various violations of duty and usurpation of power and was imprisoned in the Bastille. In March 1766 Don Antonio de Ulloa arrived at New Orleans with one small frigate and ninety soldiers. He declined to present his credentials to the Superior Council and refused to recognize any authority save that vested in Charles Aubri, who as senior Captain of the garrison had succeeded d'Abadie when the latter died in 1765. Aubri ruled Louisiana both as the French Commandant and as the representative of Ulloa until late in 1768, when the Spaniard was driven from New Orleans by a revolt which was largely the result of his vacillating attitude and the general fear and uncertainty of Spain's intentions regarding the colony. The principal conspirators were Nicolas Chauvin de la Frénière, the Attorney-General; Foucault, who had succeeded Rochemore as Intendant-Commissary; Jean Baptiste Noyan, a nephew of the founder of New Orleans; and a dozen others, all prominent merchants and planters. A memorial describing the sorry state of the province and imploring the aid of the French King was sent with a delegation to Paris, but before anything could be done there, open hostilities developed in New Orleans. On the night of October 28, 1768 the guns at

Tchoupitoulas gate were spiked, and bands of Acadians headed by Noyan, and of farmers from the German coast commanded by Joseph Villeré, a merchant, entered the city. Ulloa and his troops sought refuge aboard the Spanish frigate lying in the river, and on November 1 the ship's cable was cut and she sailed for Havana. With the expulsion of Ulloa the colonists considered that they had thrown off the yoke of Spain, and the conspirators discussed the formation of a republic. Delegates were sent to Mobile and other former French settlements now in the hands of the English, and also to the English colonies in the north, to propose a union with Louisiana and rebellion against European rule. But this project was shortlived, for on August 18, 1769 Don Alexander O'Reilly, an Irish soldier of fortune who in the service of Spain had become one of Europe's most celebrated generals, landed at New Orleans with an overwhelming force — twenty-four warships, three thousand picked soldiers, and fifty pieces of artillery. The Superior Council immediately recognized these as proper credentials, and with impressive ceremonies in the Place d'Armes, O'Reilly took possession of Louisiana in the name of the King of Spain.

CHAPTER II

IN THE DAYS OF THE DONS

O'REILLY PUT an immediate end to the activities of the revolutionists by the arrest of twelve of the principal leaders of the movement, who were taken into custody by Spanish soldiers while attending a state dinner at the Governor's mansion. All were tried and convicted, and six were condemned to the gallows. But since there was no public executioner in Louisiana, and no white man could be induced to serve in that capacity, the sentence was changed to death by shooting. One of the doomed men, Joseph Villeré, died in prison, but on October 25, 1769 the others — La Frénière, Noyan, Pierre Marquis, Joseph Milhet, and Pierre Caresse — were marched into the Place d'Armes, handcuffed and with their arms tied behind them. While the soldiers of the firing squad charged their muskets, a fire was kindled to the left of the prisoners, into which a Negro threw several bundles of papers. As they blazed up, O'Reilly's official crier, a little old man clad in a rusty black robe, walked round and round the flames, shouting in a loud voice:

"This, the memorial of the planters of Louisiana, is, by order of His Excellency Don Alexander O'Reilly, thus publicly burnt, for containing the following rebellious and atrocious doctrines: 'Liberty is the mother of commerce and population. Without liberty there are but few virtues.'"

A soldier stepped forward to bind the eyes of the condemned men, but they scornfully refused his offices. The crier announced that O'Reilly had decided to spare Noyan because of his youth, but the heroic young patriot declined to accept the pardon.

"With my comrades I fought!" he cried. "With them I die!"

As the fire dwindled to ashes, the soldiers wheeled and fired, and the five men fell dead. The crowd which had gathered to witness the execution slowly dispersed, cowed and impressed by this display of Spanish power and ruthlessness. The six remaining conspirators were imprisoned in the dungeons of Castle Morro, at Havana, but were released within a year at the request of the King of France. The property of all the convicted men was confiscated, excepting small portions which were given to their families.

O'Reilly now devoted his energies to putting in order the tangled and complicated affairs of the province. One of his first acts was to order a census of New Orleans, which showed a total population of 3,190 persons of all ages, sexes, and colors. Of this number, 1,225 were Negro slaves and sixty were domiciled Indians. (Incidentally, under the Spanish law Indians could no longer be held as slaves.) Of the free citizens, thirty-one were Negroes and sixty-eight were of mixed blood. The town contained 468 houses, all within four streets of the Mississippi. No census was taken of the rest of the province, but the number of inhabitants, including those in New Orleans, was estimated at 13,538, about half of whom were slaves. The population of Louisiana had more than doubled since the close of Bienville's administration, but most of the increase had occurred during the war with England, when hundreds of French colonists fled from the conquered territories and made their way to New Orleans and other Louisiana settlements. There had also been a considerable immigration of Acadians, who had been expelled from Nova Scotia by the English. The first group of these unhappy exiles, twenty in number, arrived early in 1764. Others followed, and between January 1 and May 13, 1765, about 650 landed at New Orleans. From there they were sent to establish settlements at Attakapas and Opelousas. A census taken in 1787 gave the number of Acadians in Louisiana as 1,587.[1]

O'Reilly abolished the Superior Council and organized in its stead, as the governing body of the city and province, "the Very Illustrious Cabildo," composed of six perpetual regidores, or aldermen; two alcaldes, or judges; an attorney-general syndic, and a clerk. Over these officials the Governor presided in person. O'Reilly also abrogated all the French statutes except the Black Code, which was retained by special proclamation as a law of the land, and substituted the system of judicial and military administration in effect in the other Spanish colonies in America. The policing of New Orleans devolved upon the troops, but the duty of maintaining law and order in the smaller settlements and in the rural districts appears to have been placed in the hands of the Santa Hermandad, or Holy Brotherhood. The members of this order, whenever they captured a culprit, acted as both judge and executioner. O'Reilly thus referred to the Brotherhood in a summary of the Spanish laws which he issued on November 25, 1769:

"The principal object of the institution of the tribunal of the Santa Hermandad (Holy Brotherhood) being to repress disorders and to prevent the robberies and assassinations committed in the unfrequented places by vagabonds and delinquents, who conceal themselves in the woods, from which they sally to attack travelers and the neighboring inhabitants, the Alcalde Mayor

[1] Descendants of the Acadians are still living, somewhat primitively, in the districts where the refugees first settled. The name has been corrupted to Cajun.

Provincial shall assemble a sufficient number of members or brothers of the Santa Hermandad, to clear his jurisdiction of the perpetrators of such evil deeds, by pursuing them with spirit, seizing, or putting them to death."

Some of the acts catalogued as crimes, and the punishments inflicted for them, illustrated the exaggerated adoration of Church and King which was characteristic of the Spain of the period. One article of O'Reilly's summary provided that "he who shall revile our Savior, or His mother the Holy Virgin Mary, shall have his tongue cut out, and his property shall be confiscated, applicable one-half to the public treasury, and the other half to the informer." Another article decreed flogging and confiscation of property for anyone who vilified the King or any other member of the royal family. If a commoner used scurrilous language to the detriment of another citizen, he was subject to a fine of 1,200 maravedis, but if a nobleman committed a similar offense the fine was 2,000 maravedis. A married woman caught in adultery and her partner in sin were delivered up to the husband to be dealt with as he pleased. The law provided, however, that he could not put one to death without inflicting the same punishment on the other.

Soon after the organization of the Cabildo, by an ordinance promulgated on February 22, 1770, O'Reilly provided the first municipal revenue for the town of New Orleans. An annual tax of forty dollars was levied upon each tavern, billiard-table, and coffee-house, and twenty dollars upon each boarding-house; and a duty of one dollar was charged against every barrel of brandy brought into the city. A special tax was assessed for the maintenance of the levee — six dollars on every boat of two hundred tons burden and over, and three dollars on every smaller craft anchoring in the port. To help meet the growing expenses of the municipality, the butchers offered to pay into the treasury annually the sum of $370, at the same time solemnly binding themselves not to increase the price of meat. The offer was accepted. On behalf of the King of Spain, O'Reilly ceded to the city two plots of ground on St. Peter and St. Ann Streets, facing the Place d'Armes and extending from Levee (now Decatur) Street to Chartres Street. Each plot had a frontage of 336 feet and a depth of 84. Soon after the cession the property was leased in perpetuity to Don Andres Almonaster y Roxas, a nobleman of Andalusia who had come to New Orleans with O'Reilly. He became the richest man in Louisiana and was the city's earliest and most generous philanthropist; to him the city owes every public building that remains from colonial days. He erected stores and a few dwellings on the sites leased from the city, and for many years the two blocks facing the Place d'Armes comprised the fashionable retail district of the city. After his death the property passed to his young daughter, Michaela, who later married Xavier Delfair, Baron de Pontalba. She lived in Paris until the French Revolution of 1848, when she fled with her family to New Orleans. About 1850 she razed the buildings which had been put up by her father, and erected two identical apartment houses on St. Peter and St. Ann Streets. For at least a quarter of a century they were the finest structures of their kind in America, and to live in them was a great mark of gentility.[1] The Baroness de Pontalba also started the movement which resulted in an act of the Legislature changing the name of the Place d'Armes to Jackson Square, and was a liberal contributor to the fund

---

[1] The Pontalba Buildings remained high-class residences for a considerable period after the Civil War. Afterwards they became cheap tenements, occupied by low-class Italian families, who destroyed much of the handsome woodwork, the marble mantels, and other fittings. In recent years the row on St. Ann Street has been acquired by the state, and that on St. Peter Street by the city. Under the direction of the Upper Pontalba Building Commission the latter has been remodeled into small apartments.

raised for the purchase of the equestrian statue of Jackson, by Clark Mills, which now stands in the center of the square.[1]

2

AFTER the baptism of blood and terror with which O'Reilly had inaugurated the rule of Spain in Louisiana, he and his successors in the executive mansion governed the province with kindness and moderation and with almost an entire absence of the political strife and chicanery which had characterized the administrations of the French governors. The prosperity and general well-being of Louisiana and her capital were far greater under the Spanish than they had ever been under the French. O'Reilly expelled the English traders who had monopolized the trade of the river and had even opened shops in New Orleans, but Don Louis de Unzaga, to whom O'Reilly transferred the gubernatorial authority at the first meeting of the Cabildo, extended the commerce of the province in other directions, and even found it expedient to countenance a contraband trade with the English, who anchored their boats across the Mississippi from New Orleans and carried on a thriving business with the tradesmen of the town.

Several American merchants from New York, Philadelphia, and Boston, who had established themselves in New Orleans during the final years of the French régime, would doubtless have suffered the fate of the English had it not been for the forethought of Oliver Pollock, of Philadelphia. Some of O'Reilly's decrees had the effect of temporarily paralyzing trade, and various commodities became very scarce throughout the province. Among them was flour,

---

[1] It was unveiled on February 9, 1856. The inscription on the base: "The Union Must and Shall Be Preserved," was cut in 1862 by order of Major-General Benjamin F. Butler, commander of the Yankee Army which occupied New Orleans after the capture of the city by Farragut.

which reached the unprecedented price of twenty dollars a barrel. At the height of the crisis a ship arrived from Baltimore with a cargo of flour consigned to Pollock. Instead of taking advantage of the colony's needs, Pollock offered the flour to O'Reilly at the latter's own price. O'Reilly bought the entire cargo at fifteen dollars a barrel, reported Pollock's generous deed to the King of Spain, and gave the merchant the right of free entry for all of his goods. During the American Revolution Pollock and others, with the aid and consent of Governor Bernardo de Gálvez, supplied the colonists with large quantities of arms and ammunition, by means of large canoes which were poled and paddled up the Mississippi and Ohio Rivers to Pittsburgh.

Twenty years after the Spaniards took possession of Louisiana, the population of the province had more than tripled, and that of New Orleans had almost doubled. According to a census taken early in 1788 under the direction of Don Estevan de Miró, who became Governor in 1783 when Gálvez was promoted to be Viceroy of Mexico, the number of inhabitants in the entire province was 42,346, including 1,700 free Negroes and about 18,000 slaves, while the population of New Orleans was reported as 5,338. So far as population and commercial importance were concerned, New Orleans had assumed the semblance of a bustling city, but its physical aspect was still that of a dirty, poorly built frontier settlement. Most of the houses were rude cabins constructed of rough-hewn cypress planks and logs, and large areas of swamp land remained within the city limits, the breeding-places of insects and reptiles. Practically all of the town's structural eyesores, however, were destroyed by two great fires which devastated New Orleans during the last fifteen years of the eighteenth century.

The first of these conflagrations occurred in the late afternoon of March 21, 1788, when a lighted candle on the altar of a chapel in the home of Don Vincente Nuñez, mili-

53

tary treasurer of the province, set fire to the draperies of
the altar and soon consumed the building. Carried on a
strong south wind, the flames spread with great rapidity,
and within an hour most of the town was afire. Because the
day was Good Friday, the priests refused to allow the church
bells to be rung; consequently no alarm could be sounded,
and the conflagration gained such headway that it could not
be checked. The fire raged for five hours, and destroyed 856
buildings, including all the stores and dwellings save a few
which fronted the river; the church, the town hall, the convent of the Capuchins, the watch-house, the prison, the
charity hospital, and the arsenal with all its contents except
750 muskets, which were saved. In his report to the Spanish
government at Madrid Miró gave a detailed account of the
losses, which he set down at $2,595,561. For two nights sev-
eral hundred people lacked adequate shelter, and many were
without food, while Miró marshaled the resources of the
province. Then the government stores were thrown open,
and rations of rice were given to all who applied, while tents
were erected in the Place d'Armes for the accommodation
of those who had lost their homes. Miró also sent ships to
Philadelphia, bearing twenty-four thousand dollars for the
purchase of flour, and removed all restrictions on trade during the period of the emergency, so that supplies came into
the city from hitherto unavailable sources.

The people of New Orleans were greatly impressed by
the promptness and efficiency with which Miró came to their
relief, and he became one of the most popular governors who
ever ruled Louisiana. He earned their gratitude to an even
greater extent about a year later, when he acted with great
promptness and energy to forestall and remove a danger
which threatened the city and which might have had an appalling effect on the prosperity of the entire province. During the late spring of 1789 Governor Miró received a long
communication from a Capuchin monk, Antonio de Sedella,

lately arrived in New Orleans on a mission which he had kept a profound secret from the officials of the colony. Sedella wrote that on December 6, 1788 he had been appointed Commissary of the Inquisition, and that he had been instructed to establish a tribunal of the Holy Office in New Orleans and discharge his functions with the utmost zeal. He wrote further that he would soon require soldiers to assist him in apprehending and punishing heretics, as his preliminary preparations had been completed.

Governor Miró received Sedella's communication late in the afternoon, and that same night the priest was roused from slumber to find a squad of soldiers at his door. Assuming that they had been sent to carry out his commands, he thanked them and praised Miró for his prompt compliance with the wishes of the Inquisition. But he suggested that they return to their barracks, as he had at present no need of their services. Instead of obeying, however, the soldiers placed the priest under arrest and took him aboard a ship which lay in the harbor. There he was kept under close guard until the next day, when the vessel sailed for Cadiz. Thus ended the only attempt of the Catholic Church to establish the Inquisition in what is now the United States. But just how narrow was the escape of the people of New Orleans from the horrors of the Holy Office was not known until half a century later, when the old calaboose which stood near the church was destroyed. Lyle Saxon wrote:

". . . Strange things came to light. There were found secret rooms, iron instruments of torture, and other indications that a private court had held meetings there. In addition to this, old newspaper files tell of the discovery of an underground passage which led from the rear of the Cathedral, or from even beyond that point in the direction of the Capuchin monastery — a passage which ended somewhere under the Calaboose. These newspaper accounts are very strange. One day the paper tells of the discovery and promises further disclosures on the following day, when the tunnel has been explored. But it is evident that some pressure was brought to bear on the editor, for there is not a line in any of the later editions of the same paper regarding this discovery. One can only draw his own conclusions." [1]

In an official dispatch to the Spanish government, dated June 3, 1789, Miró thus commented on Sedella and his activities:

"When I read the communication of that Capuchin, I shuddered. His Majesty has ordered me to foster the increase of population in this province, and to admit in it all those who would emigrate from the banks of those rivers which empty themselves into the Ohio. . . . This emigration was to be encouraged under the pledge that the new colonists should not be molested in matters of religion, provided there should be no other public mode of worship than the Catholic. The mere name of the Inquisition uttered in New Orleans not only would be sufficient to check immigration, which is successfully progressing, but would also be capable of driving away those who have recently come, and I fear that, in spite of my having sent out of the country Father Sedella, the most fatal consequences may ensue from the mere suspicion of the cause of his dismissal." [2]

---

[1] *Fabulous New Orleans;* New York, 1928; page 152.

[2] Gayarré's *History of Louisiana*, Volume III, pages 270–1. In an article in the *Louisiana Historical Quarterly* for October 1919, Clarence Wyatt Bispham, S.T.M., denied that Father Sedella attempted to establish the Inquisition. He maintained that the priest's purposes were purely political.

A few years after he had been so summarily expelled, Father Sedella returned to New Orleans, not as a torturer of the Inquisition, but as curé of the Cathedral and a simple Capuchin monk. For almost forty years his gaunt figure, clad in a loose habit of coarse brown cloth with a hempen girdle about his waist and wooden sandals on his feet, was a familiar sight in the narrow streets of the Vieux Carré. Although Father Antoine apparently conducted himself with great piety and an extraordinary devotion to duty, he was almost constantly involved in bitter altercations with his ecclesiastical superiors; and even the civil government, after the American occupation, looked upon his activities with suspicion. Early in 1805 he was suspended from duty by Father Patrick Walsh, Vicar-General of the diocese, but practically the entire Catholic community, headed by the Marquis of Casa-Calvo, Governor of Louisiana from 1799 to 1801, who had remained in New Orleans as a representative of Spain and head of the Spanish secret agents, sided with the Capuchin, and Father Walsh was compelled to reinstate him. Further efforts to dislodge Father Antoine by recourse to the Supreme Court of the territory having failed, Father Walsh wrote to Governor W. C. C. Claiborne asking for aid and complaining of the "interruption of public tranquillity" which had resulted from "the ambitions of a refractory monk," and accusing Father Antoine and the Marquis of Casa-Calvo of promoting views equally dangerous to religious and to civil order. Governor Claiborne replied that it was not the custom of the American government to interfere or take sides in religious disputes, and counseled harmony and tolerance. But Father Walsh had succeeded in implanting in the Governor's mind suspicion of Father Antoine's loyalty. He wrote to the Secretary of War at Washington:

" We have a Spanish priest here who is a very dangerous man. He rebelled against the superiors of his own church, and would even rebel, I am persuaded, against this government whenever a fit occasion may serve. This man was once sent away by the Spanish authorities for seditious practices, and I am inclined to think that I should be justifiable, should I do likewise. This seditious priest is Father Antoine. He is a great favorite of the Louisiana ladies, and has married many of them and christened all their children. He is by some citizens esteemed an accomplished hypocrite; has great influence with the people of color, and report says, embraces every opportunity to render them discontented under the American government."

Soon after sending this dispatch Governor Claiborne summoned Father Antoine to his office, and in the presence of Mayor James Pitot informed him of the reports which had been circulated. Although the priest protested his innocence, Governor Claiborne required him to take the oath of allegiance, and for several years thereafter his conduct was carefully watched. Later Governor Claiborne wrote to Washington:

" The priest declared the reports to have originated in the malice of his enemies. The division in the Catholic Church has excited many malignant passions, and it is not improbable that some injustice has been done to this individual."

Despite his encounters with the government and the dignitaries of his Church, Father Antoine became one of the best-loved men in the history of New Orleans. He died in 1829, at the age of eighty-one, and on the day of his funeral business of every description was suspended, while the members of the City Council passed an ordinance pledging themselves to wear crape on their left arms for thirty days. The body of the monk was buried in the Cathedral, in the rear of which he had lived in a rude hut of boughs and planks, but some years later was removed to "the priests' tomb" in the old St. Louis Cemetery.

3

THE second of the great fires of early New Orleans occurred on December 8, 1794, during the administration of Baron de Carondelet as Governor. Starting in a courtyard in Royal Street, where some children were playing with flint and tinder, the flames spread quickly to an adjoining hayloft and then, fanned by a north wind, swept through a large portion of the city. Two hundred and twelve buildings were destroyed, including all the stores save two, and several important governmental structures. In his report of the disaster Baron de Carondelet said that the financial losses were greater than in the fire of 1788, although fewer houses were burned. But both of these conflagrations proved to be blessings in disguise, for as Grace King says, " what lay in the ashes was, at best, but an irregular, ill-built French town," while " what arose from them was a stately Spanish city, proportioned with grace and built with solidity." [1] The old part of New Orleans is still called the French Quarter, but all of the buildings which date from colonial times are Spanish in design and architecture. The rebuilding of the city was begun immediately after both disasters, but the staggering losses and the large sums expended for relief had so depleted the provincial treasury that the government would have found it well-nigh impossible to reconstruct its administrative, judicial, and ecclesiastical edifices had not

---

[1] There is still a saying in New Orleans that the Spaniards found the city " a town of hovels and left it a city of palaces." To the outsider the " palaces " which remain from Spanish times scarcely justify the statement.

Don Andres Almonaster assumed the burden, at the cost of a great part of his fortune. Out of his private purse he rebuilt and presented to the city the schoolhouse, established in 1772 and the first public school in New Orleans; the charity hospital founded in Bienville's time by the sailor Jean Louis; the convent of the Capuchins; and the Cathedral, which was razed in 1850 to make way for the present building, which Gayarré described as "an upstart production of bad taste." The hospital alone cost Don Andres $114,000, and the Cathedral $50,000. He also built for the city a new calaboose on St. Peter between Chartres and Royal Streets, a new arsenal, a new custom-house, and a new Cabildo House.[1] A little later, also largely as a result of Don Andres's munificence, workmen began the construction of the first arcades of the so-called French Market, which is Spanish from foundation to chimney-pots.

Until the administration of Carondelet the arrangements for policing New Orleans and other settlements, and for protecting the inhabitants against the depredations of criminals, were sketchy, to say the least. A few soldiers occasionally patrolled the streets of the capital city, and in the rural districts the apprehension of evil-doers presumably remained the duty of the Santa Hermandad, although after O'Reilly's time the old records make no mention of the Holy Brotherhood. But the efforts of these forces to suppress crime and disorder, especially in New Orleans, were seldom effective; and since the Spanish officials, carrying out the government's policy of encouraging immigration, did not scan too closely the records and credentials of new-comers, the city gradually acquired a large population of thieves and vagabonds of every nationality. Robbery and murder were of frequent occurrence, while taverns, gambling-dens and

---

[1] Except for the addition of a mansard roof, the building is today substantially as it was then. Since the American occupation the structure itself has been referred to as the Cabildo.

bawdy-houses ignored the laws by which they were supposedly regulated, and kept open at all hours to accommodate drunken, brawling crowds. While perhaps not the first Spanish Governor to recognize the existence of these conditions, Carondelet was the first to take any real steps toward correcting them or to make any effort to establish a regularly organized police force. In his initial proclamation, on January 22, 1792, Carondelet provided for the division of New Orleans into four wards, each under the administration of an Alcalde de Barrio, or Commissary of Police. These officials were also to take charge of all fire-fighting apparatus and to organize companies of firemen and ax-men, for duty at conflagrations. All persons renting houses or apartments were required to give the names of new tenants to the alcalde of the district on the first day of occupancy.

In one of his early communications to the Cabildo, Carondelet recommended that provision be made for lighting the city and employing night watchmen, proposing that a chimney tax be levied to pay the costs. These suggestions were not acted upon by the Cabildo, however, until 1796, when a tax of nine reals ($1.12½) was imposed upon every chimney in the city; a body of thirteen *serenos,* or night watchmen, was organized; and eighty large lamps were purchased to be hung in the streets. The annual upkeep of watchmen and lamps was estimated at $3,898. Carondelet also reorganized the Civil Guard, which now began to patrol the city during the day in squads of four or five, each in full uniform with cocked hat, blue breeches and frock coat, and breast straps of shiny black leather supporting a cartridge box and a bayonet scabbard. His armament consisted of a short sword and a flintlock musket.

Carondelet said in a dispatch to the Spanish government at Madrid that he had inaugurated these police and crime-prevention measures because of "the frequent and almost inevitable robberies which are perpetrated in the city

61

of six thousand souls by a multitude of vagabonds of every nation," but he was actually influenced fully as much by the revolutionary spirit which had appeared in New Orleans following the beheading of Louis XVI, and Spain's declaration of war against the new French government. For several years New Orleans was a veritable hotbed of revolutionary agitation, but no actual effort was ever made to revolt against Spanish domination. The only real effect was to add to the restlessness of the Negro slaves, among whom a dangerous spirit had prevailed since the rebellion of the blacks in Santo Domingo in 1791 and the massacre of the whites. Apparently at the instigation of disaffected white men, this at length culminated in a conspiracy organized on the plantation of Julien Paydras, noted throughout Louisiana as the most indulgent of masters, in Pointe Coupée Parish, a thinly settled district about one hundred and fifty miles from New Orleans. The conspirators fixed upon April 14, 1795 as the date of the revolt. On that day all the whites in the parish, except the women and grown girls, were to be killed and an army of Negroes formed to march upon New Orleans and other settlements. But the leaders disagreed, and one of them at length revealed the details of the uprising to the authorities. All of the principal plotters, including three white men, were arrested, and twenty-five Negroes were killed when a large party of blacks attempted to rescue them. After trial the white men were banished from the province, while twenty-three Negroes were placed aboard a boat, which drifted slowly down the river from Pointe Coupée. At every parish church between that village and New Orleans, the boat stopped and one of the Negroes was hanged to a tree.

4

A YEAR after his accession to office, in 1778, Governor Bernardo de Gálvez granted to Louisiana the right to trade with any port of France and Spain, and with the thirteen British colonies then engaged in their war for independence. Apparently this ruling opened the Mississippi to the commerce of the American territories west of the Alleghanies, but actually the grant was hedged about with so many restrictions and so burdened with heavy tariffs that the only economic gain to the province was a slight increase in seaborne commerce. There was practically no expansion of trade along the Mississippi, for the Spanish government at Madrid held that Gálvez's grant did not make the river a free waterway. Spain persisted in this attitude even after the Revolution, barring American boats from the Mississippi on the ground that the United States possessed no territory on either bank. Cargoes which venturesome American traders started to New Orleans were more often than not confiscated by Spanish officials *en route,* and the few which reached the city were immediately seized by the government and sold, and the proceeds applied to the provincial treasury. Gálvez's successor, Miró, relaxed the restrictions as much as he dared in view of his definite instructions from Madrid to permit none but Spaniards to trade upon the river, but even this failed to bring American produce into New Orleans. The settlers in western America, especially the Kentuckians, who were cut off from the eastern markets by the mountains, were eager to trade with Louisiana, for they realized that their economic salvation depended upon free access to the sea by way of the river. But they distrusted the Spaniards, and the frequent seizures of boats and cargoes, even in Miró's time, kept this feeling alive and the temper of the Kentuckians at fever heat. The distress and dissatisfaction of the Americans were increased by the failure of Congress to establish a stable government in the western territories, to protect them from the Indians, or to come to their aid with strong representations to Spain for the free use of the Mississippi. Throughout the whole coun-

63

try west of the Alleghanies there was great discontent against the United States, and many factions proposed many solutions of their political and economic problems, the ultimate aim of all being to open the Mississippi to trade. Some urged an independent republic and an alliance with Spain; others advocated yielding to Spain and incorporating Kentucky as a part of Louisiana, and still others proposed that an army be formed to attack New Orleans and compel the Spanish government by force of arms to recognize American rights on the river.

To arouse this feeling of discontent had been Spain's principal object in forbidding American trade upon the Mississippi, and Miró shrewdly and energetically attempted to turn it to the advantage of his country. But above all he wished to avoid an open clash with the Kentuckians, for the defenses of New Orleans were in no better condition than during the time of the French, and they could scarcely have withstood the assault of even such a poorly equipped army as might have marched out of Kentucky. Miró carried on his intrigues, all aimed to detach Kentucky from the Union, without much hope of success until 1787, when he acquired a powerful and unscrupulous ally in the person of General James Wilkinson, an American officer during the Revolution who later became commander-in-chief of the regular Army and one of the commissioners to accept Louisiana from the French. Wilkinson had been an intimate friend of Benedict Arnold, and a member of the notorious Conway Cabal which had attempted to discredit George Washington and elevate General Horatio Gates to the supreme command of the Continental armies. In 1784 Wilkinson resigned from the Army and settled at Louisville, and soon obtained great influence over the Kentucky militia, the only really organized faction in the territory. He used his power to sow discord, and to stir up the Kentuckians against Congress. Wilkinson believed that he could quickly amass a fortune if he could secure exclusive trading rights at New Orleans, and apparently he made his plans with that end in view. He chose a spectacular method of bringing himself to the attention of the Spanish Governor of Louisiana. In 1787 he loaded a flatboat with bacon, flour, butter, and tobacco and sent it down the river to New Orleans. The cargo was seized at Natchez by the Spanish Commandant, but was released, and the flatboat allowed to proceed, when Wilkinson gave the official a pair of blooded horses.

At New Orleans the flatboat was again seized by the authorities, but one of Wilkinson's agents, a merchant, told Governor Miró that Wilkinson's merchandise had been sent down the river in order that its confiscation might give the American an excuse to lead his " wild Kentuckians " in an assault upon New Orleans. Miró at once released the cargo and allowed it to be sold. He also gave Wilkinson an audience, at which Wilkinson assured him that the Kentucky and Cumberland territories could easily be induced to secede from the United States and seek the protection of Spain, and that a secessionist movement in North Carolina, which resulted in the establishment of the shortlived state of Frankland, could also be manipulated for the benefit of Spain. Later Wilkinson amplified his assertions in a written memorial which he presented to Miró. The result of the interview was that Wilkinson became an agent of the Spanish government, and was thereafter referred to, in the correspondence between Miró and Madrid, as " Number Thirteen." He agreed to do all in his power to detach the western territories from the United States and bring them under the rule of Spain. In return for this treachery to his country, he received trading concessions and a pension from the Spanish government of two thousand dollars a year. The first commercial fruits of Wilkinson's schemes ripened early in 1788, when he was permitted to load a flatboat at New Orleans with manufactured goods and send it up the river to the Kentucky markets — the first cargo of the sort ever to ascend the Mississippi.

None of Wilkinson's flamboyant promises materialized, and his importance as a secret agent rapidly declined. After the Baron de Carondelet succeeded Miró as Governor late in 1791, Wilkinson's status appears to have been simply that of a paid spy, whose information was very often received by the Spanish authorities with a considerable degree of skepticism. Nor did Wilkinson's exclusive trading privileges prove to be the gold mine that he had expected. He shared his concession with friends in Kentucky, and several cargoes were shipped to New Orleans. But even of these Miró and Carondelet were compelled to seize and confiscate a considerable number, because of their orders from Spain and the watchful eye which the Madrid government kept upon the river. Profits were thus uncertain, and Wilkinson's group became increasingly loath to take chances with their boats and merchandise. Whatever potential value Wilkinson's concession might have possessed vanished utterly in 1795, when on October 20 delegates of the United States and Spain signed at Madrid a treaty which declared the Mississippi free to American commerce and made New Orleans a port of deposit for three years. Meanwhile Wilkinson had been reinstated in the United States Army, with a commission as Lieutenant-Colonel, and had been assigned to the Western Department under General Anthony Wayne. He became a Brigadier-General in 1792, and succeeded to the supreme command when Wayne died in 1796. During all these years Wilkinson continued his intrigues on behalf of Spain, and as late as 1800 was still receiving his pension from the Spanish government.[1]

---

[1] Wilkinson became Governor of Louisiana in 1805, and in the fall of that year informed the government of Aaron Burr's plan to establish an empire in the Southwest. Burr declared that Wilkinson had been associated with him in the scheme, and in 1811 Wilkinson was court-martialed, charged with aiding

Trade was brisk upon the Mississippi during the three years that followed the signing of the treaty, for the Kentuckians assumed that the arrangement was permanent, and invested heavily in boats and other equipment. But at the end of the three-year period the Spanish government forbade the further use of New Orleans and refused to name another port of deposit as provided by the treaty. American commerce could still move down the river, but there was no place where the cargoes could be sold or deposited to await transfer to seagoing ships. This breach of the Madrid treaty aroused the Kentuckians to new heights of anger and distrust, and throughout the country a movement to capture New Orleans began to assume definite shape, while President Adams ordered three regiments of regular troops to the Ohio River, and twelve others to be made ready for active service. The threat of war remained until Louisiana became a part of the United States and the Mississippi River an American waterway.

5

ON October 1, 1800 Louisiana was retroceded by Spain to France, but it was almost three years before the French government again took possession of the country. Meanwhile New Orleans and the remainder of the province were in much the same situation as they had been thirty years before — virtually abandoned by one country and as yet unclaimed by another. Nominally Spain remained in possession, and continued to govern the colony, but almost at once there was a lessening in the severity of law enforcement, in consequence of which the criminal element, which now formed a large proportion of the city's population, gained

---

Burr and with being in the pay of Spain. He was acquitted, certain correspondence with the Spanish government, which later established his guilt, not being available to the court. He was discharged from the Army a few years later, and died near Mexico City in 1825.

a foothold in New Orleans from which it was not dislodged for more than a hundred years. Bands of robbers roamed the streets, paying scant heed to the feeble efforts of the Civil Guard and the *serenos* to check their depredations; and while legitimate business languished because of the uncertainties which surrounded the province's trade and currency, there was a great increase in the number of low taverns, gambling-halls, coffee-houses, bagnios, and especially resorts of the type called *cabarets,* which combined groceries, dram-shops, gambling-dens, and houses of prostitution under one roof. Perhaps the most celebrated of these places was the Maison Coquet, situated on Royal Street in the heart of New Orleans, which advertised by posters at the street corners with, as was stated on the placards, "the express permission of the Honorable Civil Governor of the city."

The French Colonial Prefect, Pierre Clément de Laussat, arrived at New Orleans on March 20, 1803, to prepare for the coming of a French army commanded by General Victor, who would receive the province, on behalf of France, from the Spanish Governor. Instead of General Victor, however, a French vessel brought to New Orleans, in July, official notification that Louisiana had been purchased by the United States. On November 3, 1803, in the Hall of the Cabildo, Laussat received the keys of the city from Governor Salcedo, and the province was transformed from Spain to France. The Spanish troops garrisoned in New Orleans immediately boarded transports and sailed for Havana. To protect the city from the rioting and looting which had been freely threatened among the lower and criminal classes, New Orleans was patrolled night and day for the next two months by a battalion of three hundred men, organized by the American Consul, Daniel Clark, and composed of Creoles and Americans resident in the city. While awaiting the arrival of the American commissioners and their troops,

Laussat began the organization of a municipal government. Étienne de Boré, who had done so much for the commerce of Louisiana by his success in granulating the juice of the sugar-cane, was appointed Mayor. A Municipal Council replaced the Cabildo, and a company of militia was formed. The existing laws, including Bienville's Black Code, were retained, except such parts as might be inconsistent with the statutes of the United States, and the new Council adopted police regulations, in 108 articles, by which the conduct of the people was strictly regulated. Among other things, they forbade cursing, and driving carts on Sunday. Several of the new ordinances related to the conduct of the slaves and of the soldiers and sailors. One forbade any member of these classes to be abroad in the city after eight o'clock at night in the winter, or nine o'clock in the summer, without a written pass from his master or commanding officer. A cannon was fired each night in the Place d'Armes as a signal for the slaves to seek their homes, and for the soldiers and sailors to return to their barracks and ships. In 1850 the gun was removed to Congo Square, and the signal was given there until 1862, when the custom was abolished by the officers of the Union Army which occupied New Orleans after the capture of the city by Farragut. Thereafter the fire-bell was tolled nightly, a practice which was continued for more than forty years, long after the reason for it had been forgotten.

6

ON December 17, 1803 the American commissioners, General James Wilkinson and W. C. C. Claiborne, Governor of the Mississippi Territory, who became the first Governor of Louisiana, camped two miles above New Orleans with troops from Ohio, Kentucky, and Tennessee. On December 20 they entered the city and, with ceremonies in the Place d'Armes, took possession of the province on behalf of the United States.

When New Orleans became, in name at least, an American municipality, it was a compactly built little city of about 4,000 houses and 10,000 inhabitants, of whom some 5,000 were whites, 2,000 free Negroes, and the remainder slaves. From Levee (Decatur) Street the town was 600 yards in depth, although the houses beyond Dauphine Street in that direction were few in number. The settled area extended along the river front for about 1,200 yards. The stockade enclosed most of the town, with forts at the four corners, and the present Rampart Street was a line of palisaded fortifications, while what is now Canal Street, one of the famous thoroughfares of the world, was a moat filled with water, ending in a military gate on the Tchoupitoulas Road, near the levee. All of the public buildings, of which the Cabildo, the Arsenal, and the French Market remain today substantially as they were then, faced the Place d'Armes, which was no more than a grass plot, barren of trees and shrubbery. A wooden gallows stood, stark and terrible, about where the statue of General Jackson now gallantly bestrides a bronze charger. On Chartres Street, facing the Cabildo, were the instruments of punishment most frequently used — the pillories. There were two of these devices. One imprisoned the head and hands of the culprit, while the other held only the fingers of one or both hands with the first joints bent. An offender sentenced to exposure in the pillory for stealing sat on a low platform, while from his neck dangled a placard on which was written:

"My name is ———. I am a thief. I stole from ———. Sentenced to ——— days' exposure at the pillory."

The practice of thus exposing whites to the ridicule of the town, and to the rotten fruit and other missiles hurled by boys and the riff-raff, was abolished about 1827, but the pillory was still in use as a punishment for Negroes as late as 1847.

The homes of the wealthier citizens of New Orleans at

the beginning of the nineteenth century were generally of stucco over wood, although many were of brick roofed with slate or tiles. They were from one to three stories in height and were built in the Spanish style, around courtyards or patios. The house occupied by the Spanish governors, at Toulouse and Levee Streets, was a commodious one-story structure, more like an inn than a dwelling. On one side was a narrow garden, while along the other was a low gallery screened by lattice-work. The kitchens and stables were enclosed in the back yard. The Louisiana Legislature held its sessions in the building for several years, until it was destroyed by fire in 1827. The houses of the middle and poorer classes, farther back from the river, were of wood, with shingled roofs, and many were elevated on posts from eight to fifteen feet above the ground, a practice which was originally begun to keep frogs, snakes, and alligators out of the family's living-quarters. In the courtyard of every dwelling was a well from five to fifteen feet deep, and many of the wealthier residents possessed two or three, but the water obtained from them was decidedly not potable. Nor was it fit for many other uses. Drinking-water, and that used for washing clothes, was brought into the city from the Mississippi River and sold from carts and wagons, at the rate of four buckets for six and a quarter cents, or fifty cents a hogshead. It was either filtered through porous stone or poured into large earthenware jars and cleared by lime, alum, or charcoal.

When Governor Claiborne made his official report on the conditions of New Orleans and Louisiana, he noted that besides wholesale and retail stores, the city possessed a sawmill with two saws turned by horses, a wooden-horse riding-circus for children, a French theater, two banks, a custom-house, navy yard, and other government buildings, various ecclesiastical structures, a newspaper, and several cotton-presses, a few of which were operated by horse or steam power. The theater was Le Théâtre St. Pierre, in St. Peter Street, established in 1792 by a company of French and Canadian actors, refugees from Santo Domingo, who late in 1791 had given the first professional dramatic performance ever seen in New Orleans. Within a few months of its opening the St. Pierre was closed by the Spanish authorities because the actors insisted upon interpolating French revolutionary songs at unexpected points in their performances. It was reopened in 1803, shortly before the American occupation. The newspaper was *Le Moniteur de la Louisiane,* published in French and first issued in 1794 by a Santo Domingo refugee under the patronage of Carondelet. It appeared once a week, had a very small circulation, and was filled with government orders and proclamations, business advertisements, bills of lading, and occasionally an item of foreign or political news. But local happenings were wholly ignored. The first English newspaper, *The Louisiana Gazette,* was established on July 27, 1804, by John Mowry. It was a small folio sheet, badly printed, and was issued twice a week until 1810, when a daily edition was published for the first time. Besides the journalists and the actors, the creative arts in New Orleans at the time of the purchase of Louisiana were principally represented by Julien Poydras, in whose honor a street was named, author of the first poem published in Louisiana; and a painter whose name is variously recorded as Ferdinand Latizar, Joachim Salazar, and Ferdinand Salizar. He painted the portrait of many a Louisiana notable, and at least one example of his work is preserved in the State Museum.

CHAPTER III

DOWN THE RIVER TO DIXIE

THE ACQUISITION of Louisiana by the United States occurred at the height of the great migration from the Atlantic seaboard into the fertile valleys of the Ohio and Mississippi Rivers, a movement which began soon after the end of the American Revolution and continued in full swing for more than half a century, to the amazement of historians and other observers who could find no economic reason for such an extraordinary shifting of population, since the East was neither crowded nor unprosperous.[1] When the treaty of peace was signed with England, and the thirteen colonies became an independent nation, there were not more than 12,000 settlers in the western country. But in 1800 the Federal census placed the combined population of the territories of Ohio, Kentucky, Mississippi, and Tennessee at 380,772, and by another twenty years almost 2,000,000 persons had struggled across the Alleghenies and were bringing thousands of acres of rich land under cultivation, and building towns and cities in the wilderness. During this period the center of population in the United States shifted from forty miles northwest by west of Washington to a point sixteen

---

[1] In his *The Outlaw Years*, Robert M. Coates tells of a French professor who advanced the theory that the movement occurred because " man, like the squirrel in a cage, is irresistibly impelled to step westward by reason of the earth's rotation eastward." Other " scientists " spoke of " mystic forces " and " far-seeing powers."

miles east of Moorefield, West Virginia, a westward movement of more than fifty miles.

Manufactured goods of every description were needed
by the settlers, who had produce of the country to offer in
exchange. For all of this vast area New Orleans was the
natural market and export outlet; the cost of the long haul
across the mountains to the eastern cities was well-nigh pro-
hibitive. The Louisiana Purchase had opened the Mississippi
to American commerce without fear of confiscation or op-
pressive duties, and the accession ceremonies had scarcely
been concluded when both that river and the Ohio and all
of their important tributaries fairly swarmed with floating
cargoes consigned to the merchants of New Orleans and
destined both for domestic consumption and for transfer to
the seagoing vessels which awaited the flood of trade at their
mooring-place in front of the Place d'Armes. So great was
the demand for ships that the tonnage utilizing the port of
New Orleans increased almost fifty per cent during the first
year that Louisiana was a part of the United States.

The traders of the western territories loaded their
goods in an infinite variety of boats — canoes, keelboats,
covered skiffs or Mackinaws, rafts; huge flatboats or
barges, known in the vernacular as arks, broadhorns, and
Kentucky flats; ferryboats, also called sleds, which were
fitted with roofs when carrying passengers; pirogues hollowed from the trunks of large trees and fastened together
by twos and fours with heavy planks; scows propelled by
horses and cattle in treadmills; and occasionally a small,
flat-bottomed boat which moved briskly along under the
pressure of a paddle-wheel operated by a man turning a
crank. Except those which were worked by animals, none
had any motive power other than human muscle and the
natural current of the river. These extraordinary vessels,
most of them outlandish in appearance and impossible by
every criterion of engineering and convenience, moved

slowly and precariously between the wooded shores of the Ohio and the muddy banks of the Mississippi — jouncing through the rapids, whirling madly in the treacherous currents; slithering round the bends, sliding off sandbars, and miraculously avoiding snags and sawyers,[1] or piling up on rocks and mudbanks with great holes stove in their bottoms.

The craft principally used after the first few years had shown the utter impracticability of most of the designs were the flatboat and the keelboat, which were built in Ohio river towns and sold at the standard rate of a dollar a foot. The aristocrat of early Mississippi River navigation was the keelboat, because by virtue of its keel, usually a four-inch oaken timber, it could both ascend and descend the river. A typical keelboat was from fourteen to eighteen feet wide, fifty to seventy feet long, and pointed at both bow and stern. It carried up to seventy tons of freight in the cargo box, which utilized the four feet of the hold and extended another four or five feet above the level of the deck. A curved roof of heavy plank was built over the boat, which was decked at either end for a distance of eight to ten feet. On the forward deck was a windlass or a capstan, which was used to pull the boat off sandbars and to help warp it through the rapids and stretches of swift water. Along each side of the cargo box was an eighteen-inch walk, with cleats from twenty-eight to thirty inches apart. The equipment of some keelboats included huge sweeps twenty feet long, requiring at least two men to handle them, which were hung in oaken frames over the sides. On the Ohio the keelboat, also known as the packet-boat, reached dimensions that were truly Gargantuan. Many were more than a hundred feet long and twenty-five feet wide, with a passenger cabin aft and a huge cargo box forward. These monsters carried crews of from

---

[1] A sawyer is a tree which has fallen into the water so that its branches project above the surface, and which rises and falls with a rocking or swaying motion.

75

seventy to one hundred men, but even with every man working to the limit of his endurance, a month was required to make the round trip between Cincinnati and Pittsburgh. Many of the packet-boats were armed with small cannon, and the advertisements of sailings emphasized the fact that all of the crews were "very skillful in the use of weapons."

From an old print

A KEELBOAT ON THE MISSISSIPPI

The keelboat was usually floated downstream, since the current carried it along faster than any motive power man had yet devised, but the passage of ascent was made in a variety of ways, depending upon the size of the crew and the equipment of the boat. In high water some were bushwhacked up the river — that is, the boat was kept close to shore, and the crew moved it along by pulling on the bushes which grew on the bank. Others used the cordelle, a line varying in length from five hundred to a thousand feet, which was fastened to a thirty-foot mast in the center of the boat and pulled by men on shore, from twenty to forty of whom were needed for the task. In forest country the cordelle was tied to a tree and the boat pulled by a warp to that point, where it was anchored or tied fast while a new warp was being laid. The principal method of ascending the river in a keelboat, however, was by poling. For this work poles eighteen to twenty feet long were used, with a wooden crutch or knob on one end and an iron shoe on the other. Ten to twenty men on either side of the boat set the iron shoes against the bottom of the river, and the crutches or knobs against their shoulders, and then walked toward the stern, thus propelling the boat upstream. As each pair reached the stern they ran back over the top of the cargo box to the bow, so that with a crew of twenty men there were always sixteen poling and four returning to the bow. The sweeps were usually employed only as a supplementary source of power, for it was almost impossible to find men strong enough to make much headway against the current with the sweeps alone. But whatever way of ascent was used, it was a long and back-breaking journey; from three to five months were required to take a loaded keelboat from New Orleans to the falls of the Ohio at Louisville.

The flatboat, of which a greater number were in service than of any other type of river vessel, was simply an oblong ark with a curved roof to shed the rain, and sometimes a curved bow, with a great oar or sweep projecting from either side, whence the name " broadhorn." Occasionally these oars were used to increase the speed of the boat, but their main purpose was to shove the unwieldy craft off sand-bars and mudbanks. The flatboat varied in length from forty to one hundred feet, and in width from fifteen to twenty-five. It was constructed of massive timbers and thick planks and was designed to support the weight of from thirty to one hundred tons of freight. The hold was usually about four feet deep, and was built with a cargo box similar to that of the keelboat. Many of the flatboats were fitted with pens for horses, cattle, and hogs, and great numbers of animals were thus conveyed to the markets at Natchez and New Orleans. These craft were also used to carry immigrants to the rich down-river country. "Flatboats of this description," says an old guide-book to New Orleans, "fitted up for the descent of families to the lower country, were fitted with a stove, comfortable apartment, beds and arrangements for commodious habitancy; and in them ladies, servants, cattle, horses, sheep, dogs, poultry, all floating on the same bottom, and on the roof, the looms, spinning-wheels, and domestic implements of the family, were carried down the river to New Orleans."

On none of the river boats, not even the well-appointed family craft, was any provision made for the comfort of members of the crew. They ate and slept on the open deck. In summer they wore no clothing save a pair of heavy brogans studded with spikes and trousers of linsey-woolsey, a coarse cloth made from linen and wool; and in winter they wrapped themselves from head to foot in furs, which were so plentiful and cheap that no man, whatever his class, need be without a fur coat. Their food was bread and meat, which they ate from a great pan set down among them; and their drink was Monongahela rye whisky, the universal tipple of the wilderness, known on the Mississippi simply as "good old Nongela." No boat captain who failed to include a keg of whisky among his provisions could ship a crew at any price. With a tin cup chained to it, the keg stood in the center of the boat, and any man could help himself whenever he was so minded.

The boatmen of the early 1800's survived enormous quantities of raw whisky and bad food, and hardships which to our modern minds seem almost unendurable. As a class they were probably the roughest, toughest, and most ferocious of all the pioneers who helped carve an empire from the western wilderness. When they were not working the boats, or drunk, they were fighting, and a fracas between two flatboat bullies was a fearsome thing to see; to them it meant mayhem in all its ramifications — biting, gouging, kicking, stamping, stabbing, clubbing, anything which might maim or mutilate an opponent was considered fair and above-board. Before a fight began, certain established conventions were observed. Facing each other in the ring formed by their fellows, the gladiators strutted about, leaped into the air, cracked their heels together, and shouted their war-cries, each striving to outdo the other in ferocity of expression and in his claims of an extraordinary ancestry.

"I'm a child of the snapping-turtle!"

"I was raised with the alligators and weaned on panthers' milk!"

"I can outrun, outjump, outshoot, throw down, drag out, and lick any man in the country!"

"I'm a roaring rip-snorter and chock-full of fight!"

"I'm a pizen wolf from Bitter Creek and this is my night to howl!"

"I can wrastle a buffalo and chaw the ear off a grizzly!"

Spectacular and flamboyant boasting, perhaps, but they made good on it, for no more efficient rough-and-tumble fighters ever performed anywhere than the men who worked the boats in the early days of commerce on the Ohio and the Mississippi rivers. When they had tormented each other into furious rages, the fight was on, and it didn't stop until one or the other of the combatants had cried enough. If a man's tongue was yanked out, or if he had been otherwise rendered incapable of speech, his friends might shout the humiliating word on his behalf. Each boat crew had its champion, who wore a red turkey-feather in his hair or cap, a badge which was a standing challenge to every other bully on the river. Challenges were always issued and accepted when two or more boats moored for the night at the river settlements, and the combat between the rival champions was invariably fol-

79

lowed by free-for-all fighting and rioting which drove respectable citizens behind the barricaded doors of their homes. There they tremblingly awaited the departure of the boats at dawn, and then timidly ventured forth to see how much of their town had been left intact. When only one boat tied up at a town, the champion of that particular crew sought a fight with the local bully, a quest which was seldom successful, for even the most courageous of the town fighters fled into the woods whenever a flatboat came in sight on the river. Out of this strategic retreat by the landsmen came a ballad which was popular along the Mississippi for many years, and which was shouted by the flatboat champion as he stamped up and down the levee, a tin cup filled to the brim with whisky in either hand and his red turkey-feather bobbing in the breeze. In various versions it is still sung by professional hill-billies:

> I'm looking for the bully,
> The bully of the town;
> I'm looking for the bully,
> But the bully can't be found;
> I'm looking for the bully of the town.
>
> And when I walk this levee round,
> I'm looking for the bully of the town.

Every flatboat man possessed two major ambitions. One was to become the acknowledged champion of the river, the only bully who dared wear a red turkey-feather in his hat. The other was to visit New Orleans for a spree of whole-hearted wallowing in the fleshpots, for which exercise the town offered infinitely more facilities than any other city west of the Allegheny Mountains. Men frequently shipped aboard cargo boats for no other remuneration than a guarantee that eventually the craft would tie up along Tchoupitoulas Street. From the source of the Mississippi to its several mouths,

New Orleans was lovingly known among the rank and file of the flatboat crews as the City of Sin. But the captains and the sober traders gave the town another nickname — they called it Dixie. Originally this word was applied only to New Orleans; not until the Civil War, when D. D. Emmett's famous song, written in 1859, became the favorite battle-song of the Confederacy, was it in general use to designate the entire South. It came about in this fashion:

A few years after Louisiana became a part of the United States, at a time when the American monetary system was in a chaotic condition, one of the New Orleans banks began issuing ten-dollar notes, one side of which was printed in English and the other in French. On the latter, in large letters, was the French word for ten, *dix*. Since the proper pronunciation of French was not one of the accomplishments of the river men, one of these notes was known simply as a dix; collectively they were dixies, a name which was soon applied to the city of issue as well.

Among the flatboat men heroes appeared whose names soon became legend and whose exploits, improved and enlarged upon at each telling, approached the fantastic. Mike Fink was the most celebrated of these giants, and in the course of time he was so enwrapped in tradition that he became a combination of Samson, Ulysses, Paul Bunyan, and Jack the Giant-Killer. No man lived whom Mike Fink couldn't whip with one hand tied behind his back; blindfolded, he was still the best rifle-shot in the world; hopping on one foot, the fastest runner; with his little finger he could lift more than a score of the strongest men; he regularly drank a gallon of whisky a day. But Mike Fink was an Ohio River man and exercised his peculiar talents principally on boats operating between Cincinnati and Louisville. There is no record that he was ever south of St. Louis, and in the lore of New Orleans he is known only by hearsay.

Down river the great heroes were Bill Sedley, a six-foot-two Kentuckian who boasted that his heart was as big as an apple barrel, but " if I'm again yer, look out "; and Annie Christmas, a woman who tipped the scales at two hundred and fifty pounds, stood six feet and eight inches in her bare feet, and cherished a small but carefully trimmed mustache. And of these two Annie Christmas was by far the greater, for Bill Sedley killed two men in a New Orleans dive and fled into the Indian country, while Annie Christmas remained on the river and year by year added to her laurels. Sometimes she dressed as a man and pulled a sweep or hauled on a cordelle, or worked on the levee as a sort of super-stevedore. Again, she donned skirts, shaved her mustache, and became the captain of a floating brothel, catering to the emotional needs of the lusty river men. The tales that were told along the New Orleans levee about Annie Christmas and her cargo of scarlet women are both unbelievable and unprintable. One, however, was that on every cruise Annie offered a keg of whisky as a prize to the strumpet who could satisfactorily entertain the most men in a given time. Needless to say, the prize was always won by Annie herself.

The strength of Annie Christmas was prodigious; she thought nothing of walking off a flatboat with a barrel of flour under each arm and a third balanced on her head. Single-handed, she towed a loaded keelboat from New Orleans to Natchez; moreover, she made the trip on the dead run, and the boat skimmed over the water like a swallow. From St. Louis to New Orleans a man who performed an unusual feat of strength was said to be " as strong as Annie Christmas." She was a great and fearless fighter, too; she whipped every bully on the river, and her admirers said that the real reason Mike Fink was never seen on the lower Mississippi was because Annie Christmas had sent word to him that if he ever appeared in her territory she would send him home lashed to the bottom of a keelboat. She commemorated her exploits in the field of mayhem with a necklace which she wore about her neck on festive occasions, and to which she added one bead for every nose or ear chawed off and two for every eye gouged out. Legend says that when Annie died her necklace was thirty feet long. It could have been longer, but she counted only white men.

Unlike most white folk-heroes, Annie Christmas was also a demigod among the Negroes. But in the pantheon of the darkies she was a coal-black Negress with twelve coal-black sons, each seven feet tall, all of whom came into the world at one birth. In the white version of the Annie Christmas saga, she was murdered in a New Orleans gambling-house, but Negro tradition permits no such commonplace end. The Negroes have it that she killed herself for love, first bedecking herself in her gory necklace and all her other finery. Her body was placed in a coal-black coffin and taken to the river in a coal-black hearse drawn by six coal-black horses, while her twelve coal-black sons, in black from head to toe, walked six on either side of the somber vehicle. At the levee the coffin was reverently placed aboard a coal-black barge, and in the dark of the moon Annie Christmas's twelve coal-black sons floated it down the river to the sea. And none of them was ever seen again.

2

THE dangers of a voyage down the river were by no means confined to those provided by nature. Both the Ohio and the Mississippi teemed with pirates, who falsely marked the channels in the hope of driving the flats and keelboats ashore or against the rocks; or, this failing, attacked them from canoes and skiffs. If a cargo boat was captured, all on board were murdered, and the craft, manned by a new crew, was sent on its way to be sold for the benefit of the pirate chieftain. The worst of these marauders were concentrated along the Kentucky shore of the Ohio from the town of Red

Bank down to the little settlement of Smithland, the most treacherous section of the river, filled with snags, sawyers, riffles, rocks, and unexpected changes in the current. River piracy in this area appears to have begun with the activities of Bully Wilson, a Virginian, who established himself at a cave near the head of Hurricane Bars, some sixty miles below Red Bank, and set up a sign designed to lure thirsty travelers ashore:

WILSON'S LIQUOR VAULT

and

HOUSE FOR ENTERTAINMENT

At first Wilson's place was known as Cave Inn, but this was soon changed to Cave-in-Rock, and it became notorious as the resort and hiding-place of the most bloodthirsty of the robbers, slave-stealers, and murderers who roamed the wilderness. At the height of his career Bully Wilson is said to have commanded the allegiance of between eighty and one hundred desperate ruffians, and his forces could always be augmented by visiting outlaws eager to take part in a foray against the river traffic. Agents of Wilson waited upstream, offering to pilot boats through the Bars. Once aboard, they ran the craft on the beach at Cave-in-Rock, where they were easily captured by the pirates. If the offer of a pilot was refused and the passage of the Bars made in safety, Wilson's men set out after the escaping boat in skiffs and canoes. If it was captured, all on board were killed.

Wilson's principal rival was a whiskered giant named Fluger, who claimed to have been a colonel in the American Army during the Revolution and who was known throughout the West as Colonel Plug. His favorite method of operation began with secreting himself aboard a flatboat while it was tied up for the night. When the boat got under way he began digging out the calking between the planks and boring holes in the bottom, timing this work so that the scuttled boat would start to sink opposite his hide-away. Then, in response to a signal, members of his gang rowed out in skiffs, ostensibly to the rescue. But they rescued only Colonel Plug and the cargo; the crew and passengers were left to drown, and if they offered resistance they were shot or

From an old print

RIVER PIRATES

clubbed. Colonel Plug pursued his career successfully for many years, but at length met a fitting end. He bored one hole too many, and the boat on which he was working sank before his pirates could reach it. Unable to escape from the hold, Colonel Plug went to the bottom.

Outlaw chieftains of the caliber of Wilson and Colonel Plug seldom hesitated to attack even the huge flatboats and keelboats which carried crews of from thirty to sixty men, but a majority of the gangs which infested the rivers confined their attentions to the smaller craft. Most of the attacks were repulsed or avoided by skillful boatmanship, and sometimes, as on a historic occasion in 1823, the pirates were

85

dealt with in a summary fashion that frightened their fellows and made the rivers comparatively safe for a few months. In July 1824 the crews of a dozen flatboats, numbering about eighty men, hid in the cargo box of a single boat, which, apparently heavily loaded, was floated down the Mississippi toward an island near the mouth of Red River, which for years had been one of the strongholds of the pirates. Only a small crew was visible, and the boat was clearly being worked with considerable difficulty. Opposite the island the pirates, some thirty strong, swarmed to the attack in canoes and skiffs, and as they boarded the boat the hidden men rushed out of the cargo box and fell upon them. Ten were killed in the first few minutes of fighting, and more than a dozen were captured. Then a score of sharpshooters armed with rifles took up stations atop the cargo box, and the captives were blindfolded and forced to walk the plank in twenty feet of water. As they rose to the surface, struggling and spluttering, the riflemen shot them. In telling of the affair many years later one of the marksmen, who said he had won the bottle of whisky offered as a prize to the man who made the best score, remarked:

"They was the most put-out bunch of pirates you ever seed!"

If the trading boats slipped through the clutches of the white outlaws, they still had to reckon with the Indians. Bands of savages, many of them led by renegade white men, lurked around almost every bend. They attacked the boats in canoes, shot at the crews from the banks, and tried by every conceivable means to induce them to come ashore. If they did, they were promptly murdered, their cargoes stolen, and the boats either burned or set adrift. One of the favorite practices of the Indians was to don ragged American clothing, cover their faces with flour, and hail the flatboats from the water's edge, simulating white men in distress and pleading for help.

Despite the multitudinous perils of the passage, how-ever, the boats continued to arrive at New Orleans, right side up and with their cargoes intact, in ever increasing num-bers. For almost thirty years more than a thousand boats a year were floated down the Mississippi to the flatboat anchorage in front of Tchoupitoulas Street, where they were moored to posts driven into the mud. Sometimes there were so many of these craft in port that it was possible to walk a mile without leaving their decks.

3

SINCE the flatboat was a floater, with no equipment for navigating upstream, it was usually broken up and sold for lumber when its destination was reached. Their means of conveyance having been disposed of, the men who had brought the boat down the river set out for their homes by land, traveling the Natchez Trace through the Indian coun-try to Nashville and thence by way of the Wilderness Road to Louisville and other towns on the Ohio River. The provi-dent among them — the captains, the traders, and the re-spectable family men — journeyed on horseback in heavily armed groups, their commercial gains safe in their saddle-bags or in money-belts buckled about their waists. The im-provident and spendthrift, having left most of their earn-ings in the gambling-houses and dives of New Orleans, walked, or made their way northward by the curious method known as "whipsawing." Three such men would pool their resources and buy a horse, and after securing transportation across Lake Pontchartrain, one would mount the animal and ride for two hours, while his comrades followed on foot. At the end of the two-hour period the rider would dismount, tie the animal to a tree, and start walking. When the one whose turn it was to ride second, as previously determined by lot, reached the spot, he mounted the horse and likewise rode for two hours, leaving the animal for the third man.

In this fashion they continued day and night until they reached their homes or the horse died — or until they were robbed and murdered, for traveling through the cane-brakes and forests of the Natchez Trace and the Wilderness Road, especially the former, was at least as dangerous as attempting the passage of the Ohio and the Mississippi. For fifty years or more the Trace, which from Natchez to Nashville was no more than a narrow path, was infested by gangs of bandits whose peers, so far as brutality and blood-lust are concerned, have yet to make their appearance upon the American criminal scene. Among them were such celebrated outlaws as the brothers Micajah and Wiley Harpe, better known as Big and Little Harpe, whose wanton butcheries of men, women, and children made the Natchez Trace a road of fear and horror for more than a decade; Samuel Mason, who turned to banditry in middle age after an honorable career as a soldier and a Kentucky Justice of the Peace and who boastingly carved, on a tree at the scene of a murder, the legend which identified his handiwork: " Done by Mason of the Woods "; and Joseph Thompson Hare, who began his career picking pockets in New Orleans.

All of these men, and many others of the same stripe, eventually met fitting ends. Soon after the robbery of a mail-coach near Havre de Grace, Maryland, Hare was captured in a Baltimore tailor-shop while bargaining for a coat which he described in his memoirs as " in the style of an officer's, at the price of $75, very dashy." He was hanged at Baltimore on September 10, 1818. Big Harpe was decapitated by a man whose wife and children he had murdered, and his head was nailed in the fork of a tree on the Trace near the settlement of Robertson's Lick, in Kentucky. Little Harpe, calling himself Setton, joined Mason's gang after the capture and death of his brother, and late in 1803 he and Sam Mays, another of Mason's men, tomahawked their chieftain and cut off his head, which, packed in clay, they took to Natchez, where they claimed a reward. While parleying with the officials they were accused of stealing horses, and Setton was recognized as Little Harpe. Both Mays and Little Harpe were hanged at Greenville, Mississippi, on February 8, 1804. Their heads were cut off and stuck on poles, and that of Harpe was displayed on the Trace north of Greenville, while Mays's head was exhibited south of the town. The bodies of the bandits were buried in the town cemetery, to the great indignation of the citizens. On the night of the burial, groups of men went to the graveyard, dug up the respectable dead interred there, and buried them again in a field beyond the town.

The most spectacular of the bandits who prowled the Natchez Trace was John A. Murrel, a Tennesseean and probably the most extraordinary criminal America has yet produced. As a wholesale murderer his exploits have never been equaled even by modern gangsters. The exact number of men who met death at his hands was never determined, but it has been estimated at from three hundred to five hundred. Of these the great majority were Negroes, for one of Murrel's most lucrative activities was stealing slaves and reselling them. But if he failed to find a ready market for his human loot, or if he had stolen the same slave so often that further dealings with him had become dangerous, the Negro was murdered. For some fifteen years Murrel operated along the Trace, sometimes traveling in the guise of a Methodist preacher, and again as an elegantly attired gentleman, and not until the last two or three years was he even suspected of being a bandit. This was partly due to the fact that in Tennessee he and his brother maintained a well-equipped plantation, the legitimate operation of which would have made them wealthy men; but chiefly it was because he left few traces of his crimes. When Murrel robbed, he killed; he eliminated the chance of subsequent identification by a man whose money he had taken. Most of his murders were committed with a knife, and when his victim was dead Murrel disemboweled him, filled the abdominal cavity with sand and stones, and sunk the body in the nearest creek or river.

Murrel became a familiar figure in the coffee-houses, cabarets, and bordellos of New Orleans, where he repaired at frequent intervals to enjoy the pleasures of the flesh, but only his agents and accomplices, who gave him information about the departure of money-laden travelers for the north, knew him as the butcher of the Natchez Trace. Everyone else who saw him dawdling about the town supposed him to be a wealthy Tennessee planter, with a somewhat bizarre taste in clothing. But while he was enjoying himself in New Orleans, Murrel was engaged in formulating one of the most grandiose schemes ever conceived by a criminal mind — nothing less than the fomenting of a rebellion among the slaves, and the sacking of New Orleans, Memphis, Nashville, Natchez, and other cities of the South and Southwest by the underworld while the authorities and respectable citizens were trying to quell the Negro uprising. And after the capture of the cities, Murrel proposed to establish an underworld empire, with himself as supreme ruler and New Orleans as his capital. He perfected his plans during the latter part of 1832 in a three-day conference in the home of one of his New Orleans accomplices, and immediately began the formation of a gigantic organization which he called the Clan. Headquarters were established in a log house in a swamp on the Arkansas side of the Mississippi River, opposite the town of Randolph, Tennessee. Some idea of the sort of rule Murrel had in mind for the people of the to-be-conquered cities may be gained from the fact that after building this house he imported a dozen women from the Memphis red light district and set aside part of the structure as a private bagnio for himself and his principal lieutenants.

By the middle of 1833 Murrel had completed the organization of the Clan. Under his immediate command he had three hundred and eighty selected criminals, every one of them a murderer, who were to officer the bands of ruffians with whom alliances had been made in the cities. From the Ohio River to New Orleans his agents were busy sowing discord among the Negroes, promising them loot and white women in abundance, and cementing the allegiance of shady merchants and planters and the politicians who had already begun to cast their disreputable shadows across the western territories. So that there might be plenty of time to complete all arrangements, Christmas Day 1835 was decided upon as the time when the slaves were to rise and murder their masters, and Natchez was chosen as the first city to feel the iron hand of the underworld.

Two circumstances combined to defeat Murrel's extraordinary plot and rob it of whatever chance of success it might have had. Early in 1834 he stole two Negroes from a preacher near Jackson, Tennessee, and when he fell in with a young man named Virgil Stewart, who had volunteered to search for the missing slaves, Murrel began boasting of his exploits. Stewart led him on, professed admiration and envy when Murrel revealed his identity, and accompanied the bandit to the log house in Arkansas, where Murrel told him of the Clan and the proposed rebellion. Murrel himself proposed to lead the attack upon New Orleans; he had " always wanted to smash that city." When Murrel returned to Tennessee, Stewart was still with him and procured his arrest. In July 1834 Murrel was tried and sent to prison for ten years, but only for stealing Negroes. Stewart's tale of the Clan was so fantastic that no one would believe it for almost a year, when a Negro nurse-girl in Tennessee was overheard to tell a fellow-slave that she would not kill the white baby entrusted to her care.

The girl confessed all she knew about the conspiracy, as did other slaves with whom she had talked about it. Thoroughly aroused to their danger, the planters organized bands of Regulators, which swept through Tennessee arresting, and in many cases summarily executing, all who had been named as having had dealings with Murrel or his agents. Investigations were begun in all the towns and cities, and the authorities soon learned that although its leader was in prison, the Clan had not abandoned the great scheme or changed Murrel's plans except to advance the date of the uprising to the Fourth of July 1835. On that day minor outbreaks occurred in the underworld districts of Memphis, Nashville, and Natchez, but they were easily suppressed. In Tennessee a score of Negroes and half as many white men — some of the latter, planters and merchants of considerable prominence — were hanged for participation in the conspiracy. Murrel himself remained in prison and served his term, but his mind gave way under confinement, and when he was released he was an imbecile. He was last heard of a year or so later in the Gut, the red-light district of Memphis.[1]

4

T H E only knowledge of Americans possessed by the Creoles [2] of early New Orleans had been gained by observation of the men who came down the Mississippi from the western territories and by association with a few merchants and an occasional traveler from New York, Boston, or Philadel-

---

[1] A very fine and complete account of the activities of Murrel and other robbers of the Trace may be found in *The Outlaw Years*, by Robert M. Coates; New York, 1930.

[2] The word Creole comes from the Spanish, and was unknown in Louisiana during the French occupation. Properly, it meant native, so that any native of Louisiana was a Creole. In practice, however, the title was applied only to descendants of the original French and Spanish settlers, and, for convenience, to the native Negroes, live stock, etc. It was used as a noun only in speaking of a white man; otherwise as an adjective, as " Creole Negroes," " Creole horses," " Creole cattle," etc. In modern New Orleans, among the whites, it has the same meaning as in earlier times, but among the Negroes octoroons are known as Creoles.

phia. The merchants and travelers were regarded as at least semi-civilized beings and were well liked as long as they kept their places and remembered that they were outlanders, and not French or Spanish aristocrats. But they were seldom admitted to the best Creole society, and even before Louisiana was purchased by the United States a feeling of intense animosity had developed between the natives and the American new-comers. The word *Américain* was used by the Creoles as a term of opprobrium and as a synonym for boorishness and sharp practice. American women were snubbed by the haughty Creole ladies and excluded from the social life of the city, while American men were followed in the streets by ragamuffins, who jeered at them and derisively sang an insulting quatrain:

> 'Méricain coquin,
> 'Billé en nanquin,
> Voleur di pain
> Chez Miché d'Aquin!

The antagonism of the Creoles toward the Americans was not dissipated until the latter immigrated to New Orleans and Louisiana in such numbers that the natives finally realized that all sorts of people were required to make a nation. Business brought them together, and the inevitable intermarriages did the rest. Scarcely a decade after the Louisiana Purchase, Creoles and Americans fought shoulder to shoulder against the British at the Battle of New Orleans. But before the rapprochement begun then had been completed, the Americans had established a society of their own and had built themselves a separate city, traces of which may still be found in the so-called garden district a few blocks above Canal Street. In this section occurred New Orleans' greatest business and residential development, while the Vieux Carré, better known as the French Quarter, eventually became more or less the playground of the tourist, and until comparatively recent years, when it was at last overtaken by structural decrepitude and an appalling dinginess, retained something of the quaint charm of an old Spanish town.

Although the Creoles of New Orleans came in time to accept the American merchants and other business men as their equals, they never had any feelings but dislike and distrust for the Americans who came down the river from the wilderness. Added to these was the fear which had persisted from the time of Spanish rule, when a day seldom passed without its rumor that the wild Kentuckians were swarming down the Mississippi to loot the city. All of the inhabitants of the western country were known in New Orleans by the generic name of *Kaintock* and were regarded as blustering barbarians whose presence could be tolerated only because of urgent economic necessity. To the Creole a *Kaintock*, with his fighting and drinking and his insistence upon animal ancestry, was the embodiment of coarseness and vulgarity; he was a hobgoblin with which to frighten children. Ill-behaved little boys and girls were told that the *Kaintocks* would get them if they weren't careful, and Creole mothers scolded their offspring thus:

"*Toi, tu n'es qu'un mauvais Kaintock!*"

It was with good reason that the Creoles feared and disliked the *Kaintocks,* for the robustious river men, thousands of whom came ashore at New Orleans every year, caused more trouble than any other class in the history of the city. With a singleness of purpose which would have been admirable if exerted in less immoral pursuits, the flatboat bullies devoted themselves to the activities which combined to form what they called a frolic — drinking, fighting, gambling, and carousing in the resorts which the shrewd *entrepreneurs* of the underworld had established for their entertainment. Singly and in groups they issued from the dives and literally terrorized the town, invading and fre-quently wrecking the respectable coffee-houses, cabarets, restaurants, and theaters; and attended on these excursions by a horde of thieves and garroters who pillaged and mur-dered while the flatboat men kept the police and citizens fully occupied. The police were utterly unable to cope with such ferocious brawlers as the bullies of the Mississippi, and failed to maintain even a semblance of order in the city when the river men went on a rampage. The force of *gens d'armes* organized in 1803 by the French Colonial Prefect Laussat and the first Mayor of New Orleans, Étienne de Boré, and composed principally of mulattoes and former Spanish sol-diers, were beaten so often by the rioting flatboat crews that a strong prejudice against them arose among the respectable portion of the population. The editor of the *Orleans Ga-zette*, in a long article cataloguing their shortcomings, called the force a nuisance and demanded that it be abolished. Early in 1806, at the request of Mayor George Watkins, the Municipal Council disbanded the *gens d'armes* and organ-ized the *garde de ville*, consisting of three officers and twenty men to guard the city proper, and two officers and eight men for the outlying districts.

Contemplating the numbers and equipment of the *garde de ville*—each man was armed with a half-pike and a heavy saber suspended from a black leather cross-belt—the people of New Orleans felt that at last the authorities had provided adequate protection for the city, and that the ex-cesses of the flatboat men, and the epidemic of robberies and murders, would now be checked. The new force went on duty March 14, 1806, and less than two months later had its first encounter with the river bullies and the ruffians from the underworld districts. Sallying forth from the watch-houses to suppress a disturbance caused by brawling flatboat men, the doughty heroes of the *garde de ville* were disarmed and badly beaten. As punishment for their cowardice, the

Municipal Council formally deprived them of their weapons, while the Grand Jury handed up a report censuring them for their failure to maintain order and declaring that New Orleans was " at the mercy of brigands to loot and pillage at pleasure." As evidence of inefficiency the report mentioned the fact that the body of a murdered man, killed by footpads, had lain in the street for three days, while the police took no notice of the crime.

Two years after the formation of the *garde de ville* it was suppressed by the Municipal Council as incompetent, but was immediately reorganized with a force of eight men, known as constables. It was supplemented by a militia patrol of citizens similar to a body which had been formed in 1804 to guard the rural districts near the city. This system remained in effect for some fifteen years, with slight changes in organization and increases in personnel — by 1822, when the population of New Orleans had increased to about twenty-eight thousand, the night watch alone numbered fifty men, who were assisted by as many citizens organized by squares, each square under the command of a commissioner. One of the old ordinances imposed a fine of ten dollars upon anyone " who refuses to walk the square watch " when ordered to do so by the commissioner of his square. From this somewhat cumbersome organization eventually grew an efficient police department, but during the years in which it was in the early stages of development, the flatboat men continued their periodic forays into the respectable sections of the city. Every mayor and grand jury referred bitterly to the fact that the deviltry of the river bullies formed the greatest menace to the peace of New Orleans, and in 1818 Governor Jacques Villeré, in his message to the Legislature, called attention in scathing terms to the riots and disorders fomented by the river men, and the inability of the city authorities to suppress them. The ire of the Governor had been thoroughly aroused by one of the most flagrant of all the rowdy exploits of the flatboat crews — an attack upon Gaëtano's Circus, which had been showing in New Orleans so long — apparently it first appeared in the city soon after the American occupation — that it had become almost an institution. Its many wonders were celebrated in a song, of innumerable verses, which the Negroes sang on the streets and in the market-places. It began:

" 'Tis Monsieur Gaëtano
   Who comes out from Havana
   With his horses and his monkeys!
He has a man who dances in a sack;
He has one who dances on his hands;
He has another who drinks wine on horseback;
He has also a pretty young lady
Who rides a horse without bridle or saddle.
To tell you all about it I am not able —
But I remember one who swallowed a sword.
There are all sorts of animals, too —
They did not show to nigger folk
What they showed to the trash — the burnt-backs
Who make so much noise — nor what they had to
   amuse
All those fine ladies and gentlemen,
Who take all their little children along with them
   To see Monsieur Gaëtano,
   Who lives in Havana
   With his horses and his monkeys." [1]

Gaëtano had set up his show in a tent in Circus Square, at Rampart and Orleans Streets, which as Congo Square played an important part in the Voodoo terrors of early

---

[1] From George W. Cable's collection of Negro folk-songs. Quoted by Lafcadio Hearn in the *Historical Sketch Book and Guide to New Orleans;* New York, 1885; pages 297–8.

97

New Orleans. On a summer night in 1817 a gang of some fifty flatboat men filled themselves with "good old Nongela" at the saloons on Tchoupitoulas Street and then, led by the redoubtable Bill Sedley, started to Circus Square. A score of constables who ventured to dispute the passage of Rampart Street were soundly whipped, and the bullies reached the square soon after Gaëtano had begun his performance. The flatboat men rushed into the tent, and within a few seconds the place was in an uproar. Women and children fled screaming into the street, while the few men in the audience attacked the rowdies with their sword-canes and fists. But they were outnumbered and soon retreated. Many were badly beaten and cut, for the river men were armed not only with their own knives and bludgeons, but also with the sabers and pikes they had captured from the constables. As soon as the audience had been driven from the tent, Bill Sedley and his ruffians released all the animals from their cages and destroyed the seats and the apparatus of the circus. Luckily, Gaëtano possessed but two beasts which might have been dangerous — an ancient tiger and a bison. Both of these Bill Sedley slew with a club, a feat which greatly enhanced his renown upon the river. The wreck of the circus was so complete that Gaëtano made no attempt to reopen his show. He gathered the few belongings that remained to him and sailed for Havana.

5

THE invasion of the river men probably stimulated the growth of the New Orleans underworld to a greater degree than any other economic reason or population movement in its history. During the first twenty years of the American occupation, the number of inhabitants in New Orleans more than quadrupled, and it has been estimated that from one-third to one-fourth of the increase was composed of thieves, ruffians, vagabonds, and prostitutes who, with the removal of all restrictions upon immigration, had flocked into the city from the four corners of the earth.. For a period of some thirty years or more the lowest and most vicious elements of New Orleans' population specialized in catering to the vices and appetites of the *Kaintocks;* after three or four months on the river, the flatboat crews came ashore demanding women and liquor, and the underworld saw to it that there was always an ample supply of both commodities. Opportunities for the gratification of their desires were provided even before they set foot on land, for a score of flatboats, their cargoes unloaded and the boats themselves sold for what they would bring, had been transformed into saloons and rude bagnios, where the prostitutes entertained their visitors in narrow cubicles built into the cargo boxes, or, sometimes, openly on deck under tarpaulins. Along Tchoupitoulas Street, until the development of the new or American section of the city and the growing importance of the river trade made that thoroughfare an important business street, was a row of similar dives, though slightly more pretentious.

But the brawling bully of the flatboats looked upon Tchoupitoulas Street and the floating resorts merely as appetizers and regarded his destructive forays into the French Quarter as minor enterprises, undertaken partly to satisfy his exhibitionism and partly to vex the lordly Creole. What he considered the real pleasures of a New Orleans frolic were enjoyed in a section known as the Swamp, on Girod Street a dozen blocks from the river, near the Protestant Cemetery at Cypress and South Liberty Streets. The Swamp was the favorite haunt of the flatboat men, and with the possible exception of Gallatin Street, which was in the heyday of its fame immediately before and after the Civil War, was the toughest, most vicious area that ever flourished in New Orleans. There the flatboat men and the ruffians of the underworld reigned supreme and the art and practice of mayhem reached their fullest development. Scores of fights

99

occurred in the Swamp every night, and over a period of many years the district is said to have averaged half a dozen murders a week, none of which were ever investigated by the municipal authorities, or, for that matter, even reported. The police never ventured into the section; it was a tradition of the Swamp that for twenty years no officer of the law had set foot within its boundaries. The only law recognized on Girod Street was that which any man might promulgate by means of bludgeon, knife, pistol, or the weapons with which nature had endowed him — brawny fists, stamping feet, and a set of sharp teeth.

The Swamp comprised an area of half a dozen blocks, crowded with saloons, dance-halls, gambling-dens, bordellos, and so-called hotels, all housed in shacks with low gable roofs, built of rough cypress planks or lumber from old flatboats. Most of the bars in the drinking-places were simply boards laid across two or more kegs, and the other furniture was of the same rude sort. Practically the only attempt at decoration was a red curtain at every window; the red lantern which hung before the door was more in the nature of an advertisement. Frequently all of the various enterprises of the Swamp were under one roof, and in many the standard rates were so low that for a picayune (six cents) a boatman could get a drink, a woman, and a bed for the night — and the practical certainty of being robbed, and perhaps murdered, as soon as he fell asleep. The gambling-dives offered principally faro and roulette, but the games were so crooked that a man had about as much chance of winning as he had of performing the legendary feats of Annie Christmas. If by some miscalculation he did win a few coins, he was knocked on the head or knifed as soon as he left the place, for attached to every such establishment were ruffians who were even more adept than the flatboat men in the use of the bludgeon and the dagger. Sometimes a winner was accused of cheating and was immediately and forcibly relieved of his

gains with a great show of indignation. If he failed to sur-
vive the beating or stabbing, his body was laid out on the
floor or the bar and exposed as an example until olfactory
warnings suggested its removal, when it was carted to the
river and thrown in. This method of discouraging ambitious
gamblers was especially favored by the management of a
dive which bore the curious name of House of Rest for
Weary Boatmen, for many years probably the most vicious
resort in the Swamp.

From this teeming cesspool of iniquity issued the prowl-
ing bands of thieves, footpads, and firebugs which made life
and the possession of property more precarious in early
New Orleans than in any other city in America. Robberies
and holdups were so frequent as to be commonplace events,
and many of them were preceded by incendiary fires, for
gangs of arsonists set fire to houses in order that looting
might more easily be carried on during the excitement of
extinguishing the flames. The boldest of these gangs operated in 1827 and 1828, and early in the latter year concocted a scheme to burn and pillage the entire respectable
portion of the city. Plans for the holocaust were evidently
prepared in great detail, but before they could be carried
out a woman who had been arrested in Mobile confessed
the details of the plot to the Mayor of that city, who immediately notified the Mayor of New Orleans, Count Louis
Philippe de Roffignac. The *garde de ville* succeeded in arresting four of the conspirators — two Negroes and two
white men — but the others sought refuge in the Swamp
and were never apprehended. Prior to this time New Orleans
possessed a few clumsy fire-engines, but there were no firemen trained to operate them, although a force of thirty fire
commissioners, authorized to carry white truncheons as in-
signia of office, had been organized in 1816. These officials
were supposed to attend all fires and direct the work of the
citizens in fighting the flames, but this method was repeatedly

proved inefficient and was abandoned after the scare caused by the discovery of the great arson plot. In April 1829, Volunteer Company No. 1 was formed as the result of the appeal of the people for better protection against fire. This was the beginning of the Volunteer Fire Department, which rendered good service until 1855. Early in that year a paid department was organized, but it was very inefficient and was soon disbanded. Late in 1855 the Fireman's Charitable Association was given a contract, at $70,000 a year, to protect the city from fire, and this system was followed until 1890, when the present department was organized.

One of the most celebrated establishments of the Swamp in the days of its evil glory, and a favorite resort of the river men, was the Sure Enuf Hotel, the proprietor of which was Mother Colby, a waddling old harridan who weighed almost as much as Annie Christmas but lacked almost two feet of Annie's height. The Sure Enuf occupied a two-story shack with a low gabled roof. Downstairs the room opening into the street was the bar, and behind that was a large chamber in which the most remunerative activities of the place were conducted. The center of this room was devoted to gambling, with faro and roulette tables. One corner was partitioned off by thin boards, and served Mother Colby as a kitchen, dining-room and sleeping-quarters. Another corner was divided by curtains into small cubicles, where Mother Colby's guests, upon payment of a picayune, might repair with women who were brought in from the street as required. The second floor, really an attic, was a single large room with bunks built around it. The man who occupied the bunk in the center of the floor, where it was possible to stand while preparing for bed, paid a bit (twelve and a half cents) for his lodging, while the others, who had to crawl to and from their bunks under the gables, paid a picayune each. Similar sleeping-arrangements were provided at most of the other Swamp hotels, and frequently the plutocrat in the center bunk was murdered for the money which he was presumed to possess.

In the summer of 1822 Mother Colby leased the bar-room and gambling privileges of the Sure Enuf to two Mexican brothers, Juan and Rafe Contreras, and devoted herself to the management of the hotel and a new bordello which she had opened in another part of the Swamp. A few days after the transfer Bill Sedley came into the Sure Enuf bar-room and began drinking with a dozen flatboat men, among them Aleck Masters, a Kentuckian who was less than five feet tall, but was almost as broad and thick, and whose reputation as a fighter was second only to that of Bill Sedley himself. Sedley had a few drinks of " good old Nongela," and then went into the back room to gamble, but after a brief whirl at the faro game he came into the bar-room and said to Masters:

" I be danged if I ain't a yellow bantam pullet but I seen Rafe Contreras deal a keerd from his sleeve!"

Masters advised Sedley to take a knife to the Mexican and teach him manners, and Sedley had more drinks, brooded awhile, and then returned to the gambling-room. A moment later a pistol-shot was heard, and the ball whistled through the doorway and over the heads of the men at the bar. They rushed into the street, and Juan Contreras, who had been tending bar, locked and bolted the door, shutting himself, his brother, and Bill Sedley inside. And then from the Sure Enuf came the sounds of a mighty commotion — pistol-shots, heavy thuds, and the crashing of furniture; and over it all rose Bill Sedley's battle-cry, known and feared on the Mississippi from St. Louis to New Orleans:

" I'm a child of the snapping-turtle, I am!"

Aleck Masters tried to get into the place and, as he phrased it, " see fair play," but the front door was secure against him, and to reach the back entrance it was necessary to climb a fence. Masters was too short to accomplish this feat, and no one would give him a lift. He finally obtained a heavy timber from a near-by house and was about to use it as a battering ram when the door was flung open and a jubilant voice cried:

"Gentlemen, walk in! It's free drinks today! The American eagle has lit on the Alleghenies!"

The crowd pushed into the bar-room, to find Bill Sedley standing inside the doorway. One arm had been broken by a pistol ball, his clothing was ripped and torn in a score of places, and he was bleeding from half a dozen cuts. But he was still a child of the snapping-turtle and as full of fight as ever. He gestured grandly toward the stock of liquor behind the bar.

"Help yourselves, gentlemen," he invited, "and drink hearty. The proprietor of this here place has gone on a journey and left me in charge!"

Juan Contreras lay on the floor beneath a heavy chair, dead from a knife-wound, and his brother Rafe was sprawled across the faro table, Bill Sedley's knife still buried to the hilt in his heart. The bodies were laid out on the floor of the bar-room, while Bill Sedley boasted loudly of his handiwork and served free drinks to all comers as long as the liquor lasted. Mother Colby came running to protect her property, but Aleck Masters knocked her down with a bottle and then tied her with a rope and laid her beside the Contreras brothers. The carousing continued until late in the afternoon, when reports reached the Sure Enuf that the friends of the Mexicans were gathering to exact vengeance. For once in his life Bill Sedley deemed discretion the better part of valor. He fled across Lake Pontchartrain and headed northward along the Natchez Trace. News of his exploits along the upper Mississippi and the Ohio drifted south from time to time, but unless he came incognito, Bill Sedley never again appeared in New Orleans. For several months friends of the Contreras maintained a regular patrol of the Swamp; heavily armed, they went nightly from dive to dive, looking for the redoubtable river bully.

The Sure Enuf Hotel remained one of the popular resorts of the Swamp for many years. Mother Colby operated it for another decade, and later it came into the hands of Frederick Krause, a Girod Street character better known as Crazy Bill, who died in 1855 when a practical joker buckled about his waist a money-belt filled with brimstone and powder and then set it on fire. In front of the Sure Enuf early in 1845 occurred a famous fight between four Girod Street hoodlums, in which Jim Rogers gouged out both of Bob McBride's eyes, and Bill Curry bit off one of Jim Rider's ears and part of his jaw. But in time the Sure Enuf, the House of Rest for Weary Boatmen, and all the other buildings of the Swamp reached an appalling state of dilapidation. A writer in the *Picayune* for July 24, 1852 described them as " leaning against one another as if for support, and looking not unlike vicious old age clinging with desperate tenacity to existence while tottering on the verge of destruction." Nevertheless, despite its material decay, the Swamp remained a slum and underworld quarter until after the beginning of the twentieth century. As late as 1888 the New Orleans newspapers complained that the population of Girod Street was composed principally of thieves and prostitutes, and that from Magazine Street to the levee the thoroughfare was crowded with saloons, barrel houses, bagnios, dance-halls, and other low resorts.

6

FOR the flatboat men, and for the prosperity of the Swamp as well, the handwriting on the wall was the success of Robert Fulton in navigating a steamboat up the Hudson River, from New York to Albany, in 1807. Three years later Fulton designed a boat for service on the lower Mississippi, built it at Pittsburgh with capital furnished by himself and Robert R. Livingston, and named it the *New Orleans*. Late in 1811 the vessel left Pittsburgh under her own power and after an epoch-making voyage down the Ohio and Mississippi Rivers arrived at New Orleans on January 12, 1812. She sank within a year when her boiler exploded, but before that mishap occurred made three profitable round trips between Natchez and New Orleans. Her top speed upstream was supposed to be three miles an hour, but actually her engine seldom produced sufficient power to push her against the current at that rate. Usually she averaged less than two miles, but even that was so much better than any keelboat powered by human muscle could do that it was considered little short of miraculous. Three other river steamers were built before 1814 — the *Comet,* the *Vesuvius* and the *Enterprise,* and by 1820 sixty had been constructed and were in active service. In 1834 there were 230 steamboats, with an average tonnage of about 170, engaged in the Mississippi River trade, and within another decade this number had been increased to 450. These boats reduced the time between New Orleans and the falls of the Ohio at Louisville to about one-fifteenth of that required by the fastest of the keelboats. As early as 1817 the *Enterprise* made the trip in twenty-five days, two hours, and four minutes, and some twenty years later, in 1838, the *Diana* steamed the distance in five days, twenty-three hours, and sixteen minutes, winning the prize of five hundred dollars in gold which the Post Office Department had offered to the first boat running from New Orleans to Louisville in less than six days. In 1858 the *A. L. Shotwell* established a new record of four days, nine hours, and nineteen minutes. The time between New Orleans and Natchez was reduced from the five days and ten hours required by the *Comet* in 1814 to ten hours, thirty-six minutes, and forty-seven seconds, by the *Robert E. Lee* in 1870.

Such competition was too much for the flats and keelboats and all the other craft which depended for motive power upon strong men and the current. They soon began to vanish from the river, although they were still used to some extent until the Civil War. But by 1840 a flatboat on the Mississippi was a rarity instead of a common spectacle, and the riotous river bully was no longer a disturbing factor in the life of New Orleans.

The early Mississippi River steamboats were built for carrying freight only, as it was presumed that everyone would be afraid to ride on the " swimming volcanoes." The contrary proved to be true, however, and almost immediately there was a great demand for passage. One of the first boats to cater extensively to this traffic and to provide suitable accommodations was the second *New Orleans,* designed by Robert Fulton in 1815 and built at Pittsburgh at a cost of $65,000, of which $20,000 was for the machinery. She was 140 feet long and 28 feet wide, and was capable of a speed of four miles an hour upstream and ten miles downstream. Four-foot logs were used as fuel, and when steaming at top speed the furnace of the *New Orleans* consumed six cords of wood in twenty-four hours. She was manned by a crew of twenty-four, including four officers, and could carry two hundred tons of freight and about fifty passengers. The quarters of the latter were thus described in 1817 by J. G. Flugel, a German trader who was in the United States for fifteen years, from 1803 to 1818, and afterwards was American Consul at Leipzig for more than twenty years: [1]

" The ladies cabin is below deck, it being the most retired place. It is elegantly fitted up. The windows are ornamented with white curtains and the beds, twenty

[1] A portion of Flugel's journal was published in the *Louisiana Historical Quarterly* for July 1924.

in number, with red bombazette curtains and fringes
and mosquito bars, besides sofas, chairs, looking-
glasses, etc., and an elegant carpet ornaments the floor.
This cabin is 30 feet in length. Above deck is an elegant
round-house of 42 feet in length and 28 in breadth for
the gentlemen. This room for the convenience of the
passengers is provided with 26 berths in 13 state-
rooms . . . with mattresses of Spanish moss (in which
the woods of Louisiana abound). Other necessary bed-
clothes are handsomely flowered. Each berth had a
window. Sofas or settees and chairs, two large tables,
a large gilt framed looking-glass, several elegantly finished recommendation cards and the regulations of the
boat in gilt frames, — all these adorn the room, and
finally an elegant carpet covers the floor. . . . As the
climate is exceptionally hot and would scarcely be en-
durable in the summer months on board a steamboat
where the heat of the fire and the boilers would be
sufficient to prevent persons from traveling or, at least,
would render them uncomfortable while traveling, the
boat is completely covered with awning at that time,
and above the round-house is an elegantly decorated
walk with iron railings and nettings. . . . There the
gentlemen passengers sit comfortably and have a commanding view over the boat, river, and land, and enjoy the cool breeze. The awnings, the Captain tells
me, have no tendency to impede progress. The sight
of these swimming volcanoes on water is very agree-
able. They generally have colors at their poop and the
American eagle and stars give a very handsome effect.
A swivel-gun is carried to signalize their arrival and
departure."

The regulations of the boat were intended for the
guidance of the gentlemen passengers only, as in those days

ladies were really ladies, and it was inconceivable that a member of the gentler sex should conduct herself in an unseemly manner. Some of the regulations follow:

> " No gentleman passenger shall descend the stairs leading to, or enter the lady's cabin unless with the permission of all the ladies, to be obtained through the Captain, under the penalty of two dollars for each offense. . . .
>
> " No gentleman shall lie down in a berth with his shoes or boots on under penalty of one dollar for each offense. . . .
>
> " Cards and games of every description are prohibited in the cabin after ten o'clock at night. . . .
>
> " At noon, every day, three persons to be chosen by a majority of the passengers shall form a court to determine on all penalties incurred and the amount collected shall be expended in wine for the whole company after dinner. . . .
>
> " It is particularly requested that gentlemen will not spit on the cabin floors as boxes are provided for that purpose."

Passengers upstream from New Orleans paid $16 to Baton Rouge and $30 to Natchez; downstream the fare was $11 to Baton Rouge and $15 to New Orleans. The twenty-four persons who comprised the crew of the boat received $9,720 a year in wages, including the captain's salary of $2,500. " Their maintenance is very costly in this part of the country," wrote Flugel, " since everything especially provisions are high, for one pays from $20 to $45 per month for board in New Orleans. The expenses in case of damage to machinery, which now and then occur, no one can state, but the final and total expenses are very great. The income obtained is proportionately great, for the Captain told me that

109

on one trip from New Orleans to Natchez, the net proceeds amounted to no less than $4000. There is within the bounds of knowledge no business in any part of the globe which is more lucrative than this, but it will not be so in a few years hence, for I know the enterprise of the Americans, and the rivers as far as they may be navigable will be crowded with steamboats, and their enterprise will be slackened in the course of time."

Elegant and impressive as the fittings of the *New Orleans* appear to have been, they were downright tawdry compared to the magnificent appointments of the " floating palaces " — they were so described by enraptured journalists and awe-stricken travelers — whose paddle-wheels churned the muddy waters of the Mississippi when steamboat navigation was at the height of its importance. From about 1830 until the railroads began to monopolize both passenger and freight traffic in the Ohio and Mississippi River valleys, the river steamboats were famous the world over as the ultimate in luxurious travel. Every berth on the best vessels was equipped with an enormous feather bed and pillows filled with the softest down; thick rugs and carpets of the finest weaves covered the floors of the cabins and saloons, and the other furnishings were of gilt and plush; each gentleman passenger had his own personal spittoon, gilded and richly ornamented; and the cuisine was probably the best in America. " The saloons extend the length of the vessel, two hundred feet or so," says an old New Orleans guide-book, " and are as handsomely fitted up as elegant carpets, magnificent furniture, and grand pianos can make them. . . . The company on the steamboat, indeed, live as if in a floating hotel, with all the pleasures and enjoyments of hotel life." Enormous sums were expended on the fittings of these boats, and there was intense rivalry among owners and captains, each striving to outdo the others in providing comforts and luxuries for his passengers.

The great evil of early steamboat travel on the Mississippi was racing. Every captain was immensely proud of his boat and, regardless of her actual performances, maintained to the bitter end that she was the fastest vessel on the river. The result was that when two steamboats left port at the same time, or neared each other going in the same direction, there was a race. Most of these contests of speed and boatmanship were impromptu, but many were carefully arranged. For the latter races the boats were stripped of all fittings and superstructures which might retard their speed, and all business, both freight and passenger, was refused. In order to generate steam rapidly, the furnaces under the boilers were fed with pine knots dipped in tar. Among the Negroes, however, a firm belief prevailed that the fires were fueled with well-fattened slaves, and that at a crucial moment in the race a steamboat captain did not hesitate to give the command: "Throw in another nigger!" But whatever was used, the excess steam frequently burst the boiler or blew off the cylinder heads, wrecking the boat and scalding passengers and members of the crew. One of the first of these disasters occurred in 1816, when the boiler of the *Washington* exploded near Marietta, Ohio, and fatally injured seven men. The steamboat was repaired and returned to service on the Mississippi, and about a year later, on May 4, 1817, her captain was challenged to a race when she came alongside the *Constitution* near Bayou Sara, about 175 miles from New Orleans. The engineers of both boats jammed as much fuel as possible into the furnaces, and a few hundred yards from the starting-point the cylinder head of the *Constitution* blew off under the increased pressure, releasing a cloud of steam which was visible for several miles up and down the river. Eleven passengers were scalded, and by next morning all were dead.

During the 1830's and the 1840's a steamboat seldom went up the river without being challenged to a trial of speed. Many of these races, widely heralded in advance and elaborately prepared for, were regarded as important sporting events, on which huge sums of money were wagered by the sports in the river towns. None of the contests of this period, however, attracted as much attention as the great race in 1870 between the *Natchez* and the *Robert E. Lee,* the most famous boats on the river. There had always been considerable rivalry between the commanders of these vessels — Captain Thomas P. Leathers of the *Natchez* and Captain John W. Cannon of the *Lee* — and when Captain Cannon learned in June 1870 that the *Natchez* had steamed the distance from New Orleans to St. Louis, a distance of 1,278 miles, with a full cargo of freight and passengers, in three days, twenty-one hours, and fifty-eight minutes, he determined to beat this time with the *Robert E. Lee.* Before the *Natchez* returned from St. Louis, Captain Cannon made extensive preparations for the race. He removed from the *Robert E. Lee* all of her upper works that could be spared, refused all freight and passenger business, and engaged the steamer *Frank Pargoud* to precede the *Lee* and wait for her a hundred miles up the river with a supply of coal, which had long since supplanted wood, and even niggers, as steamboat fuel. Captain Cannon also arranged with dealers *en route* to have flatboats laden with coal lying in the middle of the Mississippi, ready to be taken in tow while the fuel was being transferred to the *Lee.*

Captain Leathers of the *Natchez* made no unusual arrangements whatever. He took aboard several hundred tons of freight and a few passengers, and at five minutes past five on the afternoon of June 30, 1870 backed the *Natchez* away from the New Orleans levee, five minutes behind the *Robert E. Lee.* Several steamers crowded with passengers had already gone up the river to watch the passing of the racing boats under full steam, and practically the entire populations of Vicksburg, Memphis, and other cities turned out *en masse* and lined the banks as the steamboats roared up the river, great clouds of smoke pouring from their stacks. All over the United States, newspapers displayed bulletins describing the progress of the race, and the time of passing Vicksburg, Memphis, and Cairo was cabled to Europe, where the interest was almost as great as in this country.

The *Robert E. Lee* was ten minutes ahead at Natchez, slightly less than four hundred miles from New Orleans, and maintained a lead throughout the race. Between Memphis and Cairo the *Natchez* ran into a fog and grounded, which delayed her for six hours and definitely put her out of the contest. The *Lee* proceeded to St. Louis at racing speed, and at the end of the run was greeted by a crowd of thirty thousand persons, who crowded the wharves and the housetops. She had made the voyage in three days, eighteen hours, and fourteen minutes, a record which was never beaten. It was estimated that a million dollars changed hands on the race, although many bets were declared drawn on the ground that when the *Frank Pargoud* transferred her cargo of coal she added her power to that of the *Lee* for a hundred miles. Practical river men generally regarded the *Natchez* as the faster boat, and Captain Cannon of the *Lee* as the more resourceful skipper.

CHAPTER IV

LE CRÉOLE S'AMUSE

DURING THE greater part of the first half-century in which Louisiana was a part of the United States, the new or American section of New Orleans above Canal Street was the site of the most sordid and vicious of the underworld districts, while the more legitimate gayety of the town was largely concentrated in the Vieux Carré, which, though Spanish in its physical aspects, was still predominantly French in spirit and custom. In that area were located the pits for cock-fighting; the elegantly appointed gambling-houses; the best of the cafés and coffee-houses; the fashionable cabarets and bordellos, which were operated with such circumspection that almost no record of their existence remains; the eating-places which were already developing the cuisine that was destined to spread the fame of New Orleans throughout the world; the ballrooms; and most of the theaters — all of them, in fact, until James H. Caldwell, recognized as the real father of the American drama in New Orleans, opened the American Theater on May 14, 1823, and successfully presented plays in English. Caldwell erected his theater, which was the first building in the city to be lighted by gas, in the middle of a swamp on Camp Street, about two hundred feet above Canal. Play-goers either donned boots furnished by the theater management and splashed through the swamp from Canal Street, or carefully made their way along a rickety plank walk, about two and one-half feet wide, made of old flatboat gunwales.

But the hardy inhabitants of New Orleans had become inured to mud and water by long experience. The principal streets of the Vieux Carré, as laid out by Bienville's engineers, were only thirty-eight feet wide and were alternately quagmires and beds of stifling dust. Because of the scarcity of stone, no attempt was made to pave them until 1821, when the Municipal Council offered $250 a ton for rock brought to New Orleans as ship ballast. A year later a cobble-stone pavement was laid for a few blocks on St. Charles Avenue.[1] The banquettes, or sidewalks, were simply planks, or sometimes a single log, pegged into the ground. In some streets wooden drains served as gutters, while in others open ditches on either side answered the same purpose. Into them were thrown garbage and refuse of every description, the result being that except in times of high wind an almost unbearable stench hung over the town. The drains and ditches were supposed to be cleaned daily by Negro convicts from the calaboose, who performed their labor under the burden of iron collars, and heavy chains attached to their ankles.

During the rainy seasons the black, loamy soil became very greasy and slippery. At these periods many of the streets were impassable by vehicles, and some of them, choked with water and debris from the overflowing drains, could not be negotiated even by men in boots. The pedestrian was frequently compelled to make long detours to reach his destination, and if he happened to be a stranger he received scant help from the inhabitants in finding his way about. As yet the street names were merely words in the municipal records at the Cabildo, unknown to anyone save perhaps the custodian of the archives. The various thor-

---

[1] Originally this thoroughfare was St. Charles Street, but to avoid confusion I have referred to it throughout this book as " Avenue," as it is today.

oughfares were identified locally by the names of prominent residents. As late as 1815 New Orleans was still lighted by Carondelet's oil lamps, which swung from projecting arms nailed to wooden posts. The illumination thus furnished was very slight, and the citizen who ventured abroad at night prudently carried a lantern, a custom which was not generally abandoned, because of the slow development of the municipal lighting system, until about 1837. When a family of early New Orleans went out in the evening to a ball or other social function, it presented a picturesque spectacle as it slowly made its uncertain way through the streets. First came slaves bearing lanterns, and the shoes, silk stockings, and other articles of full dress which were donned only when the destination had been reached; and lastly the members of the family in boots and raincoats, each gentleman carrying his own personal lantern.

Despite the discomforts and inconveniences of getting about after nightfall, the masquerades and fancy-dress balls, upon which New Orleans' early reputation for gayety was principally based, were so largely attended that they were held almost nightly during the winter season, until Lent put an end to the year's festivities. But even more popular than the balls, and almost the only event of a social character in which everyone participated regardless of class distinction, were the charivaris with which the weddings of prominent citizens were celebrated, and the newly-weds tormented for hours, sometimes days. When the young widow of Don Andres Almonaster y Roxas remarried a few years after the death of her husband in 1798, the charivari continued for three days and attracted large crowds from the country districts many miles from the city. The house wherein the bride had sought refuge with her new spouse was surrounded by thousands of persons, all shouting at the tops of their voices and producing also an infinite variety of other noises. " Many were in disguise dresses and masks," wrote a traveler who was in New Orleans at the time, "and hundreds were on horseback; and all had some kind of noisy musical instrument, as old kettles, shovels and tongs, and clanging metals. Some of the crowd drew along in a cart effigies of the widow's former husband and of her present husband. The former husband's effigy was lying in a coffin, while the widow, represented by a living person, sat near it. As Madame did not receive this rude mob very courteously, she became unpopular, and was forced to make a public gift of three thousand dollars in solid coin for an out-door mass."

Throughout the first decade of the American occupation the fashionable balls and masquerades continued to be held in a plain wooden building, about eighty feet wide, on Condé (later Chartres) Street near Dumaine, which was first used as a ballroom about 1790. It was also the scene of New Orleans' first theatrical performance by professionals. Along the sides of the hall, ascending gradually in several tiers, were the boxes in which sat the mothers and chaperons of the Creole belles; and the young girls who were permitted to watch but not to dance. Below the boxes were rows of seats for the ladies who had become wearied while treading the fatiguing measures of the *contre-danses,* and behind these was a space about three feet wide and running the full length of the building. There the Creole gentlemen awaited their turns upon the dance-floor — the forerunner of the modern stag line. Young men predominated in this group, and all wore, almost as a uniform, long coats of gay colors, and boots with fancy stitching. Each carried a sword-cane or a *colchemarde,* a French sword wide near the hilt and tapering suddenly to a rapier-like blade — a popular weapon of the period. Innumerable quarrels arose among the high-spirited Creole youths waiting impatiently for places in the dance figures, and a quarrel in those times could have but one ending — a duel. If one young man carelessly brushed against another, or accidentally trod on his toes, or danced with a young lady without first learning who had appointed himself her protector and obtaining his consent — any of these circumstances, and scores of others equally trivial, were sufficient cause for a challenge, which was issued and accepted even if the men concerned were the best of friends. Arrangements were quickly made, and the duelists and their seconds quietly left the ballroom and repaired to St. Anthony's Square, just behind the Cathedral, in which was a cleared space concealed from the street by a heavy growth of shrubbery. There they fought, strictly according to the code, with their sword-canes or *colchemardes*. Honor was satisfied with the first blood, however slight the wound, and the victor returned to the ballroom, while the vanquished duelist hurried home to bandage his hurts.

Many of the controversies which started in the old ballroom involved more than two men, and frequently rapiers flashed on the dance-floor, while the ladies fled screaming to the protection of their chaperons, and the military guard of the city stamped heavily into the hall to quell the incipient riot. One disturbance, which occurred while Don Manuel de Salcedo was Governor of Louisiana, formed a significant commentary on the ill feeling that had existed between the Creoles and their Spanish rulers since the days of Don Alexander O'Reilly. Moreover, it brought out rather clearly one of the American traits which had caused the new-comers from the United States to be regarded with distrust and suspicion — a tendency to reap the benefits without doing any of the fighting or hard work. One night early in 1802 the eldest son of the Spanish Governor, a roistering young blade who had often used his father's position to further his love-affairs and other schemes, entered the ballroom and commanded the musicians to play English *contredanses* instead of French. Out of respect to the Governor's son, the dancers at first made no protest and patiently went through the unfamiliar evolutions of half a dozen of the English dances. They then formed seven sets of a French *contre-danse,* but before the movement began, the young Spaniard cried:

"*Contre-danses anglaises!*"

The orchestra obediently switched to the English music, but the dancers refused to change the sets. Instead they set up a shout of "*Contre-danses françaises!*" while the Governor's son and his adherents continued to cry: "*Contre-danses anglaises!*" At the height of the confusion the Spaniard ordered the musicians to stop playing, which they did. What followed was thus described by a traveler who visited New Orleans soon afterwards:

"The Spanish officer who was deputed to preserve good order at this place, thought only of pleasing the Governor's son, and ordered up his guard composed of twelve grenadiers, who entered the room with swords at their sides and with fixed bayonets. It is even said that, the tumult having redoubled at the sight of this guard, he gave the order to fire on the crowd unless it should disperse at once; but that is only what people say. Imagine, now, the terror of the women, and the fury of the men, whose numbers were increased by the addition of their friends who flocked in from the gaming-halls. The grenadiers on one side and the players and dancers on the other were about to come to blows; on the one hand were guns, bayonets and sabres — on the other, swords, benches, chairs, and whatever could be conveniently utilized as a weapon of offense or defense. During all this squabble, what was done by several Americans, peaceably disposed individuals, accustomed to the prudent and advantageous role of neutrality, and who had pronounced for neither the English nor the French *contre-danses*? They carried away from the battle-field the ladies who had fainted, and, loaded with these precious burdens, they made a path for themselves through the bayonets and swords and reached the street. M——, a French merchant of the city, running from a gaming-room to the assistance of his wife, found her already outside of the dancing hall in a fainting condition, and in the arms of four Americans who were carrying her off.

"The confusion was at its height, and the scene seemed about to be transformed into a bloody one, in which the farce begun by the Governor's son should end in a tragedy. It was at this critical moment that three young Frenchmen who had but recently arrived in the city ascended into the boxes that lined the hall, and harangued the company with eloquence and firmness, urging peace and harmony, in the interest of the sex whose cause they had espoused. They succeeded, like new Mentors, in calming the agitation of all alike, pacifying the minds of the antagonists, and restoring order and concord. Even the dancing was resumed and continued the rest of the night in the presence of the old Governor, who repaired to the spot to affirm by his presence the happy pacification that had been effected; the victory remained to the French *contre-danses*, and the officer of the guard escaped with the simple penalty of being put under arrest the next day."

The functions at the old Condé Street ballroom appear to have been sufficiently gay and frolicsome, and even exciting, to suit the most exacting taste. Much of the excitement was lacking, however, after October 27, 1817, when the Municipal Council passed, and for some years rigidly enforced, an ordinance which forbade anyone to carry a sword-cane or other weapon into a ballroom under penalty of a five-dollar fine. But there was nothing magnificent about the social affairs of early New Orleans, for with true Gallic thrift the pleasure-loving Creoles indulged in no needless expense and in no extravagances whatsoever. Admission to the balls was never more than fifty cents, while ladies paid nothing, and the orchestra was composed of two or three wandering gypsies whose pay for the night's work seldom amounted to more than two dollars. "All," wrote a traveler in 1804, "is cheaply done. The ladies' dresses are mostly of white muslin, and sometimes silk of gay colors, but never costly, and always neatly and modestly made. . . . The ladies at no time wear caps, turbans or bonnets. No bonnets are ever seen on the streets. They cover their hair with a graceful veil. They are beautiful in person, in gesture, and in action. Nearly all are brunettes."

Various circumstances soon brought about a radical change in the dress of the fashionable ladies of New Orleans. The prosperity that accompanied the American occupation of Louisiana, the natural growth and development of the town, and the importation of new ideas from the cities of the eastern seaboard, all played their parts in the transformation. But the love of luxury and display was introduced into New Orleans principally by refugees from Santo Domingo, who fled to Cuba during the slave rebellions in 1791 and from Cuba to New Orleans in 1809 and 1810, when France and Spain were at war. In these two years more than ten thousand Santo Domingans, white and black, arrived in the city, more than half of them during two months in 1809. The atmosphere of tropical ease and languor which surrounded the Santo Domingo women exerted a profound influence upon the Creole ladies. Within a few years the plain muslins and modest veils had given way to bright-colored silks, transparent taffetas, velvets, richly embroidered cloths, expensive laces, and gay bonnets and turbans. The Condé Street ballroom likewise became outmoded, and Creole society transferred its allegiance to the new St. Philip Theater, which had opened its doors on January 30, 1808 and which for more than ten years was the fashionable rendezvous of the city. This was the finest place of amusement yet erected in New Orleans — the auditorium could accommodate seven hundred persons, and there were two rows of boxes and a parquet, over which a floor was laid for the balls. In this building in 1810 occurred the first public celebration of the Fourth of July ever held in New Orleans, and in 1817 the stage of the St. Philip was the scene of the city's first theatrical performance in English, under the direction of N. Ludlow, who had leased the playhouse for a year. When the English season expired, however, the St. Philip was unable to regain its former position as a French theater, and the character of its patronage gradually changed — in 1826 the young Duke of Saxe-Weimar, who wrote a book about his travels in America, called it a " den of ruffians," and described a fight, following a masquerade, in which twenty persons were injured. In 1832 the existence of the St. Philip as a theater came to an end. A permanent floor was installed in the parquet, and it became the Washington Ballroom. For many years it was a favorite resort of the *demi-monde*.

The decline of the St. Philip Theater was due partly to a natural change in the theater-going habits of the Creole population and partly to the meteoric rise of the Théâtre d'Orléans, on Orleans Street between Bourbon and Royal. A small theater had been built on this site in 1809, in which were given French plays and a few operas, although the latter were not very well received because of the mediocre talent employed. This playhouse burned in 1813, and the land on which it had stood was acquired by John Davis, an *émigré* from Santo Domingo, who immediately erected a new theater at a cost of eighty thousand dollars, which he called the Théâtre d'Orléans, and which was considered one of the finest structures of the kind in America. French plays and an occasional performance in English were given, and Davis also organized a musical stock company which offered seasons of light opera in French. Grand opera was introduced into New Orleans in 1837, when Madame Julia Calvé made her American début under the direction of Davis's son, Pierre, better known as Toto, who had inherited the property when his father died. Associated with Toto Davis in the management of the theater was Charles Boudousquie, subsequently the husband of Madame Calvé, who was largely responsible for the continued growth and popularity of opera in New Orleans.

The Théâtre d'Orléans prospered from the day its doors opened, despite the handicap of a series of city ordinances, enacted between 1815 and 1830, which regulated it and other playhouses to an extraordinary degree. Under one of these laws, passed by the Municipal Council on June 8, 1816, it was necessary for a theater manager to submit the script of every play to the Mayor for approval, and the Mayor, if he liked it, fixed the day and hour of the performance. If he didn't like it, no production was made. The same law imposed a fine of from five to fifty dollars upon any actor or actress who failed to appear upon the stage at the exact time called for in his or her part. Another ordinance, adopted on January 22, 1846, provided that the time between acts must not exceed fifteen minutes, nor the interval between two pieces on the same program more than twenty minutes; but if one of the pieces had "grand scenery" the interval might be lengthened to thirty minutes. Violations of these provisions were punished by a fine of twenty-five dollars imposed upon the manager of the theater, "who may have recourse against the mechanist, actor, actress or any other person employed at the theatre, who may have occasioned the delay." This ordinance also regulated the applause, forbidding anyone to "make a noise at said shows or theatres, whether by striking on the floor, the benches or boxes, or in any other manner," under penalty of a fine of twenty-five dollars. The Mayor or his representative attended every performance to see that the laws were obeyed, and the theater manager was required to hold the best seats in the house at the disposal of His Honor.

With the introduction of grand opera the popularity of the Théâtre d'Orléans greatly increased, and the playhouse became the one place in New Orleans where everybody with any pretensions to social standing must be seen. Four operas were sung each week, two *grande* and two *comique,* while the remaining evenings were devoted to vaudeville and musical comedy for the entertainment of *hoi polloi.* The fashionable performances were those of Tuesday and Saturday evenings, when full dress was obligatory except in the parquet, the only part of the house open to non-subscribers. Even there a gentleman was expected to wear white kid gloves and a full-dress coat, although the boots and pants that went with them were his own business. The best location, from which it was possible both to see and to be seen, was the dress circle, which was divided into stalls, each containing four seats. In the rear of the stalls were two rows of single seats, flanked by loges. The latter were so arranged that curtains could be drawn before them. They were usually occupied by families which were still in mourning, and were thus tacitly acknowledged to be in strict privacy. No visits were made to them during the intermissions except by special invitation. According to an old New Orleans guide-book, " the display of beauty and exquisite taste in dress, on Tuesdays and Saturdays, was something positively startling to a stranger — the jet black hair, the sparkling eyes, the pure complexions, the superb costumes with low-cut corsages showing the round, beautiful arms, the gay and animated features on all sides, presented a picture which has never been equalled in any other theatre in the country. Never overdressed, and generally wearing white or some other light color, the purest camelias half-hid amidst their brilliant masses of jet black hair, they re. sembled in grouping and appearance the beautiful concep-tion of the artist, Winterhalter, in his celebrated painting of the Empress Eugénie and the ladies of her court. . . . Refinement, intellect and culture were visible on every side."

Such heart-warming spectacles were on display twice weekly at the Théâtre d'Orléans until 1859, when Bou-dousquie, unable to obtain proper terms for a renewal of the lease, became manager of the celebrated French Opera House, erected that year at Bourbon and Toulouse Streets. The new building in its turn became the darling of society, and with the exception of the Civil War period, and a few years when financial difficulties prevented, opera was sung there until 1914, by companies which ranged from first-rate to terrible. In 1916 the Opera House was bought and pre-sented to Tulane University by an anonymous donor, and on December 2, 1919 it was destroyed by fire. After the de-parture of Boudousquie, opera also remained the principal form of entertainment at the Théâtre d'Orléans, and regu-lar seasons were given there by stock and traveling com-panies until late in 1866, when the building burned. A year later the owner of the Louisa Street Cemetery bought the ruins and utilized the bricks to make burial ovens.[1]

2

SOME four or five years after the erection of the Théâtre d'Orléans, John Davis constructed, at a cost of sixty thou-sand dollars, an addition or wing which he called the Orleans Ballroom. The greater part of this considerable sum was expended upon the embellishment of the interior; viewed from the street, the ballroom was " a building of unimpos-

---

[1] New Orleans *Times*, November 26, 1867.

ing appearance, whose wide, low façade, utterly devoid of
the adorning graces of architecture, is plain to ugliness."
Inside, however, the structure was elaborately decorated
with crystal chandeliers, costly paintings and statuary, and
inlays and paneling of fine woods. In the rear of the ballroom was a wide stairway leading to a flagged courtyard
where wines and cordials were served on festive occasions.
The ground floor was cut up into private card- and recep-
tion-rooms of varying sizes. The principal feature of the
building, however, was the ballroom itself — a long, gaud-
ily ornamented chamber with a lofty ceiling, balconies which
overlooked the gardens in the rear of the St. Louis Cathedral, and a floor constructed of three thicknesses of cypress
topped by a layer of quarter-sawed oak. At the time it was
regarded as the finest dance-floor in the United States. This
part of Davis's establishment achieved even greater renown
than did the Théâtre d'Orléans, for it was the scene of the
most magnificent of the *Bals du Cordon Bleu,* better known
as the Quadroon Balls, the most celebrated of all the entertainments of early New Orleans and the most shushed by
Louisiana historians.

" During the *ancien régime* in Louisiana," wrote Grace
King, "the pure-blooded African was never called coloured, but always negro. The *gens de couleur,* coloured people, were a class apart, separated from and superior to
the negroes, ennobled, were it by only one drop of white
blood in their veins. The caste seems to have existed from
the first introduction of slaves. . . . From the first appearance of *gens de couleur* in the colony, dates the class,
gens de couleur libres." [1] No more satisfactory explanation
than this of the origin of the free blacks has been given by
any Louisiana historian, although Lyle Saxon boldly ventured the opinion that " in those first far-off days when
there were no white women in the colony, there were nu-

---

[1] *New Orleans, the Place and the People,* pages 333, 334.

merous mulatto children born to negro slave-women." [1] In
many instances the father set these women free, and since
under the law children always shared the condition of their
mother, they became free also, and so swelled the ranks
of the *gens de couleur libres*. As Miss King says, they formed
a part of the population at a very early date in the history
of Louisiana. They are specifically mentioned in the Black
Code, promulgated by Bienville in 1724, six years after the
founding of New Orleans, and are therein forbidden to
marry either their own slaves or slaves owned by white men.
They were also referred to, as we have seen, in the Marquis
de Vaudreuil's police regulations, issued in 1751.

These free men and women of color — after the
American occupation they were commonly designated, in
the newspapers and in many legal documents, simply by the
initials " f.m.c." and " f.w.c." — never formed more than
a small proportion of the population until the Civil War,
when, theoretically at least, all Negroes became free. The
census of New Orleans taken in 1769 by order of Don
Alexander O'Reilly placed the number of free Negroes
living in the city at thirty-one; probably there were not more
than a hundred in the whole of Louisiana. Twenty years
later another census made by command of the Spanish Governor Don Estevan Miró placed the free colored population of the province at 1,700. There was a considerable influx of free Negroes after Louisiana became a part of the
United States, especially during 1809 and 1810, when about
3,000 Santo Domingo blacks, who had taken no part in the
slave insurrections on that island, arrived from Cuba and
other West Indian islands where they had sought refuge.
In two months of 1809 alone 1,977 of these people landed
at New Orleans, among them a few characters who Mayor
Joseph Mather said had been represented to him as " dangerous to the peace of the territory."

[1] *Fabulous New Orleans,* pages 179–80.

From the beginning of their existence in Louisiana, the free people of color maintained a society of their own, in which class lines were as rigidly drawn as among the whites. The griffe [1] looked down upon the pure-blooded Negro; the mulatto regarded the griffe with scorn and was in turn spurned by the quadroon; while the octoroon refused to have social relations with any of the others. The majority of all these strata of free colored society, and especially the men, were industrious and law-abiding citizens. "By 1830," wrote Charles Gayarré, Louisiana's foremost historian, "some of these *gens de couleur* had arrived at such a degree of wealth as to own cotton and sugar plantations with numerous slaves. They educated their children, as they had been educated, in France. Those who chose to remain there attained, many of them, distinction in scientific and literary circles. In New Orleans they became musicians, merchants, and money and real estate brokers. The humbler classes were mechanics; they monopolized the trade of shoemakers, a trade for which, even to this day, they have a special vocation; they were barbers, tailors, carpenters, upholsterers. They were notably successful hunters and supplied the city with game. As tailors, they were almost exclusively patronized by the *élite,* so much so that the Legoasters', the Dumas', the Clovis', the Lacroix', acquired individually fortunes of several hundred thousands of dollars. . . . At the Orleans theatre they attended their mothers, wives, and sisters in the second tier, reserved exclusively for them, and where no white person of either sex would have been permitted to intrude." [2]

While the free men of color were always, in the main, modest and retiring and, in the Southern phrase, "knew their places," their quadroon sisters were far from being

---

[1] The offspring of a mulatto and a Negro.

[2] From an unpublished manuscript quoted by Grace King in *New Orleans, the Place and the People,* pages 344–5.

content to hide their shining lights under the proverbial bushel. At a time when the ladies of the best Creole families clad themselves in shapeless garments of extraordinary drabness, the quadroon women were notorious for the elegance of their raiment, their silks and satins, their plumes and jewelry; at the theater and the circus their gaudy sartorial displays but emphasized the plainness of the white ladies. As early as 1786 the beauty and arrogance of the quadroons attracted the unfavorable attention of the authorities. In his *Bando de buen gobierno*,[1] issued on June 2 of that year, Governor Miró warned the free women of color that their idleness, "resulting from their dependence for a livelihood on incontinence and libertinism," would not be tolerated. He ordered them to employ themselves in honest labor, threatened to have sent out of the colony all who failed to do so, and further warned them that he would consider "excessive attention to dress as an evidence of misconduct." The proclamation also pointed out that the prescribed distinction in the head-dress of women of color was not being observed; he forbade them to wear plumes or jewelry, and required them to have their hair bound in a kerchief. With these and other laws the quadroon women were kept more or less under restraint during the remainder of Spanish rule in Louisiana, but the regulations were considerably relaxed after the American occupation, and the quadroons bloomed anew in all their beauty.

Most of the quadroon girls who formed such a disturbing factor in the social and family life of early New Orleans lived in little one-story white houses along the present line of Rampart Street. Few, if any, were prostitutes; so far as circumstances permitted, their rearing had been identical with that of white girls. Fundamentally, the aims of the quadroons and the Creole maidens were likewise identical — to attract a white man, preferably rich, who

---

[1] A proclamation issued by a Spanish governor on assuming office.

would protect them from the storms and hardships of life. The main difference lay in the fact that to the white girl this protection meant marriage, and children born with the blessing of Church and State; while the quadroon could hope for nothing better than to become the white man's mistress. And rare indeed was the young Creole gentleman who didn't have a quadroon sweetheart cozily installed in one of the little houses " near the ramparts," where he supported her in a style commensurate with his wealth. So long as the relations between them continued — nearly always for many years and frequently for life — the quadroon almost invariably remained faithful to her lover. And when the connection was broken, by the marriage of the white man or for some other reason, she usually received a competence sufficient to maintain her for the rest of her life or set her up in business. They became modistes or hairdressers, owned slaves whose labors brought them in a comfortable revenue, and in later years had a practical monopoly of the business of operating high-class boarding-houses for white bachelors.

Harriet Martineau, an English author who traveled extensively in the United States from 1834 to 1836, made a careful study of the quadroon situation during her sojourn in New Orleans. In her book *Society in America,* published in 1837, she said that she had been assured " by ladies who cannot be mistaken " that the connection between white men and the quadroons was " all but universal." She wrote further:

" The quadroon girls of New Orleans are brought up by their mothers to be what they have been; the mistresses of white gentlemen. The boys are some of them sent to France; some placed on land in the back of the state. . . . They marry women of a somewhat darker color than their own; the women of their own color objecting to them, ' *ils sont si dégoutants!* ' The girls are highly educated, externally, and are, probably, as beautiful and accomplished a set of women as can be found. Every young man early selects one, and establishes her in one of those pretty and peculiar houses, whole rows of which may be seen in the Ramparts. The connection now and then lasts for life; usually for several years. In the latter case, when the time comes for the gentleman to take a white wife, the dreadful news reaches his quadroon partner, either by letter entitling her to call the house and furniture her own, or by the newspaper which announces the marriage. The quadroon women are rarely known to form a second connection. Some men continue the connection after marriage. Every quadroon woman believes that her partner will prove an exception to the rule of desertion. Every white lady believes that her husband has been an exception to the rule of seduction."

To permit the white gentlemen to make the selections of which Miss Martineau wrote was the main purpose of the Quadroon Balls. In reality, these functions were glorified slave marts, to which the mothers of the quadroon girls brought their daughters, dressed in their finery, and paraded them for inspection. If a white man fancied one of the girls, he made the preliminary arrangements with her mother and was then permitted to pay court to the damsel of his choice. If the girl accepted him as her lover, he installed her in one of the little houses on Rampart Street. Most of these establishments were maintained by young bachelors, but the married men of early New Orleans were by no means immune to the amorous excitement aroused by the beautiful quadroons. The frequent straying of the benedict from the family fireside was largely due to the polygamous nature of the male, but it was also partly because of the rigorous marriage customs observed among the

Creoles. Love seldom entered into a match among the best people of early New Orleans; quite often the two young people most concerned never even saw each other until informed by their parents that they were to marry, when they were allowed a few moments alone to exchange vows and rings. But until the actual marriage ceremony was performed, the girl was closely guarded by her mother and strictly chaperoned wherever she went. Rebellion against the family dictum was extremely rare. And the attractions of a Creole home were generally insufficient to keep the husband interested or to prevent wandering from the connubial couch. A French traveler who visited New Orleans in 1803 and 1804 observed that with all their beauty the Creole women possessed none of the arts of coquetry; they were devoted to their families, and "their husbands easily tire of the monotony of their society, and seek amusement elsewhere."

The origin of the Quadroon Balls, and the name of the genius who first organized them, are unknown and probably always will be. Scarcely any references to these functions or to the quadroon women appear in the newspapers of the period, and Louisiana historians, with few exceptions, have either ignored them or given them extremely brief mention, and that in the highest possible pitch of indignation and disapproval. Even so sober a writer as Grace King declared that "in regard to family purity, domestic peace, and household dignity," the quadroon women were "the most insidious and the deadliest foes a community ever possessed." Distinguished foreigners who visited New Orleans were always taken to see the Quadroon Balls by their hosts, and all of them, to judge from the comments in their journals and other published works, were enraptured by the beauty and charm of the quadroons. The Duke of Saxe-Weimar found them the most beautiful women on earth, and observed that large numbers were almost white — "nay," he wrote, "many of them have as fair a complexion as many

of the haughty Creole females." [1] An English traveler described the quadroon women as the most beautiful he had
ever seen, " resembling the higher orders of women among
the high-class Hindoos; lovely countenances, full, dark, liquid eyes, lips of coral, teeth of pearl, sylphlike figures; their
beautifully rounded limbs, exquisite gait, and ease of manner might furnish models for a Venus or Hebe." The Duke
of Saxe-Weimar attended both the Quadroon Balls and
the fashionable white subscription masked balls which were
given at the Orleans Ballroom after the Tuesday and Friday performances at the Théâtre d'Orléans, and found the
quadroon *soirée* " much more decent than the masked ball."
When he returned to the white function, he " could not refrain from making comparisons, which in no wise redounded
to the advantage of the white assembly." [2] The young Duke
also observed that whenever the dates of the white and
quadroon affairs conflicted, the gentlemen flocked almost
en masse to the latter, so that at the white balls many young
ladies were condemned to be wallflowers, or, as he put it,
" left to make tapestry."

During the latter part of the Spanish régime and the
early years of the American occupation, the Quadroon Balls
were held in the old Condé Street ballroom not oftener than
once a fortnight. Later a few were given at the little theater
in St. Peter Street, but about 1810 they were transferred to
the new St. Philip Theater, and were a fixture at that playhouse for some twenty years. When the St. Philip was
transformed into the Washington Ballroom in 1832 and
began to cater to the *demi-monde,* the Quadroon Balls began to be held in the Orleans Ballroom, which for years had
been the scene of the most fashionable of the white social

---

[1] *Travels through North America during the Years 1825 and 1826,* by
His Highness Bernhard, Duke of Saxe-Weimar Eisenach; two volumes; Philadelphia, 1828; Volume I, page 61.

[2] Ibid., page 63.

festivities. The quadroons and the Creoles shared the resort until the City Exchange, later the St. Louis Hotel, opened in 1838 and became almost at once a fashionable rendezvous. Thereafter the quadroons practically had the Orleans Ballroom to themselves. It was during this period that these functions were in the heyday of their notoriety, celebrated throughout the United States as the most brilliant entertainments to be found in New Orleans. Two and sometimes three balls were given each week, at which every gentleman paid two dollars admission, double the price paid at the white balls and masquerades. In no sense were the Quadroon Balls orgies; almost invariably, as the Duke of Saxe-Weimar found, they were much more decently conducted than the white social affairs. Only white men were admitted, and every effort was made to limit the guests to men of means and social standing. More duels probably originated there than at any other place in New Orleans, for the Creole was even quicker to resent a fancied slight or insult to his colored mistress than to his white wife or fiancée. As Lyle Saxon has said, "many a young Creole, whose marble slab in the Old St. Louis Cemetery testifies that he 'fell in a duel,' lies there because of his attentions to a quadroon girl whose official 'protector' objected to his flirtation." [1]

The Quadroon Balls began to decline in popularity about 1850; by that time New Orleans was rapidly becoming Americanized and was a metropolitan city of almost 125,000 population; it had simply outgrown such exotic displays. The Civil War completed the rout of the quadroons and the destruction of their hopes. Many of them, left without protectors when their lovers flocked to defend the Confederacy, and with no provision for their future, married men of their own race. But such marriages were usually unsuccessful; in 1864 alone six quadroon women were murdered in New Orleans by their jealous black hus-

---

[1] *Fabulous New Orleans*, page 185.

bands. After the Civil War most of them appear to have removed to Northern cities, where many crossed the border-line and passed as whites. The New Orleans *Times,* on May 23, 1879, said that for at least fifteen years they " have disappeared from public gaze, and if they exist at all, those of the new generation are utterly shut out from the outside world." The Orleans Ballroom was saved from the fire which destroyed the Théâtre d'Orléans in 1866, and for several years after the Civil War was used as the Criminal Courtroom of the Parish of Orleans. In 1881 the building was purchased by the Sisters of the Holy Family, an order of Negro nuns founded in 1842. Above the stairway on which once had trailed the silks and satins of the beautiful quadroons, the Sisters placed this inscription: "I have chosen rather to be an abject in the house of the Lord than to dwell in the temple with the sinners." Today the old ballroom is used as the assembly hall of the order's convent.

3

T H E cafés and coffee-houses of early New Orleans were described by the Duke of Saxe-Weimar as places " where the lower classes amused themselves," but many resorts of this type were also much patronized by the American and Creole merchants and other business men. Wearing striped jackets, their hats cocked on one side with an air of defiance, and swinging their sword-sticks, they gathered each evening to argue politics or discuss commercial affairs over *apéritifs* or after-dinner cordials. Most of the popular cafés and coffee-houses were on Royal and Chartres Streets, the principal thoroughfares of the French Quarter, with the exception of the Café des Améliorations at Rampart and Toulouse Streets, and the Absinthe House at Bienville and Bourbon. The latter, which was operated as a high-class bar-room for almost a hundred years, is still standing, and tradition points to it as the place wherein General Andrew

Jackson and the pirate Jean Lafitte planned the Battle of
New Orleans over an absinthe frappé. The tale loses plausi-
bility, however, when two facts are considered — Lafitte
had nothing to do with Jackson's plans, and the Absinthe
House, erected in 1798 as a private dwelling, did not become a saloon until 1826, a decade after the battle had been
fought and some eight or nine years after Lafitte had left
New Orleans.[1]

The Café des Améliorations was frequented principally by elderly, unreconstructed Creoles who refused to
admit that American possession of Louisiana was final. For
years they met daily at the café, where they concocted fantastic schemes for the capture of the state government, the
expulsion of the American barbarians, and the restoration
of the territory to France. The most vociferous of these fire-
eaters was an old gentleman known as the Chevalier, who
was one of the odd characters of the time. With a dog
and a monkey which remained his constant companions, the
Chevalier first appeared in New Orleans about 1795, having removed to the city from an upstate settlement. He not
only hated the Americans, but abhorred the ideas of equality
which had developed even among the Creoles after the
French Revolution, and was horrified at the popular dress
of the period, especially the increasingly popular pantaloons
and the custom of appearing in public without a wig. To the
day of his death his attire consisted of the habiliments of a
gentleman of an almost forgotten generation — powdered
wig and queue, knee breeches, silk stockings, frizzled cuffs
and shirt-front, and silver buckles on his slippers. Most of
the Chevalier's means were dissipated in the furtherance of
chimerical schemes for the liberation of Louisiana, and about

---

[1] During prohibition times the bar of the Absinthe House was removed
to another establishment two blocks down Bourbon Street. This place is now
a saloon, and advertises as " The Old Absinthe House Bar." The original resort
also reopened as a bar-room after repeal.

1800, to recoup his fortunes, he opened a candy- and cake-shop on Chartres Street near Dumaine. His stock included a plantation delicacy called the praline, the first of that famous confection ever offered for sale in New Orleans.

Within a block of the Chevalier's candy-store was the Café des Refugés, also known as the Café des Émigrés, which was the favorite rendezvous of the French planters who had fled from Santo Domingo. It was famous for a cordial called *le petit gouave,* the recipe of which is unknown in modern New Orleans. The Café des Exilés, immortalized by George W. Cable in his romances of early Louisiana, was at Royal and St. Ann Streets. Its name indicates the character of its patronage. A dozen other similar resorts, each with its special clientele, were scattered about the Vieux Carré. But the most popular of all the cafés and coffee-houses was La Bourse de Maspero, or Maspero's Exchange, which was a two-story wooden building, ninety feet long on St. Louis Street, with the main entrance on Chartres. It was built during the first decade of the nineteenth century by Pierre Maspero and for many years was the principal resort of the city's merchants and brokers, who transacted much of their business under its hospitable roof. The Exchange was often visited by Andrew Jackson when he was in New Orleans, and after the War of 1812 it became, in the popular mind, another of the innumerable places where Jackson planned the defense of the city against the British. As a matter of fact, Jackson did hold several meetings with his officers, to discuss the strategy of the campaign, in a room on the second floor. The whole of the first story was given over to the café and the kitchens. A bar ran the full length of the room, and scattered about the sanded floor were a large number of small tables. One corner, where several tables had been pushed together, was reserved for the journalists of the town. For many years the mail was distributed only once daily, and that at eleven o'clock at night; it was the custom of the editors and reporters to meet for lunch every day and discuss the news. The resort prospered under Maspero's ownership until early in 1838, when he sold it to James Hewlett, a well-known sporting man of the period, who became the first manager of the City Exchange, at Royal and St. Louis Streets, which as the St. Louis Hotel won an enduring place in New Orleans and Louisiana history.

Hewlett changed the name of La Bourse de Maspero to Hewlett's Exchange and made many alterations in the building and its equipment. He covered the sanded floor, typical of the coffee-houses of the time, with cypress, and installed a new bar, the finest in the city. He also enlarged the kitchen and restaurant facilities, and established an auction mart, where daily from noon to three o'clock stocks, real estate, and other properties were sold by auctioneers who cried their wares in three languages — English, French, and Spanish. On Saturdays the auction block was given over to the sale of slaves. The rooms upstairs became, under Hewlett's management, a handsomely appointed gambling-house and billiard-hall, while his partner, Hicks, opened a cockpit in a small building which adjoined the Exchange on Chartres Street. Hewlett also financed an Englishman who opened, on St. Louis Street behind the Exchange, a type of resort new to New Orleans, which was regarded as a great curiosity — a place where beer only was sold.

The original plans of the City Exchange, as prepared by the architect J. N. de Pouilly, called for the construction of an enormous building to cover the entire block bounded by Royal, Toulouse, Chartres, and St. Louis Streets. Work on the structure was begun in 1836 with materials imported from France, but the money crisis of 1837 compelled the promoters to modify their plans, and the size of the building was greatly reduced. When the Exchange opened, in the summer of 1838, it occupied only the St. Louis Street side of the square. The principal entrance, on St. Louis Street, opened into a vestibule 127 feet wide and 40 feet deep. The ballrooms were on the second floor, with separate entrances on both Royal and St. Louis Streets. The main feature of the hotel, however, was the Rotunda, a circular apartment with a high domed ceiling, in the center of the building. The Rotunda soon replaced Hewlett's Exchange as the principal auction mart of the city and until the Civil War was also a favorite place for political mass meetings.

Maspero was assisted in the management of the City Exchange by a Spaniard named Alvarez, whose particular province was the bar and restaurant. From the cooking-pots of an unknown genius employed in the kitchens of the Exchange is said to have emerged, for the first time, that gastronomical miracle called Louisiana Gumbo, originally known as Gombo, the natural result of the union of Marseilles *bouillabaisse* and Creole imagination. Besides introducing this masterpiece to the restaurant menus of New Orleans, Alvarez has another claim to fame — some time in the fall of 1838 he placed upon the bar of the City Exchange the first free lunch ever served in New Orleans, and probably in America as well. The menu consisted of soup, a piece of beef or ham with potatoes, meat pie, and oyster patties. At first a plate of lunch was handed to the customer with whatever drink he had ordered, but later the food was placed on a separate counter and anyone could help himself to as much as he desired. The innovation proved so popular that it was quickly copied by all the first-class bars in New Orleans and soon spread to other cities. Before many years bar-rooms all over the country were serving free elaborate repasts which compared favorably with the menus of the best restaurants.

Alvarez succeeded Maspero as manager of the City Exchange early in 1840, and the bar and restaurant were placed under the direction of Joseph Santini, who is still recalled in New Orleans as the inventor of two drinks which were very popular for a long period — the Crusta and Santini's Pousse-Café.[1]

The City Exchange was destroyed by fire early in 1841, but was immediately rebuilt from the original plans, and opened about a year later as the St. Louis Hotel. Alvarez was replaced as manager by James Hewlett, under whose direction the St. Louis entered upon an era of great splendor and prosperity. Its only rival was the St. Charles, in the American quarter of the town on St. Charles Avenue at Common Street, which opened its doors on Washington's Birthday 1837. With "its immense dome and Corinthian portico," the St. Charles was regarded as one of the architectural wonders of the New World — many travelers compared it to St. Peter's in Rome and to the palace of the Czar in St. Petersburg. Not the least of its many attractions was the famous gold service, valued at sixteen thousand dollars, which was used on special occasions of great ceremony. For some time in 1862, after the capture of New Orleans by Admiral Farragut, the hotel was the headquarters of General Benjamin Butler, commander of the Yankee Army which occupied the city. The St. Charles was twice destroyed by fire during its career as one of the city's principal hotels — on January 18, 1851 and April 28, 1894. The present structure was erected after the 1894 conflagration.

There was little to choose between the bars and restaurants and the purely hotel services of the St. Charles and the St. Louis, but the latter, located in the heart of the French Quarter and lavishly supported by the Creoles, soon became the center of the city's social life and supplanted the Orleans Ballroom as the scene of the fashionable balls and masquerades. Soon after the reopening of the St. Louis,

---

[1] Directions for mixing these old-time favorites may be found in *The Bon Vivant's Companion, or How to Mix Drinks*, by Professor Jerry Thomas; New York, 1928.

Hewlett inaugurated a series of subscription balls which became famous throughout the country as the acme of elegance and magnificence and as the most expensive entertainments in the country. Perhaps the most notable of these functions was that given in honor of Henry Clay during the winter of 1842–3, when two hundred subscribers each paid a hundred dollars, so that the ball and supper cost the then enormous sum of twenty thousand dollars. In the public rooms of the St. Louis were held also the most important of the balls with which New Orleans celebrated the winter carnival season, and, later, the functions of the organizations which participated in the observance of Mardi Gras. This celebration, for more than a century the best-known feature of New Orleans life, was introduced into the city in 1827 by a group of young men who organized a street procession of maskers. It was very successful and was repeated each year until 1837, when allegorical floats made their first appearance on the streets. The idea of such a pageant had been originally developed in Mobile by an organization called the Cowbellions. The second parade of this character in New Orleans was held in 1839, but nothing very ambitious was attempted until 1857, when the formation of the Mystic Krewe of Comus, the first of the organizations which now dominate the Mardi Gras celebration, placed the carnival on a firm footing and gave it practically the form in which it exists today.

The St. Louis Hotel continued to operate, under various owners, for several years after the Civil War, but unsuccessfully, and in 1874 the National Building Association bought the property from the Citizens' Bank and immediately resold it to the State of Louisiana for $253,000. For the next eight years the hotel was used as the state Capitol and was the scene of the meetings of the notorious " black-and-tan " Legislature, and of the disturbances which accompanied the efforts of the White League in 1874 to overthrow the carpet baggers and regain control of the state government. The building was closed in 1882 when the state capital was transferred to Baton Rouge, and two years later it was leased by the state to R. J. Rivers, who had previously been manager of the St. Charles. Rivers remodeled the structure and reopened it as the Hotel Royal. He operated the hotel for some eight years and then abandoned the project. A few years later the state sold the property, but no other tenant was ever found for it. During the bubonic plague scare of 1914 the old building was condemned as a breeder of rats and other vermin, and rather than expend the money necessary to make repairs, the owner had it razed.

4

NOWHERE else in North America, and for that matter in few European cities, was the so-called Code of Honor regarded with such reverence and the duello so universally practiced as in New Orleans during the hundred years that preceded the Civil War. The fashionable society functions, the theater, the opera, and the Quadroon Balls were, as we have seen, extraordinarily productive of these encounters; but their origin was not to be found exclusively in social slights and effronts, nor in differences of opinion regarding the merits of some dramatic or operatic artist. As Lyle Saxon wrote, "the word 'honor' hung in the air like the refrain of a popular song." In the words of a contemporary journalist, "the least breach of etiquette, the most venial sin against politeness, the least suspicion thrown out of unfair dealing, even a bit of awkwardness, are causes sufficient for a cartel, which none dares refuse." The custom reached such heights of absurdity, in fact, that duels were fought simply because the moonlight shone invitingly on the greensward, or because two or more young men, spring stirring in their veins, felt the urge to exchange thrusts, although no altercation had arisen; and for no reason at all. Gayarré tells the story of six young Creoles who were promenading the almost deserted streets of New Orleans late one night, after a ball, when one exclaimed: "Oh, what a beautiful night! What a splendid level ground for a joust! Suppose we pair off, draw our swords, and make this night memorable by a spontaneous display of bravery and skill!" Whereupon the light-headed young idiots fought until two of their number lay dead upon the field.

Quarrels among the Creoles never ended in fisticuffs; the unwritten laws of New Orleans society absolutely forbade the striking of a blow, and the man who so far forgot himself was commonly barred from the privilege of the duello and "exposed to the ignominy of being refused a meeting." Iron-clad rules and precedents governed every detail of the altercation and the duel, and all points of procedure were settled with such exactness that when the adversaries finally faced each other they were " in full equality both socially and morally." In early French and Spanish times the weapons principally used were the *colchemarde,* the rapier, and the broadsword, and occasionally the cumbersome pistol of the period, and there were comparatively few fatalities. When the Americans came to Louisiana, however, and were compelled by circumstances to adopt a custom utterly foreign to their natures, they added to the code the unique idea that the primary purpose in fighting a duel was to kill. With this in mind they introduced the rifle and the shotgun, and thereafter many duelists faced one another and fired at will with deadly squirrel rifles and double-barreled shotguns loaded with slugs. Some Americans had even more curious notions, and in accepting challenges from the haughty Creoles stipulated that the duels be fought with a variety of weapons ranging from clubs to axes. One of these freak combats was waged about 1810, in which the adversaries were armed with eight-foot sections of three-by-three cypress timber. They knocked each other senseless.

One of the famous duelists of early New Orleans was Bernard Marigny, a member of one of Louisiana's oldest and most influential families, who was a master swordsman and a crack shot with a pistol. He was elected to the state Legislature in 1817 as a member of the House of Representatives and took an active and a leading part in the many disputes that arose between the Creoles and the Americans. At the same time Catahoula Parish was represented by James Humble, a blacksmith and a former resident of Georgia, who was noted for his great stature — he stood almost seven feet in his stockings. The Georgian replied to one of Marigny's most impassioned speeches, and made various allusions so pointed and personal that the Creole considered himself grievously insulted, and challenged the blacksmith to a duel. Humble sought the advice of a friend.

" I will not fight him," he said. " I know nothing of this dueling business."

" You must," his friend protested. " No gentleman can refuse a challenge."

" I'm not a gentleman," Humble retorted. " I'm only a blacksmith."

Humble was assured that he would be ruined both politically and socially if he declined to meet the Creole. His friend pointed out that as the challenged person the blacksmith had the choice of weapons and could so choose as to put himself on equal terms with his adversary. Humble considered the matter for a day or two and then sent this reply to Marigny:

" I accept your challenge, and in the exercise of my privilege I stipulate that the duel shall take place in Lake Pontchartrain in six feet of water, sledge-hammers to be used as weapons."

Since Marigny was less than five feet and eight inches tall and so slight that he could scarcely lift a sledge-hammer, this was giving Humble an equal chance with a vengeance.

The Creole's friends urged him to stand on a box and run the risk of having his skull cracked by the huge blacksmith's hammer, but Marigny declared that it was impossible for him to fight a man with such a sense of humor. Instead he apologized to Humble, and the two became firm friends.

The first regulations issued by Bienville for the government of Louisiana forbade dueling, and they were strengthened by each succeeding French and Spanish governor, all of whom issued proclamations solemnly deploring the custom and announcing that the laws would be enforced. The Spanish Governor Miró in particular, in his *Bando de buen gobierno,* declared that he would rigorously enforce the regulations against dueling and against " those who carry about their persons dirks, pistols, and other weapons." Heavy penalties were provided, but rarely inflicted, for violation of the anti-dueling statutes. Even more stringent laws were enacted after Louisiana became a part of the United States, and in 1848, as the result of widespread agitation by various religious bodies, an article was inserted in the state Constitution disenfranchising duelists. This provision was never enforced, however, and was eventually repealed. Not even the highest officials of the colony, and later of the state, paid any attention to the laws which prohibited a meeting on the field of honor — they never hesitated to send or accept challenges, and many occupants of the executive mansion themselves engaged in combats with their political opponents and personal enemies. Until the Civil War there was scarcely a man in public life in New Orleans or Louisiana who had not fought at least one duel; most of them had engaged in several. The first American Governor of Louisiana, W. C. C. Claiborne, left the gubernatorial chair to fight Daniel Clark, a member of Congress who had been American Consul at New Orleans during the final years of the Spanish régime; and Claiborne's secretary and brother-in-law, Micajah Lewis, was killed in a duel by a man whom he had called to account for a bitter attack upon the Governor's policies. Emile La Sère, Representative in Congress from New Orleans, fought eighteen duels in the course of his political career; and George A. Waggaman, United States Senator from Louisiana, was killed in 1843 by Dennis Prieur, who had been Mayor of New Orleans from 1828 to 1838, in a meeting that grew out of the violent political contest waged that year by the Whigs and the Democrats.

Another famous duel that resulted from this campaign was fought the same year by Hueston, editor of the Baton Rouge *Gazette,* a Whig organ, and Alcee La Branche, Democratic candidate for Congress from the Second District in New Orleans, who had been Speaker of the state House of Representatives, and the first Chargé d'Affaires to Texas. It so happened that La Branche had never fought a duel, and the *Gazette* published an article taunting the voters of the Second District with having as their candidate a man destitute of spirit and manhood. La Branche considered that Hueston had insulted him, his party, his friends, his family, and the voters of New Orleans. When Hueston visited the city soon afterwards, La Branche accosted him in the billiard-room of the St. Charles Hotel and demanded an apology. Hueston refused, and La Branche knocked him down with a billiard cue, inflicting injuries that kept the editor in bed for several days. While he was recuperating, arrangements for a duel were made by friends of the two men. The weapons chosen were double-barreled shotguns loaded with ball. Forty yards was the distance agreed upon, and the word was to be given by Colonel W. H. McArdle, editor of the New Orleans *Tropic* and one of Hueston's friends. He was to say: "Fire — one, two, three, four, five!" and the combatants were to fire both barrels between the words " fire " and " five."

The duel began at dawn, in the presence of a large crowd. Both men discharged their pieces simultaneously.

Hueston's bullets went wide of the mark, but one of the slugs from La Branche's gun passed through the editor's hat and another through his coat. A second exchange of shots produced no injuries, and Hueston's second, Richard Hagan, suggested that either the distance be shortened or the duelists retired. Neither suggestion, however, was accepted. General John L. Lewis, La Branche's second, said that his principal was satisfied, and suggested that the duel end, but Hueston would not consent; he said he was determined to kill or be killed. Accordingly, preparations were made for the third exchange of shots, in which Hueston received a slight scalp wound. His own seconds then suggested that since he had been hurt, he should retire from the field. His reply was to summon the surgeon to his side.

" Feel my pulse," he directed, " and say whether it does not beat steady and regular."

The surgeon could distinguish nothing wrong with Hueston's pulse, but he expressed the opinion that the affair should end. Hueston, however, remained obdurate, and the guns were loaded for the fourth exchange. As the word was given, Hueston immediately discharged both barrels without effect, and La Branche fired once, his seventh shot of the duel, whereat Hueston dropped his gun and reeled forward. La Branche fired again before he saw that his adversary had been hurt, and Hueston fell to the ground, shot through both lungs. He was taken to the city, where he died after a few hours of intense agony.

A few weeks after this sanguinary encounter there occurred one of the most extraordinary of the rifle duels, in which the participants were an English cotton-buyer named Wright and Colonel S. L. Oakey, a wholesale and commission merchant, who had removed to New Orleans from New York in the early 1830's. Colonel Oakey was described by a contemporary journalist as " a man of courtly and knightly bearing, with a love of the drama and a taste for military display." His difficulty with Wright grew out of a series of letters in the Vicksburg *Sentinel,* which accused the cotton factors of New Orleans of unfair business methods. For the publication of these and similar articles the editor of the *Sentinel* was later killed in a duel by General D. W. Adams. Colonel Oakey assumed the championship of the New Orleans factors and, having traced the authorship of the letters to Wright, challenged the buyer to a duel. Wright, who had often boasted of his skill with the rifle, chose that weapon. Colonel Oakey not only had never fired a rifle, but had never even held one in his hands. Moreover, he refused to practice. When the duelists faced each other at a distance of sixty yards, Colonel Oakey's second handed him a Yager, afterwards known as the Mississippi rifle, and showed him how to manipulate the action. When the word was given, Wright fired hurriedly and wildly, while Colonel Oakey calmly raised his rifle and shot the cotton-buyer through the heart.

During the French and Spanish days in New Orleans most of the duels were fought in the cleared space in the center of St. Anthony's Square, behind the Cathedral. Later a favorite spot was a place on the Metarie Road called *Les Trois Capelines,* from three large trees that grew there, so draped with Spanish moss that they resembled the capes worn by the women of the period. The most celebrated of all the dueling-grounds, however, was a grove of giant live oaks, called simply the Oaks, on the plantation of Louis Allard, in those days a considerable distance from the city.[1] No attempt has ever been made to estimate the number of duels that were fought beneath the spreading branches of the great oaks, but the number would undoubtedly run into the thousands, and the fatalities into the hundreds. Frequently half a dozen combats were waged on the same

---

[1] The Oaks are still standing in City Park. Louis Allard is buried under one of the trees.

day; on a single Sunday in 1837 ten duels were fought under the Oaks between sunrise and noon, three of which ended fatally. On this spot Mandeville Marigny fought his brother-in-law, Alexander Graithe, to settle some point of family honor; and there General William de Buys, owner of the famous slave and Negro folk-hero Bras Coupé, seconded his son in a duel and half an hour later was seconded by the younger de Buys when he met his own antagonist. In later years the grove was the scene of the famous duel between Colonel Schaumberg of the United States Army and Alexander Cuvilier, who fought with broadswords on horseback. Colonel Schaumberg's horse was killed by a tremendous stroke delivered by Cuvilier, but neither of the duelists was injured.

It was under the Oaks, too, that the Chevalier Tomasi, a distinguished European scientist, was taught by an indignant Creole not to disparage the Mississippi River. The Chevalier arrived in New Orleans about 1840, full of knowledge and opinions, both of which he dispensed freely, vocally and in a series of newspaper articles. His pronunciamentos were interlarded with sly references to the correction girls and to the *filles à la cassette* and flat statements upholding the superiority of the French, so that the Creoles found him very offensive. During a coffee-house discussion one evening the Chevalier stated dogmatically that the Mississippi River should either be compelled to flow peacefully in a designated channel or be stopped altogether, as, he said, had been done with several rivers in Europe. A Creole ventured the opinion that works which would hold back the smaller streams of Europe would have no effect on so mighty a river as the Mississippi.

" How little you know of the world! " said the Chevalier. " Know that there are rivers in Europe so large that the Mississippi is a mere rill, figuratively speaking."

"Sir," said the enraged Creole, " I will never allow

149

the Mississippi to be insulted or disparaged in my presence by an arrogant pretender to knowledge."

He emphasized this patriotic outburst by flinging his glove in the Chevalier's face and was immediately challenged to a duel. They met under the Oaks at dawn, and the Creole upheld the honor and dignity of the Mississippi by

From an old print

A DUEL UNDER THE OAKS

slashing the French scientist across the mouth. But the Chevalier Tomasi had an explanation, more or less scientific, for his defeat.

"I should have killed my antagonist," he declared, "but for the miserable character of your American steel. My sword doubled like lead."

The golden age of dueling in New Orleans was from about 1830 until the Civil War. During that period at least fifty *maîtres d'armes* operated fencing academies in Exchange Alley, a short narrow street running from Canal to

Conti between Royal and Bourbon Streets. In the New Orleans of their day they occupied much the same position that champion prize-fighters do in more modern times. Crowds followed them in the street, in the cafés and coffee-houses they were the darlings of the waiters, and the young Creoles aped their mannerisms and strove to emulate their skill with the rapier and broadsword. "Some of the fencing masters," wrote Lyle Saxon, "affected the manners of dandies, dressed extravagantly, carried their handkerchiefs in their sleeves, and attempted to get a foothold in society." [1] Few succeeded in this latter design, for while the young bloods of the town lingered at the academies to sip wine with the *maîtres d'armes,* they did not invite the professional swordsmen to meet their mothers and sisters.

Among the most celebrated of these dangerous dandies were Marcel Dauphin, whose skill availed him but little in the end, for he was killed in a duel with shotguns; Pépé Lulla, a Spaniard; Gilbert Rosière, called Titi by his pupils; and Bastile Croquère. The last named, who lived in an old house on the corner of Conti Street and Exchange Alley, was a mulatto and is said to have been the handsomest man in New Orleans. He habitually wore a suit of the finest green broadcloth, snow-white shirts, and a wide black stock about his throat. He possessed a notable collection of cameos and was considered an authority upon the subject; when in gala attire his raiment was embellished by cameo rings, breast-pins, and bracelets. He fought many duels in France, where he was educated, but none in New Orleans; because he was a man of color no white man would have accepted his challenge or even quarreled with him. But he was a miraculous swordsman and a wonderful teacher, and men of the best Creole families went to him for instruction and crossed swords with him in private bouts. Pépé Lulla is said to have been even more accomplished than Croquère and was per-

---

[1] *Fabulous New Orleans,* page 191.

haps the finest swordsman who ever drew blade in New
Orleans. When dueling declined, the Spanish master settled
on a truck farm in the vicinity of Louisa and St. Claude
Streets. Later his property became the Louisa Street Cemetery, afterwards called St. Vincent de Paul. Lulla was buried
there with his wife and daughter.

Gilbert Rosière was a native of Bordeaux, a lawyer,
and a graduate of a French university. He came to New
Orleans to practice law, but being of a wild and carefree
disposition, he fell in with a set of gay young men and became a leader in their escapades. Instead of establishing a
law office he opened a fencing academy, and at the outset of
his career attracted considerable local renown by fighting
seven duels in one week. He earned a fortune by teaching
young Army officers to fence during the Mexican War, but
it was soon squandered. His contemporaries describe him
as gay, witty, and somewhat irascible and, for all his record
as a duelist, so tender-hearted that he could not harm a fly.
He frequently wept at the theater and the opera — and
killed several men who laughed at his displays of emotion.

In the spring of 1840 the professional swordsmen held
a grand *assaut d'armes* at the old St. Philip Theater, in
which only those who had diplomas from recognized fencing schools were eligible to compete. Pépé Lulla was barred
because he could show no papers, and in a real duel later
he wounded the man who had objected to him. Poulaga, an
Italian expert with the broadsword, was defeated in an ex-
hibition match by Captain Thimecourt, who had been a cavalry officer in the French Army. Enraged, Poulaga slapped
Thimecourt's face and was immediately challenged. They
fought under the Oaks one of the bloodiest duels ever seen
on that historic spot; Captain Thimecourt literally hacked
the Italian to pieces. Besides these and other encounters
among the professionals, twenty duels between young gen-

tlemen of the town grew out of the display of skill by the fencing masters.

Many of the *maîtres d'armes* and practically all of their pupils joined the Confederate Army when the Civil War began. When they returned to New Orleans they found that dueling was no longer in fashion; new social and civic viewpoints had arisen, and there was no place for the duello amidst the problems and tribulations of the reconstruction period. Thereafter the laws against the practice were rigidly enforced, and only an occasional duel was fought. One of the last of which there is public record was a meeting in February 1887, on the Arnould plantation in Jefferson Parish, between André L. Roman, editor, and Emile Rivoire, business manager, of the *Trait d'Union,* a New Orleans French newspaper. The duel was fought in the rain with pistols at fifteen paces, and the weapons were loaded under the shelter of umbrellas. Several shots were exchanged, but neither of the duelists was injured.

CHAPTER V

THE TERROR OF THE GULF

Piracy in the grand manner, as practiced by such renowned freebooters as Sir Henry Morgan and the infamous Blackbeard, came to an end in the Gulf of Mexico about the middle of the eighteenth century, when the western seas were swept clean by combined fleets of the three principal European powers — England, France, and Spain. But the commerce of the Gulf continued to be plundered, under the flimsy guise of legality, by the privateers — armed ships whose captains carried letters of marque issued by nations at war, and were thus empowered to attack and capture vessels flying the enemy flag. Under the maritime laws a privateer could keep both a captured ship and its cargo, provided he brought the prize into a port of the country to which he claimed allegiance and had the seizure formally approved by an admiralty court. He could then sell his loot wherever he pleased. Within a few years after the turn of the nineteenth century the Gulf of Mexico fairly swarmed with piratical craft, most of which operated safely within international law by flying the flag of the Republic of Cartagena, now one of the principal seaports of Colombia, which had revolted against the rule of Spain. These privateers were supposed to prey only upon Spanish commerce; actually, they attacked every ship they met, regardless of nationality, to which they were superior in armament. And with the crew of the captured vessel murdered and the ship

itself scuttled, there was no evidence left to tell the tale.
After the American occupation of Louisiana had made
the Mississippi River a free waterway and opened the western territories to trade, New Orleans became more than
ever the principal market of the pirates and privateers. Instead of making the long voyage to Cartagena for an admiralty court hearing, the freebooters began bringing their
prizes directly to New Orleans. This necessitated smuggling
the cargoes ashore, as only goods which had been legally
condemned as a prize of war could be cleared through the
United States customs. And since smuggling required considerable preparation and a certain measure of organization, the privateers perceived the need of a base within easy
sailing distance of New Orleans and yet so nearly inaccessi-
ble as to be comparatively safe from prying warships. They
found it some sixty miles south of the city in the Bay of Barataria, one of the innumerable indentations in the coast of
Louisiana, separated from the Gulf by the islands Grande
Terre and Grand Isle, between which flowed a passage deep
enough for seagoing vessels, provided the pilot knew the
channel. At the northern end of the bay a dozen bayous led
into the swamps. From this marine labyrinth smugglers had
been operating almost continuously since the early days of
French rule, and into it pirates had often fled to escape pursuing warships. Blackbeard himself sought refuge there for
several days in 1718, a few months before his ship was sunk,
and himself slain, off the coast of Carolina.

On Grand Terre, behind a fringe of trees which further screened their activities from the Gulf, the privateers
set up their headquarters and gradually developed an establishment which supplied the merchants of New Orleans with
contraband goods of every description, at prices so low that
the legitimate importers could not compete. And around the
smuggling establishment arose a colony of hard and desperate ruffians, for Grand Terre soon became a rendezvous

not only of the privateers, smugglers, and pirates, but of criminals and adventurers of high and low degree. Fights, robberies, and fatal brawls over the division of booty became common, and the merchants of New Orleans began to be afraid to visit the island to bargain for goods, or to have other dealings with the privateers. Business at Grand Terre was done in a helter-skelter fashion, every man for himself. What the Baratarians needed most was someone who could bring order out of the chaos into which they had fallen, co-ordinate their efforts, and direct their depredations.

This Moses of the freebooters appeared in the person of Jean Lafitte, around whom so much legend and tradition has clustered that he has become the most romantic figure in all the history of New Orleans; a street has been named for him, the site of his blacksmith-shop in St. Philip Street between Bourbon and Dauphine has become a tourist shrine, and today he forms one of the principal talking-points of the civic boosters who attempt to help visitors recapture the spirit of the old city. Within the last fifty years Lafitte has been the subject of a vast literature; more has probably been written about him than about any other person who ever trod the streets of New Orleans, with the possible exception of Andrew Jackson. When a Louisiana historian or journalist can find no other work for his idle pen, he writes about the man who is in process of becoming the great folk-hero of New Orleans. As the saying goes, Lafitte has been analyzed, explained, and interpreted up one side and down the other. Innumerable books and articles have proved conclusively that he was a pirate, a murderer, and a great villain; others just as numerous have proved just as conclusively that he was no pirate at all, but a staunch patriot, a much misunderstood man, a gentleman smuggler, and a privateer who operated strictly within his legal rights. A former president of the Louisiana Historical Society once declared that "there is no character to compare him with except that of Robin Hood, whom he surpassed in audacity and success." Some accounts of Lafitte have it that he was the son of a sailor, and himself followed the sea from childhood; others that he was the scapegrace son of a noble French family, that his real name was not Lafitte, that Pierre was not his brother, but the child of an old family servant, and that Jean's parents were beheaded during the French Revolution. His birthplace and the circumstances of his death have been, and are, matters of violent dispute. He appears to have been born in a dozen different French cities, and to have died in as many places in the West Indies — he succumbed to natural causes, he was murdered by rebellious followers, and he was slain at sea in battle with an English sloop-of-war. But the latest chapter of the Lafitte saga, the author of which drew upon the vast volumes of material already written as well as upon his own original researches, says flatly that Lafitte was born at Bordeaux in 1780, that nothing is known of his family, and that he died alone, embittered and forgotten, at the Yucatan village of Teljas in 1826.[1]

Upon the person of this mysterious and romantic corsair have been bestowed as many descriptions as there are versions of his birth and the manner of his death. Grace King, one of the most careful of historians, wrote that he was "described by a kind of general authority as a man of fair complexion, with black hair and eyes, wearing his beard clean shaven from the front of his face." Another writer says that he was "a well-formed, handsome man, about six feet two inches in height, strongly built, with large hazel eyes and black hair, and generally wore a mustache." Still another describes him as rather slight, with small, almost feminine hands and feet. And a fourth has it that Lafitte

---

[1] *Jean Lafitte, Gentleman Smuggler,* by Mitchell V. Charnley; New York, 1934.

was tall and well formed, and inventories a peculiarity of which no one else appears to have knowledge — " when conversing upon a serious subject, he would stand for hours with one eye shut; at such times, his appearance was harsh." And so on *ad infinitum*. As the Louisiana darkies say, " you pays your money and you takes your choice."

Unheralded, but accompanied by rumors that they had captained great piratical expeditions in the Indian Ocean, Jean Lafitte and his brother Pierre first appeared in New Orleans some time in 1806 and, with the financial backing of the capitalist Sauvinet, established the blacksmith-shop in St. Philip Street. Using the smithy, and later a fine store which they opened in Royal Street, as blinds, but deceiving no one, they operated for some two years as smugglers' agents. The brothers prospered greatly and entertained lavishly in their mansion at Bourbon and St. Philip Streets. Jean Lafitte, especially, made many friends and became a welcome and prominent figure in the nightly discussions of the merchants and the gentry in the cafés and coffee-houses; for he was a man of great personal charm, he had considerable education — he spoke English, French, Spanish, and Italian fluently and correctly — and possessed to a remarkable degree the knack of forming warm friendships, and the ability to lead men and dominate any gathering of which he was a part. But though the profits were great and life in New Orleans very pleasant, the ambitious and methodical Lafitte soon became dissatisfied with the slipshod manner in which the smugglers and privateers conducted their affairs; he saw clearly that a guiding hand was needed to prevent the establishment at Barataria from collapsing of its own weight. His dissatisfaction became acute when on January 1, 1808 a new element entered the smuggling field. On that date a law went into effect prohibiting the importation of slaves into the United States. Throughout the South the prices of Negroes rose immediately — plantation-owners gladly paid from eight hundred to a thousand dollars for an able-bodied black man who could be bought for twenty dollars on the African coast, or for three hundred dollars in Cuba, which was now the headquarters of the legal slave trade. Negroes thus suddenly became extremely important articles of merchandise, and smuggling them into Louisiana was immensely profitable.

Lafitte's mind was made up when he learned that actual warfare threatened between the smugglers and a group of privateers who had seized a cargo of slaves imported by the former and were offering them for sale at a dollar a pound. He left the business at New Orleans in the hands of his brother Pierre and went to Grand Terre, a two-day journey by pirogue and barge through the bayous and marshes. Lafitte found some hard men on the little island — such renowned pirates and privateers as René Béluche and Dominique You, better known as Captain Dominique, who had been artillerymen in the armies of Napoleon and who later became Lafitte's principal lieutenants; Chighizola, called *Nez Coupé* — Cut Nose — because of a saber-slash which had disfigured his face; and Vincent Gambi, a surly, hot-tempered Italian who boasted that he was an out-and-out bloody private and no puling privateer, who had murdered a score of men with a broad-ax, and who was finally killed by his own men with his own ax as he lay asleep on a pile of stolen gold. These were the most important leaders of the Grand Terre colony, but there were many others of almost equal prominence, besides their followers and the smugglers — between four hundred and five hundred lawless, desperate ruffians. In addition there were perhaps two hundred women, who were even worse than their sinful sisters of the Swamp and Tchoupitoulas Street. Alone Lafitte faced the smugglers and privateers, calmly catalogued their faults and enumerated their mistakes, and pointed out to them the road to greater prosperity. Such were the po-

159

tency of his arguments and the compelling power of his personality that within a week they had accepted his leadership. Curiously enough, they unofficially bestowed upon him a title exactly similar to that which a man acquires today when he gets a community under his thumb — they called him the Bos, or Boss.

Lafitte ruled Grand Terre and the Bay of Barataria for almost a decade, and only once was his supremacy even questioned. At one of his early conferences with the privateer captains he warned them that every Baratarian ship must have letters of marque from a country at war with Spain, and that only Spanish vessels were to be attacked. Vincent Gambi dissented and left the conference, and Lafitte soon learned that he was striving to encourage his own men to revolt against Lafitte's leadership. Presently one of Gambi's lieutenants approached, pistol in hand, and called loudly for Lafitte. When the Bos appeared, the man cried: " The men of Gambi take orders only from Gambi!"

Without a word Lafitte drew a pistol and shot the man dead. This was a reply that was thoroughly understood by every ruffian on Grand Terre, and there was no further talk of rebellion.

Whatever else Jean Lafitte may or may not have been, he was beyond question a genius at organizing. Within an amazingly short time he had united the warring factions of Grand Terre and put their piratical enterprises upon a sound business basis; they cruised when and where he directed, and placed their loot in his hands for disposal. More and more of the Gulf pirates and privateers joined the Lafitte trust; a year after he had landed at Grand Terre he had a thousand men under his command; and fifty ships, all flying the flag of Cartagena, swept the shipping lanes of the Gulf and came directly to Barataria with their prizes. In every respect Lafitte greatly enlarged and improved the Grand Terre establishment. Thatched cottages were built for the pirates and their women; and gambling-houses, cafés, and bordellos were opened so that the pirates might have the sort of entertainment for which they pined. Enormous warehouses were erected, and a new barracoon or slave quarters, wherein lay in chains the Negroes taken from captured slavers, awaiting purchasers. In the center of the colony Lafitte built himself a mansion of brick and stone, equipped with the finest of furniture, plate, linens, and carpets, all stolen by his pirates. There he entertained his cronies from New Orleans, and the plantation-owners and slave-dealers, astonishing all by the luxury amidst which he lived.

Once a week, and sometimes oftener, slave auctions were held; occasionally as many as four hundred Negroes were sold in one day and then smuggled into Louisiana, either by their new owners or by Lafitte's agents. In New Orleans Pierre Lafitte, operating the store in Royal Street, and the smithy, wherein particularly fine specimens of the wild African were tamed and trained and so brought higher prices, took orders for goods and slaves and displayed a fine line of samples. Many New Orleans merchants, however, soon formed the habit of going to Grand Terre to buy; there they were lavishly entertained by Jean Lafitte and could make their own selections directly from the stocks in the warehouses. They were safe on Grand Terre now, and Lafitte guaranteed delivery of whatever they bought; a fleet of barges maintained regular schedules between Grand Terre and New Orleans and Donaldsonville, the distributing-center for the up-river country.

So extraordinary were Lafitte's abilities and so efficiently did he operate the Barataria establishment that by the beginning of 1813 practically all of the New Orleans stores were being supplied with his smuggled merchandise, and the legitimate commerce of the city had suffered to an alarming degree. It was clear that within a few more years

Lafitte would have a practical monopoly of Louisiana's import trade, as well as most of the commerce of the whole
valley of the Mississippi. The government of the United
States made a few half-hearted attempts to check the Baratarians, and several inconsequential seizures were made by
revenue boats, but the comparative failure of these expeditions only increased Lafitte's prestige. When Governor
W. C. C. Claiborne issued a proclamation early in 1813 denouncing the Baratarians as pirates and warning the people
of New Orleans to have no further dealings with them, Lafitte made a point of returning to the city. There he and
Pierre embarked upon a season of entertainment, securing
the attendance of the most prominent merchants at their
dinners. They appeared upon the streets and in the cafés,
surrounded by admiring and influential friends, and boldly
announced in the newspapers the dates of forthcoming sales
of slaves and other merchandise. And a few months later,
when Governor Claiborne issued another proclamation,
which was posted in prominent places in New Orleans, offering a reward of five hundred dollars for the arrest and delivery of Jean Lafitte to the Sheriff of the Parish of Orleans,
the Bos of the pirates countered with a proclamation of his
own, couched in heavy legal verbiage and posted in equally
prominent locations in the city, in which he offered a reward
of fifteen hundred dollars for the arrest of Governor Claiborne and the delivery of his person at Grand Terre.

Governor Claiborne then attempted criminal proceed-
ings, and the Grand Jury returned indictments against Jean
Lafitte and other Baratarians, charging them with piracy.
Pierre Lafitte, indicted as "an aider and abettor," was arrested and lodged without bail in the Calaboose. Jean Lafitte immediately retained the two most prominent members
of the Louisiana bar, John R. Grymes and Edward Livingston, the latter a brother of the Chancellor Livingston who
administered the oath of office to George Washington, and

offered them twenty thousand dollars each to defend his brother. Grymes was District Attorney of the Parish of Orleans at the time, and resigned to earn the fat fee. When his successor in office said in open court that Grymes had been " seduced by the blood-stained gold of pirates," Grymes challenged him to a duel, shot him through the hip, and crippled him for life. But the combined skill of Grymes and Livingston failed to obtain the dismissal of the indictment against Pierre Lafitte, and the pirate's brother remained in jail for several months, when he was freed in a mysterious jail-break. Nevertheless Jean Lafitte made no attempt to avoid payment of the forty thousand dollars he had promised the lawyers. On the contrary, he invited them to Grand Terre, that he might pay and thank them in person for their efforts. Grymes, who was notorious in New Orleans as a gambler and a playboy, accepted eagerly, but Livingston declined, and deputized Grymes to collect his fee at a commission of ten per cent. Grymes received the money the day he arrived at the pirate's establishment, but he lingered on the island, charmed by Lafitte's hospitality, and nightly gambled with the pirate chieftain. At the end of a few days the twenty thousand dollars Grymes had collected for himself was back in Lafitte's strong-box, together with the two-thousand-dollar commission from Livingston.

Although Lafitte was now at the height of his power, actually his star had already begun to wane. As early as 1811 his popularity had suffered a setback when a slave rebellion in the Parish of St. John the Baptist, some forty miles from New Orleans, was traced to Negroes who had been purchased at Grand Terre. He had apparently regained the lost ground, but a feeling of distrust was slowly developing. And many citizens, viewing the increasing arrogance of Lafitte and his associates, and the decline of legitimate trade, had begun to wonder what the end would be. Furthermore, the national government, harried though it was by the successes of the British in the War of 1812, had at last listened to Governor Claiborne and was preparing to send a strong force against the Baratarians. This expedition, consisting of six gunboats and several smaller but heavily armed vessels, sailed from New Orleans in September 1814, under command of Commodore Patterson of the United States Navy. The Baratarians were aware that the vessels were being fitted for active service, but had supposed the preparations to be directed against the British. Consequently they were taken completely by surprise, and after a brief fight Commodore Patterson destroyed the establishment at Grand Terre and captured nine ships and a hundred prisoners, among them René Béluche and Dominique You. Jean and Pierre Lafitte, with several hundred of their followers, escaped into the bayous and marshes.

But so far as Jean Lafitte's personal fortunes were concerned, fate had again played into his hand. A few days before Commodore Patterson attacked Grand Terre, an English ship appeared in the Bay of Barataria, and after a long conversation with Lafitte the commander of the vessel offered the pirate leader thirty thousand dollars in gold and a captaincy in the British Navy if he would enlist his Baratarians on the side of the British in an attack upon New Orleans. Lafitte asked for time to consider, and learned what he could of the English plans. After the British ship had gone he sent to Governor Claiborne a full account of what had occurred. He offered to join the American Army or Navy with his men and aid in repelling the invasion. In return he asked for " an act of oblivion for all that has been done hitherto." Claiborne called a conference of Army and Navy officials, expressed his belief that Lafitte's warning of a British attack was true, and urged the acceptance of Lafitte's offer and the recall of Commodore Patterson's expedition. But the weight of opinion was against him. No reply was made to Lafitte, and Patterson sailed as ordered. When

Lafitte, fleeing after Patterson's successful attack, reached New Orleans, he called upon Claiborne and renewed his offer. Claiborne referred the matter to General Jackson, then at Mobile, and Jackson, who had already denounced the Baratarians as " hellish banditti," rejected it with scorn. But when Jackson arrived at New Orleans, Lafitte again renewed his offer. And knowing by this time the appalling weakness of the city's defenses, Jackson accepted. Dominique You, René Béluche, and other captive Baratarians were released from jail and with the brothers Lafitte were mustered into the American Army. The character of the service they rendered at the Battle of New Orleans was thus summarized by Jackson in his dispatch of January 21, 1815:

" Captains Dominique and Béluche, lately commanding privateers at Barataria, with part of their former crews and many brave citizens of New Orleans, were stationed at Batteries Three and Four. The general cannot avoid giving his warm approbation of the manner in which these gentlemen have uniformly conducted themselves while under his command, and of the gallantry with which they redeemed the pledge they gave at the opening of the campaign to defend the country. The brothers Lafitte have exhibited the same courage and fidelity, and the general promises that the government shall be duly apprised of their conduct."

The roaring of the guns had scarcely subsided on the plain of Chalmette before Lafitte's lawyers, Grymes and Livingston, had begun suit to recover for their client the vessels which Patterson had captured at Grand Terre. At the same time the Attorney-General of the state, John Dick, suggested to Governor Claiborne that the quashing of all charges against the Baratarians would be a fitting and popular gesture. Meanwhile both the Governor and General

Jackson had notified President Madison of the meritorious conduct of the pirates and privateers during the Battle of New Orleans, and on February 6, 1815 the President signed a proclamation giving a free and full pardon to every Baratarian who could produce a statement from Claiborne that he had participated in the engagement with the British. The brothers Lafitte, Dominique You, René Béluche, Cut Nose Chighizola, and even the ferocious Gambi thus became free citizens of the United States in the full enjoyment of their liberties. There are many reasons to believe that Jean Lafitte, after the battle and the destruction of his base at Grand Terre, intended to set himself up as a gentleman in New Orleans and engage in legitimate business, but even before he was pardoned an incident occurred which had much to do with determining his future. At the great Victory Ball given on January 23, 1815 to celebrate the defeat of the British Army, Lafitte approached a group which included General Jackson, Governor Claiborne, and Generals Coffee and de Flaugeac. Jackson and Claiborne greeted him warmly, but it so happened that as Lafitte reached the group, de Flaugeac turned his back to speak to a friend; and when the Governor introduced Lafitte to General Coffee, the latter hesitated an instant before extending his hand. Whereupon Lafitte drew himself up, glared haughtily at General Coffee, and said coldly:

" Lafitte the pirate! "

Although both General Coffee and General de Flaugeac apologized and assured Lafitte that they had intended no discourtesy, the incident is said to have convinced the Baratarian that no matter what giddy heights of social and business success he might reach in New Orleans, he would always be " Lafitte the pirate." He immediately made plans to leave New Orleans, and when the ships which had been seized at Grand Terre were suddenly offered by the government at public auction, they were bought by Lafitte's backer, the capitalist Sauvinet. And a few weeks after he had been pardoned by President Madison, Lafitte sailed away to start a new career as a corsair. With him went a hundred Baratarians upon whom life in the city had already palled, and the best of his former captains — Dominique You and René Béluche, Cut Nose Chighizola, and the terrible Gambi. But almost immediately they began to leave him. You and Cut Nose returned to peaceful pursuits in New Orleans; Béluche, upon the recommendation of General Jackson, obtained a commission as Commodore in the Navy of Venezuela; and Gambi again became, as he had always boasted he would, a real pirate, and plundered and sank a score of ships before he was killed some four years later.

Jean and Pierre Lafitte attempted to establish a new base of operations at Port-au-Prince, but the Governor of that city compelled them to leave after replenishing their supplies of food and water. For the next three years the brothers roamed the Gulf of Mexico, searching for a suitable location on which to build an establishment and occasionally seizing a Spanish vessel and smuggling the cargo into Louisiana. In 1816 Jean Lafitte founded a small colony on an island off the coast of Texas and called it Campeachy, under the impression that it was in the bay of that name. When he learned his mistake, he changed the name of the new establishment to Galvez-town, which eventually became Galveston. There he prospered for several years, building himself a big red house and attracting to his banner several hundred of the same sort of men he had commanded at Grand Terre. Meanwhile he intrigued with Spain and leaders of the various revolutionary movements in Texas and Mexico, and even sent Pierre to Washington to sound out sentiment there. He was striving desperately to obtain assurances of the support and protection which he knew would in time become necessary if he was to continue his operations. But all of his intrigues failed of success, and his schemes began gradually to collapse. Instead of developing into an orderly community such as Grand Terre had been, Galveston became almost at once the refuge not only of pirates and privateers, but also of vicious criminals and fugitives from the United States and the Gulf ports.

These men, and many of Lafitte's followers with them, took matters into their own hands; instead of preying only upon commerce specified in their letters of marque, they resorted to downright piracy and attacked vessels indiscriminately, regardless of nationality. Early in September 1819 Lafitte purchased at New Orleans a new schooner, which he named the *Bravo*, and sent two of his lieutenants, Jean Desfargues and Robert Johnson, with a crew of sixteen men, to sail the vessel to Galveston. Although the ship carried no privateer's commission, she attacked a Spanish merchant vessel in the Gulf near the mouths of the Mississippi. Desfargues, Johnson, and their men were still looting the Spaniard when the American revenue cutter *Alabama* appeared, captured them and the *Bravo* after a sharp fight, and took both ship and pirates to New Orleans. There the eighteen men were immediately tried in the United States District Court, found guilty of piracy, and sentenced to hang. Jean Lafitte rushed to New Orleans to secure legal aid for his followers. Pierre was already there, and the brothers, joined by old friends and many planters who feared the loss of profitable business in slaves and other contraband which Lafitte made possible, caused such a stir that the authorities ordered out the militia to prevent a threatened attack on the prison. In the end, however, the Lafittes accomplished little or nothing. Reprieves were granted to all of the condemned men, and one, John Tuckers, was pardoned by President Monroe. But after the reprieves had expired, the remaining seventeen, including Johnson and Desfargues, were duly hanged in the Place d'Armes as pirates.

The beginning of the end of the Galveston establishment came late in 1820, when a desperado named Brown plundered an American vessel in Matagorda Bay. Brown's trail led plainly to Lafitte's colony, and although Lafitte tried Brown and hanged him on an island in the harbor, the government at Washington decided that Galveston must be destroyed. Early in 1821 an American war-brig anchored before Lafitte's establishment, and Lafitte was told that he must evacuate the island at the end of three months. The brig returned on May 11, 1821 and found Lafitte busy supervising the destruction of the colony. Fire was applied to the wreckage, and in the glare of the conflagration Lafitte and his followers, in three ships, sailed out of Galveston harbor. Two of his vessels deserted him a few days later when he refused to attack a convoy of Spanish merchantmen, and thereafter the romantic figure who had once been " the terror of the Gulf " was a petty pirate and thief. His base was a small collection of squalid huts on Mugeres Island, off the coast of Yucatan, from which he made occasional forays against small towns and coastwise trading vessels. In 1826 he crossed to the little Indian village of Teljas, on the mainland, where, in his forty-seventh year, he died of fever after a few days' illness in a native hut.

Lafitte's most celebrated lieutenant, Dominique You, spent the remaining years of his life in New Orleans, where he became a well-known and popular figure in the cafés and coffee-houses. He died in abject poverty, at the age of fifty-five, on November 15, 1830, in his home at Love and Mandeville Streets, and was buried in the old St. Louis Cemetery No. 1. On the day of his funeral all business houses in New Orleans were closed, the city's flags hung at half-staff, and old Dominique was interred with full military honors. Participating in the ceremonies were the Louisiana Legion, the crack organization of volunteers, and the Orleans Artillery, of which the ex-pirate had been one of the founders. Today Dominique You is recalled in New Orleans principally as one of the important conspirators in a legendary plot to rescue Napoleon from the island of St. Helena and bring him to New Orleans. According to tradition, for the support of which no conclusive evidence has ever been found, the plot was conceived by Nicholas Girod, who was Mayor of New Orleans from 1812 to 1815 and who built a fine house at Chartres and St. Louis Streets especially for the Emperor's occupancy. This building is still pointed out to tourists as the "Napoleon House," and sometimes an enthusiastic citizen insists that Napoleon actually lived in it, but, unfortunately for the legend, the house was actually erected several years before the date ascribed to the conspiracy. The tale further runs that from Napoleon's sympathizers in New Orleans, St. Louis, and Charleston, Girod and his associates raised sufficient money to purchase the *Seraphine,* a schooner of some two hundred tons, supposed at the time to be one of the fastest ships in the world. The vessel was equipped and provisioned and placed under the command of Dominique You, who recruited a crew from among the pardoned Baratarians. But three days before the scheduled departure of the *Seraphine* word reached New Orleans that Napoleon had died at St. Helena, on May 5, 1821.

Both before and after the days of Lafitte's pirate trust an occasional independent freebooter flashed across the horizon of notoriety, but usually he was quickly subdued by a revenue cutter or one of Lafitte's vessels, for the latter permitted no encroaching upon his preserves. One of the most successful of the free-lances of the early days was a tall, dark villain who called himself Blackbeard II, owned a small sloop and half a dozen pirogues, and operated in the vicinity of the English Turn, on the lower Mississippi. He was especially renowned for his enormous black mustache, the ends of which he tied behind his ears when he went into action; and for the dress of his followers, who wore long red stockings and red caps, and carried each as many knives, pistols, and cutlasses as he could stow upon his person. The last pirate to arouse any apprehension in the Gulf was Captain James Cole Denham, better known as King Cole, who was active in Mississippi Sound for some ten years after 1870. Cole captained a small sloop, on which he always carried a coach and a team of horses, and robbed coastal villages and small bayou trading boats. His principal base was the cabin of Red Sam Williams, a Sound fisherman, and his most notable exploit was a raid on the town of Gainesville, Mississippi. To accomplish this feat he tied up his sloop at the Gainesville wharf, loaded his men into a coach, and drove from store to store, levying tribute. He was captured at Mobile in 1881, and after trial in Jackson, Mississippi, was sentenced to seven years in prison. He served two years and then escaped. He was supposed to have reached New Orleans, and the *Picayune* said positively that he was " lurking in this city," but apparently he was not recaptured. After his escape he appeared no more in the public eye.

CHAPTER VI

FILIBUSTERS

THE NATURAL successors of the Baratarians in the affections of New Orleans were the professional adventurers and soldiers of fortune — the swashbuckling filibusters who frequented the cafés and coffee-houses and mingled with the merchants and the Creole gentlemen on terms of patronizing friendship. During the first fifteen years or so of the nineteenth century, most of the pioneer filibusters commonly took their pleasure and carried on their involved intrigues in Turpin's Cabaret and Coffee-House, a long, low wooden building at Marigny Street and the levee, opposite the mansion of the Marigny family, which was also a favorite rendezvous of the Baratarians. When United States vessels destroyed Lafitte's establishment at Grand Terre and dispersed his followers, and Turpin's closed its doors, the filibusters transferred their interminable plotting to Maspero's Exchange. For several years they were familiar figures in the bar-room and café of that celebrated resort, and many a filibustering scheme was hatched over its little tables. But the foremost filibuster rendezvous in New Orleans was Banks' Arcade on Magazine Street near Gravier, a three-story building with a bar-room, a glass-roofed courtyard, and an auction mart, which was erected by Thomas Banks in 1833. For almost thirty years the Arcade was a hive of conspiracy. The rooms on the second and third floors were used for the secret meetings of the plotters, recruiting for filibustering campaigns was carried on openly over clinking glasses in the bar-room; and in the spacious courtyard and auction mart were held the mass meetings, sponsored principally by Governor John A. Quitman and United States Senator John Henderson of Mississippi, at which orators advocated freedom for Texas and Cuba and, later, annexation to the United States.

Almost any sort of revolutionary movement was sure of a sympathetic hearing in New Orleans, and a soldier of fortune who wished to organize a filibustering campaign found no lack of financial backing, or of recruits among the adventure-loving young men of the city. It has been estimated that over a period of some sixty years no fewer than ten thousand men left New Orleans to follow the fortunes of the filibusters, while at least half a million dollars was contributed by merchants and public men to arm and equip the various expeditions and to further ambitious schemes of invasion and conquest, practically all of which were hopeless from their inception. Since most of the campaigns were directed against Spanish territory, filibustering with New Orleans as the base of operations was conducted surreptitiously until after Louisiana had become a part of the United States. Even during the Spanish domination of Louisiana, however, a few companies were recruited in New Orleans; and as early as 1799 the American Philip Nolan [1] secretly visited New Orleans and enlisted a score of young Creoles, who followed him in an unsuccessful invasion of Texas. A dozen years later a much larger number, recruited with the knowledge if not the actual assistance of the American authorities, marched openly out of New Orleans and into Texas under the banners of Bernardo Gutierrez and Augustus Magee, who captured San Antonio and defeated several Spanish armies, but were eventually

---

[1] Not to be confused with the character of the same name in Edward Everett Hale's famous story *The Man Without a Country*.

crushed. And when General James Long organized the third of this series of abortive invasions in 1819, at least half of his large force were Louisianians, most of whom had been enlisted in New Orleans.

Long was a Virginia doctor with a large private fortune and a taste for military glory and high adventure. During the spring of 1819 he organized at Natchez a force of seventy-five Mississippians and Louisianians, armed and equipped them at his own expense, and in June crossed the Sabine River into Texas and marched to the town of Nacogdoches, where he established his headquarters. There he formed a "Supreme Council," which immediately elected him President of Texas. Long's biographers have never been able to make quite clear how he expected to overcome Spanish power in Mexico with such a small expedition, although he undoubtedly expected the Texans to rally to his support. But reinforcements from local sources failed to materialize, and Long attempted to form an alliance with Jean Lafitte at Galveston. He sent Colonel James Gaines, one of his aides, as head of a mission to the pirate chieftain, bearing a letter couched in pompous terms and suggesting that Lafitte accept " a commission and patent of reprisals from our government to cruise under the flag of Texas." Lafitte made an equivocal reply, indicating clearly, however, that he would never consent to subordinate himself to an upstart filibuster. Long sent another emissary, Horatio Biglow, to continue the negotiations with Lafitte, but Biglow got drunk the day he arrived at Galveston and remained in that condition for several weeks. Lafitte gave him all the liquor he wanted, but refused flatly to discuss affairs of state with him. Long finally threw dignity to the winds and himself went to Galveston to solicit Lafitte's assistance. He was much impressed by the visible evidence of Lafitte's power. " Doubloons," he told a friend afterwards, " were as plentiful as biscuits." When Long agreed to make Galveston a free port — after Texas had been wrested from Spain — and Lafitte governor of the city, the pirate leader agreed to the suggested alliance. Long at once hastened to New Orleans, opened a recruiting office at Maspero's Exchange, and soon enlisted a large force, with which he marched to join the seventy-five men whom he had left entrenched at Nacogdoches. His agreement with Lafitte was made while the pirate was carrying on his intrigues with every government that would lend an ear — he was acting as secret agent for both Spain and the Mexican patriots — and it is doubtful if he ever intended to assist the filibuster. In any event, he never did, and when a Spanish army attacked Nacogdoches in the late autumn of 1819, Long was disastrously defeated and driven back across the Sabine into Louisiana.

The filibustering spirit, always strong in New Orleans, was given a tremendous impetus by the Texas Revolution. Aroused by the impassioned speeches made by orators at the frequent mass meetings in Banks' Arcade, several thousand of the city's young men, both Creoles and Americans, went to Texas singly, in small groups, and as members of large, well-equipped companies and enlisted in the insurgent armies commanded by Davy Crockett, James Bowie, William Barret Travis, and other Texas heroes. Bowie, a noted character of the southwestern frontier, was especially popular with these volunteers, for he was a Louisianian by adoption, had lived in the state for many years, and was well known in New Orleans. Bowie was born in Burke County, Georgia, according to some authorities, and in Logan County, Kentucky, according to others. All agree, however, that in 1802, when a small child, he was brought to Louisiana by his parents, who settled in Chatahoula Parish. In 1818 Bowie and his two brothers, Resin and John, joined forces with Jean Lafitte, and both on their own account and as Lafitte's agents smuggled Negro slaves into New Orleans and other Louisiana towns — a highly profitable business that netted them a profit of sixty-five thousand dollars in less than two years. In later years Bowie thus explained how he and his brothers operated:

"At that time each state was allowed to regulate the laws covering smuggled slaves in its own territory. In Louisiana the law said that smuggled slaves, when they were captured, must be sold at auction by the customs officers. Half of the sale price always went to the informers who 'denounced' them to the officers. So we bought Negroes from Galveston at a dollar a pound — $140 was the average price — and we took them, by boat or overland, to Louisiana. New Orleans was a favorite market. There we organized slave-handling companies which, immediately on arrival of a consignment, 'denounced' it and turned it over to the customs officials. At the auction which followed the companies bought back their own slaves, and at once received half their purchase money because they had informed the customs officers. Then the companies took the slaves direct to the plantations, sometimes carrying them far up the Mississippi, to resell them to planters. In this manner we often got prices of $1,000 for prime Negroes." [1]

Bowie severed his connection with Lafitte a few months before the latter destroyed his Galveston establishment at the command of an American naval officer and for the next few years divided his time principally between Natchez and New Orleans. During the late summer of 1827 he acquired considerable notoriety because of his participation in an extraordinary fracas near Natchez. In August of that year a duel was arranged between a Dr. Maddox and Samuel

---

[1] *Jean Lafitte, Gentleman Smuggler*, by Mitchell V. Charnley, page 185.

Wells, both of Natchez, and the spot chosen for the combat was a low sandbar in the Mississippi just beyond the state line. Each principal, when he appeared on the bar, was accompanied by a score of friends, all heavily armed. After the duelists had fired two exchanges without damage, quarrels arose among the onlookers, and a general mêlée ensued in which six men were killed and fifteen wounded. Bowie was shot early in the engagement, but succeeded in killing Major Norris Wright with a knife which he had himself crudely fashioned from a large blacksmith's rasp. This unique weapon attracted so much attention that Bowie sent it to a Philadelphia cutlery-manufacturer, who shaped and polished it according to Bowie's instruction and christened it the "bowie-knife."[1] A year or so after the fight on the sandbar Bowie removed to Texas, where he took a prominent part in the revolution against Mexico. He was butchered by the Mexican General Santa Anna, together with Crockett and Travis, after the fall of the Alamo on March 6, 1836.

Of all the soldiers of fortune who operated out of New Orleans, perhaps the most popular was a Venezuelan, General Narciso Lopez, who had risen to high rank in the Spanish Army before he turned filibuster and twice attempted the conquest of Cuba with expeditions composed mainly of Mississippians and Louisianians and financed in large measure by business and political leaders of the two states. General Lopez was born in Caracas in 1798 or 1799, the son of a rich merchant. When his countrymen revolted against Spain, he entered the Royal Army, and by the time the war was ended and Venezuela had become a republic, Lopez had advanced to the grade of Colonel, although he had barely

---

[1] A real bowie-knife has a blade from ten to fifteen inches long, with a single cutting edge, and a straight back throughout most of its length. The back then curves concavely to the point, while the edge curves convexly. Bowie pronounced his name "booee."

attained his majority. After the Spaniards evacuated Venezuela, Lopez went to Cuba and then to Spain, where he
served in the first Carlist War. In 1839 he was commissioned
Major-General and appointed Governor of Valencia. Two
years later he went to Cuba with the new Governor-General
of the island, Don Geronimo Valdes, and held various important posts until 1843, when Valdes's successor, Don Leopold O'Donnell, a descendant of the O'Donnells who fled
from Ireland and settled in Spain after the Battle of the
Boyne, relieved him of all offices and commands and retired
him to private life. In 1848 Lopez joined the Cuban revolutionary party which favored annexation by the United
States, and was one of the leaders in a conspiracy against the
Spanish government. When the plot was discovered, Lopez
escaped to New York, where he helped form the Cuban
Junta, the most important members of which were himself
and General Ambrosio Gonzales, a lawyer who had represented the Cuban insurgents in Washington for several
years. Lopez and his associates immediately began the organization of a military expedition against Cuba, but their
plans were frustrated by a proclamation issued by President
Zachary Taylor in August 1849.

Soon after the collapse of this scheme, at a White
House reception, General Gonzales met Senator Henderson
of Mississippi, who had already been associated with Governor Quitman of that state in various movements for the
conquest of Mexico and the liberation of Cuba from Spanish rule. Henderson suggested to Gonzales that the Cuban
Junta transfer its activities to New Orleans, assuring him
that Lopez could easily recruit, in Louisiana and Mississippi,
as many men as might be required for a filibustering expedition, and that money and supplies would likewise be forthcoming. Henderson also introduced to Gonzales a group
of young Kentuckians, all veterans of the Mexican War and
all eager to join Lopez's forces. Among them was Colonel

Theodore O'Hara, editor of the Louisville *Democrat*, who later served on the staff of General Albert Sidney Johnston of the Confederate Army and wrote the famous war-poem, *Bivouac of the Dead.* O'Hara and his companions were authorized to enlist soldiers in Kentucky and transport them to New Orleans for service under Lopez in Cuba.

Lopez arrived at New Orleans early in 1850 and found practically the entire city enthusiastically in favor of the aims of the Cuban Junta. His headquarters at Banks' Arcade were literally besieged by former officers of the American Army clamoring for places in the expedition. From among the many applicants who sought the honor of raising skeleton regiments, Lopez chose Colonel Bunch and Lieutenant-Colonel Smith, a son of Justice C. Pinkney Smith of Mississippi, and Colonel Robert Wheat of New Orleans, all of whom had served with greatest distinction in the war with Mexico. Colonels Bunch and Smith were authorized to recruit a force of men in Mississippi, while to Colonel Wheat was entrusted the task of enlisting a regiment in New Orleans and Louisiana. Colonel Wheat also provided his own means of transportation, purchasing the brig *Susan Loud* with money subscribed by his friends. Meanwhile Lopez had raised about forty thousand dollars and had bought the steamer *Creole* and the bark *Georgina,* together with rifles, ammunition, uniforms, and other equipment. With about six hundred men aboard, the little fleet of three vessels sailed from New Orleans in the early spring of 1850 for a rendezvous at the islands of Mugeres and Contoy, off the coast of Yucatan, the former of which had been Jean Lafitte's last base of operations. There the expedition landed, and the recruits were organized into companies, armed, and drilled.

About forty of the men refused to go farther and were left behind on Contoy Island, with the *Susan Loud* and the *Georgina,* while Lopez embarked the remainder of his force in the *Creole* and sailed for the Cuban port of Cárdenas,

179

arriving there on the night of May 19, 1850. Lopez had expected to take the Spanish garrison by surprise, but entering
the harbor without a pilot, the *Creole* went aground on the
shoals a few yards from the Cárdenas wharf. A landing was
finally effected, but there was so much delay and confusion
that the Spaniards had time to prepare their defense. Lopez
finally took the barracks and the railroad station by storm,
but with the loss of so many men killed and wounded —
among the latter were Colonels Wheat and O'Hara — that
he was unable to follow up the victory and push inland. Before Spanish reinforcements could arrive, however, Lopez
succeeded in getting the *Creole* off the shoals, and his men
aboard the vessel. The *Creole* then steamed at full speed
for the eastern shore of Cuba, where Lopez expected to
make contact with native insurgents. But before this ob-
jective was reached, the Spanish warship *Pizzaro* hove in
sight, and since the *Creole* carried no guns, Lopez was compelled to run for it. The steamer found refuge in the harbor
of Key West before the *Pizzaro* could bring her guns to
bear. Upon his return to New Orleans, Lopez, Henderson,
and Quitman, who resigned as Governor of Mississippi
when he was indicted, were tried in the United States District Court for violating the neutrality laws of 1818. Henderson was acquitted, and in the trials of Lopez and Quitman
the juries failed to agree on verdicts. The government then
abandoned the prosecution, and both men were released.

Instead of returning to New Orleans in the *Georgina*
and *Susan Loud,* the forty men whom Lopez had left on
Contoy tarried on the island, and word of their presence was
carried to Havana by Spanish fishing-smacks. Warships took
them off, and they were imprisoned in the dungeons of
Morro Castle. They had a brief period of fame as the
" Contoy Prisoners " while the American and Spanish governments exchanged a series of diplomatic notes. The Spaniards seemed determined to hang them, but they were finally

released, mainly through the efforts of Daniel M. Barringer of North Carolina, the American Minister to Spain.

New Orleans' appetite for vicarious adventure was only whetted by the failure of Lopez's campaign. When the filibuster was released by the United States government after trial, he was the most popular man in the city, and when he began to prepare for a new invasion of Cuba, all classes of the population, and the newspapers, rushed to his support. To raise funds Lopez issued bonds, bearing interest at the rate of six per cent, redeemable after an independent government had been established in Cuba, and secured by the public lands and property of the island. A great number of these bonds were sold in New Orleans, and apparently no one questioned Lopez's right to issue them. Once the " securities " had been placed on sale, Lopez began to recruit officers and men for his expedition, assuring all applicants that the task of conquering Cuba would be mere child's play, and that his first campaign had been nothing more than a reconnoitering venture. He also publicly announced that the Cubans were already in open revolt against Spain, and that as soon as he landed on the island, many of the Spanish troops would desert to his standard, neither of which statements was based on actual fact. To each common soldier Lopez promised to pay, once victory had been won, the sum of five thousand dollars, while every officer was to receive a confiscated sugar plantation. Lopez was to be generalissimo of the entire revolutionary movement, and the actual command of the filibuster troops was offered first to Jefferson Davis, a veteran of the war with Mexico, then a United States Senator from Mississippi and when Davis declined the honor, to Major Robert E. Lee of the United States Army. Lee also refused, although Lopez offered him cash and property, mostly on an if and when basis, amounting to more than a hundred thousand dollars. The post was finally given jointly to Colonel Robert Wheat, a veteran of the first Lopez expedition, and Colonel John Crittenden, whose uncle, John Jordan Crittenden, was Attorney-General of the United States and had previously been United States Senator and Governor of Kentucky.

Preparations for this expedition were much more elaborate than for the disastrous campaign of 1850, and the military plans especially were very extensive. Lopez was to sail from New Orleans in the fall of 1851 and land on the southeastern coast of Cuba, and at the same time General Ambrosio Gonzales was to lead an expedition from Georgia and Florida to the northeastern coast. The two armies were then to march inland, easily overcoming all opposition offered by the Spaniards, and in the center of the island effect a junction, with each other and with a native revolutionary force which Lopez said was already operating successfully against the Spanish. When this had been accomplished, Governor Quitman was to come to their aid with a new army which he was recruiting in the west and southwest. Lopez and his associates believed that with three American filibustering expeditions campaigning in Cuba, popular opinion would compel the United States government to interfere and help drive the Spaniards from the island. But Lopez's recruiting proceeded far more rapidly than did that of either Gonzales or Quitman. By July 1, 1851 Lopez was ready; all his bonds had been sold and his equipment purchased, and his men were assembled in New Orleans and waiting impatiently. About the middle of July word was received that on the 4th of the month the Cubans had risen at Puerto Príncipe and in the province of Trinidad and were driving the Spanish before them. These and other reports, all false, were later traced to spies operating under the direction of the crafty Governor-General of Cuba, Don José Gutierrez de la Concha, who was trying to hasten the departure of Lopez from New Orleans so he could destroy the filibuster before assistance could arrive.

Lopez and his associates believed the reports, and so did everyone else in New Orleans. On July 23, 1851 a great mass meeting was held in Lafayette Square, and another in Banks' Arcade on July 26, at which the speakers urged Lopez to strike at once. The newspapers added fresh fuel to the flame and increased Lopez's already fine opinion of himself, by assuring him that he was one of the great leaders of the world, and that he had the support of lovers of liberty everywhere. Said the New Orleans *Delta:*

" But one feeling, one voice, one hope prevails among all classes, that of success in the glorious struggle. Were it practicable one tithe of our fighting population would rush to the aid of the patriots. The wealthy planters of the south are among the most eager friends of Cuba. Our sugar planters, whose interest, it has been falsely alleged, would be jeopardized by the independence of Cuba, are too sensible to be deceived by such arguments, or too patriotic to be restrained by them."

Against the advice of Quitman and other experienced soldiers, who urged him to wait until the other expeditions were ready, Lopez yielded to the popular clamor and on August 3, 1851 sailed with his men, numbering about four hundred and fifty, aboard the steamer *Pampero*. A large crowd assembled at the wharf and cheered lustily when the *Pampero* backed into midstream and headed for the Gulf of Mexico. Thereafter Lopez's expedition was almost the sole topic of conversation in New Orleans; the bondholders calculated their profits, the families of Lopez's officers began to arrange their affairs with a view to taking over the confiscated sugar plantations, and the stores freely granted credit to the wives of the common soldiers, who were each to receive five thousand dollars. At Key West Lopez was told that the inhabitants of the district of Vuelta Abajo had recently risen against the Spaniards, and he decided to land his force on that part of the Cuban coast. The *Pampero* steamed for the small port of Mariel, but when about eighteen leagues from Havana, the machinery of the vessel got out of order. For several hours she floated helplessly in the Gulf Stream, finally approaching so close to Havana that she was clearly visible from the ramparts of Morro Castle. As soon as repairs had been made, the *Pampero* proceeded, and on the night of August 11–12 put in at Bahía Honda, west of Havana. There the expedition landed. Leaving Colonel Crittenden with a hundred and thirty men to guard the baggage and ammunition, Lopez marched inland with a force of three hundred, expecting at any moment to meet one of the mythical insurgent armies about which he had heard so much. He defeated a Spanish column at the village of Las Pozas, but about a hundred of his men and most of his officers were killed. He then retreated to Cafetal de Trias, where he was attacked by a large force of infantry, cavalry, and artillery. After two or three days of fighting Lopez's little army was overwhelmed and dispersed. With bloodhounds the Spaniards hunted down the Americans one by one. Lopez was captured on August 31 and taken to Havana, where he was immediately tried by court martial, convicted of high treason, and sentenced to death by the garrote — an iron collar which was placed around the neck of the victim and tightened by a screw until strangulation occurred. Lopez was thus killed at Havana on September 1, 1851. A few of his men were released, but about a hundred and fifty of them were sent to Spain, where they were imprisoned. Among these captives was Colonel Wheat, who returned to America after several months in a Spanish dungeon and joined the Mexican Army, becoming a Brigadier-General and Military Governor of Vera Cruz. He resigned this post to follow William Walker to Nicaragua and later fought throughout the Civil War as Colonel of the Louisiana Tigers, one of the crack regiments of the Confederate Army.

Colonel Crittenden's detachment at Bahía Honda was attacked by a large Spanish force a few hours after Lopez's departure and was soon routed, with the loss of eighty men killed. The remaining fifty, including Crittenden, attempted to escape in the *Pampero's* small boats, but were pursued and captured by the Spanish ship *Habanero*. They were taken to Havana and shot on August 16.

The news of Crittenden's death and Lopez's defeat reached New Orleans on August 21, when the steamer *Crescent City* arrived from Havana. On board the vessel was the secretary of the Spanish Consul in New Orleans, who carried letters written by the condemned men to their families and friends in the United States. For some unexplained reason this official refused to surrender the letters, a circumstance which, when it became known, greatly increased the excitement which already prevailed throughout the city. It was raised to fever heat later in the day when a Spanish newspaper, *La Unión*, published an extra edition containing a full account of the execution of Crittenden and his men, and an editorial vigorously denouncing American filibusters. A mob formed soon after the paper appeared on the streets, and before the police could take any effective measures to restrain the rioters, they had wrecked the offices of *La Unión*, together with six coffee-houses and two tobacco-stores owned by Spaniards. The mob also invaded the Spanish Consulate, did considerable damage to the furnishings, and carried away the sign of the Consulate and the Spanish flag. The flag was taken to Lafayette Square, where it was cut into strips and burned. No one was injured during the rioting. The Consul, escorted through the streets by the noted duelist Pépé Lulla, who marched beside him with a naked sword in each hand, fled to the home of a friend thirty miles away. Lulla was so enraged by the insult to the Spanish flag that he issued a blanket challenge to Cuban sympathizers everywhere and killed several men who were rash enough to cross swords with him.

2

THE last of the famous filibusters who made their headquarters in New Orleans and periodically aroused the city to bursts of fervid sympathy for the oppressed peoples whom the adventurers proposed to liberate, was the most celebrated of them all — William Walker, the "gray-eyed man of destiny,"[1] whose exploits in Mexico and Central America are too well known to require more than a brief recapitulation here. Walker was a native of Nashville, Tennessee, where he was born on May 8, 1824. He studied law in his home city and medicine at Heidelberg, Germany, and in 1845 came to New Orleans and established a law office at 48 Canal Street. Three years later he became editor and part owner of the New Orleans *Crescent* and, curiously enough, wrote several articles ridiculing and questioning the motives of Lopez and various American filibusters. The *Crescent* failed to prosper, and when it was sold, in the fall of 1849, Walker found himself out of a job. Meanwhile his sweetheart had died during an epidemic of yellow fever, a tragedy which produced a profound change in his character. Previously he had been of a quiet, studious disposition; he now became morose and melancholy, bellicose and quick to take offense where none had been intended. He also began to affect the long black coat and the big, floppy black hat which thereafter formed part of his civilian costume.

With nothing to keep him in New Orleans, Walker joined the California gold rush and arrived at San Francisco

---

[1] This sobriquet originated in Walker's newspaper, *El Nicaraguense*, as part of the effort to identify him with the "gray-eyed man" whom Indian tradition said would deliver the country from the Spanish.

in June 1850. He followed journalism there for a brief period, and then practiced law in Marysville, California. He led two unsuccessful filibustering expeditions into Lower California and Sonora in 1853 and 1854, and in 1855 was induced by American speculators to interfere in the domestic affairs of Nicaragua, ostensibly in aid of the Democratic party there. After considerable difficulty with the state and Federal authorities, who tried to prevent his departure, Walker sailed from San Francisco in the brig *Vesta* on May 4, 1855. With him were actually fifty-eight men, although the newspapers reported the number as fifty-six, a figure which in time came to be accepted as correct by the men themselves. This force was afterwards known in the United States as " the Fifty-six Immortals," and in Nicaragua as "the American Phalanx." The *Vesta* made a slow voyage, and not until June 16, 1855 did Walker land at Realejo, the northernmost port on the western coast of Nicaragua. There he was reinforced by a hundred and seventy native soldiers, and although defeated at Rivas in his first engagement, captured the city of Granada on October 15. Meanwhile his agents were openly recruiting for the expedition in San Francisco, New York, and New Orleans. In the last two cities advertisements were published in the newspapers to attract fighting men and "colonists" for Nicaragua. This notice appeared frequently in the New Orleans papers:

" Nicaragua —The Government of Nicaragua is desirous of having its lands settled and cultivated by an industrious class of people, and offers as an inducement to emigrants, a donation of Two Hundred and Fifty Acres of Land for single persons, and One Hundred Acres additional to persons of family. Steamers leave New Orleans for San Juan on the 11th and 26th of each month. The fare is now reduced to less than half the former rates. The undersigned will be happy to give information to those desirous of emigrating. Thos. F. Fisher, 16 Royal Street." [1]

The response to the appeals of the recruiting agents was extraordinary, especially in view of the fact that of all the filibustering expeditions which had left American shores, not one had been successful. From San Francisco volunteers were carried free of charge to Nicaragua on the ships of the Accessory Transit Company, one of Commodore Vanderbilt's enterprises, and there were always more applicants than could be accommodated. Sometimes the departure of a Transit steamer was followed by serious disturbances on the docks by those who had been refused passage. Hundreds also sailed from New York and New Orleans, and by March 1, 1865 Walker had 1,200 men under his command. They were soon reinforced by 208 men who had sailed boldly from New Orleans in April, their departure having been announced in the newspapers beforehand. With this sizable army Walker was soon in control of all Nicaragua. He caused himself to be elected President, and sent a Minister to Washington, who was recognized by President Franklin Pierce. But the many arbitrary acts by which Walker sought to replenish his depleted treasury and by which he made radical and unpopular changes in Nicaragua's fundamental law soon provoked an insurrection in which the insurgents were assisted by Costa Rica and Honduras and financed by agents of the Vanderbilts, whose property Walker had confiscated. Walker was defeated in several engagements, and finally, when hard pressed by the rebels, burned the city of Granada. On May 1, 1857 Walker and sixteen of his officers surrendered at San Juan del Sur to the commander of the American sloop of war *St. Mary,* which took the party to Panama. From there Walker re-

---

[1] Fisher followed Walker to Nicaragua and became a Colonel in the filibuster's army.

turned to the United States, landing at New Orleans on May 27. An enormous crowd lined the levee when the steamer with Walker aboard drew up to the wharf, and as soon as the filibuster stepped ashore a dozen men lifted him to their shoulders and bore him to a carriage. The cheering crowd followed him to the St. Charles Hotel, where he was compelled to make two speeches before his enthusiastic admirers would disperse. On the evening of May 29th a great mass meeting of welcome was held on the neutral ground of Canal Street, at which Walker and his staff, in full uniform, sat on a platform decorated with the Stars and Stripes and his own Nicaraguan flag. Walker spoke for two hours, defending his actions in Central America and denouncing those whom he blamed for his downfall. The newspapers next day, in their account of the mass meeting, published a fifteen-stanza poem composed by Mrs. V. E. W. McCord of New Orleans and dedicated to Walker. The last stanza follows:

All hail to thee, Chief! Heaven's blessings may rest
On the battle-scarred brow of our national guest,
And soon may our Eagle fly over the sea,
And plant there a branch of our national tree.

From New Orleans Walker went to Memphis, Louisville, Cincinnati, Washington, and finally to New York. Everywhere he was greeted as a conquering hero; when he attended a performance at Wallack's Theater in New York the orchestra played *Hail, Columbia,* and the filibuster was compelled to make a speech from his box. This hero-worship began to wane, however, when Walker issued several statements criticizing the commander of the *St. Mary,* who had rescued him from the Nicaraguan insurgents, and his popularity practically vanished when the human remnants of his expedition arrived in New York with tales of his cruelty, neglect, and indifference to their fate. Three days before the arrival of the first of these men Walker made a hurried trip to Charleston, South Carolina, and never made any effort to refute the charges. In the fall of 1857 he returned to New Orleans and took lodgings at 184 Customhouse Street (now Iberville), where he was arrested by Federal officers on an indictment charging him with violating the neutrality laws. He was released on two thousand dollars bail, and next day went to Mobile, from where he soon sailed at the head of a new expedition. Late in November 1857 he landed a hundred and thirty-two men in Nicaragua, but a few weeks later Commodore Hiram Paulding of the American steam frigate *Wabash* compelled the filibusters to surrender and took them to New York. The government was unable to prosecute Walker then, however, as President Buchanan refused to recognize him as a prisoner, on the ground that his arrest by Commander Paulding on foreign soil was illegal.

Early in 1858 Walker returned once more to New Orleans, and on May 31 was brought to trial in the United States District Court. Eminent lawyers appeared as his counsel, but Walker also addressed the jury on his own behalf. After deliberating for almost two hours, the jurors reported that there was no chance of a verdict, and the government entered a *nolle prosequi*. Walker had scarcely left the courtroom before he announced his intention of returning to Nicaragua. Instead in June of 1860 he sailed from New Orleans with a small force for Honduras, intending to incite a revolution there and use that country as a base for operations in Nicaragua. He captured the fortress of Truxillo on August 6, 1860, but a few weeks later the British warship *Icarus* appeared in the harbor and Commander Norvell Salmon demanded that Walker evacuate the town and surrender the money seized at the custom-house, which Commander Salmon declared had been mortgaged by the

Hondurans to the British government. Walker and his men destroyed the armament of the Truxillo fortress and retreated to the Tinto River, where they finally surrendered to Commander Salmon. The British officer turned Walker over unconditionally to the Hondurans, but ordered the remaining filibusters, some seventy in number, to be held as prisoners under British protection, and returned to the United States as soon as possible. Walker was confined in Truxillo for a few days, and on September 12, 1860 he was shot by a Honduran firing squad.

Many brave and reckless adventurers followed Walker to Central America, but none entered the filibuster's service with a greater reputation for daring and foolhardiness and afterwards more consistently justified his fame than Colonel Thomas Henry, who was one of " the Fifty-six Immortals " and fought throughout both the Nicaraguan and Honduran campaigns. Henry's military career began during the middle 1830's, when he enlisted as a private in the Seventh Regiment of the United States Army. He became a Sergeant in 1838 and went with his regiment to Mexico when the United States declared war against that country in 1846. Several times during the next two years he was cited and mentioned in dispatches for his displays of courage and resourcefulness. He was the first American soldier to scale the heights of Cerro Gordo on April 18, 1847, and a month later, in recognition of this exploit, he was appointed Second Lieutenant. In August of the same year he was breveted First Lieutenant for gallant conduct at Contreras and Cherubusco. During the attack upon Monterey in September 1846, Henry wagered a dinner with several of his fellow non-commissioned officers that he could ride a mule at a walk for three squares through the town in the face of the withering cross-fire of the Mexican troops. The mule was shot under him in the first hundred feet, but Henry calmly traversed the remainder of the prescribed distance on foot and returned to his command with three bullet-wounds. After the Mexican War he was stationed at an Army post in the Cherokee nation, but his amorous exploits with the squaws soon got him into trouble. He was finally attacked at a dance by a score of Cherokee braves, who left him lying on the ground with seven stab-wounds in his body. When he had recovered from these grievous hurts he resigned from the Army and went to California to join in the quest for gold. He was in San Francisco when Walker began recruiting for his first venture into Central America and was one of the first to enlist under the filibuster's standard.

In Nicaragua Colonel Henry was noted as a fighter of extraordinary daring and fierceness. He customarily went into battle with a saber in one hand and a pistol in the other, while his belt fairly bristled with reserve weapons. Without seeming to care whether he was followed, he plunged head-long into the ranks of the enemy, cutting, stabbing, and shooting, and yelling at the top of his voice. During the eight months in which Walker was beset by the combined armies of the Central American allies, Henry received eight wounds, and at least fifty during his entire career as a soldier and a filibuster. Many of them were of a serious nature, but he was a man of tremendous strength and vitality, and quickly recovered from injuries which to an ordinary man would have proved fatal. But despite his bravery and recklessness Colonel Henry possessed two serious faults — he was very quarrelsome and he drank too much. The latter habit finally cost him his life, and the former kept him from living in peace with his fellow-officers. Dueling among his men was one of Walker's greatest worries, and Colonel Henry was probably the worst offender. He fought at least half a dozen duels in Nicaragua, several of which terminated fatally for his adversaries. Nevertheless he was one of Walker's most valuable officers; he could always be relied upon in battle, and upon him devolved most of the work of training recruits.

One of Colonel Henry's enemies in Nicaragua was Major Joe Howell, a brother of Mrs. Jefferson Davis and a grandson of Richard Howell, an eminent soldier and statesman of Revolutionary times and an early Governor of New Jersey. Major Howell was a veritable giant, standing six feet and seven inches in his stocking feet. His reputation for bravery was second only to that of Colonel Henry, and like the latter he bore many wounds from knife, bullet, and arrow. The two men quarreled several times in Central America, but various circumstances — usually specific orders from Walker or the necessity of preparing for battle — prevented a duel. They never met on the field of honor until the summer of 1857, when they came to New Orleans after Walker and sixteen of his officers had surrendered to the commander of the American sloop of war *St. Mary*. One morning Howell walked into a coffee-house at Canal Street and St. Charles Avenue, on the site later occupied by Joe Walker's notorious Crescent Hall Saloon, and found Henry drinking at the bar with several friends. Henry asked him to have a drink, and Howell accepted. Both men were fairly drunk when two newsboys came into the coffee-house and started a fight. Henry bet on one, and Howell on the other. After a few minutes the former cried enough, and Henry remarked that the fight would have had a different ending if he and Howell had been the combatants, whereupon Howell shrugged his shoulders.

"Suppose we do have it," suggested Henry.

Howell promptly drew his revolver, but Henry stopped him.

"Hold on, old boy," he said. "We can't fight here. Let us meet at five o'clock this evening at the Half-Way House. Bring your navy, and I'll have mine."

Howell agreed, they ceremoniously clinked glasses, and each downed an enormous slug of whisky. Meanwhile the owner of the coffee-house had summoned the police, and two patrolmen appeared and arrested both Henry and Howell. But within an hour their release had been procured by friends anxious to see the fight. Henry continued to drink throughout the day, but Howell went to his lodgings and took a nap. He awoke about four o'clock, drank a cocktail, and against the advice of his second dressed with great care in a black alpaca coat, white shirt, and white trousers, all of which made him an excellent mark to shoot at. He then jumped into a carriage with his second and the surgeon of the occasion, who bore the appropriate name of Dr. Sam Choppin. *En route* the second undertook to give Howell some advice, but Howell only puffed at a cigarette and said:

"Tut, tut, my boy; teach your grandmother how to suck eggs!"

Practically every cab and hack in New Orleans were engaged when news of the duel spread through the city, and at least three hundred spectators had gathered when Howell arrived at the Half-Way House, a famous saloon and road-house at the end of Canal Street, half-way between the river and Lake Pontchartrain. Colonel Henry was also there, lying on one elbow in a little hollow, a glass of whisky in his hand, while he discoursed volubly to a large group of friends. Howell's second decided to attempt a settlement of the affair without bloodshed, and approached the man who was acting for Henry.

"What," he asked, "is your version of the cause of this difficulty?"

"It doesn't matter," replied Henry's second. "We are here to fight."

"Brave men don't fight for nothing, like children," protested Howell's friend. "We want to know what we are fighting about. If we are wrong we may apologize."

Henry's second conferred with his principal and returned with the information that Henry had said that there
need be no fight if Howell would apologize.

" Apologize for what? " demanded Howell's second.

" Don't know and don't care. We're ready to fight."

Further efforts to reach an amiable agreement also
failed, and arrangements were then made for the combat.
The two men were stationed ten paces apart on a narrow
path with a ditch on either side. Their heavy Navy revolvers were fully loaded, and they were instructed to fire
at will, and advance, when the signal was given. At the word
" Ready! " Howell aimed at Henry and looked steadily
along the barrel of his revolver, while Henry stood in a non-
chalant attitude, his weapon dangling at arm's length. At the
word " Fire! " both shot and missed. Howell cocked with
his right thumb and immediately fired again, his bullet
piercing Henry's left forearm as the latter's shot went wild.
Howell's third shot struck Henry in the abdomen, and
Henry's return fire kicked up the dirt at Howell's feet.
Howell then advanced one step and took careful aim, but
just as he fired, his own second threw up his arm, probably
saving Henry's life. Henry's friends set up a shout of foul
and drew their revolvers, while Howell's supporters did
likewise. A general engagement was prevented by specta-
tators who were there simply to see a fight and had no
special interest in either man.

Henry's wound was found by Dr. Choppin to be very
serious. He was carried to the Half-Way House, where he
remained for several weeks before he could be transported
to the city. He recovered in time to accompany Walker to
Honduras and fought brilliantly in the assault and capture
of the fortress of Truxillo. But a few days later, while
drunk, he entered the magazine with a lighted cigar and
attacked an officer who ordered him to leave. In the scuffle
Henry was shot in the face and his jawbone shattered. While

he lay dying in the fortress hospital, Walker spent as much time as possible at his bedside, for, as one of Walker's biographers said, the loss of Colonel Henry was greater than that of fifty ordinary specimens of the genus filibuster. Henry and other wounded men were left behind when Walker retreated to the Tinto River, and the British protected them from the vengeance of the Hondurans. Henry died only a little while before his commander faced a firing squad.

CHAPTER VII

GAMBLERS AFLOAT AND ASHORE

THE DEVELOPMENT of the steamboat and its appearance upon the Mississippi in large numbers practically put an end to the depredations of the river pirates, who not only were unable to cope with the large crews and the many passengers, but were overawed by the speed and majestic power of the new craft, and afraid of the swivel gun mounted at the bow. Although an occasional flatboat was attacked and plundered as late as the Civil War, by 1825 all of the large river gangs had vanished, and, so far as actual physical danger was concerned, travel on the Mississippi was as safe as on any of the well-policed waterways of Europe or the eastern part of the United States. But the steamboat loosed upon the river an even greater menace to the property of the traveler, for with the chugging log-burners came a horde of gamblers, who took more treasure from the Mississippi than Colonel Plug or Bully Wilson ever dreamed of stealing. These sharp-witted and nimble-fingered gentry had operated in a small way on the few flat-boats which carried passengers, but their opportunities were vastly increased when the steamboat appeared with its superior accommodations and a popularity which for many years sent every boat away from its wharf with all berths occupied. In the early days of steamboat navigation the gambler was tolerated only so long as no one complained, but he was frequently compelled to disgorge his gains, and the boat was nosed against the river bank long enough to unload him and his baggage. Socially he was a pariah, and in that respect his status was unchanged even by death; a gambler was among the eleven persons scalded to death when the cylinder head of the *Constitution* blew off near Bayou Sara in 1817, and Flugel noted in his journal that the outcast "was buried separately."

In later years, however, gambling on the river was recognized as an established institution. Many steamboat captains considered it bad luck to leave a wharf without a gambler on board, and no attempt was made to hinder him when he started operations in the main saloon, the bar, or the barber-shop. Sometimes he was even allowed to set up his game in the texas.[1] He was in his heyday from about 1835 to the Civil War, when from six hundred to eight hundred men regularly worked the big boats between New Orleans and St. Louis. During this period, the era of the "floating palaces," the gambler gave to travel on the Mississippi a picturesqueness which in earlier days had been provided by the swaggering bullies of the flatboat crews. He appears to have been an arresting spectacle; contemporary writers for the most part agree that as a class he was the best-dressed man in the United States. Certainly he was the most dazzling. His basic garments were sober enough — black soft hat, black broadcloth coat and trousers, black high-heeled boots, black tie, and white shirt. It was the manner in which he embellished this groundwork that earned him his reputation. The white shirt was cut low in the neck, with a loose collar and a bosom marvelously frilled and frizzled and only partly concealed by a fancy vest of unspeakable gaudiness, fastened with pearl, gold, or diamond buttons. At least three diamond rings encircled as many smooth fingers, and another stone, known as "the

---

[1] The texas was a structure on the hurricane deck containing the officers' cabins, with the pilot-house in front or on top.

headlight," as large as he could afford, enhanced the glory of the white shirt. In a pocket of the fancy vest was his watch, usually a big gold repeater set with gems, and attached to the watch was one end of a long gold chain which was looped about his neck and draped across his shirt-front.

Jimmy Fitzgerald, a New Orleans sharper who made — and lost — a fortune playing poker and faro on the river in the 1840's, was perhaps the best-dressed gambler of his time. He sent to Paris for his boots, possessed four overcoats and a score of expensive suits, and wore a golden chain a rod long and as big around as his little finger. When he came aboard a steamboat he was followed by three slaves bearing his raiment. He was a reckless and spectacular player, and what he made on the river he lost in the gambling-houses ashore. He was frequently known to " call the turn " at faro and, guessing incorrectly the order in which the last two cards in the box would appear, lose his wardrobe, his diamonds and golden chain, and his Negroes. But two or three weeks after such a disaster he invariably appeared on the steamboats as resplendent as ever, complaining because his new boots had not yet arrived from Paris. If Fitzgerald had any peers as a fancy dresser they were probably Gib Cohern and Jim McLane, whose mother gave him ten thousand dollars a year to stay away from home; Tom Mackey, who likewise sent to Paris for his boots; Star Davis, for whom a famous racehorse was named and who finally became a heavy drinker and was killed in a fall down a flight of stairs in a St. Louis hotel; and Napoleon Bonaparte White, who was better known as Poley. White came to New Orleans from Washington as a boy, about 1840, and became a gambler after a brief career as a steamboat engineer. After the Civil War he married and settled in New Orleans, where he operated a gambling-house on St. Charles Avenue in partnership with Sam Williams. The house prospered, but most of Poley's earnings were spent

trying to save his two sons, Benny and Jimmy, who were
described by the New Orleans *Picayune* as " desperate characters who made the old man's life a burden to him." Both
boys came to bad ends. Benny died of alcoholism in jail
while awaiting trial for a shooting, and Jimmy was last
heard of in California, where he had killed two men, one
of them in a fight over a bottle of wine. In the autumn of
1889, broke and upset by a new anti-gambling ordinance
which the police apparently intended to enforce, Poley borrowed a few dollars from a Royal Street bartender and
bought a revolver and an ounce of sulphate of morphine.
Then he called upon all of his friends and told them good-
by, saying he was going home to kill himself, which he did.

Another noted fashion-plate of the decade which preceded the Civil War was Colonel Charles Starr, a tall, handsome man of imposing presence, who was also celebrated
among the gamblers as the biggest liar on the river. To
hear him tell it, he owned at least half of the plantations
on the Mississippi from New Orleans to St. Louis and
gambled only because he was bored by his vast possessions
and uncountable wealth. He was able to impart a certain air
of verisimilitude to his boastings by hiring Negroes to meet
whatever steamboat he was traveling on at various landings
and hail him as " Massa Kunnel," representing themselves
as overseers on his broad acres and asking for instructions.
And these the Colonel always gave, pompously and in great
detail. Starr was endowed with a caustic wit and was very
popular despite his braggadocio; more stories were probably told of him than of any other gambler of his time.
Many of the anecdotes in which he figured are still used by
after-dinner speakers, though without acknowledgments to
Colonel Starr. Once when he was standing in front of a
New Orleans restaurant, ostentatiously wielding his gold-
mounted toothpick, a panhandler asked him for fifty cents
to get something to eat.

"How long did you say it was since you ate?" asked Colonel Starr.

"Two days," said the panhandler.

"Well," drawled the Colonel, "I reckon I won't give you a half-dollar, but if you go without eating for two days longer I'll give you a hundred dollars for your appetite."

On another occasion, while Colonel Starr was heavily engaged with a sumptuous dinner in a Royal Street coffee-house, a penniless gambler approached and looked wistfully at the array of savory dishes spread upon the table.

"Colonel," he begged, "won't you stake me to some of that? I'm awful hungry and I'm dead broke."

"Impossible, my boy," said Starr. "You see, I'm a capper for the house and my play doesn't go."

Colonel Starr accumulated a sizable fortune by his activities on the Mississippi, but in his later years he lost all his money in futile attempts to break the faro banks in New Orleans and St. Louis. When he was finally at the end of his resources and driven to cadging food and drink wherever he could, he entered a New Orleans restaurant, where he had been a frequent and welcome guest in the days of his prosperity, and ordered an elaborate dinner. The manager demanded payment in advance, and without a word Colonel Starr left the place. In an hour he returned with five dollars, for which he had pawned his overcoat, and ordered the best dinner obtainable for that amount. When it was served he deliberately and very carefully turned every dish upside down on the table. Then he walked out. That night he died.

2

AT least ninety per cent of the elegant tricksters who preyed upon the river traveler were known in the vernacular as "sure-thing players," which was a euphemistic way of saying that they were crooked, and ran "brace" games exclusively. They were adepts at palming cards and dealing from the bottom, called " laying the bottom stock "; and used extensively such cheating devices as vest, table, sleeve and belt holdouts, shiners for reading hands held by opponents, and poker rings fitted with needle-like points for making tiny indentations in the back of cards. These and other appliances of a like character, known to the trade as " advantage tools ", were sold by dealers in New York and Chicago, who flooded the river country with their circulars and catalogues and sent salesmen to demonstrate samples and take orders from the gamblers. Most of the big killings on the steamboats, however, were made with marked cards, or " readers ", which were planted beforehand with the bartender and sent to the gambler's table when new decks were called for. Sometimes, instead of actually marking the cards, the decks were stripped; that is, a fraction of an inch, never more than one thirty-second, was cut from the edges of all but three or four of the highest cards, with a tool called a " stripper plate ". The fact that these few cards were a trifle larger than the others passed unnoticed, but the expert manipulator, in shuffling, dealing, or cutting, could place them wherever he wished. " The benefit of these cards," said a dealer's catalogue, " can be estimated only in one way, and that is: how much money has your opponent got? For you are certain to get it, whether it is $10 or $10,000; the heavier the stakes the sooner you will break him, and he never knows what hurt him."

Of the few old-time river gamblers known as " square players ", who depended entirely upon their luck and skill, the most celebrated were Dick Hargraves, John Powell, and Major George M. White. The last named followed gambling as a profession for sixty-two years and won and lost a dozen fortunes. He began his career in New Orleans in 1825, when he was twenty years old, and dealt his last card in 1887, his hand still firm and his eye clear at eighty-two. Major White made a clear profit of thirty thousand dollars in one year — 1857 — on the Mississippi, and for several years received four hundred dollars a week to run a faro bank in New Orleans, said to have been the highest salary ever paid to a faro dealer in the United States. He died in San Francisco in the summer of 1900, at the age of ninety-five.

Hargraves, a slim, dapper man with suave and polished manners, had an extraordinary career. He came to New Orleans from England about 1840, when he was sixteen, and became a bartender, but turned to gambling when he won thirty thousand dollars in a poker game with a sugar-planter named Dupuy. Hargraves followed the river for more than a decade with phenomenal success; at one time he was said to be worth two million dollars. At the height of his prosperity and renown he became involved in an affair with the wife of a New Orleans banker and killed the banker when the latter challenged him to a duel. Then the brother of the wife sent word that he would kill Hargraves on sight. They met in a resort at Natchez-under-the-Hill, one of the famous hell-holes of the Mississippi, and the gambler killed the brother in a desperate fight. When he returned to New Orleans, Hargraves's paramour stabbed him and committed suicide. Hargraves recovered, married a girl whom he had rescued from a fire in Mobile, joined a filibustering expedition to Cuba, and when the Civil War began, became a Major in the Union Army. Soon after the end of the war he went to Denver, where he died of tuberculosis during the early 1880's.

John Powell, a native Missourian who lived in New Orleans most of the time he was ashore, was the beau ideal of the river gamblers — tall, handsome, and distinguished, well educated, always richly dressed without the vulgar flashiness of his professional colleagues, and possessing a charm of manner and personality which made him welcome in the best of society anywhere along the Mississippi — except among the haughty descendants of the casket and correction girls in New Orleans. He refused a nomination for Congress in Missouri when he was a young man, but continued to take an active interest in politics both in his native state and in Louisiana; he was a friend of Andrew Jackson and Stephen A. Douglas, and of most of the important Louisiana politicians, who often sought his counsel. During the period of his greatest success as a gambler — from about 1845 to 1858 — Powell was considered the most daring and expert poker-player on the river and was always ready to back his judgment on cards with everything he possessed. With the exception of Dick Hargraves, he was probably the most consistent winner, and the richest, of all the " square " gamblers who worked the steamboats. When he was fifty years old, in 1858, Powell owned a theater and other property in New Orleans, a hundred-thousand-dollar farm stocked with fine horses and slaves in Tennessee, and considerable real estate in St. Louis. His friends urged him to retire, but he declared that gambling was in his blood and that he would gamble until he died.

Powell's triumphs on the Mississippi, however, ended in 1858. In the late summer of that year he was one of the participants in a famous poker game aboard the steamer *Atlantic* with two other professional gamblers, "square players," and Jules Devereaux, a rich Louisiana planter. Within an hour after play had begun there was thirty-seven thousand dollars in gold in sight on the table, and on the first hand dealt Powell is said to have won eight thousand dollars. The game continued without intermission for three days, during which time the four men, drinking only the finest wines, ran up a bar bill of $791.50. Devereaux's losses are said to have been approximately a hundred thousand dollars, of which Powell won slightly more than half. A few months after this memorable adventure Powell played a two-handed game of poker with a young English tourist, and won eight thousand dollars and all of the visitor's luggage. Next morning after breakfast the Englishman came on deck, shook hands with all the passengers, and then put a pistol to his head and blew his brains out. Powell sent the young man's money and luggage to his relatives in England and retired from active gambling for a year. But when he returned to the river both his luck and his skill had deserted him; he is said never to have won another pot after his tragic triumph over the Englishman. Within another year he had lost all his property and was a shabby, desperate man. When the Civil War began he went to Seattle, where he died in poverty in 1870.

3

VIRTUALLY every known game of chance was played on the Mississippi steamboats, but the most popular were poker, faro, twenty-one or blackjack, seven-up or old sledge, three-card monte, and that hoary old stand-by which for so many years was a sure killer at the county fairs and carnivals of the Middle West — the shell game. Faro, one of the oldest of all card games, and still played pretty much according to the rules classified by Hoyle almost two hundred years ago, was better known on the river as " the tiger "; playing it was called " bucking the tiger ". It has always possessed a strange fascination for the professional gambler; the river trickster, when ashore, usually lost at faro the money he had gained at his own specialty on the steamboats. Draw and stud poker were developed on the Mississippi about 1825; before that time cold hands were played with a deck of twenty cards, from the deuce to the six, or the ten to the ace. The hands possessed the same values as now, except that a straight flush was inferior to four of a kind, and remained so until a few years after the Civil War. In those early days there were two unbeatable hands in poker — four aces, and four kings with an ace for a confidence card. In their essentials three-card monte and the shell game were very similar, since both took advantage of the fact that the hand is quicker than the eye, although proper and effective manipulation of the shells required greater dexterity. The monte operator simply displayed three cards, called "the tickets," usually two aces and a queen, threw them face down upon a flat surface, and then bet that the victim couldn't turn over "the old lady." The shell man moved a dried pea or a little rubber ball rapidly back and forth under three shells or cups of wood or metal. Then the sucker, having staked his money, was invited to lift the shell under which the pea or ball was hidden. If the gambler knew his business, it wasn't under any of them; it was between two of his fingers. Both shell- and monte-players were usually assisted by cappers, who got the game started and showed prospective victims how easy it was to win. The king of the Mississippi River shell men for many years was Jim Miner, variously known as Umbrella Jim and the Poet Gambler. The former sobriquet he earned by always beginning operations, indoors or out, rain or shine, under an umbrella; the latter by introducing his game with this bit of doggerel:

A little fun, just now and then,
Is relished by the best of men.
If you have nerve, you may have plenty;
Five draws you ten, and ten draws twenty.
Attention given, I'll show to you,
How umbrella hides the peek-a-boo.
Select your shell, the one you choose;
If right, you win; if not, you lose;
The game itself is lots of fun,

Jim's chances, though, are two to one;
And I tell you your chance is slim
To win a prize from Umbrella Jim.

The most successful of the monte operators were William Jones, better known as Canada Bill, and George Devol, who in later years described himself in his autobiography, which was first published in 1887, as " a cabin boy in 1839; could steal cards and cheat the boys at eleven; stack a deck at fourteen . . . fought more rough-and-tumble fights than any man in America, and was the most daring gambler in the world." [1] Devol and Canada Bill worked the steamboats together for many prosperous years, but lost all of their earnings playing faro and other games ashore. About 1850 they formed a partnership with two other gamblers, Tom Brown and Holly Chappell, and the four operated with great industry for several years on the Ohio and Mississippi, with frequent excursions to other navigable streams. When the combination dissolved, each man's share of the profits was more than two hundred thousand dollars. The body-servant of the quartet of sure-thing tricksters on this grand tour was an intelligent free Negro boy called Pinch, whom Devol had found shining shoes in a steamboat barbershop and had taken a fancy to. His real name was Pinckney Benton Stewart Pinchback, and he was born in Macon, Georgia, in 1837, two years before Devol ran away from his home in Marietta, Ohio, to become cabin boy on the *Wacousta*. Devol taught Pinch some of the tricks of the trade, and thereafter while Devol and his partners were fleecing the white folks in the saloon with monte, faro, and poker, the boy was on deck roping in the Negroes with a chuck-a-luck game. In after years Pinch continued to do very well for himself. He quit the river when the Civil War be-

---

[1] *Forty Years a Gambler on the Mississippi.* Republished in New York in 1926.

gan, and in 1862 ran the Confederate blockade at Yazoo City and reached New Orleans soon after the capture of the city by Farragut. Pinch immediately rose to a position of prominence among the Negroes, and after the War he organized the Fourth Ward Republican Club and became a member of his party's state committee. Thereafter he was increasingly important in carpetbag affairs. In 1868 he was elected to the state Senate and in 1871 was chosen Lieutenant Governor to fill the vacancy occasioned by the death of Oscar J. Dunn. He was acting Governor of Louisiana from December 9, 1872 to January 13, 1873, during the impeachment of Governor H. C. Warmoth, and in 1873 was elected to the United States Senate. The Senate, however, after three years of debate, refused to seat him.

While he was occupying the gubernatorial chair Pinchback repaid, in some measure, the man who had given him a start in life. Devol had won eight hundred dollars from one of the police commissioners of New Orleans at monte, and when he arrived in the city a few days later was summoned at once to police headquarters by the Chief of Police, who said he had been ordered to run the gambler out of town. Devol immediately jumped into a hack and drove to the Executive Mansion, where he saw his old boy Pinch for the first time in some fifteen years. The Governor aroused his servants, an elaborate supper was served, and he and Devol played seven-up until morning. At dawn Pinchback escorted the gambler to the door and said:

"Go to bed, George, and don't give yourself any uneasiness. I'll settle that Police Commissioner."

Devol was always the acme of sartorial perfection, but Canada Bill was conspicuous among the elegant dandies of the river by the slovenliness of his dress. Probably no man on the Mississippi looked less like a gambler. Devol described him as "a medium-sized, chicken-headed, tow-haired sort of man with mild blue eyes, and a mouth nearly from ear to ear, who walked with a shuffling, half apologetic sort of gait, and who, when his countenance was in repose, resembled an idiot. For hours he would sit in his chair, twisting his hair in little ringlets. . . . His clothes were always several sizes too large, and his face was as smooth as a woman's, and never had a particle of hair on it. . . . He had a squeaking, boyish voice, and awkward, gawky manners, and a way of asking fool questions and putting on a good-natured grin, that led everybody to believe that he was the rankest kind of a sucker — the greenest sort of country jake." But, as Devol said, Canada Bill was " a slick one." His uncouth appearance and verdant mannerisms disguised one of the shrewdest gamblers in the United States. He was by far the most expert of the monte-players and was one of the few men who could show the two aces and a queen and then, almost in the very act of throwing the cards, palm the queen and substitute a third ace. He made enormous sums of money, but he lost it all ashore, for while almost every professional gambler was an arrant sucker for some particular game, Canada Bill was a sucker for all of them. He would bet on anything and play any sort of game, and the fact that it was a " brace " made no difference; he loved gambling for its own sake.

It was Canada Bill who originated the story which has become the classic gambling anecdote. He and one of his partners were marooned for the night in a little Louisiana river town a few years before the Civil War, and after diligent search Canada Bill found a faro game and began to play. His partner urged him to stop.

" The game's crooked! " he declared.

" I know it," replied Bill, " but it's the only one in town! "

Canada Bill worked the river boats until traffic on the Mississippi was virtually stopped by the war, and then transferred his activities to the railroads. Some ten years before his death he offered one of the Southern roads twenty-five thousand dollars a year for permission to operate monte and confidence games on its trains without being molested. The offer was refused, although he promised to victimize only preachers. Canada Bill died a pauper about 1880 at Reading, Pennsylvania, and was buried by the Mayor of the city, who was afterwards reimbursed by Chicago gamblers. As two of his former associates stood watching the coffin being lowered into the grave, one of them offered to bet a thousand dollars to five hundred that Canada Bill was not in the box.

"Not with me," said the other. "I've known Bill to squeeze through tighter holes than that."

George Devol was not quite the kingpin he made himself out to be in his autobiography, but he was nevertheless an important personage among the "sure-thing players" of the Mississippi. He began gambling professionally at fifteen, while working as cabin boy on a Rio Grande steamboat piloted by his cousin, and within another year he was an accomplished cheat with a bankroll of almost three thousand dollars, which in those days was an enormous sum of money for a sixteen-year-old boy to possess. He had little more at the end of some fifty years of gambling, although in that time at least two million dollars passed through his hands, most of it going into faro banks in New Orleans, St. Louis, and Chicago. With the exception of Canada Bill Jones, Devol was probably the most proficient monte-player who ever trimmed the suckers of the steamboats. He was also remarkably skillful at poker, seven-up, and other card games, and at faro when he had the bank and could control the skullduggery. He was particularly adept at "laying the bottom stock" and ringing in cold decks; once in a friendly poker game with four other gamblers he rang in four cold decks on the same hand, dealt each of his opponents four aces, and then sat back and watched the fireworks. Within a few minutes everything the gamblers possessed was on the table, and when the showdown came, hours were required to get things straightened out.

Much of Devol's fame on the river and in New Orleans was based on his extraordinary ability as a fighter; he was probably correct in saying that he had engaged in more rough-and-tumble fights than any other man in America. He always carried a pistol, which he called Betsy Jane, but he never used it, and the only time he ever really needed it he found he had left it at his lodgings. This was in Chicago about 1868, when he became involved in a little difficulty with Johnny Lawler, a faro dealer who, when he lost, frequently became so angry that he butted his head against a wall and tried to pull off his ears. A woman friend of Devol's complained that Lawler had insulted her, and Devol knocked Lawler into a mud puddle on Clark Street, which in those days was the great gambling center of Chicago. Lawler went home and got a revolver and began shooting at Devol when the two men met at Clark and Madison Streets. The first bullet struck Devol in the hand, but three others missed because he jumped behind a telegraph pole. Lawler was convicted of assault and sentenced to the penitentiary, but obtained a new trial eight months later and was acquitted. While he was in jail his hair is said to have turned from black to snow-white.

Devol seldom hit a man with his hand; in most of his encounters he simply butted his opponent into submission with his head; and with the weight of his two-hundred-pound body behind it, his massive, dome-shaped cranium was a formidable weapon. Several doctors who examined him when he was at the height of his fame as a butter said that his skull above the forehead was more than an inch thick. " It must be pretty thick," Devol wrote, " or it would have been cracked many years ago, for I have been struck some terrible blows on my head with iron dray-pins, pokers, clubs, stone-coal and bowlders. . . . I have had to do some hard butting in my early days on account of the reputation I had made for my head. I am now [1886] nearly sixty years of age, and have quit fighting, but I can today batter down any ordinary door or stave in a liquor barrel with ' that old head of mine.' I never have my hair clipped short, for if I did I would be ashamed to take my hat off, as the lines on my old scalp look about like the railroad map of the state in which I was born."

For several years during and after the Civil War one of the attractions of Robinson's Circus was Billy Carroll, who was advertised as " the man with the thick skull, or the great butter." In the arena Carroll demolished barrels and heavy doors with his head, and butted all comers. He was never downed until Robinson's Circus played New Orleans in the winter of 1867. At the behest of Al and Gil Robinson and a New Orleans sporting man known as Dutch Jake, Carroll and Devol butted each other "just for fun." When the circus star recovered consciousness he walked over to Devol, put his hand on the gambler's head, and said:

"Gentlemen, I have found my papa at last."

4

T H E dominating vice of Creole New Orleans was a passion for gambling which has never been equaled on this side of the Atlantic Ocean. "All indulge in it," wrote the French traveler Robin,[1] who visited the town about the time of the Louisiana Purchase. " In the evening, when the business of the day is over, fortunes are lost over and over again at it." Robin attributed the prevalence of the habit to a

---

[1] The Abbé Claude C. Robin, who first came to America as chaplain to Count Rochambeau.

lack of education and intellectual activity; he expressed the opinion that since the men of New Orleans had nothing to talk about but business and politics, they turned to gambling as the most exciting way in which to spend their leisure. Whatever the reason, addiction to games of chance was so nearly universal and became so definitely a trait of Creole character as to foster a tradition that the first of the riff-raff colonists sent to Louisiana by the Mississippi Company stepped ashore with a deck of cards in his pocket and a roulette wheel under his arm. In any event, gambling was a source of worry to the provincial government at a very early date; alligators were still wallowing on the site of the Cabildo and bullfrogs croaking in the Place d'Armes when Bienville found it necessary to scold the settlers for thus frittering away their time and substance. The first public places of resort in the city — the low taverns and pot-houses of which the Marquis de Vaudreuil and succeeding French and Spanish governors complained — provided gaming-tables for the convenience of their customers and operated games which were open to all comers. The provincial authorities attempted, without success, to abate the evil by frequently issuing stern admonitions and by promulgating stringent regulations which prescribed such punishments as branding, whipping, exposure in the stocks and the pillory, and, in extreme cases, banishment from the colony. One of the most curious of the early anti-gambling laws was that enacted by New Orleans' first Municipal Council, organized by the French Colonial Prefect Laussat while awaiting the arrival of the American commissioners to take possession of the country. Under the provisions of this statute the professional gambler and the person who played with him were, on the third offense, each punished with twenty-five lashes on the bare back.

Gambling among the gentry in the early days was private, but in later years most of the games were transferred to the special rooms fitted up in connection with the higher-class cafés, ballrooms, and coffee-houses, which began to make their appearance as the town grew in wealth and population. New Orleans after all was a small and comparatively isolated community throughout the French and Spanish occupations, and there were few, if any, establishments exclusively devoted to gambling until after the Louisiana Purchase, when the settlement began to develop as a cosmopolitan city. By 1810, when there were approximately twenty-five thousand inhabitants, gambling-houses were numerous, both in the French Quarter and in the new section above Canal Street, and had become the focal points of much crime and disorder. The authorities attempted to control them during the next sixty years by alternating systems of suppression, municipal regulation, and licensing by the state Legislature, which in later periods imposed an annual tax of from five thousand to seventy-five hundred dollars on each establishment.

The professional gambler was likewise seldom encountered in early New Orleans, but he appeared in large numbers when the flatboats and keelboats began coming down the Mississippi, and Girod and Tchoupitoulas Streets bloomed as the favorite haunts of the boat crews and the rougher elements of the city's population. In both of these areas every dive, even the bordellos, furnished facilities for gambling, and practically all of them were crooked. So far as the records show, the only square game among the scores frequented by the river men was to be found in a little roulette house on Tchoupitoulas Street, operated by an old Frenchman named Grampin, who went bankrupt in an extraordinary fashion. Among his regular customers was a flatboat captain who came in every night while he was in port and bet twenty-five cents — never more and never less — on the red at roulette. One night the captain sat down, staked his coin, and leaned his head on his hand while

Grampin spun the wheel. Red won, and the money was doubled. As the captain did not pick up his winnings, Grampin again started the little ball rolling, and again it stopped on red, once more doubling the river man's stake. Again and again the frantic Frenchman spun the wheel, and each time red won, while the flatboat captain sat like a stone image, apparently oblivious both of his good fortune and of the excitement which his play was creating. At the sixteenth turn of the wheel, when the captain's winnings amounted to over eight thousand dollars on his original investment of a quarter, Grampin pushed all the money he had across the table and excitedly ordered the river man to leave. When the latter still did not move, Grampin pushed him, and he rolled stiffly from his chair to the floor. He was dead. With great promptness several members of his crew who had accompanied him to the gambling-house gathered up the body, the roulette wheel, the money, and all of the furniture and rushed from the place. When a dozen of the night watch appeared a little later, they found the old Frenchman weeping in the middle of a bare room.[1]

The professionals who operated in New Orleans were drab fellows compared with their gaudy brethren of the steamboats; in dress and demeanor they were scarcely distinguishable from the general run of citizens. Whatever color and spectacularity attached to gambling in Creole times were provided by river sharpers who occasionally stopped ashore for brief vacations from their arduous labors of fleecing the traveling sucker. For some twenty-five years after the American acquisition the gambling-houses of New Orleans were as shabby and unpretentious as their proprietors — small places in the side streets, fitted with rou-

---

[1] The story of the man who made a bet and then died is told of all great gambling centers, but Jonathan Green, a reformed gambler who in 1857 wrote a book exposing the iniquities of the business, says this actually happened in New Orleans.

lette wheels and a few tables at which card games were played. The first of the sumptuously appointed "palaces of chance," which became famous as the most pleasant places in the United States in which to lose money, was opened at Orleans and Bourbon Streets in 1827 by John Davis, impresario of the Théâtre d'Orléans and owner of the notorious Orleans Ballroom, who had considerable social and political influence. He established also a branch, of equal magnificence, on Bayou St. John, about a mile from the city, which was operated only from Saturday noon to early Monday morning. On Sunday evening an elaborate dinner was served free to all players. The Orleans Street house, however, was open day and night seven days a week, with croupiers and dealers working in four-hour shifts. Although Davis started both of these establishments during one of the periods in which gambling was being rigorously suppressed, he was not molested by the authorities, and he had the field practically to himself until 1832, when the Legislature legalized gambling in New Orleans and thus permitted any man to open a place who would pay the license fee of seventy-five hundred dollars a year. Under the protection of this law a score of high-class places appeared within a year, among them such noted resorts as Hewlett's, Toussaint's, and St. Cyr's on Chartres Street, and Pradat's, Elkin's and Charton's on Canal Street.

In the public casinos of these establishments there were a dozen ways by which a man and his money might be parted, but the most popular methods were faro, roulette, and *vingt-et-un,* from which came the American game of blackjack. The proprietors, following Davis's example, also provided small private rooms for the convenience of the aristocrats and officials who refused to lower themselves by gambling with *hoi polloi.* Most of these exclusives were devotees of *écarté* and brag, the latter an ancient card game from which poker probably developed. There was no limit in the gambling-houses of this period, and sometimes the play was for very high stakes, especially in the private rooms. A loss of twenty-five thousand dollars at a single sitting was not uncommon, and many men of wealth and prominence poured from fifty to a hundred thousand dollars a year across the gaming-tables. Others became paupers almost overnight, staking their plantations, their city real estate, their slaves, and everything of value they possessed. As a Louisiana historian said, " captains of vessels lost their salaries, ship-owners their cargoes, planters the money which they had gained from the sale of the years' crops." Members of the Marigny family are said to have gambled so heavily, and so unsuccessfully, that in order to pay their losses they were compelled to break up their famous plantation and sell a large part of the land as building lots. Perhaps the most consistent loser in New Orleans history was Colonel John R. Grymes, the noted lawyer who had acquired considerable notoriety by his defense of the pirate Jean Lafitte. Colonel Grymes's law practice brought him a large income, but he dissipated it at the gaming-tables and died a poor man. Tradition has it that although he gambled at every opportunity, not once did he win a hand, and that for more than a decade his losses averaged fifty thousand dollars a year.

A puritanical bloc in the state Legislature, headed by Representative Larrimore of the Parish of St. Tammany, succeeded in 1835 in forcing the passage of a law which repealed the licensing act of 1832 and made the keeper of a gambling-house liable to a fine of from five to ten thousand dollars or imprisonment from one to five years. Scant attention was paid to the new statute in New Orleans, where public opinion was decidedly in favor of gambling, and the houses continued to operate with the connivance of the police, although a little less openly than before. Practically all of the better places, however, as well as most of the

underworld " brace " games, succumbed to the money panic
and depression of 1837, and gambling languished for almost ten years thereafter. It experienced a great revival in
1846, when New Orleans became the principal base for
the operations of the American Army in Mexico, and again
in 1849, when thousands of treasure-seekers swarmed into
the city on their way to the California gold fields. "Under
the stimulating effect of an immense and transient population," says an old New Orleans guide-book, " it will not be
wondered at that the gambling furor again broke out in
New Orleans. Gambling houses were now opened in all
directions, all over the city, near the St. Mary's Market,
near the steamship landings, near the hotels, the boarding
and lodging houses, wherever returning soldiers or emigrants quartered or congregated. None of these establishments . . . assumed any pretensions to luxury or elegance."

No exact count of the gambling-houses which crowded
New Orleans during this period was ever made, but it has
been estimated that they numbered at least five hundred,
while some four thousand dealers, croupiers, and cappers
found employment in them. None brought any revenue into
the coffers of the city except a few small places which had
been licensed to play lotto and rondo, the gamblers interested in these games having convinced the authorities that
they were harmless amusements and not gambling. In later
years lotto became known as keno, and although it is seldom heard of now, for more than half a century it was
by far the most popular of all games among the lower and
middle classes of New Orleans and other Mississippi River
cities. So many keno halls were opened, especially in St.
Charles Avenue and in Royal and Chartres Streets, that they
became nuisances, and as early as 1852 the city authorities
passed a law revoking all licenses and forbidding the playing
of keno, even privately, anywhere in the city. As late as
1888 such laws were still being enacted, and the police were

still feebly going through the motions of enforcing them, but keno retained a firm foothold in New Orleans until about the beginning of the present century, although it suffered a slight decrease in popularity during the palmy days of the Louisiana Lottery. John Philip Quinn, a reformed gambler who had operated keno halls in St. Louis, thus described how the game was conducted:

"Any number of persons may play. Each one desiring to participate in the game buys a card on which there are three horizontal rows of five numbers each, arranged altogether without regularity. The price paid for a card is commonly twenty-five cents, although sometimes the stakes are considerably higher. [John Curry ran a place in New Orleans in 1888 where the cards sold for a hundred dollars each.] None of the cards contained a higher number than ninety-nine. The conductor of the game — who is known as the 'roller' — takes his position, usually upon a raised platform, in full view of the players. Before him is placed a globe containing ninety-nine balls, numbered consecutively from one to ninety-nine, to correspond with the figures on the players' cards. The balls having been thoroughly mixed, the 'roller' presses a spring at the bottom of the globe, opening an aperture just large enough to permit one ball to drop at a time. As soon as the first one has fallen, the aperture is closed and the 'roller', in a loud voice, calls out the number inscribed upon it. If a player finds the number in either of the three horizontal rows on his card, he places a button over it. When any player has all five numbers in any one of his rows thus called out, he exclaims 'keno!' after which the 'roller' takes no more balls from the globe. His card is then inspected by one of the 'collectors' — of whom there are usually two — and if his tally is correct he is given the entire amount of money paid by all the players (which is called 'the pot') less a discount of fifteen per cent, which is retained by the house as its 'percentage.'" [1]

The great popularity of keno was due partly to the smallness of the individual stakes, which made it an excellent poor man's game, and partly to the general impression that it was square. As a matter of fact, it was usually played honestly, for, as Quinn said, the bank incurred no risk whatever, and its sure percentage was enough to satisfy the cupidity of most gamblers. Cheating at keno, however, was a very simple matter; the roller simply palmed the balls as they came from the globe, and substituted others bearing numbers which were on cards previously issued to cappers, who were better known in the trade as "japs" and "pigeons."

With the exception of the keno halls, most of the houses which had preyed upon the soldiers and emigrants closed their doors when the war with Mexico ended and the excitement over California began to subside, and gambling in New Orleans returned to normal proportions. It underwent a great renaissance of luxury and splendor in the middle 1850's, when Price McGrath, James Sherwood, and Henry Perritt, who had successfully operated large establishments in St. Louis and other cities, arrived in New Orleans and invaded the field. They formed a partnership under the firm name of McGrath & Company, acquired the property at No. 4 Carondelet Street — in after years the headquarters of the Boston Club — refurnished it at a cost of seventy thousand dollars and opened a gambling-house which for richness of appointment and elegance and variety of service outshone even John Davis's famous place of an earlier day. It is said to have been the first resort of the

---

[1] *Fools of Fortune,* page 251.

kind in America wherein the croupiers and dealers were required to wear evening dress, and the sumptuous buffet suppers served free each evening were celebrated all over the country. Besides being one of the most splendidly equipped gambling-houses in the United States, the establishment of McGrath & Company was perhaps the most honest; no cappers were employed, and the partners really tried to keep from the tables men who could not afford to lose.

The great success of the policy pursued by McGrath & Company influenced the dozen other large houses which were opened about the same time, and New Orleans enjoyed some half-dozen years of remarkably upright gambling, when the river tricksters who occasionally came ashore and attempted to operate " brace " games were decidedly unpopular. Among the noted establishments which attempted to compete with McGrath & Company were those operated by Augustus Lauraine and his partner, Charles Cassidy, who was also the New Orleans correspondent of the *Spirit of the Times* of New York and wrote racing news under the nom de plume of Larkin; Sam Levy, Montiro, and Lorenzo Lewis, better known as Count Lorenzo because of the elegance of his apparel. The most exclusive house of the period was kept by a Frenchman named Curtius, at Toulouse and Chartres Streets. No one was admitted without character references and a formal introduction from someone known to Curtius. Each player paid fifty cents an hour, which entitled him to dinner and as much wine as he wished to drink. The only games allowed were boston, chess, and poker, and at poker there was a betting limit of a hundred dollars on a single hand. The house operated by Lauraine and Cassidy was the scene, about 1860, of a wild gambling spree by the representative of a large Greek importing firm. He is said to have gambled steadily for four days and nights, with only a few hours' rest, and to have lost eighty thousand dollars in one night's play. His losses during the four days amounted to about two hundred and fifty thousand dollars. He paid with drafts on his firm, which led to its suspension and the consequent loss of his job.

All of the large houses ceased operations in 1861, when the Civil War began and the Confederate military authorities practically assumed control of the city. Of the five men at whose establishments most of the gambling had been done, only two, Henry Perritt and James Sherwood, remained in New Orleans. Perritt equipped and sent to the front in Virginia a military company known as the Perritt Guards, and Sherwood likewise furnished arms, money, and clothing to several organizations. Cassidy went to New York and became a journalist, while Lauraine tried his luck in several cities before finally settling down in Dallas, Texas. McGrath returned to his native state, Kentucky, where he established a stock farm and raised thoroughbreds. Among them was the celebrated Tom Bowling, which for many years held the record for one and one-half miles. Carrying 104 pounds, he set a mark of 2.34¾ at Lexington, Kentucky, on May 12, 1874.

Many of the river gamblers abandoned their labors on the steamboats at the outbreak of hostilities between the North and the South and sought refuge in New Orleans. With the gamblers who had remained in the city they formed a military company called the Wilson Rangers, but better known among the gamblers themselves as the Blackleg Cavalry. The *True Delta* of October 23, 1861 said proudly that "a finer-mounted troop of cavalry, we think, can hardly be found anywhere in the South than the Wilson Rangers, of this city. . . . From what we have seen of them at drill, we judge them to be a valuable support to our army of gulf coast defense." But George Devol in his autobiography has a different tale to tell of the Wilson Rangers:

" I was a member of the company. We armed and equipped ourselves, and the ladies said we were the finest looking set of men in the army. . . . When we were ordered out to drill (which was every day), we would mount our fine horses, gallop out back of the city, and the first orders we would receive from our commanding officer would be ' Dismount! Hitch horses! March! Hunt shade! Begin playing!' . . . in less than ten minutes there would not be a man in the sun. They were all in the shade, seated on the ground in little groups of four, five and six; and in each group could be seen a little book of tactics (or at least it looked like a book at a distance). We would remain in the shade until the cool of the evening, when the orders would be given: ' Cease playing! Put up books! Prepare to mount! Mount! March!' When we would get back to the city, the people would come out, cheer, wave handkerchiefs and present us with bouquets; for we had been out drilling in the hot sun, preparing to protect their homes from the Northern invaders. . . . The citizens called us their defenders; and we did defend them, so long as there was no hostile foe within five hundred miles of them."[1]

The gamblers' company was ordered on active service in April 1862, when Farragut's fleet launched its attack upon the Confederate forts, and was sent down the river with other detachments to engage a large Federal land force which was reported to be marching on the city. " As we went through the streets," wrote Devol, " the ladies presented us with bouquets, and cheered us; but there was but little cheer in that fine body of gamblers." The Rangers were some six miles below the city when one of the Federal

[1] *Forty Years a Gambler on the Mississippi*, 1926 edition, pages 123-4.

ships saluted them with a salvo of canister, whereupon the doughty gamblers retreated at full speed. "When we got back to the city," Devol went on, "we dismounted without orders . . . cut the buttons off our coats, buried our sabers, and tried to make ourselves look as much like peaceful citizens as possible; for we had enough of military glory, and were tired of war."[1]

On the morning of April 24, 1862 the fire-alarm bells, with twelve strokes four times repeated, notified the people of New Orleans that Farragut's ships had passed the forts and that the last defenses of the city had crumbled. Immediately the town was thrown into a condition bordering on frenzy, for it was popularly believed that New Orleans, if it fell into the hands of the Yankees, was destined to suffer the fate of Carthage. Business was suspended, and thousands of citizens rushed to the levees to watch the conquering fleet steam up the river. Governor Thomas O. Moore and other state and city officials at once prepared to leave, and General Mansfield Lovell, in command of the Confederate land forces, seized all available steamers, loaded them with ordnance and other military stores, and dispatched them up the river to safety. He also issued orders to burn all the cotton in the city, all steamers not needed by the Confederate Army, and all shipyards. Fifteen thousand bales of cotton were burned in the streets and on the levees, steamboats at the wharves loaded with cotton were set on fire and cut adrift, and great quantities of provisions were piled in heaps ready for the torch. In the midst of the preparations for evacuation, rioting and looting began, and soon thousands of men and women were scrambling and fighting for spoil of every description, and particularly for the barrels of sugar and molasses and cases of meat; molasses flowed through the gutters like water.

---

[1] Ibid., page 125.

Confederate troops tried to check the trouble, but the people paid little attention to them; the looting continued until the plunder on the levee had been carried away.

"The merchants expected that the Yankees would sack the city," wrote Devol, "so they threw open their stores and told everybody to take all they wanted. . . . I hired a dray (for which I had to pay $10), and loaded it down to the guards. We put on hogsheads of sugar, twenty-five hams, a sack of coffee, box of tea, firkin of butter, barrel of potatoes, some hominy, beans, canned fruit, etc. I would have put on more, but the dray wouldn't hold it. . . . After laying in my stock, I went down to the river to see the fleet come in, and there were all of our company, but they did not make the slightest resistance. The Captain said, 'It's no use trying to bluff them fellows, for they have got a full hand.' "[1]

5

MAJOR-GENERAL Benjamin F. Butler, in command of the Yankee Army which co-operated with Farragut, took possession of New Orleans on May 1, 1862, and was the despotic ruler of the conquered city until December 16, when he was recalled by the War Department at Washington. In those seven months he succeeded in making himself the most thoroughly despised man in all the history of New Orleans; he is still referred to there as Butler the Beast, and if one-twentieth of the stories told about him are true he was veritably a scoundrel of the deepest dye. Even the most biased of Northern historians, except, of course, his official apologist, James Parton,[2] admit that Butler was a rapacious and unscrupulous politician who used his military

---

[1] Ibid., page 126.

[2] Parton wrote a book called *General Butler in New Orleans, a History of the Administration of the Department of the Gulf in the Year 1862*, which is as thorough a job of whitewashing as can be found in American literature.

power to feather not only his own nest but those of his friends and relatives as well. His brother, A. J. Butler, who was called Colonel although he had no connection with the Army, made two million dollars in New Orleans by various means, among them trading with the enemy, and the General is said to have left the stricken city with an even greater fortune. What he wanted he took, under the guise of military confiscation. Butler is chiefly remembered in New Orleans today for the hanging of W. B. Mumford for pulling down an American flag; and for the infamous General Order No. 28, better known as the Woman Order. From the day he entered the city Butler was greatly incensed by the attitude of the New Orleans ladies who, as Kendall wrote, "made a point of wearing Confederate colors on their hats and dresses, of playing or singing Southern songs when Federal troops were within hearing, and of manifesting their dislike by withdrawing from omnibus, street car, or church pew whenever Federal officers entered these places." [1] Parton says they went even further to show their contempt for the Yankees, pretending illness when the invaders came in sight, and ostentatiously drawing away their skirts to avoid contamination. To put them in their proper places as inhabitants of a conquered city, Butler issued this order:

Headquarters, Department of the Gulf.
New Orleans, May 15, 1862.

General Order No. 28:

As the officers and soldiers of the United States have been subject to repeated insults from the women (calling themselves ladies) of New Orleans, in return for the most scrupulous non-interference and courtesy on our part, it is ordered that hereafter when any

---

[1] *History of New Orleans*, Volume I, page 277.

female shall, by word, gesture, or movement, insult or show contempt for any officer or soldier of the United States, she shall be regarded and held liable to be treated as a woman of the town plying her vocation.

By Command of   Major-General Butler.
George C. Strong, A. A. G., Chief of Staff.

This meant that upon complaint of any member of the Yankee military forces any woman in New Orleans could be arrested, held overnight in the calaboose, brought before a magistrate the next day, and fined five dollars. Probably no other action by an American military commander ever aroused such a world-wide storm of resentment and indignation as this extraordinary display of vindictiveness. President Jefferson Davis of the Confederate States proclaimed Butler an outlaw and put a price on his head; many Northern newspapers denounced the order as an outrageous and gratuitous insult; Lord Palmerston in the British Parliament characterized it as "infamous"; Mayor John T. Monroe of New Orleans protested vigorously and was summarily removed from office; and in Washington the Secretary of State, William H. Seward, apologized to the British Chargé for "a phraseology which could be mistaken or perverted." Except for the protest by the Mayor, the only active measures in New Orleans were taken by the women of the red-light district, who, curiously enough, resented the order even more than did the ladies at whom it was directed. A large number of portraits of Butler had been distributed soon after he entered the city, and most of them eventually found their way into the houses of prostitution. A few days after the issuance of the Woman Order, General Butler learned that his portraits were being put to an extraordinary use — the prostitutes had pasted them to the bottoms, inside, of their tinkle-pots! A detachment of soldiers raided the red-light district, confiscated these utensils, and destroyed them; tradition has it that on many the General himself wielded the hammer.[1]

Butler promulgated two orders which directly affected the gamblers of New Orleans. One, issued through regular military channels, closed all of the gambling-houses; the other, circulated privately, permitted any gambler to reopen who would pay a license fee to the Provost Marshal and accept the General's brother, "Colonel" Butler, as a full but silent partner. Most of the establishments reopened under this arrangement, and from this source the "Colonel" received huge payments each week until the General was transferred and all of the Butler enterprises collapsed. The General's military successors failed to molest the gamblers, and they enjoyed great prosperity for some two years. But practically all of them were Southerners, and they took a keen delight in fleecing the officers and paymasters of the Federal Army, most of whom were inveterate gamblers, despite frequent warnings and a few cases of punishment. George Devol, who was operating the old Oakland race-track, with gambling-games going full tilt in the grand stand, when Butler entered New Orleans, was fined one thousand dollars and sentenced to a year in prison for showing Federal officers a few tricks at three-card monte, and Butler confiscated all the horses at the track, worth about fifty thousand dollars. The General's brother is said to have shipped the animals across Lake Pontchartrain and sold them to the Confederate Army. Devol was released after six months by the Military Governor of the state, General George F. Shepley, and celebrated his freedom by winning nineteen thousand dollars from a Federal paymaster at poker and monte.

The patriotic gamblers made such heavy inroads on the funds of the Army that early in 1864 all the gambling-

---

[1] This story has been current in New Orleans since the war, and is given here for what it is worth. Naturally, there is no historical confirmation of it.

houses in New Orleans were closed by order of General Stephen A. Hulburt, who had succeeded General Nathaniel P. Banks as commander of the Department of the Gulf. They remained closed, under strict military observation, until the Federal Army evacuated the city and left New Orleans and Louisiana to the tender mercies of the carpet-baggers. They were not generally reopened until 1869, when the Legislature elected after a civil government had been formed, as corrupt a body of men as ever disgraced the legislative halls of America, passed a law which legalized gambling and levied a tax of five thousand dollars upon each house. A year before this statute was enacted, however, the Legislature had placed opportunities for gambling in the way of virtually every man, woman, and child in the United States by granting a charter to an institution which became famous as one of the most successful gambling schemes in American history—the Louisiana State Lottery Company. In return for an annual contribution of forty thousand dollars for the support of the Charity Hospital in New Orleans, and whatever private disbursements were necessary to maintain its political influence, the company was granted a monopoly of the lottery business for twenty-five years. Subsequent charters extended this period, and also gave the company a monopoly of the policy game, which is still played extensively in all American cities, especially among the Negroes. Policy was in its heyday in New Orleans during the 1880's when the whole city went mad over the game; every day long lines of both whites and Negroes stood before the company's booths in Canal, Royal, and other principal streets waiting to bet their nickels, dimes, and quarters.

The Lottery Company appears to have had hard sledding for the first ten years, due largely to competition from established lotteries in Alabama, Kentucky, and other states, but the great success and popularity of policy enhanced its prestige, and thereafter it was extraordinarily prosperous. At one time, when the question of renewing the charter was being debated, the company was able to offer the state an annual payment of $1,250,000. By dint of expert lobbying, and the lavish expenditure of money, the Lottery Company acquired tremendous political power and, despite strenuous and well-organized opposition, maintained its existence until 1907. It was finally put out of business by the national government, which not only closed the mails to the company's tickets and to publications bearing its advertisements, but actively prosecuted its agents under a law, passed in 1895 by Congress, which prohibited the interstate transportation of lottery tickets.

The Louisiana Lottery began with the issuance of twenty-five-cent tickets and a capital prize of $3,750. As the demand increased, this was changed to a fifty-cent ticket and a $7,500 prize. At the height of its fame and prosperity, when tickets were sold in vast numbers all over the United States — in Chicago alone the monthly sales amounted to $85,000, and in Boston $50,000 — drawings were held daily, semi-monthly, and semi-annually, with a grand prize, awarded semi-annually on a $40 ticket, of $600,000. There were also prizes of $15,000 on a $1 ticket, $30,000 on a $2 ticket, $75,000 on a $5 ticket, $150,000 on a $10 ticket, and $300,000 on a $20 ticket. The yearly total of the daily drawings was $20,000,000, and of the others about $28,000,000. There is no record of a single person winning the grand prize, but a New Orleans barber once won the prize of $300,000 on a whole $20 ticket, and was promptly paid. Until the last few years of its existence, when the company called itself the Honduras National Lottery and operated clandestinely, a winning ticket was as good as a certified check and was cashed anywhere by banks and express companies. The company gained the confidence of the whole nation by having its drawings supervised by commissioners in whom there was universal confidence. The first of these officials were General P. G. T. Beauregard and General Jubal A. Early, renowned military leaders of the Confederacy, who were each paid thirty thousand dollars a year for about two days' work a month. When they died the task of supervising the drawings was assumed by General W. L. Cabell of Texas, known throughout the south as "Old Tige," who had likewise been a noted commander in the Confederate Army. General Cabell's salary, however, was only six thousand dollars a year.

6

WHEN the Legislature legalized gambling in 1869, New Orleans had a population of almost two hundred thousand, a large part of which was composed of carpetbaggers who had amassed riches by exploiting the city and state, and was able to support more gambling-houses than at any previous time in its history. And it soon had the opportunity to do so; the local gamblers at once opened places, and sharpers from all over the United States flocked into the one city in the country where their business was not only legitimate, but free from all inspection and supervision. Many of the new houses paid the required tax, but at least an equal number avoided it through connivance with corrupt police and officials. Within a few weeks after the passage of the law New Orleans had blossomed into one vast gambling-hell; games of every description, most of them crooked, ran wide open on all the principal streets of the French Quarter and of the section above Canal Street. On St. Charles Avenue alone between City Hall and Canal Street, there were forty resorts, popularly known as "the forty thieves", which never closed their doors. Many were housed in three-story buildings, with faro on the first floor, roulette on the second, and keno on the third, while on all floors were small rooms devoted to poker, *vingt-et-un,* and other games. The front doors of these places opened directly into the street, with no screens, and the sidewalks fairly swarmed with cappers and runners who tried to entice passers-by inside, and with shell and monte men who made their pitches and worked openly, unmolested by the police. At the same time a plague of confidence men invaded the hotels, railroad stations, and steamboat landings, and even stores and offices, in their bold search for victims. In all this carnival of iniquity the gamblers played no favorites; octogenarians and boys in short pants were fleeced with the same impartiality.

But the statute which the gamblers had greeted with such glee, and for the passage of which they had so liberally endowed needy legislators, proved their undoing. Within six months so many resorts had been opened by strangers that the old-time honest gamblers of New Orleans found themselves facing bankruptcy by reason of ruinous competition, while their carefully built-up reputations for squareness were being rapidly demolished by the excesses of the sure-thing operators. Under the leadership of Bill Franklin, who ran an ornate place at Common Street and St. Charles Avenue — the rooms were papered in green and gold and all of the chairs and tables were heavily gilded — a conference was held, and the gamblers decided that, whatever the cost, the newcomers must be driven from the city. A legislative committee was appointed, funds were subscribed, and New Orleans was treated to the curious spectacle of its best-known gamblers working assiduously for the repeal of the law which had legalized their business. They were successful, and at the next session of the Legislature the license system was abolished and gambling in New Orleans was once more against the law. The larger houses were closed for a few weeks while the police, with whom satisfactory arrangements had been made, were ridding the city of the undesirables; then they reopened. For almost ten years the gamblers operated quietly and with great prosperity, although the blackmail levied by the police and the politicians frequently exceeded the amounts which had been required for licenses under the law of 1869. During the late 1870's, however, sure-thing men again appeared in New Orleans from New York, St. Louis, Chicago, and other cities and opened houses which were operated with much of the blatancy that had characterized such resorts in the days of the carpetbaggers.

Perhaps the most noted of these new arrivals was Major S. A. Doran, a tremendously powerful six-footer weighing more than 225 pounds, who came to New Orleans with a reputation as a killer — he had shot a policeman in Texas, and the son of a prominent citizen in Memphis, and always carried a brace of revolvers, with which he was an excellent shot. He opened an elaborate establishment on Royal Street, where he employed as capper a young man named Charles P. Miller, later known as King of the Banco Men. Miller worked for Doran until he had accumulated a bankroll of thirty-five thousand dollars, and then went to New York and started in business for himself, opening a gambling-house in the metropolis and organizing a gang of banco and " green goods " operators. Miller's only peer at banco was Tom O'Brien, who frequently visited New Orleans to carry on various confidence schemes and to see his mistress, Annie Grey, a popular courtesan who ran a bagnio on Burgundy Street and had been engaged in the same business in New York, Paris, and Atlanta before coming to Louisiana. In time O'Brien extended his operations to Paris, and in March 1895 was arrested by the Paris police for the murder of Reed Waddell, originator of the gold-brick swindle. When O'Brien thus found himself in serious trouble, Annie Grey sold her property in New Orleans and went to Paris, where she spent her entire fortune in a successful effort to save her lover from the guillotine.

233

Major Doran ran his Royal Street resort until the latter part of 1883, when he sold the establishment and went to Hot Springs, Arkansas, where gambling was dominated by Frank Flynn and his brothers, John and Bill. Doran opened a house in defiance of the orders of the Flynns and was notified that he must close it or be killed. The Major immediately carried the war into the enemy's territory. On February 9, 1884, as the three Flynns drove down the main street of Hot Springs in a hack, Doran and four of his friends opened fire upon them from the sidewalk with rifles, shotguns, and revolvers. Frank Flynn and the hackdriver were killed, and John and Bill Flynn, together with two innocent passers-by, were wounded. Doran pleaded self-defense and was not punished, for although Frank Flynn had possessed considerable political influence when alive, once he was dead he was just an extinct gambler. The Major promptly assumed his place as the dominant figure in Hot Springs gambling circles.

The last of New Orleans' many unusual schemes to control gambling, called the " Shakespeare Plan," was inaugurated in 1881 by Mayor Joseph Shakespeare, and was probably the only system ever devised in the United States, with the exception of downright suppression, which succeeded in keeping the activities of the gamblers within reasonable bounds. When Mayor Shakespeare assumed office late in 1880 there were eighty-three large gambling-houses in New Orleans. He was frankly in favor of licensing a limited number of resorts and rigorously suppressing the remainder, but the City Council refused to pass the necessary ordinance, pointing out that gambling was forbidden by an amendment to the state Constitution, and that a crime could not be licensed. Regulation by the police, under the Mayor's direction, was then attempted. Early in 1881 the gamblers were told that their resorts would be closed upon the first complaint, and less than a month later, after the fleecing of a visiting French nobleman had created a sensation, the police closed every gambling-house in the city except those in the area bounded by 'Camp, Chartres, St. Louis, Bourbon, Carondelet, and Gravier Streets, wherein were located the most important establishments. The Mayor then summoned the operators of these places and broached his plan. He suggested that they pay him a fixed sum each month, in return for which he agreed to prevent the police from molesting or blackmailing them. He further promised that they would not be prosecuted, and that no competing houses would be permitted to open. On their part the gamblers agreed to run honest games, to restrict participation in them to adults, and to abide by whatever rules the Mayor saw fit to promulgate. From the beginning the plan was a success. The first payments were made in May 1881, and the total for the first year was thirty thousand dollars. Most of the fund was applied to the erection and upkeep of the Shakespeare Almshouse, a project in which the Mayor had been interested for several years, and the remainder was used for the maintenance of a small force of private detectives, whose only duties were to inspect the gambling-houses at frequent intervals and see that the games were conducted honestly.

The Shakespeare Plan continued in effect throughout the administration of W. J. Behan, and during most of the term of J. Valsin Guillotte, from 1884 to 1888. About 1885, however, politicians and city officials, anxious to increase the payments, permitted several crooked gamblers to open houses and began to divert the fund from the purpose for which it had been intended. In that year, out of $20,000 collected, the Almshouse received only $4,875. The diversion of the fund continued for the next two years, and although an investigation disclosed that there was probably no criminal intent on the part of those responsible, a scandal resulted which was fully aired in the newspapers.

Finally, soon after the payments of February 1887, the Grand Jury declared that the city officials and politicians were using the money "as a sort of contingent or secret service fund," a finding which certainly covered a multitude of sins. The Grand Jury also indicted thirty-five gamblers, but the cases were nol-prossed by the District Attorney, Lionel Adams, who told the court that "these men express their sincere regret at being thus, without notice, dragged as criminals before the court after having contributed nearly $200,000 to a deserving charity." Although the gamblers were released, they refused to make any further contributions, declaring that they could see no reason for paying if they were to be liable to prosecution. Shakespeare tried to reinstate the plan when he again became Mayor in 1888, but could gain no support from either the gamblers or the respectable elements which had previously favored it as the best way out of a bad mess. In the end the Mayor was compelled to fall back upon the system of control which is still in effect, not only in New Orleans but in most other American cities; semi-toleration until the gamblers become too bold, then systematic raids and prosecutions until they seek cover.

CHAPTER VIII

CONGO SQUARE

THROUGHOUT THE hundred years or more in which the French and Spanish dominated Louisiana, there was little if any relaxing of the rigid discipline by which the Negro slaves of the province were kept under control. In New Orleans it was the usual practice among slave-owners to lock the black chattels in their quarters soon after sunset, with armed sentinels posted about the building to see that none attempted to leave before daybreak. On many plantations the slaves commonly worked in the fields laden with chains and guarded by overseers with guns and whips, the latter of which were used freely to punish laziness, malingering, or any of a score of other faults, real and imaginary, while packs of hounds were kept in readiness to pursue runaways. The lot of the slave on some of the large French and Spanish estates, particularly those in the back country away from the protection afforded by the settlements, was scarcely more pleasant than it had been in the slave camp which the French government established in a swamp near New Orleans after Bienville proved that the new town would be permanent. To this camp the early cargoes of *Africains bruts* were brought directly from the slave ships, and there they were either tamed or killed. If the former, the men were taught to use the hoe, the ax, the plow, and other tools and implements, and the women were trained in the rudiments of housekeeping. Manacled in groups to a long, heavy chain and frequently burdened with the additional weight of an iron collar, the men labored in the fields from dawn to dark under the watchful eyes of soldiers, who drove them to and from their quarters like cattle. Except for an occasional fine specimen who was kept at stud, their rations were meager to the point of scarcity, and their clothing likewise; in the summer months they were clad only in cotton trousers, and during the damp, biting Louisiana winters they wore thin blanket robes with hoods, and shoes called "quantiers," pieces of rawhide cut to lace over toes and ankle somewhat in the manner of the modern snowshoe harness.

Since the fear of a Negro uprising was omnipresent in early New Orleans and Louisiana, many laws were promulgated by the French governors to prevent both the free colored people and the Negro slaves from assembling in large or small groups and to limit as much as possible the black man's intercourse with his kind. The thirteenth article of Bienville's Black Code forbade slaves belonging to different masters "to gather in crowds either by day or by night, under the pretext of a wedding, or for any other cause, either at the dwelling or on the grounds of one of their masters, and much less on the highways or in secluded places." Slaves who thus transgressed were whipped, and for frequent offenses of this nature the Code provided that " the offenders shall be branded with the mark of the flower de luce, and should there be aggravating circumstances, capital punishment may be applied at the discretion of our judges." The Marquis de Vaudreuil also called attention to the perils inherent in assemblages of slaves, and thus dealt with the subject in the police regulations which he issued in 1751:

"We forbid all the inhabitants or citizens of this colony to permit on their plantations, or at their places

238

of residence, or elsewhere, any assembly of Negroes or Negresses, either under pretext of dancing, or for any other cause; that is to say, excepting the Negroes whom they may own themselves. We forbid them to allow their slaves to go out of their plantations or premises for similar purposes, because His Majesty has prohibited all assemblies of the kind. . . . We also forbid the town or country Negroes to assemble in the town of New Orleans, or in its vicinity, or elsewhere, under any pretext whatever, under the penalty, for said Negroes, of being imprisoned and whipped. . . . Should any inhabitant or citizen of the province permit on his plantation or premises an assembly of Negroes other than his own, under any pretext whatever, he shall, for the first offense, pay one hundred crowns to the treasury of the church, and for the next offense of this kind, be sentenced to work for life on the King's galleys."

Various laws of a similar character, all designed to insure as far as practicable the isolation of the individual Negro, were enacted and rigidly enforced by the Spanish governors and the Cabildo. The slaves in Louisiana had no freedom of movement whatsoever until the coming of the Americans, who brought to bear upon the whole question of slavery a new viewpoint, entirely different from that of the French and Spanish, which gradually compelled the liberalization of the laws and customs regulating the life of the black man. Recognizing the value of recreation and a measure of social intercourse in keeping the Negro contented with his lot, the American authorities, soon after the Louisiana Purchase, began to allow the slaves to gather for dancing. These assemblies appear to have begun about 1805 and at first were held in various places in and near the city, among them an abandoned brickyard in Dumaine

239

Street. The most celebrated of all the slave rendezvous, however, was a large open space at Rampart and Orleans Streets, part of which had been indicated on the maps of Bienville's engineers as a public square. In early times the field was used by the Oumas Indians as the place of cele-brating their corn feasts, and consequently, in the eyes of the red man, was holy ground. When the slaves began to use the site for dancing, the whole area was popularly known as the Place des Nègres, and later as the Congo Plains; and the square itself, to which the slaves were restricted when the Plains were divided into building lots, was called Congo Square, and is still so known among the Negroes of New Orleans. Its official name, however, was never any-thing but Circus Square until after the Civil War, when it was changed to Beauregard Square in honor of General P. G. T. Beauregard of the Confederate Army, who was born near New Orleans. Until the latter part of 1820, when grass, shrubs, and sycamore-trees were planted by order of Mayor Louis Philippe Roffignac, the square was merely an expanse of barren, dusty ground, rutted and pitted by the shuffling of hundreds of black feet.

During the first decade or so after the American occu-pation of Louisiana, the slaves of New Orleans were al-lowed to congregate every Saturday and Sunday afternoon at whatever place they chose to assemble, and frequently were permitted to continue their merriment far into the night. The result was that often a dozen dances were in progress in as many vacant lots in different parts of the city, and the authorities received many complaints from householders who had been kept awake, and from slave-owners whose Negroes had failed to return home at seemly hours. On October 15, 1817 the Municipal Council adopted an ordinance directing that "the assembles of slaves for the purpose of dancing or other merriment, shall take place only on Sundays, and solely in such open or public places as shall be appointed by the Mayor." Congo Square was designated by the Mayor as the only place to which the slaves might resort, and thereafter all such gatherings were held under strict police supervision. The dancing was stopped at sunset, and all slaves were driven out of the square and sent home. Under these and other regulations, the custom of permitting slave dancing in Congo Square continued for more than twenty years, when it was abolished for reasons which the old city records do not make clear. It was resumed in 1845, when this ordinance was adopted:

"Whereas, numerous citizens have requested the Council of Municipality No. One, to grant permission to slaves to assemble on Sundays on Circus Square, for the purpose of dancing.

"Whereas, when such a merriment takes place before sunset and is not offensive to public decency, it can be tolerated; provided, it being under police inspection.

"Resolved that from the 1st of May to the 31st of August of each year, the slaves, provided with a written consent of their master, be permitted to assemble Sundays on the Circus Square for the purpose of dancing from 4 to 6½ o'clock, P.M.

"Resolved that it shall be the duty of the commissaries of police of the 3rd and 5th wards, of the commanding officer at Post Trèmé and five men of the day police, to watch that no police ordinance be violated during the time allowed to Negroes to dance on Circus Square."

The weekly concourse of slaves in Congo Square reached the height of its popularity and renown during the fifteen years which preceded the Civil War; sometimes there were almost as many white spectators surrounding the

241

square to watch the slaves "dance Congo" as there were black dancers weaving and stamping under the sycamore-trees. Even in earlier days a Congo dance was considered one of the unique attractions of New Orleans; visitors were always taken to see the slaves at play, and in their eyes the spectacle ranked second only to a Quadroon Ball as a colorful, exotic display. "The Circus public square," wrote the editor of New Orleans' first directory, published in 1822, "is very noted on account of its being the place where the Congo and other Negroes dance, carouse and debauch on the Sabbath, to the great injury of the morals of the rising generation; it is a foolish custom, that elicits the ridicule of most respectable persons who visit the city; but if it is not considered good policy to abolish the practice entirely, surely they could be ordered to assemble at some place more distant from the houses, by which means the evil would be measurably remedied." Not many contemporary observers agreed with this estimate of the slave gatherings; practically all of them, and a vast majority of the people of New Orleans, appear to have looked upon the Sunday afternoon dancing as innocent merriment and as a beneficial outlet for the energies and repressions acquired during a week of hard labor. And if the police supervision was as strict as the old records indicate, it is difficult to see how any considerable degree of debauchery could have crept in.

The slaves usually began to assemble in Congo Square an hour or so before the time fixed for the dancing, the men strutting proudly in the cast-off finery of their masters, and the women in dotted calicoes, with bright-colored Madras kerchiefs tied about their hair to form the popular head-dress which the Creoles called the *tignon*. With them were their children, in nondescript garments relieved by bright feathers or bits of gay ribbon. On the outskirts of the chattering crowd were the hawkers of refreshments, some with great trays slung around their necks and others with deal tables screened from the sun by cotton awnings, and all offering ginger beer, pies, lemonade, and little ginger cakes called "mulatto's belly." At a signal from a police official, the slaves were summoned to the center of the square by the prolonged rattling of two huge beef bones upon the head of a cask, out of which had been fashioned a sort of drum or tambourine called the bamboula. As the dancers took their places, the rattling settled into a steady drumming, which the Negro who wielded the bones maintained, without a pause and with no break in the rhythm, until sunset put an end to the festivities. The favorite dances of the slaves were the Calinda, a variation of which was also used in the Voodoo ceremonies, and the Dance of the Bamboula, both of which were primarily based on the primitive dances of the African jungle, but with copious borrowings from the *contre-danses* of the French. The movements of the Calinda and the Dance of the Bamboula were very similar, but for the evolutions of the latter the male dancers attached bits of tin or other metal to ribbons tied about their ankles. Thus accoutered, they pranced back and forth, leaping into the air and stamping in unison, occasionally shouting "Dansez Bamboula! Badoum! Badoum!" while the women, scarcely lifting their feet from the ground, swayed their bodies from side to side and chanted an ancient song as monotonous as a dirge. Beyond the groups of dancers were the children, leaping and cavorting in imitation of their elders, so that the entire square was an almost solid mass of black bodies stamping and swaying to the rhythmic beat of the bones upon the cask, the frenzied chanting of the women, and the clanging of the pieces of metal which dangled from the ankles of the men.[1]

The Congo Plains must have presented an extraordi-

---

[1] Louis Moreau Gottschalk, a noted New Orleans composer, based one of his best-known compositions, *La Bamboula*, on what he heard and saw in Congo Square as a boy.

nary spectacle on these festive occasions, but the pictur-esqueness of the scene was lost on at least one European traveler who recorded his impressions of the dancing. J. G. Flugel, the German trader already quoted, saw the slaves "dance Congo" in February 1817 and was content to record in his journal that "their dances certainly are curious, particularly to a European." He saw them again in April of the same year, and thus described them:

"Their postures and movements somewhat re-sembled those of monkeys. One might by a little imagi-nation take them for a group of baboons. Yet as these poor wretches are entirely ignorant of anything like civilization (for their masters withhold everything from them that in the least might add to the cultiva-tion of their minds) one must not be surprised at their actions. The recreation is at least natural and they are free in comparison with those poor wretches, slaves of their passions. I saw today among the crowd Gilde-meister of Bremen, clerk or partner of Teetzmann. He told me that three of the negroes in the group closest to us were formerly kings or chiefs in Congo. I perceive in them a more genteel address. They are richly ornamented and dance extremely well." [1]

2

ONE of the famous Bamboula dancers of the early days, and also an expert wielder of the beef bones, was a gigantic Negro owned by General William de Buys, who is said to have been the first to attach little bells to his ankles instead of the customary bits of metal. He could leap higher and shout louder than any of the other slaves who stamped and cavorted in the dance; his stamping, indeed, shook the ground, and when he cried: "Badoum! Badoum!" the

---

[1] The *Louisiana Historical Quarterly* for July 1924, page 432.

tops of the sycamore-trees trembled and swayed in the wind caused by his mighty bellowings. And in his ham-like fists the beef bones rattled upon the head of the Bamboula drum with a crashing roar that resembled nothing less than a salvo of artillery fire. His name during the period of his fame as a Bamboula artist was Squier; a few years later, as Bras Coupé and the Brigand of the Swamp, he acquired a different sort of renown.

General de Buys was well known in New Orleans as a remarkably kind and indulgent master; he petted, coddled, and spoiled the Negro Squier, taught him to shoot, and permitted him to go alone on hunting expeditions in the forests adjacent to the city. And Squier practiced assiduously with the General's rifle; premonition, he said afterwards, warned him that he would eventually lose an arm, and so he became an expert marksman with either hand alone. The taste of freedom which Squier experienced on his journeys into the woods after game was too much for him. He began running away, and received only slight punishment when he was captured and returned to General de Buys. Early in 1834 Squier was shot by a patrol of planters searching the swamps for runaway slaves, and his right arm was amputated, whence the sobriquet Bras Coupé, by which he was thereafter known. As soon as his injury had healed, Bras Coupé fled into the swamps and organized a gang of escaped blacks and a few renegade white men, whom he led on frequent robbing and murdering forays on the outskirts of the city, with an occasional venture into the thickly settled residential districts. He was New Orleans' most feared outlaw for nearly three years, and the successor of the *Kaintock* as the hobgoblin with which nurses and mothers frightened the Creole children. Reviewing his career, the *Picayune* after his death described him as " a semi-devil and a fiend in human shape," and said that his life had been " one of crime and depravity."

Among the slaves Bras Coupé soon became a legendary figure endowed with superhuman powers; in the folklore of the New Orleans Negroes he was installed alongside the redoubtable Annie Christmas and in many respects was accounted her superior. He was, of course, fireproof and invulnerable to wounds, for he was familiar with the miraculous herbs described by the French travelers Bossu, Perrin du Lac, and Baudry des Lozières, and with many others which these avid searchers after botanical wonders had not discovered. Hunters returned to New Orleans from the swamps and told how, having encountered Bras Coupé, they fired at him, only to see their bullets flatten against his chest; some even said that the missiles had bounced off the iron-like body of the outlaw and whizzed dangerously close to their own heads, while Bras Coupé laughed derisively and strode grandly into the farthest reaches of the swamps. And according to the slave tradition, detachments of soldiers sent after him vanished in a cloud of mist. Moreover, his very glance paralyzed, if he so wished, and he fed on human flesh.

The popular belief in Bras Coupé's invulnerability received a rude shock when, on April 6, 1837, he was wounded by two hunters who braved his magical powers and shot him near the Bayou St. John. And it was dissipated entirely on July 19 of the same year. On that day a Spanish fisherman named Francisco Garcia, who was known to the slaves as a friend of Bras Coupé's, drove slowly through the streets of New Orleans a cart drawn by a decrepit mule, and watched with tender solicitude an ungainly bundle, wrapped in old sacks, which jounced in the bed of the vehicle. Garcia stopped in front of the Cabildo and carried his bundle into the office of Mayor Dennis Prieur, where he unwrapped it and disclosed the body of Bras Coupé. The fisherman told the authorities that on the day before, the 18th, he was fishing in the Bayou St. John when Bras Coupé fired at him and missed, whereupon the indignant fisherman went ashore and beat out the brigand's brains with a club. The truth, however, appears to have been that Bras Coupé was slain as he slept in the fisherman's hut. Garcia demanded the immediate payment of the two-thousand-dollar reward which he had heard had been offered for Bras Coupé dead or alive, but he received only two hundred and fifty dollars. The body of the outlaw was exposed in the Place d'Armes for two days, and several thousand slaves were compelled to march past and look at it, as a warning.

3

THERE were a few slave-owners in early New Orleans who consistently refused to permit their black people to attend the gatherings in Congo Square, and one of them was Madame Delphine Lalaurie, the wife of Dr. Louis Lalaurie, whose mansion at Royal and Hospital Streets was one of the most magnificent in the city. Madame Lalaurie's slaves, in fact, with the exception of a sleek, handsome mulatto who was her butler and coachman, were seldom seen in public at all, and when they did appear, even her friends remarked that they looked cowed and beaten and were thin to the point of emaciation. The mulatto butler, however, was always plump and well fed; he was clearly Madame Lalaurie's favorite. Later it was hinted that his position in the household was even higher than that of trusted servant. It seems that it should have been obvious even to the obtuse white officials that there was something queer about the Lalauries, but the dancers of Congo Square, among whom ran swift undercurrents of gossip and information, knew of the extraordinary happenings in the Royal Street mansion long before they came to the knowledge of the authorities, or at any rate before the authorities dared take any action. For Madame Lalaurie was a McCarty, a member of a very powerful New Orleans family, and herself so prominent in

247

society that when Lafayette visited the city in 1825 she entertained him at dinner. She was famous throughout Louisiana as a charming and gracious hostess, and is said to have been one of the most beautiful women of the New Orleans of her time. Her husband—he was her third—was a meek, mousy little man, wholly under her domination. And so were her two daughters, one of whom was a cripple.

This bewitching and engaging creature, who entertained the great of New Orleans at her sumptuous table and fascinated her guests by the brilliance of her wit, in reality had the heart of a sadistic demon and was unquestionably mad. A little of the truth about Madame Lalaurie became known about the beginning of 1833, when a neighbor, a woman, described to the police what she had seen on a moonlight night a few days before. She was looking out of her window, she said, when a little Negro girl ran screaming out of the Lalaurie mansion into the courtyard, followed by Madame Lalaurie lashing her savagely with a heavy whip. The child made the circuit of the courtyard and then fled back into the house, pursued by Madame Lalaurie, and the neighbor heard them as they ran through the house, the sounds of shrieks and pattering footsteps punctuated by the crack of the whip-lash as it found its mark. Presently they appeared on the roof, and the child, beaten to the eaves by a rain of blows, leaped wildly into space and shattered her body upon the flagstones of the courtyard. The police found the broken corpse at the bottom of an old well on the Lalaurie premises, and Madame Lalaurie was summoned to court, where she was fined and all her slaves taken from her. But the confiscated Negroes, when sold by the Sheriff at public auction, were bought by Madame Lalaurie's relatives and immediately returned to her. She resumed her sadistic cruelties and practiced them without restraint or interference until April 10, 1834.

On the morning of that day fire broke out in the Lalaurie mansion. It spread rapidly, and within a few minutes the main part of the house was filled with smoke, and streamers of flame were darting from the windows. The alarm bell was rung, and a large crowd began to gather, while the firemen hurried to the scene with their buckets and primitive fire-engines. Neighbors and friends of the Lalauries rushed into the house and began to carry out the furniture, while Madame Lalaurie calmly pointed out the pieces she wished saved. Several men, headed by Judge J. F. Canonge of the Criminal Court, went into the kitchen, where they found Madame Lalaurie's cook, a seventy-year-old Negress, kneeling in the center of the room, manacled to the end of a twenty-foot chain. The links were broken and the slave was carried to the street, and Judge Canonge asked Dr. Lalaurie if there were any more slaves in the house who might be in danger from the fire. Dr. Lalaurie suggested " in insulting tones " that Judge Canonge mind his own business. Meanwhile the cook, who later confessed that she had fired the house, preferring death to Madame Lalaurie's cruelty, had told the police that other slaves were confined in the garret. Judge Canonge and Felix Lefebvre, with several other men, started upstairs, smashing several locked doors which barred the way. When they reached the attic, they found seven slaves, four men and three women. All were naked and laden with heavy chains riveted to iron bands fastened about their necks, waists, and ankles. In addition, two wore iron collars with sharp edges and studded with spikes which had pierced their flesh and caused horrible wounds. Several were manacled in positions which had crippled them for life. The floor of the attic was littered with instruments of torture, sufficiently numerous to cover a long table when they were displayed later in the courtyard of the calaboose. One by one the slaves were led or carried into the street. The crowd pressed food upon them when they said they had not eaten for a week, and two ate and died; the others were taken to the calaboose, where they were attended by physicians. When they were well enough, they talked. Some of them had been chained in the attic for five months; others for shorter periods. Daily, and sometimes oftener, Madame Lalaurie came into the attic and beat them with iron bars and heavy whips, or gouged their flesh with sharp instruments. Frequently she was accompanied by the mulatto butler, who wielded the whip and otherwise assisted in the torture while she watched in ecstasy.

By the time the last of the manacled slaves had been rescued, the fire was extinguished and the furniture carried back into the house. More than two thousand persons were now gathered before the mansion, and they waited patiently, expecting the police or soldiers to appear and take the Lalauries away to prison. But nothing happened. Hours passed, and still there was no indication that the city authorities intended to do anything about the situation which had been exposed. Dr. Lalaurie had vanished, but through the windows the crowd could see Madame Lalaurie as she moved about, chatting with friends and directing the replacing of the furniture. Late in the afternoon, just before dusk, angry murmurs began to arise from the crowd, whereupon the mulatto butler promptly closed and barred the heavy door of the house and the iron gates of the courtyard. Angered, the crowd now became a vengeful mob, milled uncertainly for a few moments, and then swayed forward, battering vainly upon the stone walls of the building. But the men in the front ranks fell back as the gates were suddenly flung open, and a carriage emerged from the courtyard, drawn by a team of black horses at a plunging gallop. On the box was the mulatto, lashing with his whip the frantic horses and the faces of the men who clutched vainly at the rocking carriage, while crouched in the back seat was the veiled figure of Madame Lalaurie. The carriage moved swiftly up Hospital Street and turned into Bayou Road — and Madame Lalaurie was gone.

Several hundred men streamed down the road, yelling and cursing, but the remainder of the mob turned its attention to the house. The doors and windows were quickly smashed, and the rioters thronged into the mansion and began their work of destruction. Furniture was thrown into the street, where it was destroyed or carried away; pictures and hangings were pulled from the walls; carpets were ripped up and slashed; the mahogany balustrades were torn away; the wainscoting was hacked and gouged; and every pane of glass in the building was broken. Part of the mob, as one of the newspapers said next day, was "in the very act of pulling down the walls," while other rioters had begun to loot neighboring houses, when Sheriff John Holland appeared with a posse of deputies and a detachment of United States troops. Soon afterwards the mob dispersed.

Meanwhile, according to the most plausible account of Madame Lalaurie's movements, the mulatto coachman had driven her to St. John Bayou, where her husband was waiting with a small schooner, in which they sailed at once for Mandeville, on Lake Pontchartrain. Once his mistress was aboard the vessel, the mulatto drove back toward New Orleans, but on the Bayou Road met a mob which killed him and destroyed the carriage. From Mandeville the Lalauries went to New York, but left there for Paris when they were recognized and hissed at a theater. Madame Lalaurie is said to have been killed a few years later while boar-hunting at Pau.

The mansion on Royal Street was rebuilt, but it was a haunted house from the moment Madame Lalaurie's carriage dashed through the courtyard gates. Tenants usually left after a few months, and many of them complained that at night they heard the footsteps of the Negro child who had jumped from the roof, and the clanking of chains in the garret. In later years the building was successively a school for whites, a school for Negro girls, a gambling-house, and a cheap tenement. For several years the lower floor was occupied by the Haunted Saloon. The structure still stands, and is today the Warrington House, a refuge for friendless and penniless ex-convicts.

4

THE Sunday afternoon dances of the Negroes in Congo Square were abandoned during the troublous days that followed the capture and occupation of New Orleans by Union forces during the Civil War, and while an occasional gathering of the sort was held in reconstruction times, they were never again a regular feature of the black man's life. As late as the middle 1880's, however, a considerable number of Negroes, most of whom had been slaves, frequently assembled on Sunday afternoons in the back yard of an abandoned property far out on Dumaine Street, where they trod the measures of the Bamboula and other Congo dances, which appear to have changed little since slavery times. A correspondent of the New York *World* thus described the dancing:

"A dry-goods box and an old pork barrel formed the orchestra. These were beaten with sticks or bones, used like drumsticks so as to keep up a continuous rattle, while some old men and women chanted a song that appeared to me to be purely African in its many vowelled syllabification. . . . Owing to the noise I could not even attempt to catch the words. I asked several old women to recite them to me, but they only laughed and shook their heads. In their patois they told me — 'no use, you could never understand it. *C'est le Congo!* — it is the Congo!' The dance was certainly peculiar, and I observed that only a few old persons, who had

252

probably all been slaves, knew how to dance it. The women did not move their feet from the ground. They only writhed their bodies and swayed in undulatory motions from ankles to waist. . . . The men leaped and performed feats of gymnastic dancing which reminded me of some steps in the *jota Aragonesa*. Small bells were attached to their ankles. '*Vous ne comprenez pas cette danse-la?*' an old woman asked me. I did not altogether understand it, but it appeared to be more or less lascivious as I saw it. I offered the woman some money to recite the words of the Congo song. She consulted with another and both went off shaking their heads. I could obtain no satisfaction."

CHAPTER IX

VOODOO

THERE IS no historical record of the introduction of Voodoo worship in Louisiana, but it must have occurred at a very early date, for while the first cargoes of slaves were composed of savages from the Guinea coast of Africa, succeeding shipments came from the French colonies of Martinique, Guadeloupe, and Santo Domingo, which were veritable hotbeds of Voodooism. Although the growth of the cult in New Orleans and Louisiana appears to have been slow, it had become such a potential menace by 1782 that Governor Bernardo de Gálvez prohibited the further importation of slaves from Martinique, "as they are too much given to voudouism and make the lives of the citizens unsafe." The Baron de Carondelet, who was Governor from 1792 to 1797, similarly forbade the planters and slave-dealers to import Negroes from Santo Domingo, partly because of their addiction to Voodooism, and partly through fear that they might foment rebellion among the Louisiana slaves. And in 1803 the Municipal Council, formed by the French Colonial Prefect Laussat while awaiting the consummation of the Louisiana Purchase, refused to permit a cargo of Santo Domingo Negroes to be unloaded from the ship which had brought them to New Orleans. The bars which had been raised against the Santo Domingo blacks were lowered a few years after the American occupation, however, and at least five thousand refugee

Negroes, free and slave, arrived at New Orleans between 1806 and 1810. With this influx began the development of Voodooism as a real factor in the lives of the Louisiana Negroes. Thereafter, although slaves continued to form the great majority of the rank and file of Voodoo worshippers, the priesthood was composed almost entirely of free people of color, principally mulattoes and quadroons.

Throughout slavery times, and for some twenty years after the Civil War, the most powerful figures among the Negroes of New Orleans were the Voodoo queens, who presided over the ceremonial meetings and the ritual dances of the cult. Scarcely less influential were the Voodoo doctors, although they occupied secondary positions in the Voodoo hierarchy. Both the queens and the doctors were practitioners of black magic, and derived substantial incomes from the sale of charms, amulets, and magical powders, all guaranteed, according to the incantations pronounced over them, to cure the purchaser's every ailment, to grant his every desire, and to confound or destroy his enemies. All of these sorcerers, especially the Voodoo queens, were popularly supposed to possess vast knowledge of, and to dispense with great abandon, strange and subtle poisons, which defied detection and caused the victims to waste away and die of exhaustion. But there was never any evidence to justify this supposition, nor proof that anyone in New Orleans died at the hands of the Voodoos, although it is probably true that deaths have been hastened by fear of the sorcerers' supposed powers. So far as can be determined now, all of the concoctions sold by the Voodoo queens and doctors to their gullible clients appear to have been essentially harmless. Most of the magical powders which were to be taken internally contained a generous proportion of a strong cathartic, and while the consequences of a dose were frequently painful and distressing, they were seldom dangerous. The charms and amulets intended for external use were even less harmful, though composed of such queer ingredients as nail parings, human hair, powdered bones, and dried lizards. Even the celebrated "gris-gris," the most feared — and incidentally the most expensive — of all Voodoo magic, was seldom anything more than a little cotton or leather bag filled with powdered brick, yellow ochre, and cayenne pepper, with the occasional addition of nail parings, hair, and bits of reptile skin. Left on a doorstep in the dark of the moon, the "gris-gris" was supposed to work incalculable harm to the occupants of the house. That it never did was ascribed by the Negroes to the fact that a man who found a "gris-gris" on his premises hurried immediately to a Voodoo queen or doctor and procured a counter-charm, which invariably worked. Any Voodoo sorcerer, it appears, could always overcome the efforts of another.

The "gris-gris" and various other charms and amulets of a similar nature, as well as the magical powders, were more or less standardized, and usually sold for fixed prices. In addition to these the Voodoo queens and doctors had their own exclusive bits of sorcery, for use in stubborn cases, for which they charged as much as the traffic would bear. The special magic dispensed by the queens usually took the form of spells and incantations, uttered while in real or simulated trances, while the doctors embodied their high-powered sorcery in material objects. Many of the Voodoo queens and doctors acquired fortunes of respectable proportions, for they were consulted not only by practically all of the Negroes of New Orleans, but by great numbers of lower-class whites as well. Neurotic and repressed white women were especially easy victims of the Voodoo doctors, particularly of the stalwart mulattoes who prescribed not only charms and powders, but participation in orgiastic rites. The police raids on the premises of the black sorcerers, over a long period, frequently netted as many whites as blacks. In 1855, when Captain Eugene Mazaret of the Third District police invaded a house of the Voodoo doctor Don Pedro, he found a dozen white women and as many Negro men, the former naked except for thin camisoles, and all busily amusing themselves and one another under the direction of the magician. They were all arrested and fined, although Doctor Don Pedro protested that they were simply undergoing treatment for rheumatism. Next day the husband of one of the women committed suicide.

The first Voodoo doctor of whom there is any record in New Orleans was a huge coal-black Negro with a tattooed face, who called himself Doctor John, and who flourished during the early and middle 1840's. He was a mind-reader and a dabbler in astrology, and for special magical effects sold shells and pebbles which had been soaked for three days in an evil-smelling oil rendered from snakes, lizards, and frogs. Wrapped in a hank of human hair and carried in the pocket, one of these shells or pebbles provided blanket protection against all harm. Doctor John is said to have numbered among his clients the famous slave Pauline, a mulatto, who was the first Negro to be executed under the provisions of the Black Code after the American occupation, and the first person of any color to be hanged in the Parish Prison, which was erected behind Congo Square in 1832.[1] Pauline became the property of Peter Redeck in the autumn of 1844, and soon thereafter bought from Doctor John a love-philter with which to charm her master. She succeeded and became his mistress, although the newspapers of the time were inclined to give the credit to Pauline's handsome face and superb figure rather than to Doctor John's magic. Late in 1844 Redeck went to St. Louis on business, and in January 1845 Mayor Edgar Montegut received an anonymous letter which informed him that a white woman was being kept prisoner in her own home at 52 Bayou Road. On

---

[1] This prison served until 1895, when it was torn down and a new building erected in Tulane Avenue.

January 14 Mayor Montegut and a detachment of police went to the address, which was the home of Peter Redeck, and found Mrs. Redeck and her three children, aged two, four, and seven, confined in a cabinet by the slave Pauline, who had taken possession of the premises as soon as Redeck left for St. Louis. Mrs. Redeck told the Mayor that she and her children had been imprisoned for six weeks, during which time Pauline had beaten and starved her, and taunted her with the infidelity of her husband. Pauline was immediately tried, found guilty, and condemned to death, but because she was pregnant the execution was postponed to March 28, 1846. On that date, clad in a long white robe and white cap, her arms bound with black cord, she was hanged in the court-yard of the Parish Prison.

Some fifteen years after Doctor John had retired with a fortune, the principal Voodoo sorcerer in New Orleans was a slave, called Washington by his master but known among the Negroes as Doctor Yah Yah. His favorite magic cure-all was a mixture of Jamestown (jimpson) weed, sulphur, and honey, sipped from a glass which had been rubbed against a black cat with one white foot. But in 1861 Doctor Yah Yah gave a bottle of his concoction to an Italian and was arrested when the Italian's white physician told the police that it was a deadly poison. Doctor Yah Yah's master paid a fine of fifteen dollars, and the Doctor was sent into the country and transformed into a field hand. His place in the affections of the Negroes of New Orleans was assumed a few years later by Doctor Jack, who was especially noted for the potency of his love-charms. The most important of these, and the best seller, was a beef heart, scented with spices and perfumes and wrapped in white crape. It was well known to be infallible if left on a doorstep, and was in great demand, although it cost twenty dollars. Above Doctor Jack's bed at his home in Trémé Street hung a charmed beef heart, and the sorcerer often told his admirers that he could not die until it fell to the floor. When he died, on June 10, 1869, his wife told the police that the beef heart had fallen three days before, and that Doctor Jack had immediately sickened. One of Doctor Jack's contemporaries, whose career was cut short by a long jail sentence in 1868, was an extraordinarily unkempt old Negro known as Doctor Beauregard, who had come to New Orleans a few years earlier from Kentucky. Doctor Beauregard's hair, when combed out and untangled, reached almost to his waist, but ordinarily he wore it rolled, knotted, and tied so that it formed a great number of little bags or pockets. In these curious receptacles he carried his magical paraphernalia — pebbles, shells, dried lizards and frogs, bird skulls, bottles of snake oil, and a hoot owl's head with which he performed his greatest feats of sorcery. With the hoot owl's head Doctor Beauregard tried to charm the policeman who arrested him, but the success of the experiment was negligible.

<h2 style="text-align:center">2</h2>

THE Voodoo queens and doctors appear to have been more or less on equal footings so far as the practice of sorcery was concerned, but in all matters affecting the actual worship of the cult the queen possessed supreme authority. She fixed the time and place of every Voodoo meeting held in New Orleans during the course of the year, all of which were preparatory to the grand festival of Voodooism that began on the night of June 23 and continued into St. John's Day, which was sacred to the god of the Voodoos as well as to St. John the Baptist. In early times this festival was celebrated on the Congo Plains, but when that area was divided into streets and building lots the Voodoos transferred their most important ceremonies to the abandoned brickyard in Dumaine Street, which was also the scene of the Sunday

afternoon slave dances. Still later the Voodoo meetings were
held in a large hut, or chapel, which the members of the cult
had erected on the swampy shore of Lake Pontchartrain,
about half a mile from the lake terminus of the Pontchartrain Railway. For the preliminary gatherings of the Voodoos the queen could, if she chose, delegate her authority,
but over the festival on St. John's Eve she always presided
in person, as the connecting link between the Voodoo god
and his worshippers. Tradition says that at these and other
Voodoo meetings human sacrifices were offered, but again
tradition is unsupported by evidence; it is extremely improbable that anything of the sort ever occurred in New Orleans or elsewhere in Louisiana.

The ritual of Voodooism was likewise wholly in the
hands of the queen; she could change the form of the rites
whenever she wished, and in any manner she pleased, so
long as she retained the adoration of the serpent. Practically every Voodoo queen made radical alterations in the
ritual immediately upon her accession, and many continued
to order deletions and additions from month to month. To
these frequent changes and revisions is due the fact that the
form of Voodooism in New Orleans and Louisiana never
reached the stability found in Haiti and Martinique. They
also account for the innumerable conflicting descriptions of.
Voodoo ceremonies and dances in the literature of early
New Orleans, for one gathering of the cult seldom resembled another except in essentials.

One of the earliest of the Voodoo queens was a quadroon named Sanité Dédé, who dominated Voodooism in New
Orleans for more than a score of years after Louisiana had
become a part of the United States. She was a free woman
from Santo Domingo, and in her secular guise peddled sweet-
meats in front of the Cabildo and around the Place d'Armes.
In Sanité Dédé's time the meetings of the Voodoos were held
in the old Dumaine Street brickyard. The abandoned slave

cabins were used as dressing-rooms, while the actual ceremonies and dances were held in the brick shed, which had
been boarded up by the Negroes to form a building about
forty feet long by twenty feet wide. One of the few white
persons ever to witness a Voodoo meeting in this place was
a fifteen-year-old New Orleans boy, who on a night in 1825
was taken to the brickyard by a slave woman belonging to
his father. Many years later, when the boy had become a
wealthy planter of Plaquemine Parish, he thus described the
experience:

" An entrance door was opened at the call of Dédé,
and I witnessed a scene which, old as I am, no passage
of years can ever dim. The first thing which struck me
as we entered was a built-up square of bricks at the
upper and lower end of the shed, on each of which was
burning a fierce fire, casting a lurid light over the scene.
Along the four sides of the parallelogram of the building, were sconces, with lighted dips placed at equal dis-
tances, which barely added to the darkling light of the
two pyres. . . . Each man and woman had a white
kerchief tied around the forehead, though the heads of
the latter were covered by the traditional Madras handkerchief, with its five, nay, its seven artistic points, up-
turned to heaven. In a little while the company, some
sixty in all, had assembled. There were males and females, old and young, negroes and negresses — handsome mulatresses and quadroons. With them half a
dozen white men and two white women. . . .

" Near where I stood was an oblong table about
eight feet in length and four in width. On its right end
stood a black cat, and on its left a white one. I thought
them alive, and having a certain fondness for cats,
stretched out my hand to stroke the nearest. The touch,
that most philosophical of all the senses, soon satisfied

me that they were fine specimens of negro taxidermy. Admirably stuffed they were, too. In the center of the table there was a cypress sapling, some four feet in height, planted in the center of a firkin or keg. Immediately behind the cypress, and towering above it, was a black doll with a dress variegated by cabalistic signs and emblems, and a necklace of the vertebrae of snakes around her neck, from which depended an alligator's fang encased in silver.

"At the side of this table I recognized an old negro by the name of Zozo, well known in New Orleans as a vender of palmetto and sassafrass roots; in fact, he had a whole pharmacopoeia of simples and herbs, some salutary, but others said to be fatal. He seemed to be the corypheus of these unhallowed rites, for the signal of the beginning of the work came from him. He was astride of a cylinder made of thin cypress staves hooped with brass and headed by a sheepskin. With two sticks he droned away a monotonous ra-ta-ta, ra-ra-ta-ta, while on his left sat a negro on a low stool, who with two sheep shank bones, and a negress with the leg bones of a buzzard or turkey, beat an accompaniment on the sides of the cylinder. It was a queer second to this satanic discord. Some two feet from these archmusicians squatted a young negro vigorously twirling a long calabash. It was made of one of our Louisiana gourds a foot and a half long, and filled with pebbles.

"At a given signal the four initiates formed a crescent before Dédé, who was evidently the high priestess or Voudou queen. She made cabalistic signs over them, and sprinkled them vigorously with some liquid from a calabash in her hand, muttering under her breath. She raised her hand and Zozo dismounted from his cylinder, and from some hidden receptacle in or behind the large black doll, drew an immense snake, which he brandished wildly aloft. . . . He talked and whispered to it. At every word the reptile, with undulating body and lambent tongue, seemed to acknowledge the dominion asserted over it. In the meantime, with arms crossed and reverent eyes, the initiates had now formed a crescent around Zozo. He now compelled the snake to stand upright for about ten inches of its body. . . . In that position Zozo passed the snake over the heads and around the necks of the initiates, repeating at each pass the words which constitute the name of this African sect, ' Voudou Magnian.'

" Hardly was this last ceremony over when a long, deep howl of exultation broke from every part of the shed. Zozo back to his tam-tam, his accompaniers right and left, and the gourd musician with his rattle. A banjo player, too, sprang up, and pandemonium was unloosed. In the twinkling of an eye, on little brick foundations, boards were laid for a supper-table. . . . No benches, no seats of any kind. Some squatted on their haunches, others reclined, like the Romans, on their *trichina* when at a feast. . . . No tumblers, but before each guest a baked clay vase, with capacious and rounded belly, and a small spout, out of which the revellers drank wine or tafia (sugar-cane rum). . . . They were roused from their bacchanalia by the long, fierce call of Zozo's tam-tam. The old women removed the boards, swept away the debris of the feast, and left the space of about forty feet open for the dance.

" As the guests stood on the floor (a hardened surface of brick-dust) Zozo, leaving his tam-tam, went up to the altar — I have no other name for the place of Fetish-worship — and again drew forth the snake. He forced it to writhe and wriggle over and around the company, uttering the words which were repeated by sixty voices, ' Voudou! Voudou Magnian!' He then

twirled the snake around his head and dexterously cast
it into the blazing pile. Such a yell as arose no words can
describe. The rude instruments took up their discords,
mixed with yells. The chorus of Dante's hell had entered into the mad shouts of Africa. Then came a general call for the dance, and no dance of the witches in
the Hartzberg ever came up to it. Up sprang a magnificent specimen of human flesh — Ajona, a lithe, tall,
black woman, with a body waving and undulating like
Zozo's snake — a perfect Semiramis from the jungles
of Africa. Confining herself to a spot not more than
two feet in space, she began to sway on one and the
other side. Gradually the undulating motion was im-
parted to her body from the ankles to the hips. Then
she tore the white handkerchief from her forehead.
This was a signal, for the whole assembly sprang forward and entered the dance. The beat of the drum, the
thrum of the banjo, swelled louder and louder. Under
the passion of the hour, the women tore off their garments, and entirely nude, went on dancing — no, not
dancing, but wriggling like snakes. Above all the noise
rose the voice of Zozo:

> Houm! Dance Calinda!
> Voudou! Magnian!
>   Aie! Aie!
> Dance Calinda!

"The orgies were becoming frightful. Suddenly
the candles flared up and went out, leaving nothing but
a faint glow from the dying pyres. I had grown sick
from heat, and an indescribable horror took possession
of me. With one bound I was out of the shed, and with
all speed traversed the yard. I found the gate open, and
I was in the street and near home sooner than I can tell.

If I ever have realized a sense of the real visible presence of his majesty, the devil, it was that night among his Voudou worshippers." [1]

3

SANITÉ DÉDÉ was succeeded by the celebrated Marie Laveau, who was at once the most powerful of all the Voodoo queens and the most feared of the hobgoblins with which the mothers and nurses of early New Orleans frightened their unruly children; so awe-inspiring was the bare mention of her name that a decade after she died it still had a salutary effect upon mischievous youngsters. In Negro folk-lore Marie Laveau was ranked even higher than Bras Coupé or Annie Christmas; her magical gifts were infinitely superior to those of the one-armed outlaw, and it was recognized among the blacks that with her powers of sorcery she could easily have performed, had she wished, any of the feats attributed to the legendary heroine of the river. She dominated Voodooism in New Orleans for at least forty years, and only once was her supremacy even threatened. That was about 1850, when a quadroon woman named Rosalie, who for several years had aspired to the Voodoo throne, imported from Africa a large—almost life-size —doll which had been carved from a single tree-trunk. Painted in brilliant colors and bedecked in beads and gaudy ribbons, this doll formed such an impressive spectacle, and was so obviously a source of magic, that Rosalie began to make considerable headway in her schemes of rebellion. But Marie Laveau met the situation in a characteristically masterful manner. She simply walked into Rosalie's house on a day when the quadroon was absent, and walked out with the doll. Rosalie immediately had her arrested, but the Voodoo queen presented such an imposing and carefully pre-

[1] *Metropolitan Life Unveiled, or the Mysteries and Miseries of America's Great Cities*, by J. W. Buel; San Francisco, 1882; pages 522–30.

pared array of proof that the court decided she was the rightful owner of the doll and awarded it to her. Possession of this potent fetish, together with a magic shawl which she said had been sent to her by the Emperor of China in 1830, made her authority secure.

Marie Laveau was a free mulatto, and was born in New Orleans about 1796. On August 4, 1819, when she was in her early twenties, she was married to Jacques Paris, also a mulatto, the ceremony being performed by Père Antoine. Paris died in 1826, and a year or so afterwards Marie Laveau went to live with a mulatto named Christophe Glapion — there is no record of their marriage. She had a daughter in February 1827 — whether by Paris or by Glapion is unknown — who was named Marie and who subsequently married a man named Legendre. In her youth Marie Laveau was renowned among the free people of color for her beauty, and especially for the symmetry of her figure. By profession she was a hairdresser, and as such gained admittance to the homes of fashionable white ladies, where she learned many secrets which she never hesitated to use to her own advantage. As a lucrative side-line she acted as procuress for white gentlemen, furnishing quadroon and octoroon girls for their pleasure, and also served as go-between and letter-carrier in clandestine love-affairs among her white clients. She became a member of the Voodoo cult about the time her husband died, and usurped Sanité Dédé's place as Queen half a dozen years later. Sanité Dédé was then an old woman.

For several years after she became queen of the Voodoos, Marie Laveau spent much of her time in a flimsy shanty on Lake Pontchartrain, which was sometimes used for meetings of the cult. One day while she was there a hurricane passed over New Orleans and the lake, and the shanty was torn from its foundations and hurled into the water.

Marie Laveau sought safety on the roof, but when several of her followers tried to rescue her, she discouraged their efforts, crying out that the Voodoo god wanted her to die in the lake. She was finally induced to accept assistance, however, and according to the tale which was freely spread among the Negroes, the moment Marie Laveau reached the shore the fury of the storm abated and the lake became as smooth as the surface of a mirror.

A few years after this extraordinary manifestation Marie Laveau performed the feat which made her a woman of property and enormously enhanced her prestige among both whites and blacks. The son of a wealthy New Orleans merchant, having fallen in with bad companions, was arrested in connection with a crime, and although he was certainly innocent, the police had gathered a great deal of evidence which appeared to prove his guilt. In desperation the young man's father implored the aid of Marie Laveau. On the day of the trial the Voodoo queen placed three Guinea peppers in her mouth and went to the Cathedral, where she knelt before the altar rail for more than an hour. Then she hurried to the Cabildo, gained admittance to the courtroom, and deposited the three peppers under the judge's bench. The trial was duly held, and although the evidence was overwhelmingly against the young man, he was found not guilty. His happy father was so impressed by this display of Marie Laveau's power that he not only feed her handsomely in cash, but also gave her a cottage on St. Ann Street between Rampart and Burgundy, not far from Congo Square. This house was the home of her descendants until 1903, when it was torn down.

Marie Laveau was born a Roman Catholic, and appears to have returned to the Church — if, indeed, she ever left it — a decade or so after she became the head of Voodooism in New Orleans. Throughout the remainder of her

267

life she was extraordinarily devout and attended mass almost daily at the Cathedral. At the same time she retained her office as queen of the Voodoos, and in this guise sold vast quantities of "gris-gris" and other charms and conducted an extensive practice in sorcery so successfully that even among otherwise intelligent whites the belief was widespread that she possessed supernatural powers. So great was the fear in which she was held by the Negroes that her open allegiance to two faiths was never questioned. Nor did the Voodoos protest when she revised the ritual of the cult to include worship of the Virgin Mary and the Catholic saints, so that Voodooism became a curious mixture of West Indian fetish-worship and perverted Catholicism. Before Marie Laveau's time Voodooism in New Orleans was not only frowned upon by the authorities, but every effort was made to suppress it. But Marie Laveau surmounted this obstacle by popularizing the worship of the Voodoo god, and obviated the likelihood of police interference by inviting politicians, police officials, sporting men and newspaper reporters to attend the annual festivals on St. John's Eve. During her reign these celebrations became almost as popular among sightseers as the weekly dances of the slaves in Congo Square; frequently the white spectators outnumbered the Voodoos. Under cover of these public ceremonies, however, Marie Laveau presided over many secret meetings, either in the chapel on Lake Pontchartrain or before one of the dozen altars which the cult maintained in New Orleans, at which the real magic of Voodoo was invoked, and the dancing carried to orgiastic extremes not possible before the easily shocked whites.

Most of these gatherings were for definite purposes and were paid for by the persons on whose behalf they were held. And secret and mysterious though they were supposed to be, Marie Laveau never lost her sense of the value of publicity and occasionally admitted a reporter. The New Orleans *Times* of March 21, 1869 described a meeting of the Voodoos at the lake chapel, in which the central figure was a young white girl who had chosen this method of regaining the affections of her lover. Most of the celebrants were women, with a few quadroon men, and each carried a burning brand. Said the *Times*:

" These women were all dressed elaborately, some of them in bridal costumes, and with an extraordinary regard for the fineness and purity of their linen. At one end of the chapel a corpse was exposed. The rites having been commenced, an elderly turbaned female dressed in yellow and red [Marie Laveau], ascended a sort of dais and chanted a wild sort of fetish song, to which the others kept up an accompaniment with their voices and with a drum-like beat of their hands and feet. At the same time they commenced to move in a circle, while gradually increasing the time. As the motion gained in intensity the flowers and other ornaments disappeared from their hair, and their dresses were torn open, and each one conducted herself like a bacchante. Everyone was becoming drunk and intoxicated with the prevailing madness and excitement. As they danced in a circle, in the center of which stood a basket with a dozen hissing snakes whose heads were projecting from the cover, each corybante touched a serpent's head with her brand. In the midst of this saturnalia of witches, the pythoness of this extraordinary dance and revel was a young girl, with bare feet, and costumed *en chemise.* In one hand she held a torch, and with wild, maniacal gestures headed the band. In this awful state of nudity she continued her ever-increasing frantic movements until reason itself abandoned its earthly tenement. In a convulsive fit she finally fell, foaming at the mouth like one possessed, and it was only then that the mad carnival found a pause. The girl was torn half-dead from the scene, and she has never yet been restored to her faculties."

This was the last Voodoo ceremony over which Marie Laveau presided, for some two months later, on June 7, 1869, the Voodoos held a meeting in the chapel at Lake Pontchartrain, dethroned her on the ground that since she was well over seventy she was too old to perform the onerous duties of her high post, and crowned Malvina Latour as queen. Thereafter, until her death about ten years later, Marie Laveau devoted herself entirely to her self-imposed duties as unofficial spiritual adviser to the criminals in the condemned cells at the Parish Prison, an office which she had assumed during the early 1850's. This phase of her activity was wholly Catholic, into which she permitted no trace of Voodooism to creep. As soon as a man had been sentenced to hang, Marie Laveau made daily visits to his cell, taking him bowls of hot gombo and platters of fried fish and otherwise consoling him in every way possible. If he consented, she prepared an altar in his cell before which she prayed with him — a box about three feet square, surmounted by three smaller boxes rising pyramidically to an apex, on which the Voodoo queen always placed a small figure of the Virgin Mary.

The first execution in which Marie Laveau thus figured was that of Jean Adam and Anthony Delisle, on June 2, 1852. Adam and Delisle, who were painters, were employed early in 1852 to paint the house of the grocer Chevillon, at Craps (Burgundy) and Clouet Streets. In the course of this work they located the hiding-place of a considerable sum of money and learned that every Sunday afternoon Mrs. Chevillon attended vesper services at the Cathedral, while her husband called on friends, leaving a Negro slave girl alone in the house. Adam and Delisle finished their work on a Saturday, and the next afternoon, accompanied by Delisle's younger brother, they entered the grocer's home by the back door. While the brother kept a lookout in the courtyard, Adam and Delisle stole the money, and cut the slave girl's throat when she came upon them. The brother took the loot to hide it, while Adam and Delisle went uptown, stopping at a police station, where they were known, hoping to establish an alibi. But Delisle's brother bore a bad reputation, and the police arrested him when they learned that he had been seen in the vicinity of the Chevillon residence on the day of the murder. Adam and Delisle were likewise taken into custody, although there was no evidence against them. This was obtained, however, by the first recorded bit of real detective work in the annals of the New Orleans police — a policeman in the guise of a drunken sailor was thrown into the cell with the suspects and heard them talking about the crime. On the policeman's testimony Adam and Delisle were convicted and sentenced to hang. After the trial they confessed to Recorder Seuzeneau. Delisle's brother was sent to the penitentiary.

The day of the execution dawned bright and cloudless, and the sun was not more than an hour high when people began to gather in Orleans Street before the Parish Prison; by noon, the hour fixed for the hanging, the eager crowd comprised more than a thousand men, women, and children. In order that all might see, a platform had been erected over the passage between the prison and the old police jail, and on it was fastened the derrick-shaped gallows. The trap-door, fourteen feet above the pavement of the passage, was attached to the gallows by heavy hinges, and was held in position by a thick rope which ran on pulleys over the top of the whole construction and across a window-sill into a cell on the second floor of the prison. There it lay on a block of hard wood. In this cell stood the executioner, wearing a black domino and a black mask, ready to cut the rope with a sharp ax.

Adam and Delisle spent most of the morning praying with Marie Laveau before her improvised altar, and at eleven o'clock ate a bowl of gombo which she had brought. They were then dressed in white caps, white shirts, and white pantaloons and drank a bottle of whisky furnished by the prison authorities. When the guards came for them a few minutes before noon, Delisle was roaring drunk, and Adam was so nearly unconscious from the liquor that it was necessary to carry him. Delisle walked unsteadily across the prison courtyard and up the steps of the platform, shouting that he was a Frenchman and would die for the French flag. While the final preparations were being made, he began shouting at the crowd, alternately crying his innocence and begging everyone to attend his funeral and give him a long, fine procession. He suddenly stopped his harangue, stared upward, and then screamed and fell forward into the arms of his guards. Following his gaze, the crowd saw a huge black cloud scudding swiftly across the hitherto empty sky. In a moment it had obscured the sun, and a murky twilight descended, while a faint breeze rustled the tops of the trees and stirred up little eddies of dust in the unpaved street. Several children in the crowd screamed in sudden terror.

Adam and Delisle, their arms bound with ropes, and the latter still mumbling about his funeral and the French flag, were forced into two chairs on the trap-door. Then the black hoods were adjusted and the nooses slipped about their necks. As the chimes of the Cathedral clock began to strike twelve, the Criminal Sheriff raised his hand and signaled the executioner. And at that moment sheet lightning crashed and crackled from the black cloud, and the rain came down, as the *Picayune* said next day, " as if the floodgates of heaven were opened to deluge the world again." Above the tumult of the storm and the frantic shuffling of the crowd rose the thud of the executioner's ax against the rope which held up the trap-door. It parted, and Adam and Delisle disappeared, but the next instant the crowd saw the Sheriff and the guards on the platform rush to the opening and look down, with horror on their faces, while the ropes which should have been taut flapped loosely in the wind. The nooses, imperfectly tied, had slipped, and the momentum of the drop had pulled them over the heads of the condemned men. Pelted unmercifully by the rain, Adam lay bleeding and insensible on the stone pavement; Delisle, his right arm broken and his neck cut by the rasping rope, crawled aimlessly about, screaming with pain and fright. The mob outside the prison, unable to learn what had happened, and the more superstitious seeing in the storm a significant and terrible sign from the Almighty, surged forward in a blind panic, heedless of the torrential rain and the fearful lightning, trampling a score of children and as many women who had fainted. While policemen were beating the crowd back with their clubs, Adam and Delisle were carried into the prison, where they were revived by a physician. Ten minutes later they were again taken to the gallows, and this time everything proceeded satisfactorily. They were hanged — and a few minutes after they fell through the trap the storm had passed and the sun was shining. Next day every newspaper in New Orleans embarked upon a campaign which resulted, at the next session of the Legislature, in a law forbidding public executions.

Although Marie Laveau was not at the prison while this appalling spectacle was being enacted, it actually added to her prestige; many of her followers were convinced that she had invoked the fury of the elements to prove that Adam and Delisle were not guilty of the crime for which they had been convicted. But the Voodoo queen was quite capable of engineering bizarre effects without the aid of Nature;

sometimes her efforts to please condemned murderers and make their last hours happy and pleasant took queer forms. In 1859, when James Mullen was in the Parish Prison awaiting execution for murder, Marie Laveau brought a coffin into his cell and helped him decorate it, inside and out, with religious mottoes and pictures of angels and saints, all enclosed in a border of metallic fringe. Until he was hanged, on July 30, 1859, Mullen slept in the coffin, using for a pillow a dress which had been worn by his three-year-old daughter. A year or so later Marie Laveau was popularly believed to have poisoned, at his own request, Antoine Cambre, bouncer at the Louisiana Ballroom, who had been sentenced to hang for the murder of a lamplighter. Cambre was found dead in his cell the day before his execution was to have taken place and a few hours after Marie Laveau had given him a bowl of gombo. The Voodoo queen was also a central figure in the triple hanging in the courtyard of the Parish Prison on March 18, 1859, when Heinrick Haas, Peter Smith, and Joseph Lindsay, the last an eighteen-year-old boy, were executed for murder. Marie Laveau erected her altar in Haas's cell, prayed before it with the three men, and walked with them to the gallows. Haas had been convicted of killing his wife in their home in Craps Street and was in prison almost a year before he was hanged. Throughout that period he devoted most of his waking hours to praying with Marie Laveau and, with her assistance, decorating his cell with religious subjects. Using lead pencil, indigo, and tobacco juice, he drew eleven pictures on the walls, each eighteen by twelve inches, and on the ceiling a larger one, depicting the Host with angels praying beside it.

Another to whom the Voodoo queen attempted to bring spiritual solace during his last hours was John Bazar, a Malay, who went to Texas in 1868 and returned a year later to his home in St. Anthony Street, to find that his place in the household had been usurped by Joe Cobez, a fellow-countryman. Bazar whipped both his wife and Cobez and then vanished. He appeared again in December 1869 and beat Cobez to death with a stone when the latter asked him for ten dollars. The murder was one of the bloodiest in the criminal history of New Orleans; the police found blood-stains on the pavement of the courtyard and in every room of the house. Bazar was convicted and sentenced to hang on May 27, 1870. On the morning of that day he prayed with Marie Laveau in the prison chapel, which she had decorated, and was then led to the gallows. His arms had been bound, the noose and black hood adjusted, and the Sheriff had started to raise his hand to signal the executioner, when a messenger galloped into the courtyard with a reprieve from Governor H. C. Warmoth. Later Bazar's sentence was commuted and he was sent to the penitentiary.

But even the task of bringing religious consolation to men destined for the gallows eventually proved too much for Marie Laveau's strength. About 1875, only a little while before her death, she retired to the little cottage on St. Ann Street and was never again seen in public. George W. Cable visited her during this period of retirement and thus recorded his impressions in the *Century Magazine* for April 1886:

" I once saw, in her extreme old age, the famed Marie Laveau. Her dwelling was in a quadroon quarter of New Orleans, but a step or two from Congo Square, a small adobe cabin just off the sidewalk, scarcely higher than its close board fence. . . . In the center of a small room whose ancient cypress floor was worn with scrubbing and sprinkled with crumbs of soft brick — a Creole affectation of superior cleanliness —

275

sat quaking with feebleness in an ill-looking old rocking-chair, her body bowed, and her wild, gray witch's tresses hanging about her shriveled yellow neck, the Queen of the Voodoos. . . . They said she was over one hundred years old, and there was nothing to cast doubt upon the statement. She had shrunken away from her skin; it was like a turtle's. Yet withal one could hardly help but see that the face, now so withered, had once been handsome and commanding. There was still a faint shadow of departed beauty on the forehead, the spark of an old fire in the sunken, glistening eyes, and a vestige of imperiousness in the fine, slightly acquiline nose, and even about her silent, woebegone mouth."

4

MALVINA LATOUR was a mulatto, *café au lait* in color, whose brother became a member of the notorious "black-and-tan" Legislature which misgoverned Louisiana for several years during reconstruction times. She was about thirty years old when she received the scepter of New Orleans Voodooism from the trembling hands of Marie Laveau, and is said to have been very handsome, with a fine, fully developed figure. Her favorite costume was a dress of blue calico with white dots, and on her head a brilliant orange-colored Madras handkerchief, tied into a *tignon*. Her magical powers appear to have been much inferior to those of Marie Laveau, although one of her sorcerous exploits certainly equaled anything that her predecessor had accomplished.

Soon after her accession to the throne a pious Negro clergyman, the Reverend Mr. Turner, who was chaplain of the Louisiana Legislature, became ill of a strange malady, which caused the symptoms of delirium tremens, although he was a teetotaler. Various physicians having failed to relieve him, the Reverend Mr. Turner concluded that he was the victim of a Voodoo charm, and upon the advice of Malvina Latour's brother sought the aid of the Voodoo queen. She directed that he be carried into a Negro church and laid upon a plain board table, and that the general public be invited to watch her drive out the evil spirit which possessed the preacher. At the appointed time the Voodoo queen began her work in the presence of a large crowd, which included Lieutenant Governor Oscar J. Dunn, a Negro. She first manipulated the preacher's hands, and then she rubbed his chest with a pungent oil, meanwhile chanting a Voodoo exorcism. This concluded, she stepped back, whereupon the Reverend Mr. Turner retched violently, his mouth opened, and out popped a black mouse, which uttered a few feeble squeaks, leaped to the floor, and scampered across the room, disappearing into a knothole. The preacher was cured.

In common with previous Voodoo queens, Malvina Latour made many changes in the ritual; she cast out the Catholic features which Marie Laveau had introduced, and so far as the annual festival of St. John's Eve was concerned, abolished the snakes which had always formed the basic element of Voodoo worship. Under her leadership the yearly celebrations continued to be, as they had been in Marie Laveau's time, more or less public spectacles, to which whites were admitted upon invitation or presentation of a police pass. A journalist under the escort of Chief of Police Zach Bachemin attended the meeting of the Voodoos on St. John's Eve in 1884 and described it for an old New Orleans guide-book. The rites were observed in a large two-room house on the shore of Lake Pontchartrain, about three-fourths of a mile below Milneburg:

"Seated on the floor with their legs crossed beneath them were about twenty-five Negro men and women, the men in their shirt sleeves, and the women with their heads adorned with the traditional head handkerchief or *tignon*. In the centre of the floor there was spread a small table-cloth, at the corners of which two tallow candles were placed, being held in position by a bed of their own grease. As a centre-piece, on the cloth, there was a shallow Indian basket filled with weeds, or, as they call them, *herbes*. Around the basket were diminutive piles of white beans and corn, and just outside of these a number of small bones, whether human or not could not be told. Some curiously wrought bunches of feathers were the next ornamentation near the edge of the cloth, and outside of all several saucers with small cakes in them.

"The only person enjoying the aristocratic privilege of a chair was a bright *café au lait* woman of about forty-eight, who sat in one corner of the room looking on the scene before her with an air of dignity. She said but little, but beside her two old and wrinkled Negresses whispered to her continually. She was of extremely handsome figure. . . . On inquiry it was learned that her name was Malvina Latour, and that she was the queen.

"As soon as the visitors had squatted down in their places against the wall an old Negro man, whose wool was white with years, began scraping on a two-stringed sort of fiddle. The instrument had a long neck, and its body was not more than three inches in diameter, being covered with a brightly mottled snake skin. This was the signal to two young mulatresses beside him, who commenced to beat with their thumbs on little drums made of gourds and covered with sheepskin. These tam-tams gave forth a short, hollow note of peculiar sound, and were fit accompaniments of the primitive fiddle. As if to inspire those present with the earnestness of the occasion, the old darky rolled his

278

eyes around the room and then, stamping his foot three times, exclaimed:

"'*A présent commencez!*'

"Rising and stepping out toward the middle of the floor a tall and sinewy Negro called the attention of all to him. He looked a Hercules, and his face was anything but attractive. Nervous with restrained emotion, he commenced at first in a low voice, which gradually became louder and louder, a song, one stanza of which ran as follows:

> Mallé couri dan déser,
> Mallé marché dan savane,
> Mallé marché su piquan doré,
> Mallé oir ça ya di moin!
>
> Sangé moin dan l'abitation ci la la?
> Mo gagnain soutchien la Louisiane,
> Mallé oir ça ya di moin!

"Which can be translated as follows:

> I will wander into the desert,
> I will march through the prairie,
> I will walk upon the golden thorn —
> Who is there who can stop me?
>
> To change me from this plantation?
> I have the support of Louisiana —
> Who is there who can resist me?

"As he sang he seemed to grow in stature and his eyes began to roll in a sort of wild frenzy. There was ferocity in every word, boldness and defiance in every gesture. Keeping time to his song the tam-tams and

279

fiddle gave a weird and savagely monotonous accompaniment that it was easy to believe was not unlike the savage music of Africa. When it became time for all to join in the refrain he waved his arms, and then from every throat went up:

"'Mallé oir ça ya di moin!'

"He had hardly ended the fourth stanza before two women, uttering a loud cry, joined their leader on the floor, and these three began a march around the room. As the song progressed, an emaciated young Negro stepped out, and, amid the shouts of all, fell in behind the others. This last addition to the wild dancers was the most affected of all, and in a sort of wild delirium he picked up two of the candles and marched on with them in his hand. When he arrived opposite the queen she gave him something to drink out of a bottle. After swallowing some he retained a mouthful which, with a peculiar blowing sound, he spurted in a mist from his lips, holding the candle so as to catch the vapor. As it was alcohol it blazed up, and this attempt at necromancy was hailed with a shout.

"Then commenced the regular Voudou dance with all its twistings and contortions. Two of the women fell exhausted to the floor in a frenzy and frothing at the mouth, and the emaciated young man was carried out of the room unconscious."

Malvina Latour was the ostensible head of Voodooism in New Orleans for almost twenty years, but she lacked the power and compelling personality of Marie Laveau, and during her reign the organization of the cult began to disintegrate. Rival queens appeared and formed their own congregations, and the rightful queen's magic could not prevail against them. Also, the Voodoo doctors began to assume the duties and privileges of priests of the sect and likewise formed Voodoo groups, over which they presided at ceremonies which usually culminated in sexual orgies. One of the first insurgents was Doctor James Alexander, a tall, slim mulatto from Mississippi, who boasted that he had been born " with a caul and a gift from God in his hands." Doctor Alexander maintained an office in Orleans Street, and associated with him were Doctor Sol, otherwise Solomon Hastings, and a Negress, Annie Gould, who lived on Monroe Street near Royal and sold Voodoo charms by mail. When the police finally raided her home, in 1894, they found a score of human and dog skulls, and innumerable jars filled with dried snakes, lizards, frogs, and horned toads. Doctor Alexander's principal confederate in fleecing the gullible and superstitious, however, was a white woman, Lou Jackson, who operated an assignation house in Roman Street. He used her premises for the orgies which were staged frequently under his direction in the name of Voodoo, and if additional women were required Lou Jackson provided them. Neighbors often complained of the noise made at these gatherings, and at length, on May 28, 1889, Captain Donnelly and eight policemen of the Fifth Precinct forced their way into the house. In a large upstairs room they found ten Negro men, half-naked, lying on the floor, while fifteen white women, similarly undressed, sat on chairs ranged in a circle about them. In the center of the group was Doctor Alexander, prancing and shouting, and clad simply in a blue sash and a pair of knee-length drawers made of silk netting, with a large mesh. Said the *Times-Democrat*:

" The police were not prepared for so immoral a show, and for a few minutes could only look on in listless apathy. Recovering their self-possession, the officers quickly set about to perform their duty, and in a twinkling the men and women were being carted off to the station for safe-keeping."

Among the prisoners were two seventeen-year-old girls, one of whom was accompanied by her mother. All of the celebrants were arraigned in Recorder's Court next day and found guilty of disorderly conduct. Doctor Alexander and Lou Jackson were each fined twenty-five dollars, and each of the others two dollars and a half.

By the time Malvina Latour retired as queen of the Voodoos, about 1890, the word itself had been corrupted by the Negroes into "hoodoo," and the cult had split into a score of small groups, each with its own titular head and its own ritual and ceremonial forms. In recent years little has been heard of Voodooism in New Orleans, although occasionally the newspapers record the activities of bands of Negroes who call themselves Voodoos and celebrate various bastard versions of the old worship until they are stopped by the police. But enormous quantities of charms, amulets, and magical powders are still sold by charlatans both white and black, while many of the Negro drug-stores in New Orleans dispose of more goods of this sort than of legitimate medicines. In greatest demand are the love-potions, and various powders which are guaranteed to charm an employer into granting a raise, more time off, or some specific favor. One of the recent victims of these concoctions was Lyle Saxon, the Louisiana historian. A few years ago Mr. Saxon contemplated a trip to New York, and aroused considerable consternation in his household by announcing that he was going alone. He persisted in this attitude despite the pleadings of his house-boy to be taken along. Next morning, and every day thereafter for a week, Mr. Saxon remarked that every liquid served him, from soup to coffee, was bitter and unpalatable. He consulted a physician, who could find nothing wrong, although Mr. Saxon described certain distressing physical manifestations which he was convinced were sapping his vitality. At length Mr. Saxon called his house-boy on the carpet. After long questioning the servant admitted that he had been giving his employer daily a large dose of Boss-Fix powders, by which he hoped to hoodoo Mr. Saxon into taking him to New York. And the Boss-Fix powders, an examination showed, were about ninety per cent Epsom salts.

CHAPTER X

"AN EPOCH OF DEGENERATION"

FOR MORE than a quarter of a century after the Louisiana Purchase politics in New Orleans were probably on a higher plane than ever before or since in any city in the United States. During most of that period the Creoles still formed a majority of the population, and the Creole leaders as a rule were cultured men of dignity and integrity; their interest lay not in personal aggrandizement or petty partisan advantage, but in the welfare of the city and the state. Political campaigns were conducted with decorum and restraint; candidates ran for office on their records, or their standing in the business and professional life of the community, and not on meaningless platforms built of platitudes and demagogic promises. "A primary of the party elected delegates," wrote Kendall, " and the nominations were made at a party convention in due course — the convention having no committees on resolutions, nor much of one on credentials, since it was looked upon as an offensive insinuation to examine the right of a delegate to sit when he presented himself, and such insults could be wiped out, according to the code of the day, only in blood. After nomination there was little electioneering, as we understand the word. To canvass for votes was looked on as betokening a lack of modesty." [1] There was scant excitement in the elections of those days, but there was a great deal of honesty.

---

[1] *History of New Orleans*, by John Smith Kendall, A.M., three volumes; New York and Chicago, 1922; Volume I, page 205.

All of these virtues vanished with the coming of the American politician, then as now the curse and disgrace of the country. Louisiana had scarcely been ceded to the United States before these gentry began to infest the body politic of New Orleans and the territory with discord and corruption, manipulating the antagonism between the Creoles and the Americans — and, incidentally, keeping it alive as far as possible — to further their own schemes. By 1836 they had grown sufficiently powerful to wrest the control of New Orleans from the natives, and to force through the Louisiana Legislature a new city charter which foisted upon New Orleans one of the most curious experiments in the history of American municipal government. This charter divided the city into three sections, each with distinct municipal powers and separate corporate rights, and each governed by a recorder and a council, so that New Orleans was no longer one city, but three, although united in theory under a mayor and a general council. But the mayor was little more than a figurehead, most of the powers which formerly appertained to the office having been transferred to the recorders. The general council was composed of all the other councils sitting together, and met once a year, though it could be convened oftener at the call of the mayor. Except on police matters, and on a few unimportant points of administration, its enactments became effective only when approved by the councils of the three municipalities. It could impose a few taxes, but otherwise possessed no financial powers, and could make no appropriations. The Legislature in 1840 passed laws which somewhat increased the power of the mayor and made the general council an elective body of four members from each municipality, but the three divisions of the city maintained their separate corporate identities, and the municipal waste and confusion continued, until 1852, when the Legislature provided a new charter which consolidated the city under a mayor and a common council com-

posed of a board of aldermen and a board of assistant aldermen. This charter recognized Municipality No. Two, the
new quarter above Canal Street, as the dominant section,
and virtually completed the political rout of the Creoles.
The seat of the municipal government was removed from
the historic Cabildo to a new City Hall on Lafayette Square,
and many business firms transferred their activities to St.
Charles Street, and Camp, Carondelet, and Bacchus (Baronne) Streets, the principal thoroughfares of the American
section. The banks, prevented by their charters from leaving the French Quarter, established branches above Canal
Street.

The cumbersome and unworkable three-city form of
government, which plagued New Orleans for sixteen years
and retarded the progress of the city in almost every particular, offered extraordinary opportunities for political
trading and skullduggery, all of which were lovingly embraced by the politicians. As Kendall says, so far as politics
were concerned, " the period from 1840 to 1860 was an
epoch of steady but unadmitted degeneration."[1] It was during these twenty years that political machines succeeded in
establishing a spoils system by which patronage was controlled and the finances of the city exploited; and so gained
the foothold which enabled them to transform the municipal
government into a welter of graft, inefficiency, corruption,
and demagoguery. In short, political practice in New Orleans was thoroughly Americanized and soon became indis-
tinguishable from that of any other machine-dominated city.
On March 15, 1854 the New Orleans *Bee* put into words
what many honest citizens had known for years — that
New Orleans was ruled by " the despotism of faction," and
that " fair and equitable principles, sound policy, equal justice, and the rights of the minority have been ruthlessly sacrificed to the domination of a clique, which has seized upon

---

[1] Ibid., page 204.

and maintained power through the hateful employment of means so flagitious and corrupting as to have rendered us a hissing and a scorn in the eyes of the upright, well-organized communities." In a summary of the political situation ten days later the same newspaper declared that New Orleans was miserably governed; that party legislation alone prevailed; that the custom of awarding tax collection and other municipal services on contract was "a source of vile depravity and corruption"; that efforts "to banish elections from groggeries and barrooms are systematically flouted and derided"; and that the city had been irreparably injured by "the improvidence, recklessness, prodigality, inexperience and ignorance of the Council."

That combination of chicanery and terrorization euphemistically called "practical politics" was introduced into New Orleans at the elections of 1842 and 1844 by two of the city's most distinguished citizens — Judah P. Benjamin, later a United States Senator and a member of Jefferson Davis's Cabinet, and John M. Slidell, Benjamin's colleague in the Senate and likewise a prominent figure in the councils of the Confederacy. Benjamin was one of the principal leaders of the Whigs during the campaign of 1842, and was popularly believed to have devised a shrewd circumvention of the property clause of the state Constitution, by which the city was carried for his party. Under that clause only property-owners could qualify as voters, but Benjamin successfully maintained that ownership of a cab or carriage was sufficient, and that it could be proved by presentation of a license tax receipt. On election day these receipts were distributed by the hundreds to men who ordinarily could not have voted, and they obediently cast their ballots for the Whig ticket. Slidell originated the so-called "Plaquemine Frauds" in 1844. The chaotic election laws of the 1840's provided for no registration of voters and permitted a citizen to cast his ballot at any polling-place in the county, or

parish, in which he claimed residence. Also, a winning candidate was the one who won the greatest number of precincts,
and not necessarily the one who received the largest popular
vote. The Whigs controlled the election machinery of New
Orleans, and it was accepted as beyond question that they
would carry the city. So Slidell and his associates concentrated their energies upon the remainder of Orleans Parish,
which then included all of the present Plaquemine Parish, as
well as large areas which now form parts of other parishes.
Soon after dawn on election day several steamboats loaded
with Democrats left the New Orleans wharves and steamed
up and down the river, depositing their cargoes wherever
Democratic votes were needed. Slidell's machine thus carried enough rural precincts to overcome the heavy voting of
the Whigs in the city. A storm of protest arose from Whigs
all over the United States, but the victory was confirmed
by the state election officials, and Louisiana's electoral vote
was cast for James K. Polk and George M. Dallas, the
Democratic national ticket, while the party gained control
of the state government and retained it until the Civil War
threw Louisiana into the hands of the carpetbaggers.

Four years after Slidell's coup, in 1848, the politicians
began to use newly-arrived immigrants, especially the Irish,
as repeaters, and in other forms of illegal voting. The first
organized system of ruffianism at the polls also appeared in
1848, when the Democratic machine imported Chris Lillie,
a New York pugilist and a henchman of Captain Isaiah
Rynders, a notorious Tammany Hall leader. Lillie organized gangs of bullies, and under his competent direction they
managed the repeaters, attempted to intimidate reputable
voters, and otherwise installed Tammany election methods.
Thereafter until comparatively recent years almost every
political campaign in New Orleans was marked by rowdyism
and violence, and an independent or opposition voter who
attempted to register his preference at the polls was engag-

ing in a dangerous business. He could expect no aid from the police, for they not only failed to restrain the hoodlums, but often assisted in their acts of terrorization. The pestilential weight of the politician lay heavily upon the police department, not only " during the epoch of degeneration," but for many years afterwards; it was almost half a century after the consolidating charter of 1852 before an honest and efficient force finally emerged from the municipal chaos. The merit system had no place in a city ruled by corrupt machines; before the Civil War practically the entire personnel of the department changed with each new administration, and every policeman owed his appointment, and gave his allegiance, to a politician. And any effective organization was further prevented by the new city charters, and amendments to charters, which poured from the legislative hopper in quick succession, and which shuttled the supervision of the police back and forth between the mayor and various boards, although actual control was never relinquished by the politicians. As early as 1854, two years after the consolidation of the three municipalities, the New Orleans *Bee,* on March 22, declared that the police had already become " a source of universal and well-founded complaint," and described the force as " a mighty and odious despotism, which has been foisted upon the community . . . a powerful, well-disciplined and unscrupulous electioneering machine, employed by a skillful and reckless management to influence doubtful contests."

The crucifixion of honesty and self-respect upon the twin crosses of greedy partisanship and political hatred resulted in the demoralization of not only the police department, but virtually every other branch of the municipal government. And sometimes the confusion into which the affairs of the city had been thrown, and the waste and inefficiency with which they were conducted, had dreadful consequences. The politicians and negligent officials cannot be blamed for the fact that yellow fever invaded New Orleans in epidemics thirty-nine times between 1796 and 1906, when the disease was finally conquered, for preventive measures were then unknown to medical science. But they were certainly responsible for the conditions which permitted some of the earlier epidemics to reach such appalling proportions and which caused the city to be known throughout the world as a plague-spot. Until long after the Civil War New Orleans was unquestionably the dirtiest and unhealthiest city on the North American continent — the death-rate, even with epidemical fatalities deducted, was almost double that of New York, Boston, or even Philadelphia — and the municipal authorities consistently defeated every attempt to make it otherwise. The water supply was bad, swamps remained within the city limits, and the sanitary arrangements were unbelievably primitive. The sewerage system consisted simply of open gutters between the sidewalks and the streets. Into them filth and refuse of every description were emptied, and when they overflowed, as they frequently did in the rainy seasons, the streets became well-nigh impassable. In 1850 the General Council, sodden with politics, even rejected a plan for the daily flushing of the gutters, despite many petitions and complaints that they presented a " most disgusting aspect." As late as the early 1860's the newspapers frequently published articles pointing out that the gutters were filled with foul and stagnant water, that the scavengers neglected their duties, and that weeds grew in lush profusion along the margins of the principal streets. And not until 1880, when New Orleans had a population of more than two hundred thousand, was the first underground sewer constructed — a private main from the St. Charles Hotel to the Mississippi River. A few months later another was laid by the D. H. Holmes Company, operators of a department store, to which a few other business establishments were connected. But nothing further was done until 1892, when the city made a contract with the New Orleans Drainage & Sewerage Corporation for the installation of five miles of mains — intended to answer the needs of a city which by that time had almost two hundred and fifty thousand inhabitants.

The two most disastrous visitations of disease in the history of New Orleans — the combined cholera and yellow-fever epidemic of 1832–3 and the yellow-fever epidemic of 1853 — occurred while these conditions were at their worst. In 1832 the fever had already been raging for six weeks, causing an exodus which reduced the population from almost 80,000 to about 35,000, when the first cases of cholera were discovered on October 25. The epidemic continued in full force for fifteen days before subsiding, and in that time 6,000 deaths were reported. It was believed that at least another thousand perished of whom no record was made. The cholera reappeared in June 1833, and the yellow fever in September, and 4,000 persons died before the first of November, so that in less than twelve months the two diseases had caused the deaths of at least 10,000 persons, about one-third of those who had remained in the city. Some of the terrible scenes enacted in 1832 were described by the Reverend Theodore Clapp, a Presbyterian clergyman who witnessed twenty such epidemics during a residence in New Orleans of thirty-five years:

" On the evening of the 27th of October, it [the cholera] had made its way through every part of the city. During the ten succeeding days, reckoning from October 27th to the 6th of November, all the physicians judged that, at the lowest computation, there were five thousand deaths — an average of five hundred every day. Many died of whom no account was rendered. A great number of bodies, with bricks and stones tied to the feet, were thrown into the river. Many were privately interred in gardens and enclosures, on the

291

grounds where they expired, whose names were not recorded in the bills of mortality. Often I was kept in the burrying ground for hours in succession, by the incessant, unintermitting arrival of corpses, over whom I was requested to perform a short service. One day, I did not leave the cemetery until nine o'clock at night; the last interments were made by candle light. . . . I found at the graveyard a large pile of corpses without coffins, in horizontal layers, one above the other, like corded wood. I was told that there were more than one hundred bodies deposited there. They had been brought by unknown persons, at different hours since nine o'clock the evening previous. Large trenches were dug, into which these uncoffined corpses were thrown indiscriminately. The same day, a private hospital was found deserted; the physicians, nurses and attendants were all dead, or had run away. Not a living person was in it. The wards were filled with putrid bodies, which, by order of the Mayor, were piled in an adjacent yard, and burned, and their ashes scattered to the winds. Could a wiser disposition have been made of them?

" Many persons, even of fortune and popularity, died in their beds without aid, unnoticed and unknown, and lay there for days unburied. In almost every house might be seen the sick, the dying, and the dead, in the same room. All the stores, banks, and places of business were closed. There were no means, no instruments for carrying on the ordinary affairs of business; for all the drays, carts, carriages, hand and common wheelbarrows, as well as hearses, were employed in the transportation of corpses, instead of cotton, sugar and passengers. . . . I went, one Wednesday night, to solemnize the contract of marriage between a couple of very genteel appearance. The bride was young and possessed of the most extraordinary beauty. A few hours only had elapsed before I was summoned to perform the last offices over her coffin. . . . One family, of nine persons, supped together in perfect health; at the expiration of the next twenty-four hours, eight of the nine were dead. . . . Persons were found dead all along the streets, particularly early in the mornings. . . .

"Nature seemed to sympathize in the dreadful spectacle of human woe. A thick, dark atmosphere . . . hung over us like a mighty funereal shroud. All was still. Neither sun, nor moon, nor stars shed their blessed light. Not a breath of air moved. A hunter, who lived on the Bayou St. John, assured me that during the cholera he killed no game. Not a bird was seen winging the sky. Artificial causes of terror were superadded to the gloom which covered the heavens. The burning of tar and pitch at every corner; the firing of cannon, by order of the city authorities, along all the streets; and the frequent conflagrations which actually occurred at that dreadful period — all these conspired to add a sublimity and horror to the tremendous scene. Our wise men hoped, by the combustion of tar and gunpowder, to purify the atmosphere. . . .

"The cholera had been raging with unabated fury for fourteen days. It seemed as if the city was destined to be emptied of its inhabitants. During this time, as before stated, a thick, dark, sultry atmosphere filled our city. Everyone complained of a difficulty in breathing, which he never before experienced. The heavens were as stagnant as the mantled pool of death. There were no breezes. At the close of the fourteenth day, about eight o'clock in the evening, a smart storm, something like a tornado, came from the northwest, accompanied with heavy peals of thunder and terrific lightnings. The deadly air was displaced immediately, by that which was new, fresh, salubrious, and life-giving. The next

293

morning shone forth all bright and beautiful. The plague was stayed. In the opinion of all the medical gentlemen who were on the spot, that change of weather terminated the epidemic. At any rate, it took its departure from us that very hour. No new cases occurred after that storm. . . .[1]

During the epidemic of 1853 prominent physicians estimated that the total number of cases of yellow fever exceeded 40,000. From the first of July to the early part of November 10,300 deaths were reported, and of these 8,000 were from fever. Dr. Clapp recorded that in one period of twelve hours the burials were more than three hundred, and tells of a large boarding-house from which forty-five corpses were removed in thirteen days. The city scavengers with their carts went daily from house to house, asking if there were any to be buried; the dead were piled in the wagons and hauled away like so much cordwood. Long rows of coffins were laid in shallow trenches and hastily covered with a few shovelfuls of earth, which the daily rains soon washed away. "The details of the city reeking with filth," wrote Kendall, "the bodies of vagrant dogs poisoned after the summer custom of the city authorities, putrifying in the streets; the corpses of human beings abandoned unburied in the cemeteries; the futile firing of cannon and burning of tar-barrels in the hope of 'purifying the air,' add horror to the picture of the desolate city."[2]

2

POLITICAL tactics similar to those which had been introduced by Chris Lillie in 1848 were used to a very large extent at the municipal election of 1854, when New Orleans' first

[1] *Autobiographical Sketches and Recollections during a Thirty-five Years' Residence in New Orleans*, by Theodore Clapp; Boston, 1857.
[2] *History of New Orleans*, Volume I, p. 178.

reform movement combined with the Whigs in a determined but only partially successful effort to rescue the city from the clutches of the Democrats; and again in 1856, when the Native American or Know-Nothing Party, which probably engendered more discord and hatred than any other political development in the history of the United States, succeeded in electing the Mayor and several other important city officials. In 1854 a policeman named Mochlin was stabbed to death while leading a gang of rowdies in an attack upon reform leaders at one of the polling-places; and on the same day Steve O'Leary, Chief of Police, was shot while trying to eject from the Seventh Precinct several reformers who had come to investigate a report that 1,400 ballots had been tabulated for the Democratic candidates, although the total voting strength of the precinct was only 932. In 1856 polling-places in various parts of the city were seized by bands of armed men, Know-Nothing adherents, who permitted only voters of the proper political complexion to enter and cast their ballots. As the *True Delta* said on June 3, 1856, the election was "disgraced by violence and bloodshed"; at almost every precinct there occurred fighting and rioting, in which at least two men were killed and a score wounded. Even more serious trouble was averted when Mayor John L. Lewis issued a proclamation requesting all good citizens to hasten to City Hall and be sworn in as special policemen. Only twenty responded, but they were armed and sent to the points where the greatest danger threatened. The police were worse than useless to the Democrats on this occasion, because of an order, mistakenly issued by Mayor Lewis in the hope of reducing the probability of disorder, which compelled them to go unarmed on election day. Many members of the force resigned, and those who remained, bereft of their clubs and pistols, were unable properly to serve their political masters.

Most of the outrages committed by the Native Americans during the "epoch of degeneration" were directed against aliens and citizens of foreign birth, as one of the principal points in the credo of Know-Nothingism [1] was unalterable opposition to the absorption of foreigners into the American body politic. This fact was seldom mentioned in the New Orleans newspapers, but Governor Robert C. Wickliffe brought it into the open in 1857, when in his annual message to the Legislature he declared that " at the two last general elections many of the streets and approaches to the polls were completely in the hands of organized ruffians, who committed acts of violence upon multitudes of our naturalized citizens who dared to venture to exercise the right of suffrage." At the suggestion of Governor Wickliffe and other leaders, the Legislature passed a law which created the post of Inspector of Elections for the Parish of New Orleans. This official was especially required to supervise all elections in the city and " to prevent and suppress riots, tumults, violence, disorder and other practices tending to the intimidation of voters or disturbances in the elections." Judge John B. Cotton, who in reconstruction times became affiliated with the carpet-baggers, was appointed to the office. He carried on the work with great energy, but in the face of many obstacles. He received little or no co-operation from the city authorities or the police and was frequently threatened by fanatical Native Americans when he advocated measures which promised to interfere with their curious methods of winning a political contest. Once a mob formed to attack and burn his home, and the rioters dispersed only when they learned that Judge Cotton was prepared for them — he had sent away his family, barricaded the doors and windows, and garrisoned the house with a score of friends,

---

[1] So called because members of the order replied to all questions: " I know nothing in our principles contrary to the Constitution." The Know-Nothings were also violently opposed to the Catholic Church, but this feature of their platform was officially pretermitted in Louisiana, where about one-half of the voters were communicants of Rome.

all heavily armed. Despite all these handicaps, Judge Cotton succeeded in correcting a few of the more glaring abuses, although most of them remained for many years as accepted features of New Orleans elections.

They were still very much in evidence during the municipal campaign of 1858. Mayor Charles M. Waterman, who had been elected by the Native Americans in 1856, had quarreled with his party leaders, and refused to accept a renomination; and Recorder Gerard Stith, who in private life was foreman of the *Picayune* composing-room, became the candidate of the Know-Nothings. For reasons which were never clear, the Democrats took no active part in the contest. Nor did the Whigs make any nominations as a party; instead, they joined an independent reform movement which put forward a ticket headed by Major P. G. T. Beauregard, later a Major-General of the Confederate Army, as their candidate for Mayor. A Creole with a record of distinguished military service, and one of New Orleans' most influential citizens, Major Beauregard was probably the strongest candidate the independents could have chosen. It was admitted that he would receive a large vote by reason of his personal popularity alone, and the Native American politicians immediately took steps to prevent the independents from utilizing his natural strength. Know-Nothing ruffians intensified the campaign of terrorization which they had carried on throughout the two years in which the party was in power; while the police attended all independent meetings and took the names of those present, after which pressure was applied to induce them to change their political allegiance. The climax of Know-Nothing preparation came on June 1, 1858, when a gang of rowdies invaded the office of the Registrar of Voters and seized the registration lists. With no interference from the Registrar or the police, they kept the rolls for several days, meanwhile busily striking from them the names of voters who were known to be either

Whigs or independents. The Democrats, apparently, were not eliminated from the lists, a fact which caused many citizens to believe that the Democratic leaders and the Native Americans had reached an agreement.

The stage was thus set for a typical New Orleans election, replete with violence and bloodshed; that the performance was not given as arranged was due largely to the threat of the Vigilance Committee. The avowed purpose of this organization was to insure an honest, peaceable election and to rid New Orleans of the thugs and ruffians who had inaugurated what the *True Delta* almost a year before had described as a " reign of terror." Actually, however, the movement appears to have been a protest against the excesses of the Native Americans, a conclusion which is strengthened by the fact that a majority of the Vigilantes were Creoles and citizens of foreign birth. The formation of the Vigilance Committee was begun about March 1858, when headquarters were established in the University Building at Common and Baronne Streets, with a branch in Dryades Street. But so secretly was the work carried on that although more than a thousand men were connected with the movement in one way or another, New Orleans generally was unaware of its existence until the morning of June 3, four days before the municipal election, when the city awoke to find a large section of the French Quarter occupied by armed Vigilantes. Even then the details of the committee's organization remained mysteries. The only Vigilante leader whose name became known to the public during the five days of the uprising was Captain Johnson Kelly Duncan, a former officer of the United States Army, and a comparative new-comer to New Orleans, who had displayed no interest in municipal affairs until he suddenly appeared in the field as commander of the Vigilance Committee's armed forces.[1]

---

[1] Captain Duncan was a Pennsylvanian and a West Pointer. He resigned from the Army in January 1855, after active service in the Seminole War and

The spark which set off the Vigilante fireworks was the seizure of the registration lists by Native American rowdies. Captain Duncan and other leaders of the movement held a meeting at the University Building after it had become apparent that the city authorities intended to take no action against the perpetrators of this flagrant offense, and decided that it was time to strike if the objectives of the committee were ever to be obtained. A call was sent to all members who were subject to military service, and about midnight on the night of June 2 Captain Duncan led several hundred men into the Vieux Carré, where they took possession of the Cabildo on Jackson Square, the city lock-up, and the State Arsenal on St. Peter Street, in the rear of the Cabildo. The muskets and small arms found in the arsenal, together with large supplies of ammunition, were distributed among the Vigilantes; several pieces of artillery were wheeled into the square and set up to command the approaches to the Cabildo, and sentries were posted in Royal, Chartres, and other streets leading into that part of the city. The Vigilantes who were not on duty were quartered in the rooms of the Sixth District and Recorder's Courts in the Cabildo, and in the lock-up. Captain Duncan established his general headquarters in the Arsenal. Next morning notices appeared in several of the newspapers informing the people of New Orleans that the Vigilantes, " having resolved to free our city from the murderers who infest it . . . have assumed its temporary government." The notices further called upon " all good men and true " to join the movement, and promised that the Vigilance Committee would inflict " prompt and exemplary punishment upon well-known and notorious offenders and violators of the rights and privileges of citizens." At the same time an unsigned pronunciamento ad-

garrison duty at several posts, to accept the civilian post of Superintendent of Repairs in New Orleans, in charge of the Mint, the Marine Hospital, the Quarantine Warehouse, and the Pas à l'Outre Boarding Station.

dressed " To The Citizens of New Orleans " appeared in public places throughout the city:

" After years of disorder, outrage, and unchecked assassination, the people, unable and unwilling either to bow down in unresisting submission to a set of ruffians, or to abandon the city in which their business, their social sympathies, and their affections cluster, have at length risen in their might — have quietly taken possession of the arsenal and buildings at Jackson Square, and have established here the headquarters of a Vigilance Committee; pledging each to the other to maintain the rights unviolable of every peaceful and law-abiding citizen, restore public order, abate crime, and expel or punish, as the law may determine, such notorious robbers and assassins as the arm of the law has, either from the infidelity of its public servants, or the inefficiency of the laws themselves, left unwhipped of justice.

" For the present the ordinary machinery of police justice is suspended — the mayor and the recorders, we understand, yielding up the power they confess the inability to exercise for the preservation of public peace, and the preservation of property; and the Vigilance Committee will therefore provisionally act in their stead, administering to each and every malefactor the punishment due his crimes, without heat, prejudice or political bias. All citizens who have sympathies with this movement, and who think the time has come when New Orleans shall be preserved like all other well-ordered and civilized communities, will report themselves without delay at the Principal,[1] where the character of the movement will be explained, and the determination of the people more fully made known. All has been done noiselessly thus far; all will continue noise-

---

[1] The Cabildo was sometimes called the Principal.

lessly, dispassionately, and justly, but the ruffians who have dyed our streets in the gore of inoffending citizens, and spread terror among the peaceable, orderly and well-disposed, must leave or perish. So the people have determined — Vox Populi, vox Dei."

The intimation that the Mayor and the Recorders had yielded up their powers was not based on fact, but it might as well have been true, for the city authorities met the challenge of the Vigilance Committee with the vacillation, timidity, and fear of political consequences which have always been characteristic of American municipal governments when confronted by emergencies. Mayor Waterman was notified of the occupation of Jackson Square at five o'clock on the morning of June 3. He immediately summoned Major-General John L. Lewis, in command of the first division of the Louisiana militia, to City Hall for a conference, and ordered the Common Council to meet in special session at ten o'clock. At this meeting the Council seriously considered an extraordinary proposal to arm the Know-Nothing mob which was already clamoring at the doors of City Hall and dispatch it against the Vigilantes in Jackson Square. When Mayor Waterman declined to issue a proclamation which would have meant immediate bloodshed and would have turned over to armed rioters all that part of the city not in the hands of the Vigilance Committee, the Council adopted a resolution demanding his resignation. The Mayor refused to resign, whereupon the Council withdrew its resolution and adopted another giving him discretionary powers, thus throwing the emergency squarely into his lap. Then the statesmen adjourned, confident that they had offended no one, and that all of their political fences were still standing. None of the plans made then or thereafter by the city authorities comprehended the employment of the regular police; the force seems to have quietly disintegrated at the first sign of trouble. The policemen disappeared from the streets, and no mention of them appears until the last day of the Vigilante uprising, when they were ordered to report for duty.

While the Common Council was adding to the confu, sion, the Vigilantes were consolidating and fortifying their position. The line of sentinels was moved forward to Canal Street, and, using cotton bales and paving stones, the troops of the Vigilance Committee erected barricades in Royal and Chartres Streets, the principal thoroughfares leading into the French Quarter. Also, their numbers increased during the day; when Mayor Waterman, accompanied by General Lewis and William Freret, who had been Mayor from 1840 to 1844, went to Jackson Square on the afternoon of June 3 for a consultation with Captain Duncan, the latter had under his command between eight hundred and a thousand well-armed and well-equipped men. Many of the officers were veterans of William Walker's campaigns in Nicaragua. Mayor Waterman ordered Captain Duncan to disband his army and evacuate the Cabildo, the Arsenal, and the lock-up. The Vigilante leader refused to obey unless his men were sworn in as a special police force to serve during the election, but the Mayor said that he had not been authorized by the Council to make such appointments. He therefore returned to City Hall, and the mob there received with shouts of approval the announcement that he had rejected Captain Duncan's demands and defied the Vigilance Committee. After a conference with his advisers, Mayor Waterman decided to call out the militia and officially commanded General Lewis " to co-operate with the civil authorities in maintaining law and order," and declared that " a lawless mob has invaded the property of the city of New Orleans, and taken into their possession the State Arsenal, and military arms and munitions belonging to said city and State of Louisiana." General Lewis immediately notified the commanding officers of the First Brigade and the Louisiana Legion to muster their men for active service. The Mayor then issued warrants for the arrest of Captain Duncan and his associates, and the papers were solemnly served by the Chief of Police, Colonel Henry Forno, at the Arsenal. But since none of the Vigilantes would submit to arrest, Colonel Forno was compelled to return to City Hall without his prisoners.

The crowd which seethed in Lafayette Square now numbered several thousand men, who were vociferously demanding an immediate assault upon the stronghold of the Vigilance Committee. Mayor Waterman was finally prevailed upon to sign an order upon a large hardware and sporting-goods store for weapons, and the mob rushed to that establishment, where clerks handed out firearms and ammunition to all comers until the supply was exhausted. Instead of marching upon Jackson Square, however, the great throng of restless men returned to Lafayette Square, firing their weapons into the air and dragging with them several pieces of artillery which they had taken from the quarters of one of the militia companies. The guns were set up to command St. Charles Avenue and Camp Street. When dusk fell, the leaders of the mob posted sentinels along Canal Street, and throughout the night the picket lines of the opposing factions faced each other across that famous thoroughfare. Fortunately nothing occurred to start the fighting.

On Friday the 4th of June Mayor Waterman conferred with General Lewis at eight o'clock in the morning, and was informed that fewer than a hundred and fifty militiamen had responded to the call. General Lewis expressed the opinion that it would be impossible to enlist a force strong enough to dislodge the Vigilantes from Jackson Square. The Mayor thereupon determined to seek a compromise with the Vigilante Committee as the only way in which a conflict could be avoided, and at 9.30 o'clock went to the State Arsenal with General Lewis and two prominent citizens, C. Fellowes and

M. O. H. Norton. They remained in consultation with Captain Duncan for several hours, and early in the afternoon reached an agreement by which the city virtually accepted the demands of the Vigilance Committee. It was signed by the Mayor for the city; by General Lewis as Inspector of Elections, to which office he had succeeded Judge Cotton; by Fellowes and Norton " on the part of the Citizens "; and by Captain Duncan as President of the Executive Vigilance Committee:

NOTICE TO THE PEOPLE AND CITIZENS OF NEW ORLEANS

Office Executive Vigilance Committee
Arsenal, June 4, 1858

The Vigilance Committee, which had thoroughly organized itself, and which had temporarily seized and taken possession of the State Arsenal, and the Municipal Court and Jail, having organized with a view of freeing the city of New Orleans of the well-known and notorious " thugs," outlaws, assassins and murderers who infest it, and which Vigilance Committee organized for three months with these objects in view, hereby solemnly agree to and with the Chief City Magistrate, Mayor Waterman, and the Superintendent of Elections, Gen. Lewis, to disband the same, and immediately reorganize the same body under their legal sanction, viz: freeing the city of thugs, outlaws, assassins and murderers. The conditions of this agreement are:

1. That before disbanding we shall all have been first sworn in, under our present organization, as special election policemen under General Lewis, to act under his authority on the day of election. Our duties as special city police will be to bring up for trial, under affidavits, the notorious offenders against the law that it

was intended originally to proceed against, and free the city of, in our capacity of Vigilance Committee.

2. We are authorized to remain in a body, as at present composed and organized, and are to remain in quiet possession of our present position, in the Arsenal, until we have been truly sworn in as special police of Mayor Waterman and by General Lewis. As soon thereafter as is practicable, we will occupy such other position as is selected by us as more to our own and the public convenience, and under the legal sanction of the Mayor and Superintendent of Elections, all our future acts, so long as acting in the capacity of special city and election police, which shall not be for a less period than five days.

3. It is further understood by the parties hereto that the City shall be subject to no expense for the pay or support of said organization.

The huge crowd assembled in Lafayette Square greeted Mayor Waterman's announcement of the agreement with yells of anger and derision, and threatened him when, from the steps of City Hall, he urged " all citizens peaceably inclined " to return to their homes. After milling uncertainly about the square for half an hour or so after the Mayor had retired to his office, a large portion of the mob, numbering about three hundred men, started down St. Charles Avenue toward the Vieux Carré, with the avowed intention of driving the Vigilantes from Jackson Square. At Canal Street someone, probably a Vigilante sentry, fired a shot from the sidewalk, which wounded a man in the cheek and abruptly halted the advance. During the momentary lull, Recorder L. Adams, who had previously tried to stop the mad rush down St. Charles Avenue, loudly ordered the crowd to disperse and abandon the proposed assault. About half of the rioters obeyed the command and returned to

Lafayette Square, but the remainder of the mob marched down Royal Street in more or less orderly formation. When they came in sight of the barricades, behind which crouched armed Vigilantes supported by artillery, the rioters broke and fled through St. Louis Street to Chartres Street. Finding that thoroughfare similarly fortified, the mob retreated pell-mell to Canal Street, where many of its members narrowly escaped death at the hands of their comrades, for Native American patrols were about to fire when the identity of the fleeing men was discovered. At Lafayette Square Recorder Adams succeeded in disarming most of the mob and stored the weapons in City Hall. The only fatalities of the afternoon occurred in Jackson Square, where one man was killed and another wounded by the premature discharge of a cannon with which the Vigilantes were preparing to repel the threatened assault.

While the mob from Lafayette Square was charging into and out of the French Quarter, Mayor Waterman was in conference with a committee of fifteen citizens, headed by R. N. Ogden and Edward MacPherson, who proposed to wait upon Captain Duncan and attempt to effect a compromise which would restore control of the city to the constituted authorities. This compromise the committee had set forth in resolutions containing seven sections. Briefly, it provided for the closing of all drinking-places until after the election; the dismissal of the regular policemen (if they could be found), and the surrender of their arms; the disbanding of the Vigilance Committee and the evacuation of city and state property; and the appointment, by the Mayor and a committee of citizens, of a new police force of a thousand men for duty on election day and for police service thereafter. The Mayor expressed approval of this plan; nevertheless, as soon as the conference had adjourned he went to Jackson Square with his principal adviser, C. Fellowes, and proceeded to swear in the Vigilantes according to

306

the agreement previously made with Captain Duncan, administering the oath to all who had not fought a duel in or out of the state of Louisiana. "It was the opinion of Mr. Fellowes and myself," the Mayor said later, "that . . . the arms and property of the state and city were to be given up that evening if my part of the agreement could be performed." The task completed, Mayor Waterman decided to remain at Jackson Square, and quarters were prepared for him on the second floor of the Arsenal. In a long communication to the Common Council after the Vigilantes had finally disbanded, the Mayor thus gave his reasons for making this decision:

"As I had performed my part of the agreement, I felt it incumbent on me to remain until Captain Duncan had performed his, which was to disband his forces, to remove the barricades, and to restore to the State and to the City the property which had been taken forcible possession of. With this in view and for the purpose of consummating the agreement, I remained in the camp of the Vigilance Committee all the night, and at about four o'clock a.m. I sent for Capt. Duncan and stated that I thought it was time to commence his part of the contract. His apology was that various rumors during the night had reached him, of a threatening import, and that he thought it his duty to protect the men under his command. However, about 7 o'clock a.m., he moved the cannon from their positions into the alley and in front of the Arsenal on St. Peter Street."

No explanation of the Mayor's absence from his official post was made to the Native American mob in Lafayette Square, which knew only that he had moved bag and baggage into the camp of the enemy. Dissatisfaction with his course had been steadily increasing since the agreement with Captain Duncan was made public, and there is little doubt that his life would have been in danger if he had ventured above Canal Street. During the late afternoon unsigned posters were scattered about the city violently attacking him for coming to terms with " the traitors," and many threats against him were shouted by the crowd which seethed before City Hall. By nightfall the mob numbered at least five thousand men, and they remained in Lafayette Square until morning, firing their muskets and pistols into the air, fighting among themselves, and yelling threats and curses whenever the Mayor's name was mentioned. At intervals they were harangued by spellbinders, who denounced Mayor Waterman for his attempts at compromise, and demanded the immediate extirpation of the Vigilantes. The principal speakers were Colonel Thomas Henry, who had been one of Walker's mainstays in Nicaragua; and Colonel William Christy, a veteran of the War of 1812, who offered to lead any force that might be organized to attack Jackson Square. The response, however, was slight. At the height of the oratory the crowd was thrown into great excitement by the sound of heavy firing from the French Quarter. Believing that this presaged an advance against City Hall, officials hastily organized a force of a hundred men, who were armed and posted about the building under the command of Justice Bradford. But the attack failed to materialize, and there is no evidence that Captain Duncan had ever planned one, or at any time contemplated the extension of his lines above Canal Street. The shooting which so alarmed the Know-Nothing mob was the result of the same sort of misapprehension by the Vigilance Committee troops. Spies who had been sent to City Hall by Captain Duncan reported that an attack on Jackson Square appeared to be imminent, and later in the evening excited Vigilantes opened fire upon a dozen armed men who were seen tramping down St. Peter Street. Four men were killed and nine wounded before the Vigilance sharpshooters discovered that they were slaughtering one of their own patrols which had been inspecting the picket lines on Canal Street.

The situation in New Orleans on the morning of Saturday, June 5, was extraordinary. Only in the Fourth District, which was a considerable distance from the main business section, were conditions normal; there life and business went on much as usual, the courts functioned, and even an occasional policeman was seen about the streets performing his accustomed duties. But elsewhere in the city there were confusion, terror, and the constant threat of violence and bloodshed. Business was suspended, and all mercantile and manufacturing establishments, with the exception of a few liquor-stores, were closed and barricaded. All of the territory below Canal Street was still in the hands of the Vigilance Committee, while above that thoroughfare the Know-Nothing mob was in control; bands of armed men wandered through the First and Third Districts, potentially a much greater menace to the peace of the city than the organized, disciplined Vigilantes. Fortunately the mob lacked effective leadership, and although a few stores were looted and several naturalized citizens assaulted, there was no widespread rioting. The municipal government had practically collapsed; since the disappearance of the police and the refusal of the militiamen to answer the call to arms, it was powerless to maintain order or to enforce any decrees it might have issued. Mayor Waterman remained at Jackson Square, and throughout the morning no word was received from him at City Hall. During the early afternoon several prominent citizens called upon the Mayor and urged him to return to Lafayette Square, but he refused when they were unable to promise protection from the mob. He did, however, give Recorder Stith, the Native American candidate for Mayor, authority to enroll a special police force, but revoked this commission a few hours later, on the ground that the City

Charter forbade him to delegate his powers as head of the police department. In the meantime Recorder Stith had sworn in two hundred and fifty men, described by the Mayor afterwards as "good and respectable citizens."

The Common Council met at six o'clock in the evening of June 5, and the Board of Assistant Aldermen immediately adopted articles of impeachment against Mayor Waterman and sent them to the Board of Aldermen for trial, as required by the City Charter. These articles accused the Mayor of deserting his post, pointed out that since June 2 a portion of the city had been "in the hands of an unlawful and armed organization," and declared that Mayor Waterman had been "recreant to his duties" and had "failed, neglected and refused to enforce the laws of the United States and the ordinances of the city." The Board of Aldermen likewise adopted resolutions of impeachment, which declared that the Mayor had "abandoned the seat of the municipal government without just cause, and cannot be found nor induced to attend to his duties . . . there is no longer a Mayor of New Orleans." While the Council was considering these affairs, Recorder Stith and three other citizens called upon Mayor Waterman at Jackson Square, told him what was being done, and suggested that he accompany them to City Hall and defend himself. "The gentlemen of the Vigilance Committee," the Mayor said afterwards in his communication to the Council, "having heard that my life had been threatened, advised me not to leave their quarters without an armed escort. But, after deliberation, I concluded to go to the City Hall with the gentlemen who had called to see me. I left the Arsenal without any escort, and on my way up, the suggestion was made to stop at my rooms at the hotel. I then requested Recorder Stith . . . to go to the City Hall and inform the Council where I was, and that if my presence was required I would wait upon your honorable body."

The Council did not send for him, and it does not appear that any actual impeachment trial was ever held. Nevertheless, both the Boards of Aldermen adopted resolutions asking H. M. Summers, President of the Council, to act as Mayor, which he agreed to do on condition that the Council provide him with "all the sinews of war." Waterman, obviously frightened and confused, apparently remained in seclusion at his hotel (the St. Charles) for the next two weeks; there is no record that he visited City Hall during that period. On June 18 the Board of Assistant Aldermen, having heard the communication in which the Mayor explained and attempted to justify his course, adopted a resolution declaring that "this Board now verily believes" that Waterman "acted in all that he has done conscientiously, and, as he understood, to the best interest of his fellow-citizens and of this corporation." The resolution also withdrew and repealed the articles of impeachment, and after the Board of Aldermen had been notified of this action, the Council as a whole accepted Waterman's resignation as Mayor. Three years later, in 1861, Waterman suffered disastrous business reverses and disappeared, leaving a note which led to the conclusion that he had drowned himself in the Mississippi River.

Summers took charge of the Mayor's office about seven o'clock in the evening of Saturday, June 5. His first acts were to revoke the appointment of the Vigilantes as special policemen and to issue a proclamation denouncing the Vigilance Committee as a lawless mob and commanding it to disperse its armed forces. On Sunday, June 6, Summers ordered the regular police to report for duty (for the most part they ignored the order), dismissed Colonel Forno as Chief of Police, and appointed in his stead Colonel John A. Jacques. Except for these preparatory moves, Summers took no action against the Vigilance Committee, and Sunday passed quietly, although both the Vigilantes and the Native Americans maintained their picket lines, and a large crowd still lingered in Lafayette Square. Throughout the day there was a constant parade of city and state officials to Jackson Square, where they solemnly told Captain Duncan that all of the actions of the committee had been illegal, information which Captain Duncan received with great equanimity.

The election was held on Monday, June 7, and before the polls opened Acting Mayor Summers swore in several hundred special policemen and a large number of additional election commissioners. General John L. Lewis, apparently recognizing as still valid Mayor Waterman's appointment of the Vigilantes, notified Captain Duncan that his aid would be required only in case of extreme emergency. The effect of all these measures was to accomplish one of the principal aims of the Vigilance Committee — the election was one of the quietest and most orderly in the history of New Orleans. As had been expected, the Native Americans were victorious, capturing the mayoralty and all of the other city offices except one recordership and a few places in the Council. Two years later, in 1860, the Know-Nothings completed the conquest of the city, electing a full ticket headed by John T. Monroe, a prominent labor leader, as Mayor, and remained in power until New Orleans surrendered to the Federal fleet under Admiral Farragut, long after the Native American movement had collapsed everywhere else in the United States. Monroe was the last Mayor chosen by the people until 1866, when the Federal military authorities permitted another municipal election, at which he was again elected, though as a Democrat.

The Vigilantes began to evacuate the Arsenal and the Cabildo as soon as the polls had closed on the evening of June 7, 1858, and by four o'clock the next morning only about two hundred remained in Jackson Square. These were marched by Captain Duncan to the United States Army barracks, where they were disarmed and advised to go home.

Most of them, however, fearing the vengeance of the Know-Nothing mob — and with good reason, for a score of men suspected of participation in the activities of the Vigilance Committee were beaten during the next few days — crossed the Mississippi and hid in the swamps below Algiers until they became hungry. Fifty, most of them foreigners, then surrendered to the police, but were soon released, as were a dozen others who had previously been locked up in the Third Precinct station. When the city authorities took possession of the property in Jackson Square, bloodstains were found on the pavement in front of the Arsenal and the Cabildo, and on the carpets of the Sixth Precinct Court, while the jail and the small chambers connected with the courtrooms were in such filthy condition that Negroes worked for several days with scrubbing-brushes before they could be occupied. The city was formally notified of the dissolution of the Vigilance Committee by a card published in the *Crescent,* and signed by Captain Duncan " for self and others " :

" The object of the Vigilance Committee is today what it was when it was first formed, viz :, to deliver the city from the notorious thugs and assassins who infest it, and who are abhorred by all good citizens. The result of the late election has, therefore, not in any way changed the honest views entertained by the committee, and to prove that we have never had any political views in our organization, but only the security of all good citizens in their lives and property, we now put ourselves at the disposal of the Mayor, and at his call will assemble under arms as a special police in order to put down the rule of murderers and thugs. Yielding to public opinion relative to our possessing the State Arsenal and the Sixth District Court — but doing this only — we now hereby abandon and give up our position, and we agree thus to answer a call from the Mayor, our engagement lasting for at least three months, or longer, if found expedient."

Once the Vigilantes had actually disbanded their forces and evacuated the French Quarter, the municipal government and the newspapers proceeded on the theory of "least said, soonest mended." No investigation of the movement was ordered by the city authorities, nor did they try to learn who had provided the war-chest of thirty thousand dollars which the Vigilance Committee was reported to have spent during its campaign. Thirty of the Vigilante leaders, some of them men of wealth and prominence, left the city by steamboat on the morning of June 8, and while affidavits were sworn out against several of them, the gesture was a perfunctory one, and no real effort was ever made to apprehend them. The Coroner held inquests over the bodies of eleven persons described as having been "slain within the entrenchments," but the details of the inquiries were not published. One man was killed in Jackson Square by the premature discharge of a cannon, and four died when the Vigilantes fired upon their own patrol, but the identities of the other six and the manner in which they met death are still mysteries. Captain Duncan, the principal leader of the uprising and quite possibly its originator, escaped punishment and apparently was not even questioned. He remained in New Orleans and was professionally engaged as civil engineer, surveyor, and architect until 1860, when he was appointed chief engineer of the state Board of Public Works. At the beginning of the Civil War he entered the Confederate Army as Colonel, but was soon promoted to the rank of Brigadier-General. He was assigned to the command of Forts Jackson and St. Philip, and became a prisoner of war when those strongholds fell before Farragut's fleet in April 1862. On the following December 18 he died at Knoxville, Kentucky, in his thirty-sixth year.

CHAPTER XI

"HELL ON EARTH"

As a natural consequence of the demoralization of the police, the underworld of New Orleans grew rich and powerful, and crime of every description increased. During the twenty years prior to the Civil War, and for an even longer period after that conflict, the newspapers were almost constantly filled with reports of murders, robberies, and assaults, and of the activities of gangs of incendiaries, who frequently fired sections of the city and plundered under cover of the conflagrations. The New Orleans correspondent of the New York *Tribune,* writing under date of January 30, 1855, reported that "murders here are an everyday occurrence, and the papers daily give details of the same"; he quoted the *Delta* as saying that "a thousand murders might be committed in New Orleans, and if the murderers could not be found on the spot, our authorities would never afterward make any efforts to have them punished." In a letter from New Orleans on January 27, 1857, James Sterling, an English traveler, noted with amazement that in the First District Court alone there were then pending fourteen cases of murder, twenty of shooting and stabbing, and 340 of assault and battery. "The proportion of crime to the population," he wrote, "is, to a European, perfectly astounding." It was only a few months later that the *True Delta* [1] declared the city to be suffering from a

---

[1] The *Delta* and the *True Delta* were different newspapers, with nothing in common but enmity.

" reign of terror," and sarcastically apologized to Mayor Waterman for calling his attention to "the danger which ordinary, peaceable citizens ran whenever they ventured abroad." And on June 4, 1858, at the height of the Vigilante excitement, the *Bee* said editorially that "it is most true that our city has been infested by a band of desperadoes who have shed innocent blood and spread terror and consternation among certain classes." The Vigilance Committee had so frightened the politicians that they permitted an orderly municipal election in 1858 and again in 1860, but its activities had neither lessened the prevalence of crime nor brought about lasting reforms in the administration of the police department, although Mayor John T. Monroe, in his inaugural message in 1860, declared that he recognized the supreme importance of the force, promised to appoint the several hundred men without fear or favor, and urged that the policemen be uniformed, a measure which he continued to advocate unsuccessfully for the next decade.

More than a year after the Vigilantes made their comparatively fruitless gesture, on December 25, 1859, the *True Delta* complained that "another murder seems to have become one of the daily recurring topics of the reporters of the city papers; the record of one deed of blood has hardly dried upon the paper when another recital of crime has to follow it, each chapter a brutal and bloody continuation of the preceding." During the two years that followed this illuminating comment upon conditions in New Orleans, the Coroner held inquests over the bodies of 132 murdered persons, an average of more than one a week — and it was common knowledge that at least two-thirds of the homicides committed in the Swamp and other underworld districts were never reported to the police, nor the bodies of the victims found. In 1861, a month or so after the Civil War had begun with the firing upon Fort Sumter, Sir William Howard Russell, a noted British war-correspondent, recorded in his diary a statement made to him by the Criminal Sheriff of Orleans Parish, whom the Englishman described as a " great, burly six-foot man, with revolvers stuck in his belt. Speaking of the numerous crimes committed in New Orleans, he declared it a perfect hell on earth, and that nothing could ever put an end to the murders, manslaughters, and deadly assaults till it was made penal to carry arms." No permit was required for the possession of firearms, and men of all classes habitually carried weapons to protect their lives and property, although no one seems to have been in any real danger from a pistol or revolver in the hands of the average citizen. Said the New Orleans *Republican* on May 19, 1870:

> " Judging by the amount of poor shooting lately, it cannot be denied that our people are very inefficient marksmen. One man fires six shots at his assailant, and made only one ball tell; another fires pointblank and simply raises a skin blister; while another fires three shots and harmed, by accident, a disinterested citizen. Unless an improvement takes place, revolvers might as well be ignored."

On those rare occasions when the police did send a malefactor to jail, he was apparently coddled in a manner which would have gladdened the hearts of modern penologists; late in 1869 a Grand Jury which investigated the Parish Prison found life there so pleasant and food so abundant that " the jury believes persons are induced to violate the laws for the express purpose of being confined there."

2

THE criminals and ruffians whose unchecked depredations had transformed New Orleans into what the Criminal

Sheriff so graphically described as "a perfect hell on earth" found refuge and amusement in the scores of cheap groggeries, dance-houses, bordellos, low taverns and coffee-houses, concert-saloons and barrel-houses with which the Vieux Carré and the area above Canal Street were literally crowded. Probably no other city in the United States harbored so many unsavory resorts in proportion to the number of inhabitants; on St. Charles Avenue alone, in the half-dozen blocks between Canal Street and the City Hall at Lafayette Square, there were forty-five places where liquor was sold, and nearly all of them were thoroughly disreputable. A similar congestion of underworld rendezvous existed on many other streets, notably Gallatin in the French Quarter; and, in the American quarter, Girod Street, which still retained the evil reputation it had acquired in the heyday of the rowdy flatboat crews. Its rating as the toughest thoroughfare above Canal Street, however, was now being challenged by St. Thomas Street and Corduroy Alley, the latter a narrow byway running from St. Thomas in the direction of Rousseau Street, near the Soraparu Market, and in the heart of the district known as the Irish Channel, where the low-class Irish immigrants congregated when they began to come to New Orleans during the 1840's. Both the Alley and a large section of St. Thomas Street were lined on both sides by groggeries, and groceries which sold more whisky than food. The inhabitants spent most of their time drinking and brawling. Said the *True Delta* on July 10, 1861:

> "St. Thomas Street is keeping up its ancient reputation, especially that portion of it which boasts of Corduroy Alley. The inhabitants of the Alley appear for the most part to be an intemperate and blood-thirsty set, who are never contented unless engaged in broils, foreign or domestic, such as the breaking of a

318

stranger's pate or the blacking of a loving spouse's eye. These are the ordinary amusements of the Alley. . . . Honest people, doubtless, live on St. Thomas Street, but they must have a hard time of it if they manage to keep their skulls uncracked and their reputations unstained."

The *True Delta's* comment was occasioned by a fresh outbreak of the feud between the Lahey and Claffey families, which had kept the Irish Channel in a turmoil for several years — Bill Claffey, the most redoubtable ruffian of his clan, went on a drunken rampage in Corduroy Alley on July 4 and stabbed several Laheys and half a dozen innocent bystanders with a long sharpening-steel before he was finally shot by a policeman whom he had attacked.

Almost every conceivable type of resort had been common enough in New Orleans since the early days of the colony, and their numbers had more than kept pace with the growth of the city and the increase in the population. The barrel-house and the concert-saloon, however, were products of the Civil War period. Both were introduced into New Orleans by the Northern riff-raff which flocked into the city in the wake of Farragut's victorious fleet and added its peculiar talents and appetites to those of the criminal scum which already formed a large and dangerous part of the population.

As its name implies, the barrel-house was strictly a drinking-place, and no lower guzzle-shop was ever operated in the United States. It usually occupied a long, narrow room, with a row of racked barrels on one side, and on the other a table on which were a large number of heavy glass tumblers, or a sort of bin filled with earthenware mugs. For five cents a customer was permitted to fill a mug or a tumbler at the spigot of any of the barrels, but if he failed to refill almost immediately he was promptly ejected. If he drank until his capacity was reached, he was dragged into the alley, or, in some places, into a back room. In either event, he was robbed, and if he was unlucky enough to land in the alley, sneak thieves usually stripped him of his clothing as well as of the few coins which he might have in his pockets. Most of these dives served only brandy, Irish whisky, and wine, and the liquors which masqueraded under these honorable names were as false as the hearts of the proprietors. A barrel of neutral spirits became Irish whisky when a half-pint of creosote was dumped into it; and the wine was simply a mixture of three parts of water and one of alcohol, with coloring and flavoring materials added; in making port, for example, prunes, cherries, and burnt sugar were used, with olive oil to provide the old tawny taste. Brandy was usually manufactured from this recipe: into a barrel half-full of water put a pint of flavoring — grape juice or dried fruit — a pound of burnt sugar, a half-ounce of sulphuric acid, and a plug of chewing-tobacco for the bead and sparkle. Then fill the barrel with neutral spirits. Another ingredient which frequently found its way into the barrels was knock-out drops, by which the barrel-house proprietor made certain of the ultimate possession of the customer's money. The owner of one such establishment not only doped all of his liquor, but maintained his own staff of sneak thieves, who skulked like wolves in the alley behind his property. They worked on a percentage basis and took turns robbing the sodden wretches who were dragged from the barrel-house.

The concert-saloon, forerunner of the modern night club, provided a dance-floor upon which pleasure-seekers might kick up their heels to the music of a tinny piano and a squeaky fiddle; an occasional show performed on a rough platform without curtain or scenery; and plenty to eat and drink, served at little tables by waiter girls, popularly known as " beer-jerkers," who sometimes doubled as singers and dancers. The first resort of this character, the St. Nicho-

WORKING A SUCKER IN A CONCERT-SALOON

las, opened its doors on St. Charles Avenue about 1865. It became popular immediately, and others were soon established; during the next twenty years there were seldom fewer than fifteen scattered about the city. These places employed from one hundred to two hundred "beer-jerkers," the number varying as the popularity of the concert-saloon waxed and waned. The girls received no salaries, but were allowed to keep their tips, if any, and were paid ten per cent commission on all liquor sales. From these sources the "beer-jerker" averaged from fifteen to thirty dollars a week, an income which she usually augmented by prostitution in her leisure hours. The entertainment which vied with the waiter girls for the honor of being the main attraction of the concert-saloon generally consisted of the cancan or a somewhat similar dance called the *clodoche,* and "art poses by living models," in which the female performers wore ankle-length cotton tights with long sleeves, and closely buttoned about the throat. But these shows must have been worse than they seem to our modern minds, for on June 18, 1869, after a dozen "actresses" from the concert-saloons had been fined one dollar each, and the owners of two of the resorts placed under bonds of two hundred and fifty dollars to keep the peace for six months, the New Orleans *Times* said:

"We can state that in an experience of some years we have never observed in any of the dance-houses of Gallatin or Barracks Street, or the ball rooms of the demi-monde further downtown, the utter abandon which has characterized these places."

Besides the St. Nicholas, the best-known of the concert-saloons were the Napoleon, on St. Louis Street; the Bismarck and the New El Dorado, on St. Charles Avenue; the Pavillon on Baronne Street under the National Theater, on the site of the present De Soto Hotel; the Gem, the Tivoli, the Eden, and the Royal Palace Beer Saloon & Concert Hall, on Royal Street; the Conclave on Chartres Street; the

Buffalo Bill House at Franklin and Dryades Streets; and Wenger's Garden on Bourbon Street, the owner of which in 1869 proudly summoned the newspaper reporters to inspect a novelty which the New Orleans *Republican* described as "the remarkable machine known as the self-acting organ." The St. Nicholas, the Buffalo Bill House, and the Conclave also possessed special claims to fame — at the former it was the garish decorations, the wine-room where aerated cider sold as champagne for two dollars and a half a pint, the life-size portrait of Don Quixote in the entrance lobby, and the spectacle of the proprietor, dressed as Cervantes's character, stalking about the place keeping order with the aid of a huge cudgel. The Conclave was one of the few concert-saloons to maintain a bar as well as table service, and the arrangement of the back bar aroused much comment — it was fitted up as an exact replica of a section of burial ovens or vaults, complete with marble slabs on which were chiseled "Brandy, Whisky, Gin," etc. The bartenders were clad as undertakers, and when one of them served a customer he opened a vault in the back bar and pulled out a small silver-handled coffin filled with bottles of the desired liquor. The Conclave was always very popular among sightseers, but it never gained great favor with hard drinkers.

The Buffalo Bill House was kept by a whiskered ruffian named Bison Williams, who came to New Orleans from Cincinnati during the latter part of 1862 and ran a lunchroom on St. Charles Avenue until the end of the Civil War. He then opened his combination concert-saloon and dance-house and installed a staff of harlots and jail-birds. He scorned the "art poses by living models" which were popular entertainment at other resorts; instead he regaled his clientele with butting matches, wrestling and boxing bouts, and rat and dog fights, while the cancan and the *clodoche* as danced at the Buffalo Bill House were really indecent, and the ditties sung by the waiter girls frankly obscene. The

323

most noted of the butters who appeared under the direction of Bison Williams were two underworld characters known as Looney and Oyster Johnny, who butted one another three times a week all during the summer of 1869, ostensibly for a purse of fifty dollars. Oyster Johnny was finally proclaimed the victor in August; after forty-five minutes of butting, Looney was knocked unconscious. But when Oyster Johnny attempted to collect the money he had won, Bison Williams disclaimed knowledge of any purse; he gave Oyster Johnny a drink and a bottle of headache tablets, and then kicked him out.

Almost from the moment Bison Williams opened the doors of the Buffalo Bill House, this unsavory dive was a favorite haunt of the most vicious elements of the population and was admittedly the toughest of all the concert saloons. By the middle of 1869 it had become so notorious that several newspapers denounced it as a nuisance and demanded that the police stop the fights and robberies which occurred there every night, whereupon Bison Williams published a card pointing out the absurdity of a complaint against his place, since he had purposely established it " in the only locality in the city where decent people do not live." For several years the resort was the headquarters of Pierre Bertin and Jean Capdeville, New Orleans' most celebrated home-grown burglars, and of many other famous criminals, among them a benign-looking old gentleman variously known as Sam Gorman and Charles Steadman, who in reality was one of the shrewdest confidence men and most daring burglars in the country. Gorman was a New Yorker who spent his winters in New Orleans, and his arrival about Thanksgiving of each year usually heralded a sharp increase in the number of store and residence burglaries. When he was finally arrested in 1869 — and released after a few days for lack of evidence — he was more than seventy years old and was suffering from tuberculosis. Also, according to the *Republican,* he owned considerable real estate in New York, and had sixty thousand dollars on deposit in a Northern bank. A policeman asked him why he continued his career of crime, in view of his age, his poor health, and his excellent financial condition, and the old man replied : " Well, it's fun ! "

Bertin and Capdeville planned some of their most important burglaries over a table in a corner of the Buffalo Bill House; and there, too, they openly displayed samples and took orders for the burglar tools which they manufactured in a little machine-shop. They also made slung shots — in those days this popular and efficient weapon was simply a short piece of heavy rope with a loop at one end and a chunk of lead at the other — and, for pickpockets, large finger-rings with tiny knife-blades embedded in the settings. With these the thieves cut slits in their victims' pockets. For more than a decade Bertin and Capdeville successfully carried on their various criminal enterprises, and although they were known to the police and were frequently arrested, they were never convicted until 1871, when a jury found them guilty of " robbery with weapons," for which, under the Louisiana law, capital punishment might have been inflicted. Instead they were sentenced to life imprisonment. After a few months in the penitentiary Bertin was pardoned by Governor H. C. Warmoth, but the pardon was withdrawn and the burglar returned to prison when the Governor learned that most of the signatures on his petition had been forged.

The bawdy entertainment, the rowdy dancing and singing, and the frequent fights and robberies in the concert-saloons, together with the noise which accompanied these activities, occasioned so much complaint from the newspapers and various civic organizations that in 1870 the City Council, after ignoring many petitions, finally attempted to drive them out of business by enacting an ordinance which imposed heavy license fees upon the resorts. A tax of $100 a year was required from a concert-saloon wherein instrumental music was played, $200 if singing was added to the clatter of the piano and the whine of the fiddle, and $300 if a platform show was presented. Issuance of a license, however, was prohibited unless the applicant had obtained the written consent of the owners or lessees of one-half the frontage of the block in which his establishment was located. A few resort-owners closed their doors rather than pay the tax, but most of them paid without protest and either procured the signatures necessary to remain in their old locations or moved to other parts of the city where property-owners were more amenable to persuasion. Frequent raids by the police, and fines imposed upon the proprietors and performers, likewise failed to dislodge the concert-saloon, and it remained a disreputable feature of New Orleans life until about 1890, when it succumbed to a changing public taste in entertainment. To some extent its passing was hastened by the Sunday closing laws of 1886 and 1888, when the state and city authorities attempted to close, from midnight Saturday to midnight Sunday, not only the concert-saloons but practically everything else in New Orleans except the legitimate hotels and restaurants; when the police were ordered, in January 1887, to prepare a list of violators, they gave District Attorney Lionel Adams the names of several hundred saloon-keepers, dealers in coal and wood, shoe and clothing merchants, owners of cigar-stores, etc. The state law, which went into effect on July 31, 1888, closed the concert-saloons on week-days as well as Sundays, except from 6 p.m. to 4 a.m., and provided that none could continue in operation without the consent of a majority of the property-holders within a radius of three hundred feet from the resort's door.

The fight of the saloon-keepers and the concert-saloon proprietors against the Sunday laws was led by Joe Walker,

who ran the famous Crescent Hall Saloon at Canal Street
and St. Charles Avenue, and Otto Henry Schoenhausen,
owner of the Royal Palace Beer Saloon & Concert Hall
on Royal Street near Customhouse, now Iberville. Schoenhausen had opened this resort about 1867, but it was closed
in 1869 when he was sent to prison for the murder of Dr.
H. L. Nelson in a Canal Street confectionery. He was pardoned by Governor McEnery late in 1882, and came out of
the penitentiary with ten thousand dollars which he had acquired by lending money to the guards at usurious rates of
interest. He immediately reopened the Royal Palace, and
for some seven or eight years it was one of the most popular and at the same time one of the most disreputable resorts
in the city. He employed from fifteen to twenty waiter girls,
some of whom also sang and danced, and sold beer for five
cents a glass and forty cents a bottle, drawing all of it from
the same keg. In an attempt to circumvent the Sunday closing law Schoenhausen organized the Actors' Benevolent Association, the officers of which were his bartenders and performers. Anyone could join upon payment of two dollars,
and the Association met every Saturday at midnight at the
Royal Palace and remained in session until the same hour
on Sunday. At the same time Joe Walker formed the Citizens' Protective Association, which sponsored mass meetings of protest. Neither organization accomplished anything,
and both were abandoned by their promoters when Emile
Baumann, a former Alderman who kept a saloon at Cabal
and Chartres Streets, was convicted by a jury in 1889 of
violating the new statute. Thereafter the law was strictly
observed for several months. But enforcement was gradually relaxed, and within another year Sunday closing was
only a reformer's dream. Meanwhile, however, the concert-
saloon, against which the law was mainly directed, had
met its predestined end.

3

GALLATIN STREET today is perhaps the most peaceful and insignificant thoroughfare of the Vieux Carré, as well as one of the shortest—it extends only two blocks from Ursuline Avenue through Nicholls Street (formerly Hospital) to Barracks, and is occupied principally by weather-beaten warehouses and the storage-rooms of produce-dealers at the French Market. But for almost forty years this short stretch of dingy buildings and broken cobblestones was a worthy successor to Girod Street and the Swamp as the most vicious underworld area in New Orleans; in many respects conditions there were even worse than they had ever been in the old-time haunt of the flatboat bullies. From about 1840 to the middle 1870's Gallatin Street could boast of no legitimate business whatever; it was completely filled with barrel-houses where for five cents a man could get not a meager tumblerful of liquor, but all he could drink; dance-houses which were also bordellos and gin-mills; and sailors' boarding-houses from which seamen were occasionally shanghaied, although this particular practice appears to have been less common in New Orleans than in other American seaports. There were also a few such resorts, forming a sort of overflow, in Levee (Decatur), Peters, and other streets adjacent to Gallatin. From dawn to dusk the district slept off its debauches behind closed shutters; from dusk to dawn the dives roared full blast, and Gallatin Street was crowded with countrymen, sailors, and steamboat men seeking women and diversion. And they in their turn were sought by a horde of harlots, sneak thieves, garroters who openly carried their deadly strangling cords, and footpads with slung shots looped about their wrists. There were crime and depravity in every inch of Gallatin Street; the stranger who entered it at Ursuline Avenue

A FOOTPAD AT WORK

with money in his pocket and came out at Barracks with his wealth intact and his skull uncracked had performed a feat which bordered on the miraculous. The police occasionally entered the district during the daytime in large, heavily armed parties, but after nightfall they never went there at all. As Girod Street had done, Gallatin Street made its own law.

Of all the desperate habitués of the district, probably the most dangerous were the Live Oak Boys, so called because they carried oaken cudgels and, when not asleep or occupied in crime, basked in the shade of a big pile of live-oak knees in a shipyard at Elysian Fields Street and the river. Once during the early days of the Live Oaks the owner of the shipyard tried to drive them from his property by moving the knees, but the ruffians threatened to burn the shipyard unless the lumber was put back. It was, and there it remained for almost twenty years, the recognized headquarters of the Live Oak Boys. This aggregation of bullies, every one of whom was a thief, a drunkard, a brawler, and during his career committed at least one murder, was formed about 1858 by Red Bill Wilson, a notorious Gallatin Street rowdy who carried his knife concealed in his bushy red beard. The Live Oaks were never a criminal gang in the ordinary sense of the term; they had no regular organization and no recognized leader, and there was no division of loot. In matters of business they were arrant individualists; they initiated their own crimes, chose their own associates, and kept what they stole. When occasion offered, they robbed and even killed one another. This sort of internecine criminality cost the gang two of its most noted brawlers and thieves in 1867, when Henry Thompson, asleep at the daylight rendezvous, awakened to find his fellow Live Oak, Jimmy O'Brien, with whom he had been drunk the night before, going through his pockets. When Thompson struggled, O'Brien calmly shoved a knife into his heart and continued the search. But the murder had been seen by a Negro and a small boy, and upon their testimony O'Brien was convicted and sent to the penitentiary for twenty years. He died in prison.

It is doubtful if any of the Live Oaks ever performed a stroke of honest work. They devoted their nights to robbing and killing, or to carousing and brawling in Gallatin Street dives, and their days to loafing, sleeping, and planning new crimes. For years they were the particular bane of the dance-house proprietors; a night seldom passed that they didn't raid one or more of the resorts, either on commission from rival establishments or simply because they loved a brawl. And so great was the fear in which they were held throughout the district that when they came charging into a dance-house, fighting drunk and brandishing their oaken clubs, the bouncers, bartenders, musicians, and customers rushed pell-mell through the back door, while the harlots fled to the comparative safety of the upstairs. The Live Oaks then proceeded to wreck the place at their leisure, smashing the furniture and the musical instruments, scarring the dance-floor, robbing the till, and carrying away as much liquor as they wanted. Occasionally a dance-house owner resisted the ruffians, but he always lived to regret it — if he lived at all.

Such activities were not conducive to popularity, and the Live Oaks were welcome nowhere in the Gallatin Street district except at Bill Swan's Fireproof Coffee-House on Levee Street. Swan had been a member of the gang before he amassed sufficient money to set himself up in business, and the Live Oaks took his resort under their protection, partly for old-time's sake and partly because Swan gave them free drinks. Consequently the Fireproof was one of the most orderly places in the neighborhood, and Swan operated it profitably until about 1877, when he sold it and opened a saloon at Peters Street and Esplanade Avenue, which became the headquarters of the then popular sports of dog-fighting and rat-killing. In previous years most of these contests had been held at Hanly's Dog Pit on Baronne Street near Girod, scene of a famous battle in October 1869 between Hanly's dog Cabbage, and Twitcher, owned by Dan O'Neil, landlord of the Amsterdam Dance-House on Gallatin Street. Cabbage won after an hour and a half of fighting, in which both dogs were seriously injured. Hanly closed his pit a few years later, and both dog-fighting and ratting languished in New Orleans until they were revived by Bill Swan. They were monthly features at his place for three or four years. One held on March 10, 1879 was thus advertised by a magenta-colored handbill scattered about the streets:

"Grand national rat-killing match for $100, to take place at Bill Swan's saloon, corner Esplanade and Peters Street, third district, Sunday afternoon, at four o'clock, precisely.

"Harry Jennings, of New York, has matched a certain New York dog, whose fighting weight is twenty-three pounds, to kill twelve full-grown rats per minute, for five consecutive minutes, being one of the greatest feats a dog can accomplish — sixty full-sized rats in five minutes.

"Harry Jennings of New York, Thos. Thornton of Boston, and Tom Tugman of Philadelphia, will, on this occasion, exhibit thirty of the most celebrated champions of the U. S., from thirteen pounds up to thirty-eight pounds of weight, which dogs are open to match against any dogs living for from $500 to $1,000 a side. All the above dogs will have a set-to together according to their respective weights. Mr. Salvador Habar will also exhibit his wild Mexican boar, and is prepared to pit him against any dog produced.

"Harry Jennings will, on this occasion, exhibit twelve variegated rats.

"Admission 50¢, reserved seats $1."

In the back yard of Swan's property Jennings and his associates erected a large booth, in the center of which was a pit twelve feet long by ten feet wide, with sides two feet high and capped by a twelve-inch board which projected six inches over the pit. A good-sized crowd had gathered when Jennings, Thornton, and Tugman appeared with their dogs and seventy rats in a box covered with wire netting, but as a *Times* reporter pointed out, "the rougher element of life predominated. The men representing business interests and the gentlemen of the town might have been counted upon the fingers of either hand." The rat-box had a small trapdoor at one end, through which Jennings removed the rodents with his bare hands. He put most of them into a burlap bag, but tucked half a dozen inside his shirt and was uproariously applauded when he grimaced and complained that they were tickling him. Thus encouraged, he performed other tricks — he thrust his head into the burlap bag, swung several rats by their tails, and finally seized one by the back of the neck with his teeth and plunged about the pit, snarling and shaking his head in imitation of a terrier. The comic interlude having been concluded, Jennings took his post in a corner of the pit and, as a dog was thrown in, began shaking the rats one by one from the burlap bag. A dog named Skelper killed twenty-one rats in three minutes and forty-five seconds, but lost all interest in the slaughter and retired with a yelp of pain when one of the rodents nipped him on the nose. His place in the pit was taken by another dog, Modoc, which killed thirty-six rats in two minutes and fifty-eight seconds.[1] The remaining rodents were quickly dispatched by

---

[1] The records in this sport were held by a dog named Jacko, owned by Jimmy Shaw, a London sporting man. On May 1, 1862 Jacko killed one hun-

other dogs, but none equaled Modoc's average. The dogs wore muzzles when they fought one another, and the contests appear to have been tame and uninteresting. Mr. Salvador Habar failed to show his wild Mexican boar, nor did Harry Jennings, on this occasion, exhibit any variegated rats.

Besides Bill Swan, Henry Thompson, and Jimmy O'Brien, the Live Oak Boys included such renowned brawlers as O'Brien's brother Hugh and the latter's sons, Matt and Hugh, Jr.; Jack Lyons, Crazy Bill Anderson; the brothers Petrie — Henry, Redhead and Whitehead; Jack Lowe, Yorker Duffy, Barry Lynch, Tommy Lewis, Billy Emerson; Charley Lockerby, better known as Lagerbeer, and his son Albert; and Mike and Bill Knuckley. Most of these, as well as other members of the gang, either met violent ends or died in prison. Charley Lagerbeer was accounted the most ferocious fighter of the lot, although he was slightly less than five feet and eight inches tall. But he was thickset and extremely strong and powerful, with a little bullet head which squatted between his broad shoulders on a very short neck. He was finally shot by a saloon-keeper named Keppler, whom he killed, and died in Charity Hospital. Hugh O'Brien was killed when he tried to rob a fisherman from a rowboat on the Mississippi River. He had stolen the boat and set out from the Dumaine Street wharf with the drunken idea of being a pirate. His sons, Matt and Hugh, Jr., were then nineteen and twenty-one years old, respectively, and were already accomplished in the ways of the Live Oaks. Their development continued, and for several years they were notorious trouble-makers around Gallatin Street, although by the time their father was killed, about 1871, the gang had begun to break up. On October 2, 1886 the two brothers became involved in a bitter quarrel while drinking in Bill

---

dred rats in 5 minutes, 28 seconds, and on June 10 of the same year he disposed of two hundred in 14 minutes, 37 seconds. His best record was made on July 29, 1862, when he killed sixty rats in 2 minutes, 43 seconds.

Swan's saloon with their brother-in-law, Johnny Hackett, and Jack Lyons, one of the Gallatin Street old-timers. Hackett and Lyons tried to prevent a fight, but when Matt continued to shout abuse at his brother, Hackett handed Hugh a knife.

"Here," he said, "shut him up with this!"

Matt O'Brien abruptly stopped quarreling when he saw the knife in Hugh's hand, and after a few more drinks the brothers left the saloon, apparently on good terms, and walked together into Gallatin Street. A few yards from the corner of Barracks Street they stopped and talked for a moment, and then Matt was seen to draw a pistol and shoot Hugh in the side. "Hughey was drunk," Matt told the police when he was arrested a few hours later, "and he was goin' to do me up, and I shot him to keep him from doin' it. I didn't give him no cause, only he was drunk and wanted blood." Hugh O'Brien was not seriously hurt and left New Orleans to avoid testifying against Matt. Nevertheless, the latter was convicted of "assault less than mayhem" at his trial in November and sentenced to the penitentiary. With one of the O'Brien brothers gone and the other in prison, not more than half a dozen of the Live Oaks remained in New Orleans. They were all old men now, and, with the exception of the prosperous saloon-keeper Bill Swan, most of them had degenerated into quavering barflies who spent all their time cadging drinks and brooding on departed glories. Crazy Bill Anderson, who had earned his sobriquet by the abandon and enthusiasm with which he fought, had become a confirmed alcoholic; he was arrested for drunkenness and thrown into the calaboose several times a month. The *Picayune* thus commented on Crazy Bill's downfall on April 20, 1886:

"Now he is handled without gloves by the police, and is kicked and cuffed about like any other common drunkard. Yet, there was a day . . . when the police really feared to approach him with hostile intentions, and it usually occupied all the time, strength and attention of four able-bodied policemen."

The only one of the Live Oak Boys, again excepting the canny Bill Swan, who retained all of his faculties and who didn't seem to be trying to drink himself to death was Bill Knuckley. A reporter for the *Picayune* interviewed him in September 1886, and Knuckley told him with great gusto how he had killed William Lee, landlord of the Green Tree Dance-House in Gallatin Street. " I killed him at his own door," said Knuckley, " and the man drank his own blood. He was full and so was I. Jack Lyons was with me. To tell the truth, I feel kinder sorry I killed Lee. He was a pretty good feller, but he had my brother Mike's girl, and I wasn't going to stand for that. Lord, how he did bleed! The floor at his feet was full of blood in a minute. I just out with my knife and let him have it."

4

EXCEPT that there were no formal programs of entertainment, the dance-houses of Gallatin Street were operated in much the same fashion as the concert-saloons — the main attractions were women, liquor, and dancing. But they were infinitely lower in the scale of depravity; the only resorts New Orleans ever harbored that were comparable to them were such places in Girod Street and the Swamp as the House of Rest for Weary Boatmen and Mother Colby's Sure Enuf Hotel. They were all very much alike — a typical dance-house occupied a two- or three-storey building, the upper floors of which were partitioned into small rooms and rented by the night to streetwalkers, or by the week to the harlots of the house staff, all rents payable in advance. As a *Times* reporter wrote in 1869, after a tour of Gallatin

Street, these chambers were equipped " with furniture of the oldest and craziest patterns, and . . . were filthy and unclean to a degree which beggars description." The first floor of the dive was divided into two rooms, which formed the business part of the establishment. The bar ran across the rear of the front room, and behind it, on high stools, sat the bouncers, from two to six great rough fellows armed with clubs, slung shots, knives, and brass knuckles on both hands. Ordinary fights and even murders concerned them not at all so long as the killers dragged their own victims into the street and thus showed a decent regard for the good name of the house. The bouncers interfered promptly, however, if the brawlers threatened to damage property. The back room was the dance-hall, where music of a sort was produced by a piano, a fiddle, and sometimes a few cornets or trombones. No charge was made either for admittance or for dancing, but a man was expected to treat his lady at the bar after every dance. Whisky, the favorite tipple, sold for twenty cents a drink, but only the first two or three served to a customer were full strength; after that they were freely watered so he wouldn't get too drunk to dance. If he did, despite these precautions, he was robbed and thrown out.

As a general rule the dance-house women wore their hair loose, slippers which were badly scuffed and run down at the heel, and knee-length calico dresses with nothing underneath. Once in a while a harlot who retained a faint craving for personal adornment appeared on the dance-floor with a sash about her waist or a bit of ribbon in her hair. But she only made herself conspicuous, and her finery was soon torn away by her jeering sisters. From ten to thirty of these creatures, all drunkards and prostitutes of the lowest class, were regularly attached to a dance-house, and additional women were brought in from the street or near-by bordellos when business was exceptionally brisk. On such occasions, as the New Orleans *Times* said on July 31, 1869, " the long dance

337

hall would be filled with some two or three hundred scowling, black-bearded, red-shirted visitors coming from every port, prison and lazar-house, and presenting such a motley throng as Lafitte or any of the pirates of the Gulf might have gathered for their crews. With a piano and two or three trombones for an orchestra, and with dances so abandoned and reckless that the can can in comparison seemed maidenly and respectable, one can form an idea of what the scene was."

This same reporter described the company at one of the dance-houses as being "in a state of awful nudity," although he failed to give details of the spectacle. Such a state, however, was not uncommon in Gallatin Street. Excited by the dancing and the innumerable slugs of harsh liquor dumped down their throats, the women frequently threw off their dresses and shuffled about naked, and it was only natural that many of the men should follow their example. Sometimes it was necessary to stop the music while the bouncers cleared the dance-floor of couples who were doing everything except dance. None of the strumpets received any pay from the dance-house proprietors; their rewards were the excellent opportunities for prostitution and stealing which their employment afforded. A woman attached to the staff of a Gallatin Street dive never lacked a companion for the night, or rather for the day, since none of the resorts ever closed their doors until dawn; and the man who spent a few hours with one of them and escaped without being robbed was so rare as to be practically a unique specimen. Nor was there anything subtle about the methods of the dance-house harlots. If a man was drunk enough they simply emptied his pockets; if he wasn't, they used other means of getting his money, none of which was more effective than that employed against a foolish countryman who entered Archie Murphy's resort in March 1859 and boasted to Lizzie Collins, one of the house harpies, that he had a hundred and ten dollars in gold bound to his leg with a handkerchief. He refused to drink, but accepted with alacrity when Lizzie invited him upstairs. As they entered her darkened room three other women threw him to the floor and held him while Lizzie poured whisky into his mouth and down his throat. He was compelled either to swallow or strangle. When he was sick and helpless, Lizzie untied the handker-

From an old print

A GALLATIN STREET DANCE—HOUSE

chief and took the money and then summoned the bouncers from downstairs and had him tossed into the alley. The countryman complained to the police and the four women were brought into court, but he was unable to prove anything, and they were released. A year or so later Lizzie Collins developed a mania which proved her undoing — instead of stealing money from the men whom she took to her room, she waited until they were asleep and then cut the buttons off their pants and stored them away. The time soon came when she had a great supply of buttons but no money to pay her rent, so Archie Murphy kicked her out. Thereafter her reputation in Gallatin Street was very bad. The general opinion was that while a man might be willing to take a chance with his money, his buttons should be sacred.

339

Another of Archie Murphy's girls who made a name for herself in her particular field was Mary Jane Jackson, a husky, full-bodied strumpet whose mop of flaming red hair had earned her the sobriquet of Bricktop. As far as toughness and the ability to take care of herself in a fight were concerned, Bricktop lost nothing in comparison with the male bullies of Gallatin Street, even the most ferocious of the Live Oaks. She was never whipped, and in a career of some eight years in the bordellos and dance-houses of New Orleans she killed four men and stabbed and slung-shotted a score of others. She was born in Girod Street, about 1836, and was the natural product of her environment. At thirteen she was a prostitute, and at fourteen she was in fairly comfortable circumstances as the mistress of a Poydras Street bartender. She lived with him for three years, until she was seventeen, when he tired of her and locked her out, whereupon she charged into his saloon and gave him a terrible beating which sent him to the hospital, lacking one ear and most of his nose. Bricktop then entered a bordello in Dauphine Street, and while she was popular enough with the men — she was a handsome girl with an exceptionally fine figure — she kept the house in such a turmoil that after a few weeks she was turned into the street. She was similarly discharged from half a dozen other bagnios, and about 1865 went down to Gallatin Street and got a job in Archie Murphy's Dance-House.

Bricktop was the scourge of Gallatin Street for about a year and a half, during which period she committed two of her murders — she beat one man to death with a club, and stabbed another, known as Long Charley because of his height; he stood almost seven feet in his socks and was as thin as the proverbial beanpole. In the Long Charley killing she used her favorite knife, which had been made to her order from her own design; it had a heavy five-inch blade at each end, with a center grip handsomely mounted in German silver. With this fearsome weapon clutched in her fist, she could slash, cut, and stab in any direction without changing the position of her hand. Bricktop remained a member of Archie Murphy's staff for only a few weeks; she proved too tough even for Gallatin Street. She was almost constantly involved in fights; with few exceptions the other women were afraid of her, and the men had as little as possible to do with her because she was too handy with her knife. Murphy threw her out, and so did a dozen other dance-house proprietors who had mistakenly thought they could tame her. During the latter part of 1857 Bricktop became, of necessity, a free-lance prostitute, sneak thief, and pickpocket, and moved into a little house in Dauphine Street with three sisters in sin whose combative dispositions had likewise caused them to be barred from the Gallatin Street dance-houses — Ellen Collins, a mite of a woman but a terror in battle; America Williams, who was almost six feet tall and stronger than most men; and Delia Swift, a fiery redhead who was better known by the appropriate name of Bridget Fury. With the exception of Bricktop Jackson herself, Bridget Fury was probably the toughest woman in the New Orleans of her time. As Bricktop had done, she started young — she entered upon a life of depravity and crime at the age of twelve, in a Cincinnati dance-house where her father was a fiddler until he killed a girl and was sent to the Ohio state prison. Soon thereafter Bridget Fury came to New Orleans, where her career closely paralleled that of Bricktop Jackson. She was the first of the fearful foursome to retire from the scene of their triumphs — she murdered a man at the Poydras Street Market in 1858, and was sentenced to life imprisonment.

Bricktop Jackson committed her third murder about a year after justice had finally overtaken Bridget Fury. On November 7, 1859, accompanied by Ellen Collins and America Williams, she went into Joe Seidensahl's beer garden at Rampart and St. Peter Streets and began drinking. At the table next to them Laurent Fleury, one of Seidensahl's boarders, was eating lunch. Bricktop picked up a knife, and when Fleury told her to put it down she replied with a torrent of obscene invective and threatened to cut his heart out. Fleury, who had not recognized the redoubtable Bricktop, promptly slapped her, whereupon the three women leaped upon him, screaming with rage. In a moment he was the luckless center of a mass of swirling skirts, clutching fingers, and flashing knives. Seidensahl came to Fleury's assistance, but he was unarmed, and the women drove the two men before them into the back yard, where Seidensahl was seriously cut and Fleury was stabbed half a dozen times. He died three days later. One of Seidensahl's employees shot at the embattled harridans from an upstairs window, but they drove him away with a shower of bricks. Ellen Collins escaped before the police arrived, but Bricktop and America Williams were arrested and committed for trial. They were acquitted because the Coroner, under whose direction a very sketchy post-mortem examination had been made, was unable to say under oath what had killed Fleury. Bricktop's lawyer successfully contended that he had died of heart disease.

While she was in the Parish Prison awaiting trial, Bricktop became enamored of one of the prison turnkeys, a notorious ruffian named John Miller, who had been for more than a decade the acknowledged bully of Gretna, across the river from New Orleans. Miller was born in Gretna, and for several years had been a manager and handler of prizefighters. In 1854, when he was barely twenty-five years old, he had under his wing a heavyweight, Charley Keys, who had defeated every pugilistic aspirant on the Gretna side of the Mississippi. A match was arranged with Tom Murray, a noted bruiser of Gallatin Street, and the men met on the river bank near Miller's shanty at Freetown, afterwards called Goldsborough, between Gretna and Algiers. Keys was being beaten when Miller attacked Murray's principal backer with a knife. A general mêlée ensued, and Miller's left arm was so badly cut that amputation was necessary. When the stump healed he fastened a chain to it, and on the end of the chain welded an iron ball about the size of a baseball. With a knife in his remaining hand and the iron ball whirling about his head, Miller was a terrible opponent in a fight. He was the undisputed lord of Gretna until early in 1857, when he came to New Orleans, killed a man in a fight in Gallatin Street, and was sentenced to two years in the Parish Prison. Having served his term, he was, for some reason known only to the politicians, appointed turnkey.

When Bricktop Jackson was acquitted of the murder of Laurent Fleury and released from prison, Miller resigned his job, and the precious pair went to his shack at Freetown. There they lived for almost two years in constant turmoil, varying their domestic brawls with occasional trips to Gallatin Street, where they were about as welcome as a breath of fresh air, and where they proved that they were more than a match for the dance-house bouncers. The daily battles in which Miller and Bricktop engaged began to assume a serious aspect in October 1861, when she slashed him with her knife and went to New Orleans. Miller followed and begged her to return to him, and she finally went back to Freetown. On December 5, 1861 Miller came home with a cowhide whip and told Bricktop that she was getting too fresh and needed a good thrashing. She promptly took the whip away from him and gave him an unmerciful beating. He tried to brain her with his iron ball, but she seized it in mid-air and began to drag him toward her by the chain affixed to the stump of his left arm. Frantic with fear and rage, Miller drew a knife, but she snatched it from his hand, slammed him against the wall of the shanty, and held him by the throat while she stabbed him five times. He was dead when she let his body fall to the floor. The news of the murder didn't reach New Orleans until December 8, when the *Picayune* published a short paragraph which said simply that John Miller had been killed by Mary Jane Jackson. It concluded:

" Both were degraded beings, regular penitentiary birds, habitual drunkards, and unworthy of any further notice from honest people."

On December 9 the *Daily Crescent* thus commented on Bricktop's career:

" This woman has been concerned in several murders, and is remarkable for bestial habits and ferocious manners. By the law making an example of her the community will be rid of two nuisances."

Bricktop was sent to prison for the killing of Miller, but both she and Bridget Fury were released in September 1862, when the Military Governor of the state, General George F. Shepley, virtually emptied the penitentiary by means of blanket pardons. Bricktop apparently never returned to New Orleans, but Bridget Fury was a familiar figure about the city for another decade, although during her four years behind the bars she had lost a great deal of her belligerence. She opened a bordello in Dryades Street in the autumn of 1859, but a week or so later two Texans were robbed of $761 in the dive, and Bridget and five of her girls were brought into court. And as the *Times* said, " a more bedraggled and desperate looking set would be difficult to imagine." Bridget Fury served several months in jail for her share of the theft, and when she was released her bagnio was in other hands. Within another year she was a besotted hag, sleeping in the gutters and being arrested two or three times a week for drunkenness. All that remained of her former prosperity were the long brass pendants which her father had placed in her ears when he put her to work in the Cincinnati dance-house.

5

BESIDES Archie Murphy's place, the best-known of the dance-houses which flourished during the many years that Gallatin Street was the center of a vicious underworld district were the Green Tree, the Amsterdam, the Stockholm, the Blue Light, the Baltimore, Andy Bradley's, George Kent's; the Canton House, which was closed in 1867 when Oliver Canton kicked a sailor to death in the bar-room; and the Blue Anchor, before which hung a sign further identifying it as " Mother Burke's Den." Of all these, by far the toughest and most notorious were the Amsterdam, on Gallatin Street near Hospital (Nicholls), and the Green Tree, a three-storey building on Gallatin two doors from Barracks Street. The latter dive, distinguished by a large sign on which was painted a tree in full foliage, was opened about 1850, and for several years was operated by an old woman named Morgan, who set a pattern of conduct which was faithfully followed by succeeding landlords. A few years before the Civil War it came into the hands of Harry Rice, who ran it until the summer of 1864, when he was stoned almost to death by a mob of sailors who complained that he had un-duly watered their liquor. Rice was rescued by a detachment of United States cavalrymen, but he was so seriously injured that he closed the Green Tree and retired from Gallatin Street. The dive was reopened early in 1865 by Mary Rich, otherwise known as One-Legged Duffy, but she was mur-dered in July of that same year by her lover, Charley Duffy, who dragged her into a shed behind the resort, stabbed her five times, and for good measure beat her brains out with her own wooden leg. Then Paddy Welsh, who had been run-ning a saloon on Girod Street, came down to Gallatin Street to operate the Green Tree. He made the mistake of defying the Live Oak Boys, and the ruffians wrecked the place and warned him not to reopen it. Welsh ignored the warning, started business anew, and the next morning disappeared. A few days later his body, with the skull fractured, was found in the river.

Several months after Welsh's death the Green Tree was acquired by William Lee, who had come to New Orleans during the Civil War as a drum-major of the United States Army. Later he was a policeman for a year or so. He was killed by Bill Knuckley. The last landlord of the resort was Tom Pickett, who took over the place early in 1872 and prospered until 1876. On January 10 of the latter year the Green Tree was raided, and considerable damage was done to the furnishings, by a group of Live Oaks, among them Jack Lowe, Mike and Bill Knuckley, and Crazy Bill Anderson. Pickett drank heavily all the next day, and during the early evening put a revolver in his pocket and went hunting for the men who had wrecked his property. In Jack Smith's saloon on Levee Street he found Jack Lowe and the Knuckley brothers drinking at the bar. "I been lookin' for you fellers," Pickett said, and fired a bullet into Jack Lowe's head. He then turned his gun upon Bill Knuckley, but Mike jumped in front of his brother and was shot in the heart, while Bill Knuckley fled, probably the only time that a Live Oak ever ran from trouble. Pickett was sentenced to life imprisonment, but escaped when the state penitentiary caught fire on February 21, 1885. He was last heard of in New York.

The Amsterdam Dance-House was opened in 1845 by William Wilson, who went to California during the gold rush and was hanged there by the Vigilantes. The dive then passed through the hands of various owners, all of whom enhanced its reputation for viciousness, until about 1860, when it came into the possession of Conrad Lehman and

Dan O'Neil, the latter a well-known handler of fighting dogs. When New Orleans was captured by the Federal forces, Lehman sold his interest in the Amsterdam to O'Neil and returned to Germany. O'Neil shrewdly made peace with the Live Oak Boys and paid them to keep away, and ran the resort with great success until early in 1869, when he began to have trouble with the police. He first came to public notice in February of that year, when Molly Mason, a former Amsterdam girl who had fled with her lover and the night's receipts, returned to the resort and asked for her job back. She was received with apparent friendliness, but the first drink served to her was drugged, and when she collapsed she was stripped naked and thrown into the street, where she was dragged into an alley and cruelly abused by half a dozen men. On July 17 the police raided the Amsterdam and served upon O'Neil a warrant charging him with keeping a house of ill fame. Politicians procured O'Neil's release, but twelve of his women were fined ten dollars each. A week later police closed the Amsterdam, and the newspapers said that the action had been taken because the place had been complained of as a nuisance. O'Neil, however, probably came nearer the truth in a letter which was published in the *Times* on July 31, 1869:

> *To the reporter of the N. O. Times — About the Amsterdam Dance-House — there ain't much in it, as you have written, as appeared in your evening's edition, that's true. As for leaving there I paid, during the past five months, to the Captain of Police, $80 for each of three months, and $40 for each of two. In other words, I paid the police during that time, $320 for keeping the place open. I believe if there had been no trouble about paying up regular I would have been allowed to stay there still.*

> (*Signed*) DAN'L O'NEIL

347

O'Neil made the necessary arrangements with the police and resumed operations with a full staff of harlots and musicians, but apparently he continued to fall behind in his payments, for the resort was again closed in November. The police told the newspapers that after being given another chance O'Neil had violated an ordinance which prohibited the renting of rooms to prostitutes, and another, adopted in 1817, which forbade the owner of a ballroom to admit any person carrying a weapon.

During the summer of 1869 the Amsterdam was the object of much unfavorable attention because it became known as the favorite rendezvous of Vincent Bayonne and Pedro Abriel, burglars and professional murderers, and as the place where they had planned the crime which finally sent them to the gallows. Early in June they were approached by one of the mates of a Spanish bark then lying in the river, and offered six dollars to kill a sailor who, the mate said, had threatened him with a knife. Bayonne and Abriel made the acquaintance of the sailor, gave him a drink or two at the Amsterdam, and then took him to the levee, where Bayonne knocked him down with a club. Bayonne was about to strike again when Abriel seized his arm and cried:

"Let me finish him!"

Bayonne refused, and Abriel hit him. They fought fiercely, while their victim lay unconscious on the levee, awaiting the outcome of the strange battle. Abriel finally knocked Bayonne senseless and then proceeded to finish the sailor, stabbing him seventeen times and throwing the body into the river. Unfortunately for them, the murderers confided the gory details of the crime to Isadore Boyd, a cigarette-maker, and on Boyd's testimony were convicted and sentenced to hang. The day before the execution, accompanied by a guard, Bayonne made a tour of the Parish Prison, bidding everyone good-by. He then carefully inspected the gallows, pointed out where he wished to sit, and sprinkled the trap-door from a bottle which he said contained holy water. The next day, May 14, 1871, he and Abriel were duly hanged, and the *Times* published an account of the execution under these headlines:

EXPIATION
Execution of Bayonne and Abriel
SCENES AND INCIDENTS
Etc.   *Etc.*   *Etc.*

The Amsterdam never reopened after the police closed it in the fall of 1869, nor did the Green Tree find another tenant when Tom Pickett was sent to prison. The latter building remained vacant until about 1880, when the ground floor became a bakery and the upstairs a private residence. It was destroyed by fire on the afternoon of April 19, 1886.

CHAPTER XII

SOME LOOSE LADIES OF
BASIN STREET

THE FAME of New Orleans as the gayest place on the North American continent was spread by the ballrooms, the cafés and coffee-houses, the hotels and restaurants, the elegant gambling-establishments, and the unrestrained merriment of the Mardi Gras festival. But the fact that at the same time the city was notorious throughout the world as a veritable cesspool of sin was principally due to the prevalence of prostitution, which in turn was due to the tolerance with which it was regarded by the authorities and the people generally. This attitude, eagerly embraced by the American politician because of the protection it afforded to one of his most lucrative fields of graft, was based upon the Latin viewpoint that prostitution was an inevitable and necessary evil, to be regulated rather than suppressed; it became such a definite municipal characteristic that it persisted until comparatively recent years. From Bienville to the World War commercialized vice was the most firmly entrenched phase of underworld activity in New Orleans; it was not only big business on its own account, owning some of the best property in the city and giving employment to thousands, but was also the foundation upon which the keepers of the concert-saloons, cabarets, dance-houses, and other low resorts reared their fantastic structures of prosperity. Without the lure of the harlot it is doubtful if such districts as the Swamp and Gallatin Street, and the Franklin Street area which Bison Williams described as " the only locality in the city where decent people do not live," could have existed.

Prostitution in early New Orleans passed through two distinct periods of growth and expansion. The first occurred during the thirty years that followed the Louisiana Purchase, when the underworld was engaged almost exclusively in pandering to the lusty heroes of the flatboat crews, and of its own accord kept vice confined to the districts frequented by the river men, with the exception of a few so-called high-class places which operated with considerable circumspection in Royal, Chartres, and other streets of the French Quarter. The second period commenced in the late 1840's, when New Orleans was in the full flush of its development as an important seaport and a cosmopolitan city, and when virtually every department of the municipal government was notoriously corrupt and demoralized. It was during the early years of the latter era that prostitution began to leave the recognized underworld sections and establish itself in the new quarter above Canal Street, especially that portion lying north and northwest of St. Charles Avenue. From this vantage point it invaded the Vieux Carré as the American politicians completed the rout of the bewildered Creoles, consolidated the city under their domination, transferred the important branches of the government from the Cabildo to the new City Hall at Lafayette Square, and gradually compelled the removal of business and industrial activity to the American section.

Beyond a few meaningless and futile gestures for the benefit of the reform groups which even in New Orleans occasionally appeared on the political scene, the authorities made no attempt to halt the march of the harlots into the fine residential areas, despite the ruinous effect upon real estate and the complaints of hundreds of property-owners who were forced by the proximity of boisterous brothels to

abandon their homes. The movement was likewise encouraged rather than hampered by the Yankee military forces
during the Civil War, and by the carpetbaggers who
brought the state and city to the verge of ruin in reconstruction time. By 1870, when New Orleans had a population of
approximately 190,000, bordellos of every degree of viciousness, from the ten-dollar parlor-house to the fifteen-cent
Negro crib, were running wide open on such important
streets as Gravier, St. John, Chartres, St. Charles, Basin,
Union, Royal, Canal, Burgundy, Poydras, Baronne, Gasquet
(now Cleveland), Customhouse (now Iberville), Dryades,
Dauphine, Common, Rampart, Toulouse, St. Peter, Bienville, Villere, Conti, Camp, Bourbon, St. Louis, Trèmé
(now North Liberty), Perdido, Franklin, and a score of
others besides; except in the outlying parts of the city, there
was scarcely a block in New Orleans which did not contain
at least one brothel or assignation house.

Almost from the beginning of the American occupation, until open vice was officially abolished some twenty
years ago, the brothels, with little or no concealment, paid
tribute to the corrupt politicians, the police, and various
officials of the state and city governments. The payments
which were divided among the higher-ups varied with the
prosperity of the bagnios and the rapacity of the grafters;
sometimes, especially during the Mardi Gras celebrations,
when the city was full of strangers and the strangers full of
liquor, and in consequence free spenders, they were as high
as two hundred dollars a week for each of the large parlor-
houses, and twenty dollars for the lowest of the cribs. In
times of depression, however, the canny politicians and officials not only omitted their regular collections, but frequently
advanced money to pay the running expenses of the brothels
until business improved, when they shared heavily in the
gross income. In addition, particularly during the reconstruction period, when every conceivable source of graft was

thoroughly explored, the erection and equipment of many of the larger houses were financed by state and city officials and political leaders, and house warmings were held which were attended by the chivalry of Louisiana politics, the flower having been left at home with the children.

The rank and file of the police force, and the petty precinct officers, seldom shared in the larger spoils which accrued to their political superiors. They imposed their own levies, usually twenty-five cents a week upon each inmate of a crib, and a dollar upon the prostitute domiciled in an elegant parlor-house. Payments for officials and politicians were customarily made through trusted saloon-keepers or civilian agents, although during the reign of the carpetbaggers many statesmen went from house to house making their own collections. The money for the cop on the beat was left on the stoop on designated nights. There are still many people in New Orleans who recall the days when little piles of quarters and dollars could be seen on the doorsteps of the brothels by early risers; and newspaper reporters who remember when policemen assigned to the red-light districts came into the station-houses at weekly intervals with their pockets bulging with coins.

For sheer innocuity the laws by which the authorities pretended to regulate the conduct of the " woman notoriously abandoned to lewdness," as the old statutes described the practicing prostitute, have probably never been surpassed in an American city. Prostitution was not *per se* a crime; under an ordinance adopted in 1817 the harlot was subject to punishment only if she " shall occasion scandals or disturb the tranquillity of the neighborhood," when she could be fined twenty-five dollars or imprisoned for one month. Any person who furnished lodging to " a woman or girl of that description " was liable to a fine of fifteen dollars for each day after due notice had been given by the Mayor. Another law, passed in 1837, empowered the Mayor, upon receipt of a petition signed by three respectable citizens, to order the ejection of prostitutes from any premises against which complaint had been made. In 1845, while New Orleans was still divided into three municipalities, the Council of Municipality No. One reduced by two the number of reputable signatures required. In 1839 prostitutes were prohibited from occupying the ground floor of any building in Municipality No. One, and in 1845 they were forbidden to frequent, or drink in, any coffee-house or cabaret. These laws, which were seldom enforced, were retained in substance on the statute books of New Orleans until a very few years before the beginning of the present century. With the exception of the general vagrancy and nuisance ordinances, they were the only weapons at the disposal of the police on those rare occasions when it was deemed necessary to make a gesture against prostitution. The vagrancy and nuisance laws were principally used to hale the harlots into court and fine them — madames $25 each and their girls $10. Said the *Picayune* on July 13, 1861:

"It is about this time of the year annually that the moral sensitiveness of our police becomes suddenly alive to the immoral neighborhoods of certain portions of our city, and arrests are accordingly made to replenish the depleted treasury. It would be much better for the morality of the city if the authorities would resort at once to direct taxation."

The city had anticipated the *Picayune's* advice four years before, in 1857, when the Common Council passed Ordinance No. 3267, "concerning lewd and abandoned women," which marked the first and only attempt by an American municipality to license prostitution. Section One of this law provided "that it shall not be lawful for any woman or girl, notoriously abandoned to lewdness," to occupy any one-story building, or the lower floor of any house, within these limits:

First District — between the River, Felicity Road, Hercules Street, the New Canal, Claiborne Avenue, and Canal Street.

Second District — between the River and Basin Street, Canal and Toulouse Streets, and between the River, the Bayou St. John, Toulouse and Esplanade Streets.

Third District — between Esplanade Street, Elysian Fields Street, the River and Broad Street.

Fourth District — between the River, the Carrollton Railroad, the upper line of the District, and Felicity Road.

So far as residence in a one-story building or on the ground floor was concerned, this section, theoretically at least, banished the prostitute to the sparsely settled outskirts. A fine of twenty-five dollars was imposed for violation, with a further penalty of twenty-five dollars for each day, after the third, that the offense continued.

It was with Section Three of the ordinance that the Common Council hoped to bring into the city coffers an annual revenue of from $75,000 to $100,000. Under its provisions a prostitute might live, and a madame operate a brothel, above the first floor of any building in New Orleans if licenses were first obtained from the office of the Mayor. The annual fees were fixed at $100 for a harlot and $250 for the keeper of a bordello. Failure to procure a license was punishable by a fine of $100, half of which went to the informer.

Succeeding sections provided fines ranging from $5 to $25 for disturbing the peace, for occasioning scandals, and for drinking in coffee-houses or cabarets; prohibited white and Negro prostitutes from living in the same house, and forbade them to accost men from the doors and windows of

355

their houses, to " sit upon the steps thereof in an indecent posture," or to " stroll about the streets of the city decently attired."

This unique ordinance was adopted on March 10, 1857, signed by Mayor Charles M. Waterman and the presidents

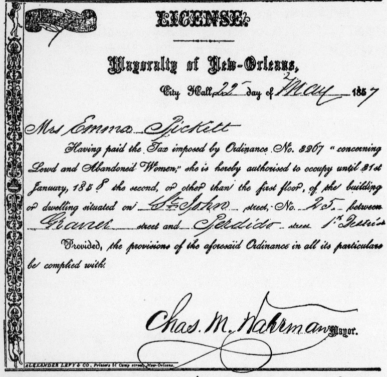

A BROTHEL-KEEPER'S LICENSE OF 1857

of the Board of Aldermen and the Board of Assistant Aldermen — H. M. Summers and John M. Hall — and went into effect on April 1. Within the next month and a half sixteen women paid the taxes and received licenses signed by the Mayor on engraved forms appropriately decorated with smiling Cupids. The seventeenth applicant was Mrs. Emma Pickett, who on May 22 applied for a license to operate a brothel at No. 25 St. John Street, between Gravier and Perdido. She paid the fee of $250 under protest, and immediately filed a suit, financed by her sister madames, to test the legality of the law. The courts eventually held that the law was unconstitutional, and ordered the authorities to return the money which had already been collected from the prostitutes. Successive appeals having failed, the city abandoned the licensing law in 1859, and not until almost forty years later was a system devised which effectually regulated prostitution in New Orleans.

2

WHILE a score of New Orleans streets acquired great celebrity as abodes of vice during the Civil War and reconstruction periods, and successfully maintained their reputations for many years thereafter, the giddy heights of world-wide notoriety were reached only by Basin Street, which began at St. Peter Street in the French Quarter, ran southward to Canal, and thence in the same general direction through the American section to Toledano Street. Although it has long since vanished from the map of New Orleans,[1] the glories of Basin Street are still celebrated in a popular blues song, often heard on the radio, which describes it as " heaven on earth," and " the place where the white and the black folks meet." As a matter of fact Basin Street was never frequented by Negroes, and it certainly was not heaven, though of course opinion may differ on that point. But for almost half a century it was the principal artery of the red-light district, a scarlet thread through the heart of New Orleans; and during the greater part of that time, after about 1880, it was entirely given over to vice from St. Louis Street to Tulane Avenue. On both sides the street was lined with the

---

[1] From Canal Street to Common Street and Tulane Avenue, Basin Street is now Elk Place. On the other side of Canal, in the French Quarter, the Southern Railway Station occupies part of the old Basin Street, and the remainder is called Crozat Street.

most pretentious, luxurious, and expensive brothels in the United States — three-story mansions of brick and brownstone, many of them built with the aid of politicians and state and city officials, and filled with mahogany and black walnut woodwork, and furniture, Oriental rugs and carpets, silver door-knobs, grand pianos, carved marble fireplaces and mantels, and copies of famous paintings and statuary. A reporter for the New Orleans *Times,* in company with a police official, visited one of the gaudy dives of Basin Street in 1869 and appears to have been greatly affected by the spectacle. Entrance to the brothel, he wrote in his paper of February 7, was " through a passageway adorned with a couple of statues representing some obscure divinities of light, and in whose hands were held lighted flambeaux. Beyond this lay the drawing-room, peopled with a few figures in glittering attire, and who, from their costumes and manners, might have been visitants from the Mountains of the Moon Neither did the decorations of the rooms, in the pictures that hung from the walls, the plated mirrors, the delicately-tinted furniture, appear to be altogether of a sub-lunar character, though evidently intended to embody a sybarite's dream — luxury and repose. The grotesque and bizarre aspect of everything — splendor without comfort, glitter and sparkle suggestive of death and decay — gave rise to singular reflections." But what the reflections were he didn't say.

Only wine and champagne were served in these sumptuous palaces; the ladies wore evening gowns, and in many houses could be seen only by appointment; and between business conferences in the luxurious boudoirs the harlots and their gentleman callers were entertained by strolling musicians, dancers, singers, and jugglers who nightly went from house to house offering refined and artistic performances. A few of the larger brothels of this period were staffed by as many as thirty women, each of whom paid her madame from thirty to fifty dollars a week for board and lodging, and as much more for laundry and incidentals. The fees paid by customers ranged from five to twenty dollars for one amatory experience and from twenty to fifty dollars if a man wished to spend the night. The latter prices included breakfast and, if necessary, cab-fare home. In later years, as Basin Street declined considerably in tone and increased prodigiously in viciousness, the rates underwent a drastic reduction. During the period of the legal segregated area plenty of women were available in Basin Street for a dollar; while the wine of an earlier day was replaced by beer, the evening gowns by Mother Hubbards or nothing at all, the juggling and dancing by erotic exhibitions and the hoochy-koochy; and the melodious outpourings of the fiddlers and guitarists gave way to the weird noises of mechanical pianos and music boxes and the efforts of such entertainers as a popular barfly called Happy Charley, who blew a tin whistle through his nose and, as he played, sang a ditty entitled " Der Nue Orleans Tuff," herewith quoted verbatim from the *Lantern* of May 14, 1887:

> I am a man dat most of yer know,
> I'm known as a knocker wherever I go.
> My fame it is fightin'; I kan't get enuff,
> All over de town dey call me a tuff;
> Yes, I'm a man dat de people all dread,
> And when I gets rowdy I paints de town red.
> I know all de cops; I stan' in wid de roughs,
> Yer kin bet yer sweet life I'm er Nu'leens tuff.

The evolution of Basin Street from an insignificant lane through the woods and swamps into an important thorough-fare began in the 1830's, during the boom times of the American quarter, when New Orleans was experiencing a phenomenal growth in population — between 1820 and 1840

359

the number of inhabitants increased from 41,000 to 102,000. For more than two decades Basin Street was one of the finest residential districts in the city, with handsome shade trees and imposing mansions occupied by wealthy American families. But unfortunately it lay directly in the path of the prostitutes when they started their northward and eastward movement from Tchoupitoulas Street and the Swamp through Common, Canal, Perdido, Union, Rampart, and other streets, where bordellos were established several years before the Civil War. A few assignation houses appear to have been in operation on Basin Street as early as 1860, but the first of the big brothels was erected about 1866 by Kate Townsend at No. 40,[1] on the present site of the Elks Club. According to an article in the New Orleans *Times* for September 22, 1870, signed "Suffering Property Holder," it was built at the joint expense of a high police official, a Recorder, and several members of the Common Council. "Indeed," the article continued, "we have understood that the lady of an Alderman, who heard that her husband visited the house, resolved to see for herself. She disguised herself and entered the house, where she found nearly the whole city government, with the President of the Board of Aldermen or the Mayor — we forget which — at the head of the table and her husband at the foot." There are, of course, no records to prove either the truth or the falsity of "Suffering Property Holder's" statements, but it is very likely that they were correct, for Kate Townsend was one of the most influential courtesans in the history of New Orleans, and for many years, particularly while the carpetbaggers were in power, her bordello was a favorite haunt of the politicians and city officials. Moreover, her successful defloration of Basin Street had paved the way for such an influx of pros-

---

[1] All addresses used in this chapter are according to the old method of numbering, which has been superseded by the centennial system, with a hundred numbers to a block.

titutes that within a few years the finest part of the thoroughfare above Canal Street had lost all semblance of respectability. Said "Suffering Property Holder" in the *Times*:

"The opening of another of those 'whited sepulchres' on Basin Street offers a fitting opportunity of calling the attention of the public, and particularly the city authorities and the police, to the condition of this fine street. Between Canal and Common Streets[1] almost every house is of bad repute, lighted up at night with music and revelry within, having a constant stream of men going in and out, and the late investigation into the homicide that took place in the den No. 40 reveals the scenes that are nightly therein enacted. To such a state has the neighborhood come that several of our most respectable citizens have had to sell their family mansions at half the price they cost to build, and have removed from the locality, and others we learn are about to follow, as they cannot permit their families longer to remain within hearing and seeing of the nightly orgies that are going on there."

Some of the prostitutes and brothel-keepers who followed Kate Townsend into Basin Street remained on that thoroughfare for many years; their names and memories of the manifold elegancies of their establishments are still preserved in the traditions of the red-light district. A swarthy beauty who called herself Minnie Haha and claimed to be a descendant of the heroine of Longfellow's poem — she is said to have had an oil painting in her parlor labeled "Mr. and Mrs. Hiawatha, Ancestors of Minnie Haha" — put a housekeeper in charge of her Union Street brothel late in 1868 and opened a swanky place on Basin Street near the

---

[1] In those days Common Street ran from the river to the city limits, but it now widens at Rampart Street and becomes Tulane Avenue.

Townsend mansion. At the curb in front of the house she installed a huge granite hitching-block equipped with gilded iron rings, with her name chiseled upon it in large letters, and attended by a uniformed Negro boy — he wore a scarlet jacket with " Minnie Haha, Welcome," embroidered on the chest in gold — to take the gentlemen's carriages. For the horses, Minnie Haha provided daily a bag of apples. More-over, when a man spent the night at Minnie Haha's he arose in the morning to find his clothing pressed and his shoes polished.

A few doors from this picturesque house of sin, at No. 18, Leila Barton operated a brothel which was described by the *Times* in 1870 as " one of the most fashionable palaces of the demi-monde." It was the scene of considerable com motion on March 5 of that year, when, according to the *Times,* "Mrs. H., wife of a well-known merchant, walked in with a new six-shooter and fired at Blanche Russell," an inmate, who Mrs. H. said was her husband's mistress. Only one cartridge exploded, however, and no one was hurt. Gentle Annie Reed opened a big house at No. 88 Basin Street about 1868, but a year or so later she removed to Customhouse Street, and No. 88 was run for many years by Kitty Johnson, who was noted for the multiplicity of her lovers. Two of them, Billy Walsh and J. J. Heley, fought a duel on the sidewalk in front of the house in 1882, while Kitty Johnson and her staff watched from the window, and in the kitchen the cook labored over a sumptuous dinner which the brothel-keeper had promised as a reward for the victor. After several shots had been exchanged Walsh was mortally wounded. " Billy Walsh was a notoriously wicked man for many years," said the *States* on August 2. " He was a cab driver, a detective, and a gambler. During his turbu-lent life in this city he was engaged in many disreputable affrays, and finally terminated his career as he lived — riot-ously and in blood."

The Mascot, 1886

"OUR HOUSES OF PROSTITUTION; THEIR
INMATES, PATRONS AND OWNERS"

Josephine Killeen was madame of a brothel at No. 45 Basin Street, opposite Kate Townsend's, where the big attraction in 1870 was the ten-year-old daughter of Molly Williams, an inmate of the resort. Mother and child were sold jointly for fifty dollars a night. When the police said this was going a bit too far and took the little girl away, Josephine Killeen denounced their action as an outrage; she protested that the child was simply helping her mother get along in the world. A similar plea was made a few weeks later by Kate Smith, who advertised by chastely engraved cards distributed in the saloons that none of the girls in her establishment near Canal Street was more than seventeen years old. In March 1870, during one of their rare periods of righteous wrath over what went on among the red lights, the police took two young girls from Kate Smith's dive, one of whom said that she had been a prostitute for four years, since she was twelve. The brothel-keeper said the girls were her sister's children, and that they were really entitled to great credit because they gave all their earnings to their mother and visited her every Sunday morning. The *Times* said on March 10, 1870: "The house has the reputation of being of the lowest character, and at the same time of having more frequenters of this age than any other house in the city." Another Basin Street brothel of more than ordinary notoriety was the three-story brick mansion at No. 21, which during the 1880's was a mulatto resort operated by Hattie Strauss and known simply as Twenty-One. When the carpetbaggers were riding roughshod over New Orleans and Louisiana, Twenty-One was run for a year or two by Hattie Hamilton, one of the three women who made Basin Street history (the others were Kate Townsend and the incredible Fanny Sweet) and the beloved of Senator James D. Beares, a member of the fantastic "black-and-tan" Legislature. In an account of Hattie Hamilton's death in 1882 the *States* described Beares as "one of the most profligate and corrupt Senators under the radical regime, and whose vote for a measure was only to be obtained by substantial pecuniary reward. His corruption was so notorious that he earned the sobriquet of 'Where does Beares come in?'"

Hattie Hamilton's maiden name was Peacock, and she is said to have been the daughter of a prosperous shopkeeper of Port Richmond, New York. On March 3, 1855 she was married in that town to Samuel W. Plume, who took her to Cuba, where their one child, a son, was born. Plume sent her back to New York when he learned that she was on the roster of a Havana call-house, and himself came to New Orleans with his son a few years later and became a policeman. In 1864 his wife appeared in New Orleans in company with a gambler who called himself " Colonel " Hamilton, and for a year or so she was a familiar figure in the cafés and theaters, while the " Colonel " cut a wide swath in the gambling-houses, and the wronged husband wearily plodded his beat and played nurse-maid to his young son. During this period of her career Hattie Hamilton was renowned in New Orleans for her charm and beauty, although when she died the *Mascot* said that she had " a glass eye and other infirmities." But when she began to acquire almost equal renown for promiscuity, " Colonel " Hamilton cast her off, and Plume divorced her in 1866 when she entered Tilly Phillips's brothel in Rampart Street. Early in 1869 she transferred her allegiance to Julia Davis's place in Customhouse Street, one of the toughest dives in the city, and in April of that year was one of three harlots arrested by Policeman Plume for fighting.

A few months after this encounter Hattie Hamilton's affairs took a turn for the better — she met the statesman Beares, and so impressed him with her beauty and skill at harlotry that he took her out of the Davis resort, bought her fine raiment, a red-wheeled carriage, and a matched pair of high-stepping horses, and installed her in style as the

madame of No. 21 Basin Street, which she staffed with a
score of beautiful and accomplished bawds. Under her expert management Twenty-One became almost immediately
one of the most popular brothels in the city, and for a while,
owing to the influence of the Senator, seriously threatened
to usurp the place of Kate Townsend's resort in the affections of the politicians. Once Twenty-One was in good running order, however, Hattie Hamilton left its affairs largely
in the hands of a housekeeper and began to spend much of
her time at the home of Senator Beares on St. Charles
Avenue, where she posed as his wife, and where they indulged in protracted drinking-bouts which continued for days
at a time. On the night of May 26, 1870 the Senator and
Hattie Hamilton began drinking heavily after dinner, and
several times during the night Beares's Negro butler, Robert
Phillips, heard them quarreling and scuffling about the room.
About dawn the Negro heard a shot, and a few minutes later
found Senator Beares lying on a couch dying from a bullet-
wound in the abdomen, while Hattie Hamilton sat in a
chair and regarded him with drunken gravity. On the floor
between them was a pistol, which disappeared during the
next few hours and was never found.

Phillips summoned the Senator's brother, George
Beares, who notified the police. Subsequent procedure in the
case was declared by the *Times* to be " altogether irregular "
and was never satisfactorily explained. Hattie Hamilton
was taken in custody, but not formally arrested, and was
released within twenty-four hours without being questioned.
George Beares refused to make a charge against the woman,
but he did accuse the Negro butler, and Phillips was arrested
as an accessory to the murder. But when he was examined
before Recorder Walsh on June 7, 1870, George Beares
said he knew nothing of the case and refused to testify, while
Patrick Clark, an intimate friend of the Senator's and a
frequent visitor to his house, swore he had never seen Phil-

lips before he appeared in court. Consequently the Negro was released and the investigation abandoned. The general belief was that both Hattie Hamilton and Phillips had become privy to so many of the Senator's secrets that his friends and relatives couldn't afford to go further into the circumstances of the killing.

Business fell off at No. 21 Basin Street following the death of Senator Beares, and after a year or so Hattie Hamilton sold the resort and opened a place at No. 158 Customhouse Street, which was a notorious dive for some ten years. She died at Old Point Comfort, Virginia, on August 9, 1882, leaving all of her property to David Jackson, owner of the Gem concert-saloon on Royal Street. The *Mascot* said that Jackson had "looked after her affairs and kept the cash books and accounts" of the brothel; according to the court records in the Succession of Hattie Hamilton, she had been his mistress since 1877. The newspapers estimated the Hamilton estate at $200,000, but an inventory at the probate of the will showed that it amounted to $2,-149.75. After the debts had been paid, only $719.20 remained as the profit of a lifetime of vice. Jackson, however, did not receive even this modest sum, for Hattie Hamilton's son, John J. Plume, appeared and contested the will, invoking against Jackson the Louisiana law of concubinage, which has frequently operated to prevent courtesans from leaving property to their lovers. Under its provisions a person cannot give or bequeath real estate to one with whom he or she has lived in open concubinage, nor more than one-tenth of the movables of the estate, which may not exceed one-tenth of the whole. Jackson contended that his relations with Hattie Hamilton had not been open, but the courts held otherwise, and he finally received $71.92 as his share of the estate.

3

KATE TOWNSEND was always very reticent about her early life, but after her death the authorities and the newspapers, searching for heirs to her considerable fortune, managed to piece together a fairly complete account of her brief career before she came to New Orleans. One point, however, remained a mystery: no one was ever found who knew why the letters " A.PIMM " were tattooed on her arm. But from prostitutes, politicians, and other disreputable characters with whom she associated and in whom she had occasionally confided when drunk, reporters and attachés of the Public Administrator's office learned that her real name was Katherine Cunningham, that she had never married, and that she was born in Liverpool in 1839, the daughter of a dock laborer. At fifteen she was barmaid in a notorious dance-house on Paradise Street in Liverpool, but according to her own story she remained a pure and innocent maiden until she was almost seventeen years old. Then she yielded to Peter Kearnaghan, a handsome young sailor whose life she had saved by felling with a pewter mug two ruffians who attacked him in the bar of the dance-house. Twins were born to her after Kearnaghan sailed away, and when he returned she gave him a beating, complained to the police, and saw him safely in jail under a six months' sentence. Then she abandoned the twins, assumed the name of Townsend, and fled to America. She arrived in New Orleans, after a few weeks in New York, early in 1857, and immediately became an inmate of Clara Fisher's brothel in Philippa Street (now Dryades), where she worked for about six months. From there she went to one of a row of two-story red-brick bagnios on Canal Street between Basin and Rampart, and then to Maggie Thompson's place on Customhouse Street, the last place in which she was just one of the girls.

In later years Kate Townsend suffered from a glandular disorder and became grossly corpulent; she weighed three hundred pounds when she died, and, according to the *States,* "when they cut her open the fat was seen to be six inches in thickness. . . . Kate was a very portly woman, and attracted general attention on the street . . . as she grew in age she became afflicted with what was properly a deformity, a voluminous bust which never failed to provoke astonishment in those who chanced to meet her." But when Kate Townsend came to New Orleans, at the age of eighteen, she was an exceedingly handsome girl with an exceptionally fine and voluptuous figure, and is said to have been the most popular young strumpet of her time; it was not until the middle 1870's, after she had developed an irascible disposition and had begun to drink heavily, that she put on flesh and her billowing bosoms became one of the sights of the red-light district. During her early years " on the turf," as the saying went, she was both thrifty and ambitious, and about 1863, when she was twenty-four, she was able to leave Maggie Thompson's, rent a house at Villere and Customhouse Streets, and open a place of her own. There she prospered and made influential friends among the politicians and city officials, and with their aid built the three-story palace of marble and brownstone at No. 40 Basin Street, which was probably the most luxurious brothel that ever opened its doors in the United States. For her own occupancy Kate Townsend reserved a suite of large rooms on the Common Street side of the building, on the first floor, which she equipped in magnificent fashion at a reputed cost of some forty thousand dollars. The fireplaces and mantels were of white marble, and the furniture, upholstered in rep and damask, was of highly polished solid black walnut, as were all of the woodwork and the floors, which were covered by velvet carpets. The bedroom utensil common to the times is said to have been heavily gilded. The sleeping-chamber of the mistress of the bordello was thus described by the *Picayune:*

" In the left hand corner was a magnificent *etagere,* upon which were statuettes, the work of renowned artists, and small articles of vertu, betraying good taste, both in selection and arrangement. A finely carved though small marble table stood next, while adjoining this was a splendid glass door *armoire,* on the shelves of which were stored a plethora of the finest linen wear and bed clothing. Next the *armoire* was a rep and damask sofa, and over the mantel was a costly French mirror with gilt frame. A large sideboard stood in the corner next a window on the other side of the chimney, and in this was stored a large quantity of silverware. Another *armoire* similar to the one just described, a table, and the bed completed the furniture of the room, saving the arm-chairs, of which there was quite a number, covered with rep and damask, with a tete-a-tetes to match. The hangings of the bed, even the mosquito bar, were of lace, and an exquisite basket of flowers hung suspended from the tester of the bed. Around the walls were suspended chaste and costly oil paintings."

The remainder of the house was furnished with the same gaudy magnificence; from cellar to garret there was a profusion of gilt, plate glass, velvet, plush, and damask. The building and its contents were said to have cost well over a hundred thousand dollars, and that at a time when two dollars a day was a high wage for a skilled carpenter, and when other labor, as well as materials, was correspondingly cheap. And the manner in which the brothel was conducted, at least for several years, was in keeping with the richness of its appointments. Elegance and an excessive formality formed the keynote of the establishment. High-class trade only was encouraged, and the rowdies who occasionally invaded the refined precincts of No. 40 were ejected by Kate Townsend in person; she was not only very strong, but when aroused was a fierce and dangerous fighter; throughout her career as a madame she acted as her own bouncer. The number of girls regularly on duty — each had one day off a week, which she usually spent at the theater or drinking in the cafés with her " fancy man " — varied from fifteen to twenty, and every one of them was a lady to her fingertips. Evening dress was the invariable rule, and bawdy talk and behavior were sternly prohibited; a spade was never a spade in Kate Townsend's bagnio. When a gentleman arrived he was met at the door by a uniformed Negro maid. If he was one of the steady clients, many of whom had charge accounts, he was ushered ceremoniously into the drawing-room, where he was expected to buy wine — at from ten to fifteen dollars a bottle — for the assembled company. If a stranger, he was shown into an anteroom and questioned by Kate Townsend, who also drank a glass of wine with him — at the modest price of two dollars a glass. If his credentials were in order, he was escorted into the drawing-room and formally presented to the ladies by his full name and style. If one of the girls struck his fancy, he communicated his desires to the madame, who conferred with the lucky strumpet. If the latter was willing — and there is no record that one of them was ever otherwise — she discreetly retired to her boudoir. Thither, after a seemly interval, the gentleman was conducted. The tariff for such an adventure was fifteen dollars, although a few of the more beautiful and popular bawds received twenty. Kate Townsend herself was occasionally available for the entertainment of a particularly distinguished client — at a price which is said to have been fifty dollars an hour.

These unusual methods of operation brought great prosperity to Kate Townsend for half a dozen years, but

371

as the power of the carpetbag politicians upon whom she principally depended began to wane, she was compelled to abandon some of her strictest rules, make drastic reductions in the rate schedule, and open the brothel to men of a lower stratum of wealth and importance. The new clients brought almost as much money into the house in the long run, but the fact that she had been forced to lower her standards so weighed on Kate Townsend's mind that she began to display the streaks of meanness and the fiery temper which were characteristic of her later years and which naturally drove away trade. The house also suffered a severe though temporary setback in 1870 when Gus Taney, a young gambler who was noted for the variety of his personal armament — he habitually carried a derringer, a revolver, a bowie-knife, a slung shot, and a gimlet-knife — was murdered in the drawing-room by Jim White, also a gambler. On the night of July 30 Taney and White, both drunk, visited Kate Townsend's place, and Taney ordered a bottle of wine, at ten dollars. When he started to pay for it he found he had only two dollars and a half.

"Never mind," said Kate, "you can pay some other time."

White said: "I can whip any damned bastard that can't pay for the wine."

Taney accused White of stealing his money, and White lunged at him. Taney drew his revolver, but before he could use it White stabbed him in the heart with a knife — it had a nine-inch blade — which he carried in a red sheath beneath his armpit. The revolver was found on the floor by the police, who gave it and the knife to Kate Townsend as souvenirs. Thereafter she slept with the knife under her pillow and carried it in her reticule wherever she went. It was the weapon with which she was herself finally murdered by Treville Egbert Sykes, member of a good New Orleans family and the son of a merchant and auctioneer of Magazine Street. She had met Sykes, who was commonly known as Bill, when she was an inmate of the red-brick brothel on Canal Street, and he was her "fancy man" for almost twenty-five years.

Sykes was very little in evidence during the highfalutin period of Kate Townsend's career, but he became increasingly prominent in her affairs after she had lost her youthful beauty and had become an irascible, obese monstrosity. He moved into the brothel in 1878 and was given a small room on the second floor. In return for his board and lodging he was supposed to bring custom to the house, to keep the accounts, and to make himself generally useful. He lived there for five years, during which time, according to his story, Kate Townsend led him "a dog's life," beating him, locking him in dark cupboards, refusing to allow him spending-money, once cutting his nose almost off with a vicious slash of her knife, and frequently threatening to "open his belly," an idea which in time became almost an obsession. The brothel-keeper, on the other hand, often complained that Sykes was jealous and a thief, and that he interfered with business. In 1878, a few months after he took up his residence in the bagnio, she had him arrested for forging her name to five checks totaling seven thousand dollars, but she soon relented and refused to prosecute.

The troubles of Kate Townsend and her "fancy man" reached a climax about the middle of October 1883, when she became infatuated with a young sport named McLern, who came often to the house, borrowed money, and was otherwise the recipient of the brothel-keeper's bounty. Sykes protested and attempted to eject McLern, and for his pains was severely beaten by his mistress and her new lover. The day after this incident Kate Townsend was in the kitchen with Molly Johnson, whose real name was Mary Buckley —

a St. Louis girl — when she suddenly picked up a heavy
butcher-knife and said:

" I've a good mind to take this knife and open Sykes's
belly ! "

Molly Johnson finally dissuaded her, and she compro-
mised by summoning Sykes into the kitchen, where she beat
him with a bread-board and ripped his clothing to tatters.
A few hours later Molly met her on the stairway, brandishing the butcher-knife.

" I went up to open Sykes's belly," she said, " but I
couldn't find him. I'll kill him yet."

On Thursday night, November 1, 1883, Kate Townsend and Molly Johnson met McLern and another man on
Canal Street, and the four got drunk in Pizzini's Café,
where Kate and McLern quarreled and McLern threatened
her with a champagne-bottle. He apologized when Kate
drew her knife, and she said:

" I've got to cut somebody. I'll go home and open
Sykes's belly ! "

When they returned to Basin Street, Molly Johnson
warned Sykes, who locked and barred his door. Next day
and the following night Kate Townsend remained in her
suite, sleeping off her hangover. On Saturday morning, November 3, Sykes arose about half past nine o'clock and went
to Kate's room. The housekeeper, Mary Philomene, a Negress, heard screams and found Sykes and Kate Townsend
fighting in the bedroom. Sykes put the servant out and locked
the door, and then from the room came shrieks and the
sounds of a terrific commotion. After several minutes the
door opened and Sykes appeared on the threshold, bleeding
from cuts on the left breast and below the left knee, and
with his clothing torn to shreds.

" Well, Mary," he said, " she's gone ! "

A few hours later the *States* appeared on the street
with a story which began thus:

374

"At half-past ten o'clock this morning a report was spread on St. Charles Street, among the sporting fraternity, that Kate Townsend, keeper of the bagnio 40 Basin Street,

HAD BEEN MURDERED BY TREVILLE SYKES, HER LOVER.

"At first everyone thought the matter a joke. A *States* reporter at once started for the place, and when he reached the corner of Canal and Basin Street it was easily seen that something had occurred, judging from the enormous crowd that had gathered together. The police were on guard on the inside, and it was with a great deal of difficulty that the writer succeeded in gaining an entrance. Going into the second parlor, on the left wing of the house, halfway across an elegant bed, with her feet resting on the floor,

LAY THE DEAD CORPSE

of Kate Townsend, covered with blood. Her body was pierced by four large-sized stab wounds, apparently inflicted with a broad sheath-knife."

Next morning the *Picayune* published an account of the tragedy under these headlines, typical of the journalism of the period:

CARVED TO DEATH!
TERRIBLE FATE OF KATE TOWNSEND
AT THE HANDS OF TREVILLE SYKES
WITH THE INSTRUMENTALITY OF A
BOWIE KNIFE
HER BREASTS AND SHOULDERS LITER-
ALLY COVERED WITH STABS

As a matter of fact there were eleven wounds in Kate Townsend's body, three of them of a fatal character. Sykes told the police that soon after he went into her room she drew

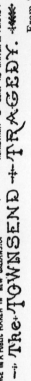

From *The Mascot*

the sheath-knife from beneath her pillow and attacked him. He wrenched the weapon from her grasp, and she renewed the assault with a pair of pruning-shears. He killed her then, he said, in self-defense. The knife and the shears were found on the floor by a policeman and displayed to the crowd, which set up a satisfactory howl of delighted horror. The body of the famous madame, attired in a six-hundred-dollar white silk dress, trimmed with lace at fifty dollars a yard, was laid out in the drawing-room, and at the funeral, on November 5, all the furniture was covered by white silk instead of the usual linen or muslin. Champagne was served to the guests in accordance with Kate Townsend's request. She was buried in a four-hundred-dollar metallic casket, one corner of which bore a silver cross inscribed with her name, the date of her death, and her age. The body was followed to Metarie Cemetery by a procession of twenty carriages. There was not a man in any of them. The Public Administrator took charge of the brothel, and soon afterwards it was leased to Molly Johnson, who operated it until her death in 1889, when the contents were sold at public auction and the house closed. Eventually the property came into the hands of the Elks.

Treville Egbert Sykes was tried for murder and acquitted, and thereupon produced a will, dated September 9, 1873, in which Kate Townsend bequeathed him her entire estate. The instrument was admitted to probate, and Sykes was appointed executor. He was removed in February 1884 for failing to deposit funds received to the credit of the estate and for withdrawing money without a court order. At the same time the Attorney-General asked the court to deprive Sykes of all interest in the estate except one-tenth of the movables on the ground that he and Kate Townsend had lived in open concubinage. Sykes fought the application with such vigor and with such an array of eminent counsel that the case established several important precedents and be-

came a *cause célèbre* in Louisiana jurisprudence. The higher
courts upheld the state law, and Kate Townsend's estate was
finally settled in 1888. According to the figures of the Public Administrator, it amounted to $81,936.45, but the *Mas-
cot* declared that this was " whittled down and hocus-pocused
with until but $33,142.65 remained to be turned into the
state treasury." Lawyers got about $30,000 of the differ-
ence, and the remainder went for court costs and other expenses. Sykes's share was $34.

4

FANNY SWEET's early activities in the Basin Street
district antedated those of Kate Townsend and Hattie
Hamilton, and she outlived both of those noted personages.
She was infinitely more versatile than either of them, for
in the final analysis they were simply ambitious bawds who
had become prosperous madames. Fanny Sweet was not
only an important figure in the field of professional harlotry
— she was also an authentic adventuress of the old school;
a devout and diligent Voodoo who pinned her faith upon a
little metal casket filled with charms and amulets; a Confederate spy; a bad-tempered harridan who carried a knife
and a brace of pistols and slept with them under her pillow;
and, if the New Orleans *True Delta* is to be believed, " a
modern Lucretia Borgia . . . a hardened murderess . . .
one of the most remarkable female desperadoes ever known
. . . subject to horrible dreams, in which her spirit seemed
to struggle with apparitions of vengeance. In such moments
she would grind her teeth together and mutter the most fearful oaths and imprecations that mortal ever heard, while
she would seize the bowie-knife that she kept under her
head and brandish it in the air. . . . Was it unlikely that
these spectres, haunting her pillow and wringing her soul
with such fear as to bring the cold sweat in large drops to
her forehead, were the dark figures that conscience disen-

tombed from their graves to pursue her even in slumber?"
At the height of her notoriety, about 1862, it was popularly
believed that Fanny Sweet had shot one man and poisoned
three or four others, that she had crippled a woman who
dared stand in her way, and that she regularly tortured her
slaves. As a matter of fact, no charge of murder or assault
was ever proved against her, although it is true that she was
frequently accused and that several of her lovers showed
a suspicious susceptibility to "congestive chills." In common with many courtesans of greater renown, she was physi-
cally very unattractive. She towered five feet and ten inches
in her stockings, her figure was lumpy, her feet and hands
huge and ungainly, and her carriage awkward. She had
large, masculine features, high cheek-bones, a prominent
nose, bushy eyebrows, a noticeable mustache, and a slightly
warty skin. Her hair was a dry, lifeless dun. But behind
thick-lensed spectacles, which she didn't need but often
wore, her eyes were a clear, sparkling blue. To atone for her
many physical defects, Fanny Sweet was endowed with a
fascination and a skill in amour which men seemed unable
to resist; she never lacked a lover, and from New Orleans
to California, and from California to New York, she left a
trail of broken hearts and flattened pocketbooks.

The *True Delta* published an exposé of Fanny Sweet
on December 8, 1861, and on the authority of a New Orleans business man who had known her as a girl, said that
her name was really Mary Robinson and that she had been
born in a small New York town in 1827. According to this
account, she strayed from the way of virtue at fourteen,
"from the promptings of her own innate wickedness and
ungovernable nature," and at fifteen, in 1842, went to New
York, where she called herself Fanny Smith and soon became known as one of the toughest little strumpets that ever
bedeviled the madames of the metropolis. She was thrown
out of half a dozen brothels for fighting and general cussed-

ness, and in 1844 came to New Orleans and entered a bagnio on Dauphine Street, between Canal and Customhouse. She was dismissed after a few weeks, when she hurled another inmate down the stairs and broke half the bones in her body, and then went to live at a large brothel on Royal Street. While there a young banker, called Mr. D. in the various accounts of her life, became infatuated with her, and she resigned her position in the bordello to become his personal mistress. Within a year after this relationship began he stole a large sum of money from his bank and fled to Havana to escape arrest.

Fanny Sweet answered the *True Delta's* revelations with the " Autobiography of Mrs. Fanny Sweet — A Card to the Public," which the newspaper published in two installments on December 15 and 22, 1861. In a great burst of elegant language she told the story of her life. She said her birthplace was England, and that she was the only child of parents who reared her " in comfort and even luxury." She failed, however, to divulge either the exact place of her birth or her real name. Her father and mother died when she was eight years old, she said, and she was brought to America by a family which settled on a farm in the Guyandot region of the present state of West Virginia. There she lived for some six years. When she was fifteen her foster-parents placed her in the care of a gentleman relative who promised to take her to a boarding-school in Cincinnati. Instead, the scoundrel seduced her, and " for two years the trusting girl waited the fulfillment of his promise to make her a wife . . . finally they were to come to New Orleans, where the long hoped for union was to be consecrated. . . . Banishing all her secret fears, she took passage with him on a steamboat, as his lawful wife. . . . At Memphis he got off to attend to some business, as he explained. The bell rang and the boat left the wharf, but he had not returned. She kept on, with anxiety, but still hoping. . . ." This was in 1846.

When she arrived in New Orleans she went to live with a man and his wife whom she had met on the boat, and who operated a book-store in Exchange Alley. There "she waited fruitlessly for him who had sworn to make her his wedded wife." When the people who had befriended her learned the awful truth they cast her out, and she was immediately given another push down the pathway of sin by a lawyer who had offered advice and assistance. He soon tired of her, and she had no recourse but the brothels, which in those days gaped wide open for "the young girl who had fallen astray," as the old song has it. From this point the stories of Fanny Sweet and the *True Delta* are substantially in agreement, although she vehemently denied any intentional wrongdoing at any time or place whatsoever. She particularly denied that she had received from Mr. D. any of the money stolen from his bank. She wrote:

"During all of her intimacy with young D., whose winning ways and kindness toward her had made her but a pliant tool of his wishes, she never received from him enough to pay her board. She was at that time supported, and most liberally, by a wealthy gentleman, Mr. P., whom she was in the habit of meeting by appointment, at the house of an old woman named Moss. . . ."

Mr. P. served his purpose and vanished from the scene, and in 1849 Fanny Sweet went to New York — she said it was her first visit to that city — and bought tickets to California for herself and "two respectable lady friends." She ran a haberdashery, at an enormous profit, in San Francisco until the great fire of May 4, 1850, and then went to Sacramento, where she became the mistress of the owner of a large building, part of which she operated as a boarding-house. "These were rough, lawless times in California," said the *True Delta,* " but she was rougher and more law-less than any, and her strong arm and iron nerve carried her through many exciting scenes . . . she became feared even among the miners, with whom she circulated as if a man, always armed to the teeth. She had many fights, and desperate encounters with them, in one of which she shot a stage-driver dead, and in another she had three of her ribs broken." Fanny Sweet's troubles with the stage-drivers and the miners culminated late in 1852, when a mob invaded her home and destroyed the furniture. She protested, and a man named Putnam slapped her, whereupon she drew a pistol and shot him. She was tried before a friendly Justice of the Peace and acquitted, and a gang of rowdies demolished the Justice's house. They threatened to hang Fanny Sweet, but she escaped while the noose was being prepared and found refuge on the prison brig moored in the Sacramento River. The Grand Jury indicted her, but she left Sacramento early in 1853 and returned to New Orleans, where she published a card announcing that she had abandoned her wicked ways and wished to be received as a respectable lady. The response was so slight that she was offended, and after a few weeks went to Aspinwall, on the Isthmus of Panama. There she captivated and married Abraham M. Hinkley, the wealthy owner of Hinkley's California Express. She appeared in New Orleans again late in 1854, with more money than ever, and bought a large brick house on St. Louis Street, with half a dozen Negroes and a gaudy carriage in which she drove about the city, clad in silks and satins and blazing with jewels. She was arrested in 1855 on a charge of mistreating her slaves, but was triumphantly vindicated, and soon thereafter went to New York, where she divorced Hinkley in 1856. A few months after she filed her suit he went to Nicaragua to join William Walker, and was killed by the Nicaraguans at Granada.

Rumors drifted south during the next few years that

Fanny Sweet was up to her old tricks in the metropolis, but she was not in New Orleans again until early in 1860, when she suddenly appeared and ensconced herself in a little house on Canal Street. It was during this period that she embraced Voodooism. She attended many of the secret meetings of the cult, bought great quantities of charms, love-potions, and amulets from Marie Laveau and the Voodoo doctors, and was among those arrested when the police broke up a Voodoo orgy late in 1860. Owing, as she believed, to the efficacy of the Voodoo magic, the victim she required appeared in the person of Mr. M., whom the *True Delta* described as " a gentleman of years and means, of high standing in both social and commercial circles . . . he lavished his wealth upon her, giving her the beautiful little property on Gasquet Street (at the corner of Basin) furnishing it with the most exquisite taste, and stocking the sideboard with the finest wines and liquors, imported. Colored servants, a carriage that was built to order in New Jersey — afterwards sold by her at auction for $1,600 — fast horses, everything that she could want at her disposal." In this palatial haven, where she and Mr. M. — he visited the house two or three times a week — were known as Mr. and Mrs. Sweet, she lived for almost two years diligently bleeding Mr. M. and operating, unknown to him, a select assignation house, providing young girls for the amusement of elderly men and then blackmailing the latter, one of whom paid her ten thousand dollars in less than a year.

When Mr. M. learned what was going on, he tried to break with his mistress, but she only laughed and pointed out that if she wished she could ruin him. He offered her a large sum to leave New Orleans. She took the money, but didn't go. Soon afterwards she asked for additional funds, and when he refused she prophesied that he would be ill. Within a few days he became violently sick with an ailment which the mystified doctors diagnosed as " congestive chills," and recovered only when he had summoned Fanny Sweet and paid through the nose for a "secret remedy." Thereafter he contributed regularly and without protest to her expenses until she had entangled the man whom she had fixed upon as his successor. This was the rich William G. Stephens, a widower with two small children, who was worth more than a hundred thousand dollars and had many irons in the commercial fire. He was known as something of a tightwad and habitually drove a shabby buggy with a little mule between the shafts. He was also a very religious man, and so careful of his good name, according to the *True Delta,* "that he would not even enter a coffee-house, much less enter any haunt of immorality." This virtuous and high-minded gentleman fell for Fanny Sweet like a ton of bricks, and she became his mistress within a week after their first meeting. To protect his reputation she closed her Gasquet Street house, donned men's clothing, and thereafter, until the end of the adventure, lived openly in the Stephens mansion as his nephew, Freddy, and was so introduced by him to his business associates. She accompanied him on trips, boldly visited the cafés and coffee-houses as a man, and in this guise acquired something of a name as a cavalier. She also supervised the education of Stephens's children, and controlled the household expenditures, which increased enormously. To a woman who recognized her she said that she was "done with petticoats forever." In August 1861 she made a business trip to New York for her lover, and while there obtained valuable information which she sold to the Confederate military authorities.

When she returned from New York, Fanny Sweet suggested to Stephens that they turn their property into cash, pool their resources, travel overland to Mexico and buy quinine and munitions of war, and then bring these supplies back into Texas and Louisiana and sell them to the Confederate Army. Stephens was quick to see the huge profits that might accrue from such a venture, and accordingly they started from New Orleans about November 1, 1861, accompanied by a man named Lincoln, one of Stephens's employees, and bearing a common purse of about sixty-five thousand dollars, of which Stephens had contributed by far the greater part. Fanny Sweet traveled as a man, having procured a passport from the Mexican Consul in the name of " Frederick J. Stephens, a subject of Great Britain." When they reached Houston, Texas, however, she suddenly decided to wear skirts and refused to go farther until Stephens had returned to New Orleans and obtained another passport for her as a female. She was now equipped to travel anywhere in Mexico either as a man or as a woman, but once they had left Houston she again put on men's clothing. Between Houston and Corpus Christi, Stephens suddenly became ill with " congestive chills," and Fanny Sweet pushed the party on at top speed toward Brownsville, where they had intended to cross into Mexico. Several miles from that city, however, he died. There seems to be grounds for the belief that Stephens acted somewhat hastily in this matter; according to Fanny Sweet's plan he should not have succumbed until the party was safely over the border, when she could easily have satisfied the Mexican authorities and gone where she pleased. Of necessity, she changed her whole plan of campaign and hurried to Brownsville, where, according to her story, the police and city officials at once engaged in a mad scramble to get what they could of Stephens's effects. Meanwhile she began clamoring for an inquest and a post-mortem examination, but at the same time so effectively distracted the officials by her frantic grief that neither was ever held. Stephens was quickly buried in a tin box, a metallic coffin not being available, and Fanny Sweet and Lincoln started to return to Louisiana, bearing most of Stephens's money.

By this time reports had reached New Orleans that

Stephens had been poisoned by Fanny Sweet, and that she was in flight through Mexico with a confederate, whereupon the *True Delta* remarked that her companion's life "would not be insured at this time for ninety-nine cents on the dollar by any insurance company in the city, and the chances are fifty to one that he will be attacked by congestive chills before they get half-way to Vera Cruz." The police searched the house on Gasquet Street and found the precious Voodoo casket, in which were several packets of white powder, believed to have been love-potions if not poison, and a lock of bloodstained hair, one of the most potent of Voodoo charms. Fanny Sweet, however, said the powder was medicine, and that the lock of hair had been taken from Hinkley's scalp "while the warm blood was yet trickling over it," and sent to her by one of his comrades as a *memento mori*. While these investigations were in progress Mayor John T. Monroe heard that Fanny Sweet and Lincoln were in Texas, and sent Detective Izzard Smith to intercept them. At Brashear City they were arrested, brought to New Orleans, and lodged in jail, while the Mayor wrote to Corpus Christi and Brownsville for information. He received a dozen letters, all of the same tenor as that of a Brownsville business man who wrote that Fanny Sweet had shown "sorrow inconsolable. . . . I would as soon believe the Angel Gabriel had descended to do violence to Stephens, as that she had made way with him, as I have heard surmised." When these testimonials were published, a great wave of sympathy for Fanny Sweet swept over New Orleans. On December 12, 1861, she and Lincoln were released, and the Attorney-General of the state announced officially that she was innocent of any connection with Stephens's death, while the *Picayune* said that there was "nothing against Fanny but her past reputation." Stephens's body was disinterred and brought to New Orleans for reburial, but the authorities refused to order an autopsy.

Fanny Sweet vanished from New Orleans when the Yankees captured the city, and is said to have spent the next few years in New York, Washington, and other Northern cities as a Confederate spy, although none of the details of her activities are known. She returned at the close of the war, reopened her house on Gasquet Street, and lived there for almost twenty years. But she got into no serious trouble, and appears to have eschewed blackmail and attended strictly to her business of running a high-class assignation house. She left New Orleans in 1889, when she was about sixty years old, and is believed to have died a few years later in Florida.

5

DURING the greater part of the period which witnessed the rise and fall of Kate Townsend, Hattie Hamilton, and Fanny Sweet, the lowest of the cribs and the cheap parlor-houses, besides those in the Girod and Gallatin Street districts, were largely concentrated on Dauphine, Burgundy, St. Louis, Conti, Customhouse, and Bienville Streets, in the French Quarter; and, in the American section, on Franklin Street and the upper end of Gasquet Street, which ran from Basin Street to Claiborne Avenue a block above Canal street. The worst dive on Gasquet Street was a two-bit crib-house known as Pig-Trough Carrie's, which flourished around 1870; while on Franklin Street were such notorious resorts as the Picayune House, McCarty's Ranch, and the combination brothel, dance-hall, and gambling-den at No. 22, much frequented by Negro burglars and footpads. In the rear of this establishment Kendrick Holland, a Negro monte thrower, ran a lunch-room and thriftily compelled his mistress, Hannah Glover, to work in the kitchen when she was not busy in the brothel division of the establishment. In her rare moments of leisure it was her habit to play seven-up, while Holland stood behind her chair and proffered advice.

He became increasingly annoyed at her lack of skill, and while watching her on the evening of August 17, 1883, he suddenly leaned forward and tapped her on the shoulder. He said:

"I'll kill you if you don't do better than that!"

On the next deal the girl made a stupid play, and Holland drew a revolver and shot her in the back of the head.

"I told her I'd do it," he said, "but she wouldn't believe me."

In the Dauphine and Burgundy Street vice areas white women and Negresses crowded together indiscriminately and were patronized by men of all races and colors, a situation which persisted for many years before and after the Civil War. As late as May 22, 1888 the *Lantern* complained that "In our daily walks through life we notice the surprising amount of co-habitation of white men with Negro women." A year or so later, on November 30, 1889, the *Mascot* presented the other side of the picture, declaring that "this thing of white girls becoming enamored of Negroes is becoming rather too common." From about 1850 to the early 1880's, except for infrequent clean-up periods, conditions in Dauphine and Burgundy Streets were so bad as to be almost unbelievable. From Canal to Toulouse Streets virtually every building was a brothel, filled with fighting, brawling strumpets of the lowest class. The whole area fairly swarmed with streetwalkers and their "fancy men," and in the absence of permanent quarters the perambulating bawds flung a piece of old carpet on the sidewalk and entertained their customers in full view of passers-by and the prostitutes in the houses, who screamed advice and abuse from the windows and kept pails of hot water handy to discourage use of the doorsteps. Inside the bordellos prices ranged from fifteen to fifty cents; on the sidewalk the standard rate was a dime. Many of these women were addicted to flagellation, and their needs in this respect were served by a professional flaggellant called Joe the Whipper, who was a familiar figure on Dauphine and Burgundy Streets for many years. He carried with him always a black bag containing the tools of his trade — switches, whips, and thin, flexible metal rods.

At No. 111 Dauphine Street was a brothel which was described by the *Picayune* in 1885 as the worst Negro dive in the city, and which at that time was the particular haunt of Red Light Liz, the sweetheart of Joe the Whipper and a noted brawler. In earlier days, however, the house had been occupied by white prostitutes, and gained considerable renown by reason of the tragic end of one of its inmates, Nellie Gaspar; and the mere presence of another, a woman known as "the notorious Fanny Peel." The latter, said to have been the most beautiful courtesan who ever appeared in New Orleans, was, according to the newspapers, the daughter of a clergyman of Troy, New York, and a graduate of the Troy Female Seminary. She was seduced at fifteen, in 1843, and immediately became a prostitute, an almost compulsory fate in those days, when a girl once ruined was ruined forever. After a career in Chicago and other cities, during which she was the mistress of several important men and accumulated a considerable fortune, she came to New Orleans in 1857 with her coachman, a free Negro, whom she immediately sold as a slave to a Louisiana planter. She entered the brothel at No. 111 Dauphine Street, but was soon dismissed because she refused to have anything to do with the men who visited the place — she said they weren't good enough for her. She went to Mobile early in 1858 and died there during the summer of that year.

Nellie Gaspar, the daughter of a London innkeeper, came to New Orleans in 1866 as a performer in Smith's European Circus. She was ruined by a smooth-tongued New Orleans scoundrel, who then put her in the Dauphine Street brothel. She was expelled because she went out too often with her lover, and went into a house on Tremé Street. After a few weeks there she became an inmate of a Customhouse Street brothel operated by Madame Schneider, who was noted for her bass voice and her demoniac temper. Meanwhile Nellie Gaspar's seducer had deserted her and she had taken a new lover. She had been at Madame Schneider's for only a few days when the man who had started her upon the career of a harlot broke into her room, stole all of her money, and beat her unmercifully with the butt of a revolver. She was still alive when found by Madame Schneider, and that big-hearted harridan put her into a small room and traded her water for dresses until her wardrobe was exhausted. Then the girl was sent to Charity Hospital, but was discharged after three days and returned to the brothel in Dauphine Street, where she died within a week.

On Burgundy Street, between Bienville and Conti, was Smoky Row — half a dozen dilapidated old houses, with batten doors held together with ropes, and peep-holes covered by movable slabs — which was notorious during the early 1870's because of the almost continuous brawling of four battling bawds known as Fightin' Mary, Kidney-Foot Jenny, One-Eyed Sal, and Gallus Lu, who lost nothing in comparison with their white sisters of the Swamp and Gallatin Street. For at least twenty years the dives of Smoky Row were as low as any with which New Orleans had ever been afflicted. They were filled with Negro prostitutes of all ages, from ten years to seventy, who wore loose, dirty Mother Hubbards cut very low in front and trailing behind. When not fighting or otherwise occupied, they sat on rickety chairs in the doorways of Smoky Row, smoking pipes and chewing tobacco. Whenever a man passed, they tried to drag him inside; if he resisted they grabbed his hat, and when he went after it, oftener than not one of the women spat tobacco juice in his eyes and another knocked him down with a club. Then he was robbed and thrown into the street.

Smoky Row maintained its existence until 1885, when so many complaints were made that the police were compelled to take some action against it. Accordingly, in July of that year the denizens of the dives were evicted. A police searching party found piles of bloodstained wallets and men's clothing, and dug in the courtyards for bodies, but without success.

6

IN addition to the brothels scattered about New Orleans, there were also the business establishments of the scores of procuresses who operated almost without hindrance until a portion of the city was legally set aside as a red-light district in 1897. These harpies supplied girls for the bordellos, and some of them did a considerable export business, sending women from New Orleans to houses of prostitution in Galveston, Atlanta, Memphis, and other Southern cities. Most of them, however, found their greatest profit in procuring young girls for men who feared to visit recognized bagnios, but were good customers of the assignation houses if all arrangements were made for them in advance and everything conducted quietly. Every procuress had her list of clients, whom she notified when new girls were brought in by her agents. In the trade the girls were known as " stock," while inexperienced children were referred to as " fresh stock," and sometimes brought extraordinarily high prices. A procuress named Louisa Murphy, a school-teacher, is said to have sold several young girls during the late 1860's for as much as eight hundred dollars each.

Although they had transacted their evil business in New Orleans from the earliest days, the procuresses seemed to have attracted little attention until the middle 1840's, when Mary Thompson was operating on Royal Street, with a cigar-store for a blind. She specialized in virgins, whom she sold for from two hundred to four hundred dollars each, but she caught a tartar in fifteen-year-old Mary Fozatte. The Thompson woman gave the girl trinkets and candy and clothes, and they became very friendly. Then the procuress sold her for three hundred and fifty dollars to an elderly gentleman who had had his order in for just such a girl for more than a year. In March 1845 she was *en route* to a Burgundy Street assignation house to deliver the purchase when the girl broke away and went home. Highly indignant, Mary Thompson had her arrested on a charge of stealing. The case was dismissed, and the girl brought suit against the procuress for attempting to injure her character. She was awarded fifty dollars damages, and the police told Mary Thompson that if she tried to sell another girl she might be punished.

During the 1880's and early 1890's the procuresses operated with greater boldness than ever before. They distributed circulars by means of mailing lists, and advertised " specials " by cards scattered about the saloons and assignation houses. Many of them, carrying bags containing photographs and other matter descriptive of their " stock," called openly at stores and offices. Competition was so keen that about 1890 a virgin could be bought for as little as fifty dollars. The leaders in the field at this time were Nellie Haley of Customhouse Street, called the Queen of the Procuresses, who was arrested in Chicago in 1893, but acquitted; Miss Carol of Baronne Street; Mother Mansfield of Bienville Street; Spanish Agnes of Burgundy Street, who ostensibly ran an employment agency; and Emma Johnson of Gasquet Street, who in later years was madame of " The Studio " on North Basin Street. Spanish Agnes came to the public notice late in 1890, when the police found that she had sent two girls, reported missing by their parents, to Abbie Allen's brothel in Galveston. The *Mascot* published this interview with Spanish Agnes in its issue of November 22, 1890:

"I frequently receive orders from the keepers of fashionable places. These ladies ask me to send them girls, or women for that matter. I always prefer to have experienced women than virtuous girls, because there is less fear of trouble. I am in correspondence with women like Molly Waters and Abbie Allen of Galveston; these people write to me for girls. Some time ago I received an order from Miss Abbie Allen to send her some girls, and soon after Miss Lena Smith [one of her field agents, who was paid five dollars for each girl procured] informed me that she could secure two nice young girls. . . . I do not like to have anything to do with innocent girls. . . . Not a very long time ago a mother brought her three daughters to me and offered them for sale. Two, she said, were bad, and the youngest still unacquainted with vice and the wickedness of the world. She demanded $25 for the girls, and expressed her belief that she ought to get more for the guileless maiden."

Spanish Agnes said she bought the three girls and made "a nice profit."

Miss Carol of Baronne Street carried on a general procuring business in girls and women, and also had a profitable side-line — she found boys for the amusement of male degenerates. There was a great influx of these men into New Orleans about 1890, and Miss Carol is said to have been the financial backer of an assignation house which was opened for their convenience on Lafayette Street near Baronne. The mister of this establishment was a man who called himself Miss Big Nellie, and the permanent roomers included Lady Richard, Lady Beulah Toto, Lady Fresh, and Chicago Belle. Balls were frequently given at the house, to which both white and Negro men were invited.

Emma Johnson had a fifteen-year-old girl for sale in May 1892 and offered the child at a bargain to a *Mascot* reporter who was investigating the activities of the procuresses. When he refused to buy she cried:

"You're a fool! The girl's a virgin! You'll never get another chance like this in New Orleans!"

CHAPTER XIII

CRIMINALS' PARADISE

T H E P O W E R of the carpetbaggers in Louisiana declined rapidly after the formation of the White League in 1874, and collapsed entirely in 1877, when Federal troops were withdrawn and the national government at Washington acknowledged the election of Francis T. Nicholls, who had been a high officer in the Confederate Army, as Governor over the Republican carpetbagger candidate, Stephen B. Packard. The state was thus " returned " to the Democrats,[1] and, as a Louisiana historian says, " assumed a normal position among the states of the Union." But so far as New Orleans was concerned, the transition from carpetbagger to Democratic machine brought no improvement. The city was destined to remain for at least another ten years burdened with debt and overrun by corrupt politicians, despite the activities of such reform agencies as the Committee of Safety, the Committee of Seventeen, the Committee of One Hundred, and the second Vigilance Committee, which was organized in 1881 " to suppress crime, to compel the authorities to perform their duties, to watch the city government," and especially to procure the punishment of dishonest officials. These organizations accomplished very little, although two of them, the Vigilantes and the Committee of

---

[1] As part of a deal, most historians believe, whereby the Democrats agreed not to contest the counting of Louisiana's electoral vote for Hayes, although actually Tilden carried the state by a substantial majority.

Safety, appear to have had the support of Mayor Joseph Shakespeare during the last year of his first term. Throughout the decade that followed the downfall of the carpetbag machine, virtually every branch of the municipal government was at least as demoralized and inefficient as during the " epoch of degeneration " before the Civil War; and the payrolls of all departments were padded with the names of hoodlums and " shoulder-hitters," who were thus paid by the city for their labors as henchmen of the politicians. The character of these men was well indicated by a statement in the *Mascot* of July 4, 1883:

> " Nowadays, leaving Negroes out of the question, nine-tenths of the criminals arrested for drunkenness and ruffianly conduct are city employees. . . . Fully a dozen of the ' toughs ' arraigned last week are drawing pay from the city."

And by the headlines in the *Picayune* of October 3, 1885, when two employees of the Department of Public Buildings, of which Patrick Mealey was Commissioner (he was also Commissioner of Police), were charged with stabbing a keeper at the House of Refuge, who had been accused of stealing several hundred pairs of shoes:

MEALEY'S COLLEGE OF CRIME
TWO OF THE FACULTY UNDER INDICTMENT
IN CRIMINAL COURT.

And further, by the action of the Grand Jury of Orleans Parish, on January 12, 1885, in calling the attention of the Governor and the Mayor to the common practice among state and city employees of " carrying revolvers and committing lawless acts." This custom bore fruit in a series of fatal affrays in which every man involved was more or less prominent in the state and city governments. The most sensational

396

of these tragedies were the killing of three men and the wounding of eight others, on December 14, 1883, in a pistol battle between groups of rival politicians, which included Robert Brewster, the Criminal Sheriff, and James D. Houston, Tax Collector for the Upper Districts; the fatal shooting of Brewster on January 12, 1885, when he and Houston attempted to horsewhip the editor of the *Mascot* for publishing an article about Houston's brother, a judge; the murder of Patrick Mealey on January 1, 1888, by John Gibson and Louis Clare, the latter a special policeman and both he and Gibson ward-heelers for the Democratic machine and notorious hoodlums besides; and the killing of Cap Murphy, a Workhouse keeper, by Patrick Ford and Policeman John Murphy at the behest of the former's brother, Recorder Thomas J. Ford, who had been selected by the machine as the next Mayor of New Orleans. For the murder of Mealey, Clare and Gibson were sent to the penitentiary for life. For shooting Cap Murphy to death, John Murphy and Patrick Ford were hanged, while Recorder Ford and two of the officers of his court were convicted of manslaughter, and received long prison sentences.

As in former years, the police department was the stepchild of the municipal budget, and the focal point of graft and corruption. Inefficiently organized, underpaid, woefully inadequate in numbers and equipment, and subject to little or no discipline, the police made scarcely any pretense of protecting the lives and property of the citizens. Patrolmen reported for duty or not as they pleased, paraded the streets in full uniform with prostitutes, and engaged in drunken carousals in public resorts, while many were the open accomplices of burglars, pickpockets, and crooked gamblers. In a memorial sent to the Legislature in 1886, the Committee of One Hundred denounced the police force as " partisan and corrupt . . . largely contributing to the criminal ranks and largely recruited from those ranks. . . . Words cannot adequately describe the utter inefficiency of the present police system. It is deficient in numbers and morale. It wants every characteristic, physical, moral and intellectual. It is badly paid and badly disciplined." The memorial caused something of a furor among the statesmen, but the members from New Orleans disposed of it in a fashion which met with the approval of the entire legislature — they simply issued a statement accusing the committee of aping the Committee of Seventeen, which had made similar charges in 1884. The *Picayune* published the statement, without comment, under this headline:

THE GALLED JADES WINCE!

Much of the demoralization of the police was due to the presence on the rolls of the department of large numbers of "specials," hoodlum favorites of the political leaders who were given jobs without regard to their records or qualifications. For example, Louis Clare, the murderer of Patrick Mealey, was appointed by Mayor J. Valsin Guillotte in July 1887, although he was well known as a ruffian and a brawler and had been arrested thirty times in one year for fighting, drunkenness, and stealing. The specials were armed and clothed with the authority of policemen, but performed no regular police duties, although they drew from twenty to forty thousand dollars a year in pay. They used their power to protect criminals, to escape arrest for ruffianism, to make themselves dangerous nuisances in the saloons and cafés, and the better to serve their political masters as thugs and bullies. One of these appointees, Theodore J. Boasso, attained high rank in the police force, but his career soon terminated in a sensational scandal.

Boasso, the son of an Italian printer, entered politics in New Orleans as a ward-heeler for Guillotte and the state machine dominated by Governor Samuel D. McEnery. His first job was as keeper in the state insane asylum, but when

From *The Mascot*

THE HANGING OF FORD AND MURPHY

CHIEF OF AIDS BOASSO AND HIS VICTIM

Guillotte was elected Mayor, in April 1884, Boasso was appointed Acting Chief of Aids, as the detectives were then called, although he was clearly unfitted for such a post. During his brief time in office he was often in trouble with his superior officers because of his haughty and overbearing manner, and was frequently accused of being in league with the sure-thing gamblers and confidence men; once when White Pine Russell, a bunko operator, was arrested for fleecing a Colorado man out of four hundred dollars, the Chief of Aids offered to return a hundred and fifty dollars if the complainant would not prosecute. Despite Boasso's open alliances with the underworld, he continued to be one of Guillotte's intimate friends and advisers. Early in June 1885 he accompanied the Mayor to a dinner party at the home of Ambrose Kuhn, a grocer, and met Kuhn's twin daughters, handsome girls of eighteen. According to the *Picayune,* Boasso " looked with lecherous eyes full on the twins," and chose Mary Catherine as his victim. Posing as a bachelor, although he had been married since 1881, he wooed the girl, and eloped with her on June 20, 1885. Boasso showed her a bogus marriage certificate, and she believed him when he said that their signatures on the document would legally make them man and wife. When Kuhn learned the truth, he rescued his daughter from Boasso's clutches, and the girl went hunting for her betrayer with a revolver. She found him in front of a saloon on St. Anthony Street and shot him in the liver and the back. When he recovered he was tried, convicted of " forging and uttering a false marriage certificate," and sentenced to fourteen years in the state penitentiary. He had served about eight years when he was pardoned by Governor Murphy J. Foster in 1894.

2

WHILE the politicians and city officials were occupied with graft, murder, and factional rows, conditions in New

Orleans, so far as crime was concerned, were about as bad
as in the days when the city was described by the Criminal
Sheriff as "a perfect hell on earth." Murder and robbery
were so common in the 1880's that the newsboys no longer
relied upon them to sell papers, and the streets and public
places of resort were so terrorized by hoodlums that they
were unsafe for decent people, and no respectable woman
dared venture out at night without a strong escort. Most of
these ruffians were organized into bands, all carried revolvers and slung shots, and many had political connections
which gave them virtual immunity from punishment; the
police might put them in jail occasionally, but the politicians
soon got them out. Their liberty was really jeopardized only
when they committed murder and so came to the attention
of the District Attorney's office, which appears to have been
an oasis of comparative honesty and efficiency in a desert of
corruption. The newspapers were filled with news of the
exploits of the hoodlums, especially of Tom Newhouse, the
redoubtable Tug Wilson, and young Tommy McGittigan,
who in 1886, at the age of eighteen, climaxed a brief but
eventful career as a ruffian with a murder, for which he was
sent to prison for life. Newhouse was a fireman until he
killed his company commander, and thereafter was never
known to work, although he was always on the payroll of
some department of the city government. He murdered a
policeman in 1878, for which he was not punished, and in
1887, after a month's spree during which he kept the vicinity
of Poydras and Prieur Streets in a state of constant commotion, he killed George Maloney, a one-legged man who was
also well known as a brawler. For this crime Newhouse went
to prison for twenty years.

Tug Wilson was probably the most notorious rowdy,
and one of the most ferocious fighters, who appeared in New
Orleans after the Civil War; he was a familiar figure in the
saloons, the red-light district, and the speakeasies from the

early 1880's until his death in 1934. He was in his heyday
during the former period, when hoodlums were the salt of
the earth in New Orleans. In some six or eight years he was
arrested more than a hundred times for fighting, drinking,
and gambling, but he was an invaluable man on election day
and actually spent very little time behind the bars. He was
extremely strong, and once broke the doors of five cells in the
police jail, one after another. At the height of his career he
always wore a plug hat and a long-tailed coat, the pockets
of which were filled with broken mugs and beer bottles, his
favorite weapons. Curiously enough, Tug Wilson appears
never to have worked for the city, although he was the perfect type of municipal employee.

Besides being afflicted with the hoodlums, New Orleans
was preyed upon by a score of well-organized gangs of
burglars, pickpockets, and sneak thieves, and at the same
time was the winter headquarters of many criminals of international renown, who lived openly at the best hotels, attended the races and the theaters, and consorted on terms of
friendship with the politicians and high officials of city and
state. Among the most distinguished of these visitors were
Ned Lyons, master cracksman, and his wife, the celebrated
Sophie Lyons, née Levy; Jim Kelly, a hotel thief better
known as the Artful Dodger; John Larney, a pickpocket
who was called Mollie Matches because he had once made
a big killing in New York while disguised as a match girl;
Big Tom Bigelow, a noted burglar who died at the St.
Charles Hotel in November 1886, while stopping there with
Little Louise Jordan, a shoplifter and sneak; Little Dave
Cummings and Billy Forrester, who robbed a Canal Street
jeweler of $83,000 and a bank in the French Quarter of
$65,000, and thereafter spent their vacations elsewhere;
Red Leary, Jack Cannon, Paddy Guerin, Jimmy Carroll,
Dutch Freddy Watson, Billy Burke, and the Lop-Eared Kid,
otherwise Charley Wilson, all burglars and cracksmen; and

Rube Burrows, Colonel Carl Hobgood, and Captain Eugene Bunch, train robbers who operated principally in Louisiana, Mississippi, and Alabama. Bunch was a firearms expert and when in New Orleans usually posed as a Texas sheriff and spent most of his time at gun-stores.

Of all this array of criminal talent, only the Artful Dodger and Jack Cannon came to grief in New Orleans. The former was sentenced to prison for five years in 1896, and Cannon received two years in 1886, after he had committed robberies at the Hotel Royal and the Hotel Gregg, and had stolen $8,000 in diamonds from a woman in May Banker's house on Union Street. Burrows was killed at Linden, Alabama, in October 1890, by Detective John McDuffie of the Southeastern Express Company, and the careers of Hobgood and Bunch came to an end when a posse cornered them near Franklinton, Louisiana, on August 22, 1892. Bunch was killed and Hobgood surrendered. Among Bunch's effects was found a bag containing a hundred pounds of pistols, masks, and burglar tools. His most celebrated exploit was the single-handed robbery of a train on the Queen & Crescent Railway, near Derby, Mississippi, on November 3, 1888, when he took $28,000 from the express car.

Among the local gangs of thieves were those captained by Yellow Henry Stewart, Irish Houlihan, Monk O'Brien, Willie Walla, and Phil Oster. The worst of the lot was Yellow Henry's mob. Another smaller but almost as dangerous gang was the Spiders, who had a hang-out, which they called the Web, in a house on Franklin Street near Poydras. They specialized in robbing the Negro gambling-houses, many of which paid them a weekly sum for protection. At the municipal election of 1884 the Spiders were used as bullies at the polls by the Guillotte machine, but two years later, having outlived their usefulness to the politicians, the Web was raided by the police and the gangsters dispersed. For several months thereafter the hang-out was occupied by a crone named Margaret Murphy, who had been a successful pickpocket for more than sixty years, operating principally at funerals. When she was finally captured in February 1887, at the age of seventy-seven, she boasted that during the two years prior to her arrest she had picked more than a hundred pockets. Phil Oster was always ready to commit a burglary when opportunity offered, but his specialty was counterfeiting, at which he was remarkably expert. He began making bogus money in 1872, when he was twenty-five years old, and continued to do so, with more or less success, for almost half a century, first with his own gang and then as a member of the mob captained by the noted Rash Shepard. Oster's last appearance in New Orleans was in November 1917, in his seventy-first year, when Secret Service men found counterfeiting apparatus in his room on Bourbon Street. The old man said to a *States* reporter:

> " I've been in the penitentiary five times. I've been pardoned as many times, and I'm proud of my record. I started making counterfeit money forty-five years ago. It took 'em fifteen years before they got me, and after I had made and spent enough money — if I had it now, well, there would be few, if any, men in New Orleans more wealthy."

The membership of the Yellow Henry gang included some of the most desperate criminals that the New Orleans underworld has yet produced; there was scarcely one of them who would not have been able to hold his own in the Swamp or Gallatin Street when those districts were at their toughest. Among them were Crooked Neck Delaney, Joe John, George Sylvester, Garibaldi Bolden; Joe Martin, an expert garroter; Prussian Charley Mader, who always wore a mask and a false beard when working; George Lehde, Pat Keeley, Jim Maroney; Tom McDonald, better known as Tom the Dog;

the Haley brothers, Red and Blue; and the notorious Frank Lyons, who is said to have been the son of Jack Lyons of Gallatin Street fame. Yellow Henry succeeded to the captaincy of the mob in 1877, when the former leader, Turpo, went to prison for ten years, and enjoyed great success until 1884. In August of that year he was arrested, together with Lyons, Sylvester, and Bolden, for the robbery of a Julia Street sailmaker. Sylvester died in the Parish Prison, but the others were sent to the penitentiary, where Yellow Henry died in July 1886, of the malaria which had given him his sobriquet. Lyons escaped in 1888, but was soon returned to prison, and there he remained until pardoned by Governor Nicholls in 1890. He then reorganized the Yellow Henry gang, and was not again molested by the authorities until August 1892, when he killed Patrolman John Hurley for trying to stop a fight at Gallatin and Hospital Streets. A few months later he was sentenced to prison for life.

3

THE Democratic machine which had inherited Louisiana from the carpetbaggers, dominated alternately by the McEnery and Nicholls factions, remained in control of New Orleans until the spring of 1888, when it was finally overthrown, so far as the city was concerned, by the most successful of New Orleans' reform movements, the Young Men's Democratic Association. Organized along the lines of the White League, the Association surrounded the polling-places with companies of riflemen, which prevented the usual ruffianism and intimidation of voters and compelled an honest election. As the *Times-Democrat* said, "the almost countless devices and election legerdemain so familiar and so often practiced by the ring, were utterly and woefully futile." The Nicholls faction carried the state, but in New Orleans the Association elected by large majorities a complete city ticket headed by Joseph Shakespeare as Mayor (he had previously filled that office from 1880 to 1882), on a platform which pledged the new officials especially " to strike from the payrolls political deadheads " and " to have the police force purged and remodeled and so fairly paid that proper men may be induced to serve." Shakespeare set to work with great vigor to reform and reorganize the department, lopping off the heads of the " hoodlum specials," increasing the pay of the patrolmen, and otherwise laying the groundwork for the present comparatively efficient police establishment. One of his first acts, a few days after the election in April 1888, was to appoint as Chief of Police David C. Hennessy, who was elected Superintendent of the force when the Police Board created by the Legislature late in 1887 began to function about the middle of 1888.

Hennessy was born on March 4, 1857, the son of a policeman who was murdered in 1869 in a St. Ann Street coffee-house. A year after the death of his father Hennessy became a messenger boy in the office of General A. S. Badger, then Chief of Police, and after a few years was appointed aid, or detective. In this latter work he was teamed with his cousin, Mike Hennessy, a former cab-driver who had been appointed special policeman by Governor Nicholls in 1877, and detective two years later. A bitter enmity, the cause of which is no longer known, existed between Mike Hennessy and the Chief of Aids, Thomas Devereaux, for whose benefit the office had been created, and the two men frequently exchanged threats. On October 31, 1881, David and Mike Hennessy met Devereaux on Gravier Street, and the latter immediately drew a revolver and fired. Mike Hennessy fell, wounded, and as Devereaux advanced to shoot again, both Mike and David Hennessy fired. Devereaux was killed. The cousins were tried and acquitted on a plea of self-defense, but were dismissed from the police force. Mike Hennessy operated a detective agency in Galveston for a year or two and then went to Houston, where he was murdered on September 29, 1886, by an assassin who was said to have come from New Orleans expressly to commit the crime. David Hennessy joined M. J. Farrell's Harbor Protection Police, a private agency, and was superintendent of that organization until his appointment by Mayor Shakespeare. And almost from the day that he took the oath as Chief of Police he was marked for death by the Stoppagherra, a branch of the Mafia, the notorious Sicilian murder society.

Sicilian criminals appeared in New Orleans soon after the beginning of the great wave of immigration from southern Europe before the Civil War, and within a few years were operating in well-organized bands in various parts of the city. As early as 1861, on June 22, the *True Delta* declared that " recent developments have satisfied the police of the city that an organized gang of Spanish and Sicilian thieves and burglars have long made their headquarters in the Second and Third Districts." Two months later the same newspaper reported the arrest of a band of Sicilian counterfeiters and again called attention to the presence in New Orleans of large numbers of Sicilian robbers and assassins. On March 19, 1869 the *Times* said that the Second District was infested by " well-known and notorious Sicilian murderers, counterfeiters and burglars, who, in the last month, have formed a sort of general co-partnership or stock company for the plunder and disturbance of the city." This " co-partnership " was the Stoppagherra Society, organized as a branch of the Mafia by four men who, driven from Palermo by the Sicilian authorities, arrived in New Orleans early in 1869. The assassins of the Stoppagherra quickly disposed of a gang of Messina men who attempted to set up a rival band in the autumn of 1869, and thereafter the Mafia was the dominating element in Italian crime, not only in New Orleans but elsewhere in the United States, for with the Louisiana metropolis as headquarters, branches were soon established in New York, San Francisco, Chicago, and other large cities. To these havens of refuge and opportunity, largely through the kind offices of politicians who found the Mafia a great help at election times, flowed a stream of criminals from Sicily and other parts of Italy. In New Orleans alone during the late 1880's, according to the Italian Consul, Pasquale Corte,[1] there were a hundred escaped Italian criminals, not one of whom had entered the country legally. Many had become naturalized citizens. These desperadoes, and other members of the Mafia, kept the Italian colony of New Orleans in a state of terror for more than twenty years, and grew rich and powerful upon the proceeds of robbery, extortion, and assassination, most of the victims being fellow-countrymen who had failed to pay the sums demanded by the Mafia leaders. A few of these killings — there were about seventy during the two decades — were committed with knives, but in most of them the murderers used a weapon known to the New Orleans police as "the Mafia gun" — a shotgun with the barrels sawed off to about eighteen inches, and the stock sawed through near the trigger and hollowed out. The stock was then fitted with hinges, and the entire gun folded up like a jackknife. It was carried inside the coat on a hook. Loaded with slugs or buckshot, it was as deadly a weapon up to thirty yards as had ever been devised.

During the period in which the Mafia was gaining a foothold in New Orleans, the chieftain of the society in Sicily was the celebrated Leoni, and his principal lieutenant was Giuseppi Esposito. The latter, who was notorious for ferocity and cruelty, was a small man, scarcely five feet and four inches in height, with a heavy black beard and mustache and a remarkably low forehead, over which the hair projected. In 1880 Leoni and his band, operating near Palermo, captured an English clergyman, the Reverend Mr. Rose,

[1] In an interview with the New York *Tribune*, quoted in the *American Law Review*, May–June, 1891.

and when no ransom was forthcoming immediately, they cut off his ears and sent them to his family. The British government made such a peremptory demand upon Italy that troops were dispatched against the brigands. Leoni was killed and many of his men captured, but Esposito and six others escaped and were smuggled aboard a ship bound for the United States. After a few weeks in New York, Esposito, in March 1881, came to New Orleans, where he rented a house in Chartres Street, assumed the name of Radzo, and bought a small lugger which he plied in the oyster trade between New Orleans and the lower coast. The boat he named *Leoni,* and flying at the masthead was the flag of the bandit chief.

When Esposito arrived in New Orleans the head of the local Mafia, according to the best information the police could obtain, was Tony Labruzzo. He was immediately deposed by Esposito, who extorted several thousand dollars from wealthy Italians and began the organization of a band of brigands in the Sicilian style, with a fleet of piratical luggers and a hide-away in the swamps where he could hold his victims for ransom. His ambitious plans, however, never matured. Labruzzo resented Esposito's assumption of command and informed the Italian Consul that the escaped bandit was in New Orleans. The Consul notified the Chief of Police, Colonel Thomas N. Boylan, and asked that Esposito be kept under surveillance until he could receive instructions from Italy. For several weeks thereafter Esposito was shadowed night and day by David and Mike Hennessy. Meanwhile James Mooney and D. Boland, private detectives of New York, were searching for Esposito on behalf of the Italian government and had traced him to New Orleans. They arrived in the city early in July 1881, and at a conference with Colonel Boylan the arrest of the brigand was decided upon. At dusk on July 5, 1881, David and Mike Hennessy captured Esposito in Jackson Square, rushed him into a carriage which Mooney and Boland had waiting, and took him to a police station. Next morning he was spirited aboard a ship for New York by Mooney and Boland, who met the boat in a skiff down the river to avoid the gangs of Mafiosi who were searching New Orleans for their leader. From New York, Esposito was sent to Italy, where he was imprisoned in irons for the remainder of his life. Ten days after Esposito's arrest Tony Labruzzo was shot down in Bienville Street by a Mafioso named Giutano Ardotta. Both of the Hennessys were warned to prepare for death, but although Mike Hennessy was killed in Houston five years later, presumably by a Mafia gunman, it was ten years before the society carried out its threats of vengeance against David Hennessy.

4

SOON after the capture of Esposito and the assassination of Labruzzo, the Mafia in New Orleans came under the domination of a faction headed by Charles Matranga and his brother Tony, the latter a saloon-keeper whose place had been an unsavory resort for many years. Although the actual strength and inner workings of the organization were never known, the police believed that by 1885 the Mafia could muster about three hundred members, that Tony Matranga was president, and that it was governed by a supreme council of twenty which prepared the extortion letters, planned the murders, and assigned the assassins. When one of the latter was summoned before the council, he found the leaders of the society dressed in black masks and dominoes, and swore a bloody oath on a human skull with daggers stuck in the eye-sockets. Under the leadership of the gifted Matrangas the Mafia invaded a new field. For several years the brothers Provenzano — George, Joe, and Peter — had enjoyed a monopoly of unloading the fruit ships from South and Central America. They held contracts with the shipping companies and employed several hundred

Italian laborers, who received forty cents an hour for day work and sixty cents at night, which in those days were reasonably high wages. The Provenzanos were rich and politically influential and, so far as was ever known, had no connection with the Mafia. On the contrary, they regularly paid tribute to the society and employed the men sent them by the Matrangas.

During the middle 1880's the Matrangas began to cast covetous eyes upon the profits of the Provenzanos. The shipping companies were notified that thereafter the Matrangas would attend to the unloading of the vessels, and the Provenzanos were ordered to leave the docks. The command was emphasized by attacks upon Provenzano men, in which several were shot. Unable to cope with the Mafia, the Provenzanos abandoned their business, and the Matrangas took charge of the docks. They immediately made enormous profits by reducing wages to ten and fifteen cents an hour and forcing the Italians, under threat of death, to work for these miserable pittances. The Provenzanos opened a grocery-store, but the Mafiosi destroyed their stock and intimidated their customers, and the venture failed. In desperation, the Provenzanos hired gunmen, and so began a vendetta, about the time that David Hennessy became Chief of Police, which resulted in half a dozen killings. The last encounter between the Provenzanos and the Matrangas occurred in April 1880, when Tony Matranga and two of his men were ambushed and wounded at Claiborne Avenue and Esplanade Street. Joe and Peter Provenzano and three other men of their faction were arrested, and after many delays their trial was set for October 17, 1890. The Matrangas employed some of the foremost lawyers in New Orleans to assist in the prosecution.

Hennessy had been a friend of George and Peter Provenzano for many years. He was convinced that they were in the right in their troubles with the Matrangas, and that the murders in the Italian colony would not end until the power of the Mafia had been destroyed. He began to collect evidence proving the existence of the society in New Orleans, and its connection with the many fatal affrays which had occurred. Late in July 1890 he received an anonymous letter warning him that the Mafia would kill him unless he ceased his activity, but he paid no attention to it. In August he wrote to the head of the Rome police for the names and photographs of several members of Esposito's band who were supposed to be in New Orleans and active in the operations of the Matrangas. Early in October Hennessy said publicly that he would present his evidence at the trial of the Provenzanos. On the night of October 15, 1890, two days before he was to appear on the witness-stand, Hennessy left his office in the Central Police Station and started for his home on Girod Street between Basin and Franklin. He was accompanied by Captain William J. O'Connor of the Boylan Protective Police, a private agency, who left him at Rampart and Girod Streets. O'Connor had walked less than a block when he heard a burst of shotgun fire, followed by three or four revolver-shots. He hurried back and found Hennessy sitting on the stoop of a house in Basin Street near Girod, bleeding profusely from four wounds in the left side of the body. As O'Connor came up, Hennessy said:

"They've given it to me, Bill, but I gave them back the best I could."

"Who did it?" cried O'Connor.

"Dagoes!" whispered Hennessy, and collapsed. He was rushed to Charity Hospital, where he died about nine o'clock on the morning of the 16th. Before the end came, Hennessy said that he had not recognized any of his assailants, but that they were all Italians, a partial identification which was sustained by various persons who had seen several of the assassins running away. A double-barreled shotgun, a typical Mafia weapon, was found in the gutter near a shed opposite Hennessy's home. From this shed the shots had been fired.

The murder of Hennessy created a tremendous sensation in New Orleans. The funeral, held from the Council Chamber of City Hall, was attended by prominent citizens and members of the state and city governments, while the streets along which the cortège passed *en route* to the cemetery were lined by thousands of people. For days there was much talk of lynching, and many Italians hastened to publish notices in the newspapers disavowing any connection with the Mafia or the suspects who were daily being arrested by the police. On Saturday, the 18th of October, the City Council held a special meeting to consider the tragedy, and approved the appointment by Mayor Shakespeare of a Citizens' Committee of Fifty, composed of some of the best-known men in New Orleans, to assist the authorities in gathering evidence. Edgar H. Farrar was appointed chairman, but resigned after a few days in favor of Walter C. Flower, who was later, in 1896, elected Mayor. About the time the committee began its work Fred Bessel, a ballader of considerable local renown, author of " The Mud Run Disaster," " The Fatal Electric Wires," and " The Wilkesbarre Cyclone," wrote a song called " The Hennessy Murder," which was printed on a black-bordered sheet and circulated by the thousands of copies. It began:

Kind friends if you will list to me a sad story I'll relate,
'Tis of the brave Chief Hennessy and how he met his fate
On that quiet Autumn Evening when all nature seemed at rest,
This good man was shot to death; may his soul rest with the blest,
Why men commit such crimes as these 'tis very hard to tell

For such Satanic fiends, there should be no place but
    Hell;
'Tis not alone the murdered man who suffered by this
    crime,
But the hearts of ALL GOOD CITIZENS LAY HURT FROM
    TIME TO TIME.

CHORUS

Chief Hennessy, he was murdered for no cause that we
    all know,
And the murderer in prison he will pine;
Why men have such a will, that for vengeance they
    can kill,
Such men with Satan surely must combine.

In the month that followed the murder the police arrested twenty-one Italians, nineteen of whom were indicted
by the Grand Jury late in November, eleven as principals
and eight as accessories to the crime. On February 16,
1891, nine of the accused — Bastion Incardona, Charles
Matranga, Antonio Bagnetto, Antonio Marchesi, Joseph
Macheca, Manuel Politz, Antonio Scaffedi, Pietro Monasterio, and Asperi Marchesi, the last-named a fourteen-year-
old boy who had signaled the coming of Hennessy — were
brought to trial in the Criminal Court before Judge Baker.
They were represented by an imposing array of eminent
counsel headed by Thomas J. Semmes and Lionel Adams,
the last-named a former District Attorney, but the most
important figure in the defense was Dominick C. O'Malley,
a private detective, whose brief career in New Orleans had
been interrupted by a ten-month sentence in the Workhouse
and nine appearances in court for carrying concealed weapons, jury-fixing, and intimidating witnesses. Lionel Adams
was a partner in O'Malley's detective agency, a fact which
caused the Grand Jury to say that "such a combination

413

Courtesy of the *Tunis-Picayune*

PROMINENT FIGURES IN THE HENNESSY CASE

Top row, left to right — Charles Matranga, Manuel Politz, Pietro Monasterio

Bottom row — John C. Wickliffe, Dominick C. O'Malley, David C. Hennessy

between a detective and a prominent criminal lawyer is unheard of before in the civilized world, and when we contemplate its possibilities for evil we stand aghast." Seventy-one jurors of the regular panel and 1,150 talesmen were summoned before the jury could be obtained, and the taking of testimony did not begin until February 28, 1891. John C. Wickliffe, one of the editors of the New Orleans *Delta,* wrote in *Frank Leslie's Illustrated Newspaper* for April 4, 1891:

> " Convinced as the people were of the guilt of the accused, they were staggered by the strength of the case made out by the State. Eye-witnesses to the killing came forward and identified many of the men on trial. Circumstantial evidence of the most conclusive sort was piled on top of this. . . . In the midst of the trial, Politz, one of the defendants, broke down and confessed that he was present at the meeting of the society when the death of Hennessy was decreed, and when the detail of murderers was made. He gave a partial list of the members, and gave their signs and signals. He confessed that Macheca, one of the defendants, had furnished the ' Mafia guns ' that were used, and had ordered him (Politz) to carry them to the house from which the assassins sallied when they killed Hennessy. This, of course, is only an outline of the confession. . . ."

During the progress of the trial the State abandoned the prosecution of Bastion Incardona, and Judge Baker directed the acquittal of Charles Matranga. Because of the boy's youth, the State also requested the Judge to so charge the jury that Asperi Marchesi's acquittal would be certain. The case went to the jury on March 12, 1891, and a verdict was handed up on the 13th. Despite the conclusive nature of the testimony, which incidentally is as apparent today as it was when presented on the witness-stand, the jury reported that it was unable to agree as to Politz, Scaffedi, and Monasterio, and acquitted the others. And almost simultaneously with the verdict came proof that the jury had been tampered with. Several talesmen admitted that they had been approached with bribes, and it became increasingly clear that Dominick O'Malley and his agents had won the case by the liberal use of Mafia gold. An investigation begun immediately by the Grand Jury resulted in the indictment of O'Malley and half a dozen other men, several of whom were later convicted.

The Italian colony received the news of the verdict with great rejoicing. Many stands in the French Market, owned by Sicilians, suddenly became gay with bunting and streamers, and in the Parish Prison the acquitted men, though still under an indictment charging conspiracy, toasted each other and their lawyers in wine sent by their friends, while scores of citizens reported to the police that they had heard Sicilians all over the city say: "The Mafia is on top now, and will run the town to suit itself." Many of the State's witnesses, who had received death warnings from the Mafia, left the city, or barricaded their homes and gathered supplies of arms and ammunition. At the lugger landing a gang of Sicilians tore down an American flag, trampled it in the mud, and then hoisted it upside down below the banner of Italy. But while all of these celebrations were in full swing, a meeting was being held in a Carondelet Street club, as a result of which this notice appeared in the morning newspapers of March 14, 1891:

MASS MEETING!

All good citizens are invited to attend a mass meeting on SATURDAY, March 14, at 10 o'clock a.m., at Clay Statue,[1]

---

[1] This statue of Henry Clay was erected in 1859 in Canal Street at the junction of Royal and St. Charles, and for many years was the common meeting-

to take steps to remedy the failure of justice in the HEN
NESSY CASE. Come prepared for action.

The notice was signed by sixty-one of New Orleans'
most prominent citizens, among them William S. Parkerson,
John M. Parker, Ulric Atkinson, Thomas Henry, N. H.
Pierson, S. P. Walmsley, Samuel B. Merwin, Walter D.
Denegre, H. R. Labouisse, James D. Houston, H. B. Ogden,
Edgar H. Farrar, Frank B. Hayne, T. D. Mather, and
John C. Wickliffe.

Long before the time set for the mass meeting, the
Clay statue was surrounded by a crowd which filled Canal
Street and extended for half a block up both Royal Street
and St. Charles Avenue. A few minutes before ten o'clock
the signers of the call appeared, marching three abreast
down Canal Street, and headed by William S. Parkerson and
John C. Wickliffe. They took up positions against the railing
around the statue, and Parkerson, Wickliffe, and Walter
Denegre ascended the steps of the pedestal. Each spoke for
three minutes, reviewing the Hennessy case and denouncing
the failure of the law to exact vengeance. They told the
crowd what they intended to do, asked for a sign of approval, and received it in a great roar of applause. The last
speaker, Wickliffe, announced that he would be second lieutenant of the execution party, James D. Houston first lieutenant, and Parkerson captain. As Wickliffe stepped down from
the pedestal the crowd turned almost as one man and
streamed in the direction of the Parish Prison at Beauregard
(Congo) Square. The signers of the call formed ranks and
marched to a Canal Street gun-store, where they armed
themselves with rifles and shotguns. Then they proceeded to
the prison.

Meanwhile Sheriff Gabriel Villere had left Captain

---

ground of New Orleans. In January 1901 it was removed to its present location
in Lafayette Square.

Lemuel Davis in charge of the prison and had gone to seek help from the military and the police. In neither place was he successful. Captain Davis locked in their cells all prisoners except the Italian suspects, who were given the run of the prison and told to find hiding-places wherever they could. When the party headed by Parkerson arrived, the mob was clamoring at the locked doors and threatening to dynamite the building. Parkerson demanded admittance, and when Captain Davis refused to open the doors, a detachment of men under command of Houston was sent round into Marais Street, where they smashed a little-used wooden door. Through this entrance Parkerson led his men, posting armed sentinels to keep out all who didn't know the password. Once inside the prison, the lynchers proceeded with great deliberation. Each member of the party had a list of the eleven Italians who were believed to be guilty of the murder of Hennessy beyond the shadow of a doubt, and he was instructed not to harm any of the others whom he might encounter. Among these latter were Charles Matranga, Bastion Incardona, and Asperi Marchesi, who were not molested.

But the eleven who had been condemned by the signers of the call were searched out and killed. Seven were shot down in the yard of the woman's department of the prison, and two were riddled with bullets as they crouched in " the dog-house," a large box under a stairway which had been the home of Captain Davis's bull-terrier. Manuel Politz was dragged from the prison and hanged to a lamp-post at Trèmé and St. Ann Streets. Antonio Bagnetto, discovered by Wickliffe shamming death in the pile of corpses in the woman's yard, was hanged to a tree in front of the prison, on Orleans Street. In less than an hour after the execution party had entered the prison, Parkerson clambered to a window-sill and announced to the mob outside that the work of the lynchers had been completed. A few minutes later he

Courtesy of the *Times-Picayune*

THE LYNCHING OF THE ITALIANS

Top, left to right — The hanging of Bagnetto, the "Dog House," the execution of Politz. (From the *Picayune*)

Bottom — The slaughter in the Women's Yard (From the *Mascot*)

marched his men out the front door into Orleans Street. He was quickly elevated to the shoulders of half a dozen men, a procession was formed, and he was thus carried through Rampart and Canal Streets at the head of cheering thousands. At the Clay statue Parkerson urged the crowd to disperse, but as it still lingered, Wickliffe made a brief speech in which he said:

"I ask you, as an endorsement of what has been done, and in pursuance of the promise which we impliedly gave the people, to return quietly to your homes. The lesson we have given will have its effect. If it does not we will repeat it."

But there was no need to repeat it. After the fearful slaughter in the Parish Prison the Mafia was never again a power in the New Orleans underworld.

Several of the newspapers denounced the lynching of the Italians and demanded investigations by the authorities, but as a whole New Orleans greeted the action of the mob with approval, and, incidentally, bought huge quantities of the poet Bessel's new song:

HENNESSY AVENGED!

Chief Hennessy now will lay at rest, his soul will be at
    ease,
It would be useless without their lives his spirit to
    appease,
They have killed and robbed among themselves, that all
    of us do know,
They cannot do it among us, for our power we now do
    show.
They killed the chief upon that night, of that we all
    have read,
And they gave him no chance for his life, that all of us
    have said,
But as song progresses with me you will agree

That they're better off where they have gone than under
    lock and key.

They show their blood and courage in the far off West,
By quickly fixing murderers, who that country do infest,
Now we have shown our Southern blood — for no-
    where will you find —
A town that would have justice and fair play of this
    kind.
We would not have the verdict given by them men of
    nerve;
It seems to us as if this case had quite a crooked curve.
The execution was gone through quickly, and done by
    gentlemen,
And everybody will agree it could never be a sin.

Great praise is due those gentlemen whom we all do
    know,
Who called upon the citizens for them their power to
    show.
No more assassins we will have sent from a foreign soil,
In New Orleans we've proved to all we're honest sons
    of toil.

In an interview telegraphed to the St. Louis *Globe-Democrat* on March 17, Mayor Shakespeare declared: " I do consider that the act was — however deplorable — a necessity and justifiable. The Italians had taken the law into their own hands and we had to do the same." Similar statements were made by other officials, while resolutions endorsing the action of the lynchers were adopted by the Cotton Exchange, the Sugar Exchange, the Stock Exchange, the Board of Trade, and the Mechanics', Lumbermen's and Dealers' Exchange. For a while, however, international complications threatened. Italy, demanding reparations and the punishment of the lynching party, recalled her Ambassador and severed diplomatic relations with the United States, and there was much talk of war in both countries. At length Italy agreed to accept an indemnity of twenty thousand dollars, which was paid out of the contingent fund of the State Department. No investigation of the lynching was ever made.

5

ABOUT 1900 the Black Hand Society attempted to take the place of the Mafia in New Orleans, but although in other cities it operated with considerable success, in New Orleans it lacked intelligent leadership and for the most part was a source of annoyance rather than of danger. A few Italians paid the blackmail demanded, but only a few of those who refused were molested; as a rule the society contented itself with sending death threats and warnings heavily embellished with black hands and crimson skulls and crossbones. No murders were ascribed to the Black Hand in New Orleans until the kidnapping of Walter Lamana, the eight-year-old son of Peter Lamana, an Italian undertaker, on June 8, 1907. Two days after the kidnapping Lamana received a letter demanding six thousand dollars ransom. Prominent Italians headed by Lawrence Frederico, a macaroni-merchant, and Philip J. Patorno, a lawyer, called a mass meeting and organized the Italian Vigilance Committee, which searched every house in the Italian quarter and employed private detectives to assist the police. But no trace of the boy was found until June 23, when his body was discovered in a dense swamp near St. Rose in St. Charles Parish, twenty miles from New Orleans. He had been killed about ten days before by a blow on the head. The police and posse of the Vigilance Committee were led to the spot by one of eight suspects. In July four of these, one a woman, were convicted at Hahnville and sent to prison for life. In November another woman and her brother were likewise found guilty and sentenced to hang. After the trial in July there was so much talk of lynching that Governor Newton C. Blanchard sent three companies of militia to Hahnville to guard the jail. A mob which had formed at Gretna was quickly dispersed by the troops, and thereafter no further trouble occurred. Nor did the Black Hand attempt any more coups in New Orleans.

CHAPTER XIV

STORYVILLE

URING THE decade in which the hoodlums, the burglar gangs, and the Mafia were the dominating elements of the New Orleans underworld, prostitution continued to spread unchecked, especially in the French Quarter, where brothels began to appear in considerable numbers on those parts of Villere, Marais, Robertson, and Basin Streets which lay north of Canal Street. As a result of New Orleans' almost universal reputation as the promised land of harlotry, hundreds of prostitutes flocked into the city from all parts of the United States, attended by the " fancy men " and other male parasites who fattened upon the shame of their fallen sisters. In all of this period the authorities, except for the closing of Smoky Row on Burgundy Street, made only one gesture against the bawdy horde. That was in September 1886, when the police succeeded in shifting most of the crib and sidewalk strumpets to the Franklin Street district by an order requiring them to vacate the ground floors of all houses on Burgundy, Customhouse, Bienville, Dauphine, St. Louis, and Conti Streets. For a while it seemed as if these historic thoroughfares might be reclaimed as residential and business streets, but the order apparently didn't affect the parlor-houses, and they continued to operate without restraint. Most of the latter resorts in this area during the late 1880's and the early 1890's were two- and three-dollar houses, although there were a few which charged five dollars and otherwise attempted to ape the palatial brothels of Basin Street. All were elegantly furnished, but it would appear that sometimes the madames neglected to pay for their velvet carpets and their plush sofas; in October 1892 the W. B. Ringrose Furniture Emporium sued Carrie Freeman, Mary O'Brien, Mattie Marshall, Nellie Williams, and Sally Levy, prominent Customhouse Street brothel-keepers, for a total of $7,493.07 for furniture which had been bought on credit, and posted guards at the houses to see that the property was not removed before trial of the suits. Mattie Marshall alone owed the Ringrose store $4,786.92, and Carrie Freeman $1,301.65. The madames seem also to have been rather fortunate in the matter of tax assessments. The *Mascot* investigated this subject in 1892 and found that many of the brothels were not assessed at all, including such notorious dives as those run by Fanny Decker, Frankie Belmont, Annie Deckert, and Annie Merritt, all on Customhouse Street. Annie Merritt, whose house was one of the worst in New Orleans, opened a saloon when prostitution was officially abolished, and conducted the business in person until she was eighty years old. From early girlhood to death she smoked from twenty to thirty big black cigars every night.

The largest assessment found by the *Mascot's* investigators among the red lights was $1,200 against Madge Leigh's house on Customhouse Street. Mamie Christine's place on the same thoroughfare — in later years she ran a resort which was noted for its circuses and other erotic exhibitions — was assessed at $300; and a similar sum was set down in the tax books against a brothel across the street from Mamie Christine's, operated by Lulu White, afterwards the madame of a famous octoroon house, Mahogany Hall, on North Basin Street. At the time she was paying taxes on the trifling assessment of $300, Lulu White owned $2,000 worth of furniture, a cut-glass chandelier which had cost $200, a carriage and a team of fine horses, and diamonds

worth more than $10,000, including a $7,400 pair of ear-
rings. Despite this and other property which she accumulated during her long professional career, Lulu White died
a pauper.

Perhaps the most popular prostitute in New Orleans
during the early 1890's was Abbie Reed — her real name
was Mary E. Hines — a strawberry blonde of striking
beauty, amiable disposition, and unusual accomplishments.
She was an inmate of one of the big brothels on Basin
Street for several years, but she was frugal and ambitious and was soon able to go into business for herself.
By the early part of 1892 she owned the bagnio at
No. 15 Burgundy Street, near Canal, and a large two-
story residence on Delord Street, which she had bought
from Mayor Shakespeare and which she operated as a high-
class assignation house. In January 1893 Abbie Reed married Jules Kuneman, grandson of a wealthy planter of St.
James Parish, who had been educated in France and Germany and whose mother lived in Paris. The wedding bells
had scarcely ceased ringing when Abbie Reed's trouble began. She left the Burgundy Street brothel in the hands of a
housekeeper and went to live with Kuneman in the house on
Delord Street. They fought almost constantly, he frequently
beat her, and in August 1893 he was arrested for knocking
her down in front of No. 15 Burgundy Street because, she
said, she had rented the property to Gertrude Livingston,
better known as Queen Gertie. Late in the following September, Kuneman slashed her with a knife he had been using
to pare his nails, so severely that she was in a hospital for
several weeks. Kuneman told the police that he had been
angered by her expressed desire to leave him and return to
Burgundy Street as a member of Queen Gertie's staff. Abbie
Reed, however, said he had attempted to kill her because she
had refused to sell all of her property and set him up in business. When she recovered from her injuries Abbie Reed dis-

posed of her two houses and went to Pensacola, Florida. She returned to New Orleans early in 1904, calling herself Countess Kuneman, and became an inmate of Fanny Lambert's brothel on North Basin Street. The *Sunday Sun* re-

HER THROAT CUT.
Jules Kunemann Attempts to Murder Abbie Reed.
From *The Mascot*

marked that "her friends will be glad to hear that she is getting along so nicely."

Queen Gertie Livingston operated the old Reed place on Burgundy Street for several years and, as she phrased it, "attracted a nice class of trade," despite the fact that her strumpets were quarrelsome and high-spirited and always fighting, either among themselves or with the madame. One of the many rows in Queen Gertie's establishment attracted considerable attention. That was in October 1894, when Cecile Torrence bit off one of Josie Vinton's fingers and was

arrested when the victim of her sharp teeth developed ery-
sipelas. Among the witnesses at Cecile Torrence's trial was
her fellow-bawd Helen Frank, who said that when the house
bouncer wanted to separate the two girls, Queen Gertie told
him to let them fight it out. When she returned to the brothel
Helen Frank had a fight with Queen Gertie over her testimony and was thrown into the street. The madame, however, held the girl's trunk until a writ of sequestration compelled her to relinquish it. " Among the things in the box,"
said the *Mascot,* " are four dozen towels, which Helen does
not think Gertie has any right to withhold, as they come under the act that provides that a workman's tools cannot be
retained." Apparently the only one of Queen Gertie's harlots
who was never involved in a fight was the principal attraction
of the establishment — a handsome girl named Josephine
Clare, but better known as Josephine Icebox. She was advertised by Queen Gertie as the coldest strumpet in the red-light
district, and a prize of ten dollars in trade was offered to the
man who could arouse her. Many men accepted the challenge, but there is no record that the reward was ever won.

2

I T was almost a century and three-quarters after Bienville
and his working party of soldiers and convicts first set foot
on the site of New Orleans before the authorities and the
people generally awoke to a realization of the fact that unless suppressive or regulatory measures were carried out,
their city would eventually be transformed into one vast
brothel. About 1890 the voice of opposition to rampant and
uncontrolled vice began to make itself heard. One of the first
to sound the tocsin in the battle against the army of harlots
was the Reverend E. A. Clay, pastor of the Dryades German
Methodist Church and President of the Society for the Prevention of Cruelty to Children, who was active for several
years in the work of rescuing young girls from the bordellos.

428

On Sunday, October 30, 1892, the Reverend Mr. Clay delivered a sermon on " Some City Pitfalls and Snares," which helped measurably to crystallize the sentiment against a continuance of open prostitution. He said:

" I am now going to speak to you, beloved, of the things which I wish could be told without words. I am going to speak of those houses of darkness and death and blackness and despair, of those human slaughter-houses, of the gravest things of all the pitfalls in the way of virtue in this great city. . . . There are over five hundred of these dark places scattered throughout this city from Carrollton to the barracks, and they run the gamut of condition from the palatial palaces of velvet and gilt down to the veriest stinking and reeking pesthole of foul hags and noisomeness. Fifteen hundred angels of death and damnation inhabit these places. They affect and imperil the virtue and honor of every girl in the city."

An attempt to establish some sort of control over prostitution in New Orleans was made in 1891 by the police department, which proposed the enactment of an ordinance providing for compulsory medical examination of " all women and girls notoriously abandoned to lewdness." Many city officials and members of the Council favored such a law, but the plan was quickly dropped when the respectable ladies of New Orleans held a mass meeting and denounced it as an insult to Southern womanhood! About a year later Alderman Harman, acting upon the suggestion of the *Mascot,* introduced an ordinance providing a segregated district and the issuance of licenses to prostitutes, but the measure fell before the united opposition of clergymen and leading women of the city, who advanced the curious argument that such a law would recognize the existence of vice. Nothing further was done until January 26, 1897, when the City Council adopted the famous ordinance introduced by Alderman Sidney Story, a well-known broker, who had made an exhaustive study of the methods by which prostitution was regulated in the large

From *The Mascot*

QUEEN GERTIE LIVINGSTON

cities of Europe. This measure set aside an area in the French Quarter wherein prostitution was to be permitted but not actually legalized. On February 8, 1897 an ordinance was introduced extending the limits of the district by including an area in the American section, but it was withdrawn because of protests from property-owners of the Third District. On July 6, 1897 the original Story ordinance was amended and re-enacted, to provide two distinct and uncon-

430

nected segregated areas, one in the French Quarter and one above Canal Street, as follows:

" BE IT ORDAINED, by the Common Council of the City of New Orleans, That Section 1, of Ordinance 13,-032 C.S., Be and the same is hereby amended as follows: From and after the first of October, 1897, it shall be unlawful for any prostitute or woman notoriously abandoned to lewdness, to occupy, inhabit, live or sleep in any house, room or closet, situated without the following limits, viz: From the South side of Customhouse Street to the North side of St. Louis Street, and from the lower or wood side of North Basin Street to the lower or wood side of Robertson Street [in the French Quarter]; 2nd: — And from the upper side of Perdido Street to the lower side of Gravier Street, and from the river side of Franklin Street to the lower or wood side of Locust Street [in the American section], provided that nothing herein shall be so construed as to authorize any lewd woman to occupy a house, room or closet in any portion of the city."

Succeeding sections provided a system of fines, ranging from five to twenty-five dollars, and imprisonment up to thirty days in default of payment, for violations of the ordinance; and authorized the Mayor to close any house, whether within or without the segregated district, which " may become dangerous to public morals," and require the occupants to move. If they failed to do so, the Mayor was given the power " to place a policeman at the door to warn away all parties who shall undertake to enter."

The limits of the French Quarter district, as set forth in the amended ordinance, were the same as in the measure adopted on January 6, except that five blocks had been added by the inclusion of St. Louis Street. For reasons which the records do not show and which city officials of the time who are still alive do not recall, no prostitutes were permitted to establish themselves in the area prescribed in the American section, and it was never used as a segregated district. The decision to confine vice entirely within the French Quarter must have been made soon after the passage of the amended act, however, for on September 1, 1897 the Council adopted an ordinance providing that " on and from the first of January, 1898, it shall be unlawful . . . to open, operate or carry on any cabaret, concert-saloon or place where can can, clodoche or similar female dancing or sensational performances are shown, without the following limits, viz, from the lower side of N. Basin Street to the lower side of N. Robertson Street, and from the south side of Customhouse Street to the north side of St. Louis Street." No provision was made for such resorts in the section of the city above Canal Street.

The passage of these ordinances, and the obvious intention of the city to enforce them, had several immediate results. There was a noticeable exodus of prostitutes who indignantly refused to be herded like cattle; rentals and property values in the proposed district doubled, and many houses throughout the city for which the harlots had been paying large sums were left tenantless. One of the owners of this latter class of property brought suit to test the constitutionality of the law and was victorious in the Civil District Court. On an appeal by the city, however, the Supreme Court of Louisiana reversed the lower tribunal and held that the municipal government had the power under the city charter to confine prostitution to any given locality. The area thus finally determined upon as a quasi-legal red-light district comprised five blocks on each of Customhouse, Bienville, Conti, and St. Louis Streets, and three on each of North Basin, Trèmé (now North Liberty), Villere, Marais, North Franklin, and North Robertson Streets — a total of thirty-eight blocks occupied solely by brothels and assignation houses, and by saloons, cabarets, and other enterprises which depended upon vice for their prosperity. The removal of prostitutes to these streets, several of which were already well filled with bordellos, began during the late summer of 1897 and was in full swing on October 1, when the Story ordinance went into effect. By the middle of 1898 the movement had been completed, and the new district, popularly known as Storyville, much to Alderman Story's disgust, was operating full blast under the sheltering shadow of the law. The brothels were now safe from interference by the police so long as they were conducted with a modicum of restraint and no crimes were committed in them. Sensible madames and crib girls, however, made assurance doubly sure by continuing the custom of leaving dollars and quarters on the doorsteps.

Within a few years Storyville had become the most celebrated red-light district in the United States and had assumed the position once held by Congo Square and the Quadroon Balls as a unique attraction of New Orleans. In other days visitors to the city were escorted to Congo Square to see the dancing of the slaves, and to the old Orleans Ballroom to watch the beautiful quadroons trail their silks and satins across the dance-floor; now they were taken " down the line " to see the plush and velvet parlors of the palatial mansions of sin, to shiver at the bawdy shows and dancing in the cabarets, and to peek through the shutters of the lowly cribs at the naked girls who sat patiently waiting for customers. In obedience to a custom which had the strength of unwritten law, a tour of the segregated area invariably began with a drink at the Arlington Annex, at Customhouse and North Basin Streets. This gateway to Storyville was the property of Thomas C. Anderson, saloon-keeper, political boss of the Fourth Ward, member of the Legislature for two terms prior to 1908, owner of at least one of the prosperous bawdy-houses of North Basin Street, and the happy posses-

433

sor of an interest in several others. In deference to this big shot of brotheldom the red-light district was sometimes called Anderson County. Besides his bagnio holdings, Anderson owned a restaurant and cabaret on Rampart Street, which he advertised as " The Real Thing," and two other saloons, the Stag on Gravier Street and the Arlington on Rampart. The Annex was by far the most important establishment in Storyville, an unofficial Town Hall where Anderson, a worthy disciple of the politicians who had made New Orleans a shambles of corruption for almost a hundred years, sat enthroned amidst his tainted dollars, dispensing political largesse and making known his wishes and commands. So far as the red-light district was concerned, he was the law and the prophets. Said Will Irwin in *Collier's Weekly* for February 29, 1908:

" Briefly, here is the reason for Tom Anderson: With a little break here and there, New Orleans has been in the grip of a ring. No large city in the United States gets such poor returns for the public money expended as New Orleans. It is ill-paved, ill-policed, behind in municipal improvements; the public money is needed for a thousand and one sinecure jobs. By the same token, no other city of the country runs vice of every kind so wide open. Tom Anderson has been a great help. Highly prosperous himself, he has not failed to divide up with the power which enabled him to be prosperous; and he has helped to make the saloon-keepers, the gamblers and the brothel-keepers generous. It was his whim to go to the Legislature, and a grateful people, recognizing his services, rewarded him."

Anderson's right-hand man in the operation of his various properties was Billy Struve, who was a young police reporter on the *Item* when he first met the king of the red lights about 1895. Struve helped Anderson organize the Astoria Club, one of the latter's first important ventures, and went to work regularly for Anderson in 1900, abandoning his newspaper career. In 1907 Anderson gave him an interest in the business. With Billy Struve's [1] expert assistance, Anderson conducted his affairs with great prosperity, and retained his political power and his prestige as first citizen of Storyville until the segregated district was abolished. Soon after prohibition came upon the land, Anderson retired from the saloon business and became interested in oil, organizing the Protection Oil Company, and later the Liberty Oil Company, which was purchased by Standard Oil. In 1928 Anderson was very ill, and after his recovery he became very religious and often expressed the wish that he had lived in a more godly manner. In September of that year he married Gertrude Hoffmire, better known as Gertrude Dix, who for several years after about 1908 had operated the brothel at No. 209 North Basin Street, owned by Anderson, and the Arlington at 225 North Basin, in which Anderson had an interest. When Anderson died, on December 10, 1931, he left his estate of some $120,000 to his widow, but the will was contested by Mrs. Irene Delsa, widow of George Delsa, at one time manager of Anderson's cabaret on Rampart Street. She claimed to be Anderson's daughter by his first wife, Emma Schwartz, whom he married in 1879 or 1880, when he was a young book-keeper of twenty-two and had not yet realized the money-making possibilities of liquor and vice. Mrs. Delsa's attorneys cited the state law of concubinage and the decisions in the Hattie Hamilton and Kate Townsend cases, but the courts held that the statute was not applicable because Anderson and Gertrude Dix had married. Mrs. Delsa was recognized as Anderson's daughter, how-

---

[1] At this writing Billy Struve is still alive and running a saloon on Rampart Street.

435

ever, and a settlement was effected by which she is said to have received a considerable part of the estate.

3

WHEN the prostitutes of New Orleans were ordered to transfer their activities to Storyville, the police made no attempt to separate the races further than forbidding white and black women to live in the same house; they might, and did, occupy adjoining premises. Although among such a fundamentally transient population there was naturally much shifting about in the course of twenty years, during the greater part of the period in which the red-light district was in existence most of the cribs, flimsy one-story wooden shanties wherein prices ranged from twenty-five cents to a dollar, were on St. Louis and Franklin Streets, with a few on Customhouse, Conti, and North Robertson; while the two-and three-dollar houses were principally located on Villere, Marais, Customhouse, and North Liberty Streets. The five-dollar establishments — there were no ten- and twenty-dollar brothels as in the days of the rich and dissolute carpet-baggers — were largely concentrated on North Basin Street. As another section of it across Canal Street had been when Kate Townsend and Minnie Haha were in their heyday, this was the swank thoroughfare of the district. Many of the North Basin Street brothels, some of them imposing mansions three and four stories in height, were conducted with considerable elegance and ceremony. Rudeness and bawdy behavior on the part of the customers were frowned upon, and drunken gentlemen were not accommodated. When a man entered the parlor he was expected to buy a drink at once — incidentally, at an enormous profit to the house — but the girls were not trotted out for inspection unless he so requested. All of the parlor houses were more or less expensively furnished and equipped, with as much gilt, plush, and velvet as the madames and their financial backers could afford. In many of them, especially on North Basin Street, were one or more rooms with mirrored walls and ceilings, which were available at special rates; and ballrooms with fine hardwood floors and curtained platforms for the circuses, indecent dancing, and other erotic displays which were given whenever sufficient money was in sight. In most of these exhibitions the ladies of the house participated; sometimes, however, specialists were called in.

A few of the best brothels regularly employed orchestras of from two to four instruments, which played each night in the ballroom from about seven o'clock to closing, which was usually at dawn. The others depended upon the groups of itinerant musicians who frequently appeared in Storyville, playing in the streets and saloons for coins and drinks. One of the most popular of these combinations — though not for dancing — was a company of boys, from twelve to fifteen years old, who called themselves the Spasm Band. They were the real creators of jazz, and the Spasm Band was the original jazz band. There were seven members besides the manager and principal organizer, Harry Gregson, who was the singer of the outfit — he crooned the popular songs of the day through a piece of gas-pipe, since he couldn't afford a proper megaphone. The musicians were Emile Lacomb, otherwise Stalebread Charley, who played a fiddle made out of a cigar-box; Willie Bussey, better known as Cajun, who performed entrancingly upon the harmonica; Charley Stein, who manipulated an old kettle, a cow-bell, a gourd filled with pebbles, and other traps and in later life became a famous drummer; Chinee, who smote the bull fiddle, at first half a barrel and later a coffin-shaped contraption built by the boys; Warm Gravy; Emile Benrod, called Whisky, and Frank Bussey, known as Monk. The three last-named played whistles and various horns, most of them home-made, and each had at least three instruments, upon which he alternated. Cajun Bussey and Stalebread Charley could play tunes upon the harmonica and the fiddle, and the others contributed whatever sounds chanced to come from their instruments.[1] These they played with the horns in hats, standing upon their heads, and interrupting themselves occasionally with lugubrious howls. In short, they apparently originated practically all of the antics with which the virtuosi of modern jazz provoke the hotcha spirit, and sometimes downright nausea. The Spasm boys even screamed " hi-de-hi " and " ho-de-ho " — and incidentally these expressions, now the exclusive howls of Negro band-leaders, were used in Mississippi River songs at least a hundred years ago.

The Spasm Band first appeared in New Orleans about 1895, and for several years the boys picked up many an honest penny playing in front of the theaters and saloons and in the brothels, and with a few formal engagements at West End, Grand Opera House, and other resorts, when they were advertised as " The Razzy Dazzy Spasm Band." Their big moment, however, came when they serenaded Sarah Bernhardt, who expressed amazement and gave them each a coin. About 1900 — the date is uncertain — Jack Robinson, owner of the Haymarket dance-hall on Customhouse Street between Dauphine and Bourbon, engaged a band of experienced, adult musicians, who imitated the antics and contortions of the Spasm Band and, moreover, used their billing — Razzy Dazzy Spasm Band. When the members of the original Spasm Band appeared at the Haymarket with their hands and pockets filled with stones and bricks and made violent protest, Robinson repainted his advertising placards to read: " Razzy Dazzy Jazzy Band! " Thus it began. And now look!

---

[1] Harry Gregson and Frank Bussey are still living in New Orleans. Gregson is a Captain of Detectives in the police department, and Bussey, at this writing, is tending bar at Royal and Toulouse Streets. Neither remembers the real name of Chinee and Warm Gravy.

4

THE doings of the New Orleans strumpets were faithfully chronicled for some thirty years in half a dozen publications, which appeared with great editorial fanfares, ran through their comparatively brief periods of success and notoriety, and vanished into the limbo of nasty journalism, to be reincarnated, perhaps, in the modern tabloids. The best-known and most influential of these were the *Mascot,* the *Sunday Sun,* and the *Blue Book.* The *Mascot* was established in 1882. It was issued every Saturday at five cents a copy, and was about the size of the present-day tabloid, with from four to six pages. For about ten years the *Mascot* was a vigorous weekly of decidedly liberal tendencies. It published sensational accounts of crime and scandal in the manner of the *Police Gazette,* but the comments of its editorial writers were clear and pungent, and it frequently performed valiant service in exposing corruption in high places. During the early 1890's the *Mascot* began to devote considerable space to the activities of the red-light district, and in 1894 established a column, called simply " Society," in which were published personal items about the prostitutes. The following, from various issues of 1894 and 1895, are fair samples:

" Madame Julia Dean has received a draft of recruits, and the fair Julia is bragging loudly of her importation. She seems to forget that the ladies played a star engagement here last winter at Mme. Haley's, and they all carry their diplomas with them.

" Several amateurs have been enjoying quite a good time of late in the residence at the rear of a grocery store on Derbigny Street.

" The bewitching Miss Ollie Martinez has become so thoroughly domesticated of late that her name is becoming missed from the society columns.

"It is safe to say that Mrs. [Madeleine] Theurer can brag of more innocent young girls having been ruined in her house than there were in any other six houses in the city."

Society.

THE ladies who are in the social swim are looking forward with pleasing anticipation, to next week's performance at the Grand. Not only the title of the play, "Daughters of Eve," pleases the darlings, but they also know that Marie Wainwright is a regular sport and they consider that the fair Marie acts as a lever for them in giving  them social prominence. The girls all pity poor, dear, Henry Greenwall, and think it is a horrid shame that luck should have turned so dreadfully upon him. His shows don't seem to take, cotton played him false and this year the ponies are playing the very deuce with him. The darlings all ascribe Henry's being as cross as a bear with a sore head to the fact that he has been unlucky lately. But unlucky in monetary matters means lucky in love, and by all accounts dear Henry is so, and it is said he swears by a folding sofa.

The society world was greatly disappointed with Wenger's New Year's ball. The ladies all declare that it was a snare and dillusion The only thing that caused the slightest fun was a peep that was obtained of Henry in a new POSE PLASTIQUE, representing the ram in the bushes that Abraham caught and sacrificed in place of his son Isaac.

Miss Carrie Freeman has favored us with a recent photograph of herself, taken since she adopted her new diet of spaggbetti. Carrie no longer sees ghosts, but she at times sees spirits.

MISS CARRIE FREEMAN.

Miss Bessie Lamothe, 9 South Franklin street, wishes her friends to understand that she did not announce that she received in a pink dress on New Years, but she desires it to be understood that she receives every night in un ROBE, blanc de nuit,

THE SOCIETY COLUMN OF *THE MASCOT*, ISSUE OF JAN. 5, 1895

The personal items and the news accounts in the *Mascot*, however, were models of propriety and choice language compared with those published in the *Sunday Sun*, which appeared in the field in 1888 and was always an out-and-out scandal sheet. It was slightly smaller than the *Mascot*, never had more than four pages, and appeared weekly, on sale at five cents in the saloons and on the news-stands every Saturday evening. The front page was invariably devoted to an account of a murder, a divorce case, or other scandal, and the story was very plainly written, usually under some such headline as this:

Wife of . . . Commits Herself in a Most
Notorious, Lewd and Outrageous Manner.

COMMITS ADULTERY

With a Person Known as . . . Who Openly
Boasts That She is His Woman.

The inside pages were filled with similar stories, and with advertisements of saloons, quack doctors, pool-rooms, shyster lawyers, restaurants, cabarets, and assignation houses, which made their announcements in this fashion:

ELEGANTLY FURNISHED
ROOMS
1320 Conti Street . . . Corner Liberty.
New Orleans, La.
MISS MAY EVANS.

The feature which really accounted for the considerable success of the *Sunday Sun* was a column headed " SCARLET WORLD," and filled with frank comment on the doings of the bawds. These excerpts are good examples of the *Sunday Sun's* journalistic style and of the content of the paper:

"Nina Jackson, who keeps the swell mansion, 1559 Customhouse Street, and who is herself one of the jolliest girls in the bunch, has gotten rid of those two tid-bits, May and Mamie, and in their stead she

441

has two of the finest and most charming ladies to be found anywhere. Queen Emmette, known as the Diamond Tooth, is one of the girls, and Etta Ross is the other.

" Nettie Garbright, who for a number of years kept a sporting house at No. 139 Customhouse Street, and retired to private life, is back on the turf again, comfortably situated at No. 1537 Customhouse Street.

" Eunice Deering, who presides at the swell mansion, No. 341 Basin Avenue, corner Conti, has increased her staff and is ready for the Carnival business. In this mansion nothing but swell women are to be seen.

" Madge Lester has returned from a trip and is back in Jessie Brown's, 1542 Customhouse Street.

" Boys, if you want to have a real jolly good time, don't overlook Miss Antonia Gonzales' establishment, for a visit to the village is incomplete without seeing Antonia and her array of beautiful young girls . . . she keeps a swell house, where nothing but the best is kept."

The *Blue Book,* most famous of all New Orleans' red-light publications, was the last of a series of directories of the district. The first of these, *The Green Book, or, Gentlemen's Guide to New Orleans,* was published in January 1895, in an edition of two thousand copies, which were quickly sold at twenty-five cents each. A few years later the *Red Book* appeared, and was similarly successful. The first issue of the *Blue Book,* supposed to have been financed by Tom Anderson, was published about 1902, and it appeared every year or so thereafter for several years. It was six by four and one-half inches, contained from forty to fifty pages, and was sold for a quarter a copy in the saloons, and by agents at the hotels, the railroad stations, and the steamboat

SCARLET WORLD.

Gay Girls' Actions.

Gilded Vice in Silk and Calico.

Interesting Items About the Every-Day Life of Women of Crimson Circles.

The Arlington Saloon, No. 12 N. Rampart street, presided over by Tom Anderson, is the principal and most popular resort for all sporting men. Everything you get there is first-class.

Miss Josie Arlington is suffering with a bad cold, but she is on deck all the same attending to business.

Tillie Thurman or Carlisle, who keeps a joint on Basin street near the corner of Conti, next to Pelican Four's truck house, is certainly a Pelican of the first water. Boys, if you are out looking for a good time and wish to save a doctor's bill we severely advise you to give the above establishment all the room possible. When it comes down to the real thing in the way of low-down tarts, then this is the house you are looking for.

Clara Henderson is now occupying the beautiful cottage 1554 Conti street, and has living with her Cleona Miller, a lovely blonde who is in the 20 karat class. Clara is well known by the rounders and is a thorough good fellow.

Lou Raymond, better known as Kackling' Lou, ought to attend to her own business and quit poking her nose into her neighbors' affairs. The way Kackling Lou has put the devil in a couple of young girls, who were doing nicely with a neighbor of hers, was a caution. Such conduct on the part of a woman as old as Kackling Lou is most mortifying. Now will you be good, you naughty old girl, and attend to your own business?

Alda Dugaot, one of Lulu White's finest, has a good one on her staff. Alda is now wearing a pair of $800 diamond ear-rings. Alda, they are very becoming.

Stella Clements, who now calls herself Stella Moore, has taken the name of a performer in Haverly's Minstrels. Are you going to do the couche-couche, Stella?

Jessie Brown is expecting two girls from Atlanta, Ga.

Daisy Merritt is having a grand, old time with her lumberman. Say, Skidoo, look out; there might be something doing there that may surprise you. Money is H—ll, you know.

Last Tuesday George S. Roddy, advance agent of "King Dodo," which is now playing at the Tulane Theatre, was out in the Tenderloin acting anything but a gentleman. He went into Maestri's row of low prostitutes, bilking them. One of the women grabbed his hat, and had it not been for the officer on the beat Mr Roddy would have fared badly. This is the recognized 50 cents colony. George, that is below the standard; did you want it cheaper?

Truxie Leroy is the latest arrival in Fanny Lambert's. Truxie comes from Evansville, Ind. She has been named the Little Casino of the house. She is a contrast of Maud Wells.

Abbey Reid, better known as the Countess Kuneman, is in Fanny Lambert's. Her friends will be glad to hear that she is getting along nicely.

Bertha Golden, the landlady who presides at 213 Basin avenue, is one of the best looking women on that thoroughfare. Bertha conducts a swell house and is known all over the country. She is surrounded by a bevy of choice girls and it goes without saying that they are beauts, entertainers, dancers, etc. The motto of this house is to give Satisfaction. Bertha herself is an entertainer, having at one time been on the stage, and her pleasing stunts are in themselves attractions which go to assist in making time fly. She has ten girls at the present time.

Estelle who occupies rooms 305 Lesin ave near Bienville has an idea of business. Estelle is a pronounced brunette and a genuine Parisian buxom and very pretty woman. Estelle has many friends who admire her for her many good qualities she possesses. She is an entertainer, speaks several languages, and is a thorough good fellow. A visit to her will not be regretted.

There is a drugstore at the corner of Customhouse and Marais streets that is selling certain drugs which are prohibited by law except when ordered by a physician. It is not lawful to sell cocaine, but it is sold here just the same.

THE SOCIETY COLUMN OF "THE SUNDAY SUN," JANUARY 31, 1904

landings. It was bound in blue paper, and the cover was decorated by a flower design and the words "Blue Book," all printed in red ink. It contained a preface, a notice that "This book must not be mailed," and a complete list of all prostitutes in residence in Storyville, both white and black, arranged by streets in some issues and alphabetically in others. There was also a list of "Late Arrivals," and a roster of the girls employed in the cabarets of the district, who were at least $99\frac{44}{100}$ per cent impure. At the top of each page of names was a decorative drawing of two women, facing each other, with a red light between them. In the front and middle portions of the *Blue Book* were advertisements of saloons, lawyers, liquor-dealers, restaurants, cabarets, breweries, cigars and tobacco, and other places and commodities, while the last fifteen or twenty pages were devoted to the announcements of the brothel-keepers, with the names of the madames and the street addresses in red. A few of the best-known houses and madames, together with excerpts from their *Blue Book* advertisements, follow:

The Phoenix, 1547 Iberville Street. Kept by Fanny Lambert. "Wine and beer house full of jolly and Pretty Ladies."

Antonia P. Gonzales, corner Villere and Iberville Streets. "The above party has always been a headliner among those who keep first-class Octoroons. She also has the distinction of being the only Singer of Opera and Female Cornetist in the Tenderloin. She has had offers after offers to leave her present vocation and take to the stage, but her vast business has kept her among her friends. Any person out for fun among a lot of pretty Creole damsels, here is the place to have it."

The Firm, 224 North Villere Street. Kept by Miss Leslie. "The Firm is also noted for its selectness. You make no mistake in visiting The Firm. Everybody must be of some importance, otherwise he cannot gain admittance."

Eunice Deering, corner Basin and Conti Streets. "Known as the idol of the society and club boys. . . . Aside from the grandeur of her establishment, she has a score of beautiful women."

Margaret Bradford, 1559 Iberville Street. "Pretty women, good time and sociability has been adopted as the counter sign of Miss Bradford's new and costly home."

Jessie Brown, 223 North Basin. "Don't be misled until you have seen Jessie Brown and her ladies."

The Cairo, 320 North Franklin. Kept by Snooks Randella. "Snooks has the distinction of keeping one of the liveliest and most elaborately furnished establishments in the city, where an array of beautiful women and good times reign supreme."

Martha Clark, 227 North Basin. "Her women are known for their cleverness and beauty. Also, in being able to entertain the most fastidious of mankind."

The Club, 327 North Franklin. Kept by Maud Hartman. "Come and join the club and meet the members."

Diana and Norma, 213–215 North Basin. "Their names have become known on both continents, because everything goes as it will, and those that cannot be satisfied there must surely be of a queer nature."

Gertrude Dix, 209 North Basin. "Miss Dix, while very young, is of a type that pleases most men of today — the witty, pretty and natty — a lady of fashion. . . . There are no words for her grandeur of feminine beauty and artistic settings."

Louise Dreyfus, 1310 Conti Street. "She has some of the most beautiful and select girls in the District — one of whom is Chiquita, the Spanish Beauty."

Blue Book

THIS BOOK MUST NOT BE MAILED

TO KNOW the right from the wrong, to be sure of yourself, go through this little book and read it carefully, and then when you visit Storyville you will know the best places to spend your money and time, as all the BEST houses are advertised. Read all the "ads."

This book contains nothing but Facts, and is of the greatest value to strangers when in this part of the city. The names of the residents will be found in this Directory, alphabetically arranged, under the headings "White" and "Colored," from alpha to omega. The names in capitals are landladies only.

You will find the boundary of the Tenderloin District, or Storyville: North side Iberville Street to south side St. Louis, and east side North Basin to west side North Robertson Street.

This is the boundary in which the women are compelled to live, according to law.

PREFACE

"Honi Soit Qui Mal y Pense"

THIS Directory and Guide of the Sporting District has been before the people on many occasions, and has proven its authority as to what is doing in the "Queer Zone."

Anyone who knows to-day from yesterday will say that the Blue Book is the right book for the right people.

WHY NEW ORLEANS SHOULD HAVE THIS DIRECTORY

Because it is the only district of its kind in the States set aside for the fast women by law.

Because it puts the stranger on a proper and safe path as to where he may go and be free from "Hold-ups," and other games usually practiced upon the stranger.

It regulates the women so that they may live in one district to themselves instead of being scattered over the city and filling our thoroughfares with street walkers.

It also gives the names of women entertainers employed in the Dance Halls and Cabarets in the District.

NAMES
STORYVILLE "400"

Basin Street

COLOR.	NAME.	ADDRESS.
W	MEEKER, FLO	209 Basin
W	Clark, Jennie	"
W	Parish, Ida	"
W	Tropp, May	"
W	Bard, Grace	"
W	Ellison, Eunice	"
W	Parker, Jeanette	"
W	Moss, Lillian	"
W	Lee, Andry,	"
W	ANGELE, MARGUERITE	213 Basin
W	Duval, Nina	"
W	Grosso, Carmen	"
W	DENIS, MARIE	217 Basin
W	Blement, Blanche	"
W	Manghi, Angeline	"
W	NICHOLLS, OLLIE	221 Basin
W	Lemcure, Violet	"
W	Douglass, Lucile	"
W	Vogt, Grace	"
W	Desmond, Carmen	"
W	Schneffer, Corinne	"
W	Thornton, Bennie	"

PAGES FROM THE BLUE BOOK

EMMA JOHNSON'S

MISS
JOSIE ARLINGTON

225 Basin Street   **Phone 1888**

The Arlington

Nowhere in this country will you find a more complete and thorough sporting establishment than the Arlington. Absolutely and unquestionably the most decorative and costly fitted out sporting palace ever placed before the American public.

The wonderful originality of everything that goes to fit out a mansion makes it the most attractive ever seen in this and the old country.

Miss Arlington recently went to an expense of nearly $5,000 in having her mansion renovated and replenished.

Within the great walls of the Arlington will be found the work of great artists from Europe and America. Many articles from the Louisiana Purchase Exposition will also be seen.

Mme. Emma Johnson

Better known as the "Parisian Queen of America," needs little introduction in this country.

Emma's "Home of All Nations," as it is commonly called, is one place of amusement you can't very well afford to miss while in the District.

Everything goes here. Pleasure is the watchword.

Business has been on such an increase at the above place of late that Mme. Johnson had to occupy an "Annex." Emma never has less than twenty pretty women of all nations, who are clever entertainers.

Remember the name, Johnson's.

Aqui si hable Espanola.

Ici on parle francais.

PHONE CONNECTION

331-333 N. Basin

MISS RAY OWENS
"STAR MANSION"

1517 Iberville Street   ✕ ✕ ✕   **Phone 1793**

By far the handsomest and most modern Sporting House in the Crescent City. The Turkish room in this mansion is the finest in the South, all the furnishings and decorations having been imported by Vantine of New York especially for Miss Owens, regardless of cost.

Miss Ray Owens' "STAR MANSION"
Iberville Street

HER LADIES ARE: MILDRED ANDERSON
GEORGIE CUMMINGS   SADIE LUSHTER
MADELINE ST. CLAIR   GLADIS WALLACE
PANSY MONTROSE, Housekeeper

SOME FAMOUS STORYVILLE RESORTS
[FROM THE BLUE BOOK]

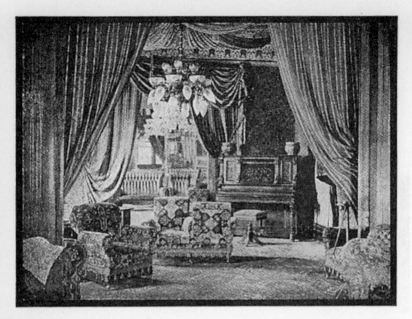

THE VIENNA PARLOR

THE MUSIC HALL

THE INTERIOR OF JOSIE ARLINGTON'S BASIN

THE AMERICAN PARLOR

A BOUDOIR

TREET BAGNIO AS ADVERTISED IN THE BLUE BOOK

Edna Hamilton, 1304 Conti Street. "As for women, she has an unexcelled array, who, aside from their beauty, are all of high class and culture."

The Studio, also known as the House of All Nations, 331–333 North Basin. Kept by Emma Johnson. "Everything goes here. Pleasure is the watchword. Remember the name, Johnson's."

Grace Lloyd, 338 North Franklin. "A visit will teach you more than pen can describe."

Olga Lodi, the Italian Queen, 321 North Basin. "Aside from the magnificence of her home, she has a score of most handsome ladies, who are a jolly crowd to be among."

Countess Willie V. Piazza, 317 North Basin. "If you have the blues, the Countess and her girls can cure them. She has, without doubt, the most handsome and intelligent octoroons in the United States. You should see them; they are all entertainers."

Mav V. Spencer, 315 North Basin. "Miss Spencer, while very young, is very charming, and, above all things a favorite with the boys — what one might say, those of the clubs. . . . You should see her girls."

Bertha Weinthal, 311 North Basin. "While still young in years, has, nevertheless, proven herself a grand woman, and has also made 'good' as a conductor of a first-class establishment."

Minnie White, 221 North Basin. "She has surrounded herself with a bevy of charming girls, each one a star, who are always willing to meet you halfway and make you feel that you are welcome."

Alice Williams, 1545 Iberville. "She has a lot of jolly good girls as guests, who are the 'goods' as one would term them. Don't overlook Alice."

The Little Annex, 217 North Basin. Kept by Lizette Smith. "She has some of the most beautiful and

select girls in the district, who know how to do things
as you like 'em.''

Lillian Irwin, 313 North Basin Street. ". . .
where swell men can be socially entertained by an array of swell ladies.''

Mary Smith, 1538 Iberville. " A pleasant time for
the boys.''

Despite the extravagant claims of their advertising,
none of these brothels were equal in reputation, in magnificence, or in the number of bawds permanently resident
on the premises, to the Arlington, which was operated at
No. 225 North Basin Street by Josie Arlington, the most
celebrated madame of her time; she was to Storyville what
Kate Townsend had been to the red-light district of an
earlier day. Josie Arlington's house was a five-dollar house
and looked it — an imposing structure of four stories, with
bay windows on three sides and a cupola on the roof;
chastely painted on the outside, but inside a riot of gilt,
plush, velvet hangings, Oriental carpets, damask chairs and
sofas, lace curtains, beveled mirrors, cut-glass chandeliers,
and Turkish corners crowded with bric-a-brac and objects
of more or less virtue. Few of the many rival establishments
housed as many as half a dozen girls, but when the roll was
called at the Arlington no fewer than ten exquisite strumpets trooped into the parlor. And during the tourist and
Mardi Gras seasons this number was often doubled. The
Blue Book was probably not far wrong when it described
the Arlington as " absolutely and unquestionably the most
decorative and costly fitted out sporting palace ever placed
before the American public . . . a palace fit for a king . . .
the most attractive ever seen in this or the old country. . . .
Within the walls of this mansion will be found the work of
great artists from Europe and America. Many articles from
various expositions will also be seen, and curios galore.''

Among the inanimate attractions of the bordello was a collection of steins which is said to have been really extraordinary. The entire collection was displayed on a shelf in the dining-room, but since the house was frequently filled with strangers, a heavy chain was passed through the handle of each stein and securely padlocked to a ring-bolt sunk into the wall.

Josie Arlington's real name was Mary Deubler. She was born in New Orleans about 1864, of German parents, and was never married. In 1881, when she was about seventeen years old, she fell in love with Philip Lobrano, an obscure sporting man who was also known as Schwarz, and was his mistress for nine years, during most of which time she was an inmate of various brothels on Customhouse and Basin Streets, under the name of Josie Alton. She never remained very long in any one place, for at this period of her career she possessed an exceedingly irascible disposition and was noted for her brawling and fighting proclivities; in 1886 she engaged in a fierce fight on Burgundy Street with a Negro prostitute, Beulah Ripley, in which she lost most of her hair, while Beulah Ripley staggered from the scene of combat minus part of her lower lip and half an ear. About 1888 Josie Arlington began calling herself Josie Lobrano, and opened a place of her own at No. 172 Customhouse Street, which soon became known as one of the toughest houses in the city, and the inmates as the most quarrelsome strumpets. On the profits of this establishment she supported several members of her family and Lobrano, who lived in the house. Lobrano hated her relatives and frequently referred to them as "a flock of vultures." On November 2, 1890, during a terrific fight in which Josie Arlington and all of her girls were involved, Lobrano shot her brother, Peter Deubler. Lobrano was tried twice, and at the second trial was acquitted. After the shooting Josie Arlington broke with her lover, changed her name to Lobrano d'Arlington, dismissed her brawling bawds, and announced that she would fill her house with gracious, amiable foreign girls, who would be at home only to gentlemen of taste and refinement. Early in 1895 a considerable stir was aroused in the red-light district by this announcement in the *Mascot:*

> " Society is graced by the presence of a bona-fide baroness, direct from the Court at St. Petersburg. The baroness is at present residing incog. at the Chateau Lobrano d'Arlington, and is known as La Belle Stewart."

Unfortunately, the baroness was exposed within a few weeks as a hoochy-koochy dancer and circus specialist who had performed on the Midway at the Chicago World's Fair, and several of Josie Arlington's other importations were likewise branded as impostors. Nevertheless, she operated the brothel in Customhouse Street with great success until Storyville was established, when she opened the Arlington. There she acquired her reputation as the snootiest madame in America, while the house became renowned as the gaudiest and grandest of bordellos. Josie Arlington ran the place for some ten years and amassed a considerable fortune, with part of which she built a thirty-five-thousand-dollar house on Esplanade Street. There was only one break in the chain of her prosperity. That was about 1905, when the interior of the Arlington was badly damaged by fire, and Josie Arlington and her girls moved into temporary quarters above Tom Anderson's Arlington Annex until repairs had been made. But she had narrowly escaped death, and she was so frightened that she began to prepare for the end. She bought a plot of ground for two thousand dollars in Metarie Cemetery and on it erected an eight-thousand-dollar tomb of red marble, with two large flambeaux on top, a cross cut in the back, and a copper door on which, in *bas relief,* was carved the figure of a kneeling woman, her arms filled with flowers.

Josie Arlington became very moody and introspective after the fire, and about 1909, it is said upon the advice of her friends Tom Anderson and John T. Brady, she leased the Arlington to Anna Casey and retired to her house on Esplanade Street. There she lived — somewhat violently according to the neighbors — with her niece, whom she had educated in a convent. On February 14, 1914, in her fiftieth year, she died, and was buried next day after a quiet funeral. Her body was followed to the cemetery by a few carriages containing flowers, Sisters of Charity, priests, and a few male friends, among them, according to the *Item,* Tom Anderson, John T. Brady, and Judge Richard Otero. The *demi-monde* sent flowers, but did not attend the funeral. A few months after Josie Arlington's death the city installed a red traffic light in the road alongside the cemetery, and at night the glow struck the two flambeaux in such a manner as to cause the perfect illusion of a red light shining above the famous brothel-keeper's tomb. Crowds gathered each evening to watch the spectacle, and it was one of the sights of the city until the red light was replaced with a white one. Josie Arlington's niece and Brady were married soon after the death of the madame, and about 1924 her bones were placed in a receiving vault and the tomb sold.

5

ON July 17, 1917 the City Council adopted an ordinance establishing a special district for Negro prostitutes in the area bounded by the upper side of Perdido Street, the lower side of Gravier, the river side of South Franklin, and the lower side of Locust Street. This act was to have become effective on August 15, but no effort was ever made to enforce it, for segregated vice in New Orleans had already been doomed by America's entrance into the World War. Early in August, Secretary of War Newton D. Baker issued an order forbidding open prostitution within five miles of an Army cantonment, and a similar ruling was made by Josephus Daniels, Secretary of the Navy, respecting naval establishments. Later in the same month Bascom Johnson, representing the War and Navy Department, visited New Orleans, inspected Storyville, and informed Mayor Martin Behrman that the orders must be obeyed. Mayor Behrman went to Washington and protested, but without success, and on September 24 and again on October 1 he was notified by Secretary Daniels that unless the red-light district was closed by the city it would be closed by the Army and the Navy. On October 2, 1917 Mayor Behrman introduced an ordinance in the City Council abolishing Storyville. "Pretermitting the pros and cons of legislative recognition of prostitution as a necessary evil in a seaport the size of New Orleans," the Mayor said, "our city government has believed that the situation could be administered more easily and satisfactorily by confining it within a prescribed area. Our experience has taught us that the reasons for this are unanswerable, but the Navy Department of the Federal government has decided otherwise."

The ordinance was adopted on October 9, and provided that after midnight of November 12, 1917 it would be unlawful to operate a brothel or assignation house anywhere in New Orleans. A few days later William Railly, president of the Citizens' League of Louisiana, which had waged an unsuccessful fight against Storyville for several years, wrote to the *Times-Picayune* that the principal brothels had been promised protection and would be permitted to reopen. Mayor Behrman immediately asked the District Attorney, C. C. Luzenberg, for a Grand Jury investigation, but proof was not forthcoming from the League.

On October 15 several fire-insurance companies canceled all policies on property in Storyville, and the State Fire Marshal began an investigation of a rumored plot to burn the district. November 10, two days before the ordinance was to go into effect, was Saturday, and a large force of police was sent to Storyville to prevent expected trouble. None, however, developed; in fact, the district was quieter than it had been for months. The usual crowd of idlers was in the streets, but there were few customers in the saloons, the cabarets, or the brothels. Many of the latter had already closed, and the red lights had been removed from the windows of others. On November 11 Gertrude Dix asked Judge F. D. King of the Civil Court for an injunction restraining the city from enforcing the closing ordinance. He refused, holding that " the subject matter of the ordinance is clearly within the police power of the city." Later in the day the Supreme Court refused to issue a writ of mandamus to compel the granting of the injunction.

The exodus from Storyville had begun two weeks before November 12, but most of the prostitutes had awaited the result of Gertrude Dix's application for a restraining order. When the news of her failure spread, wagons and vans began entering the district and hauling away whatever furniture had not been sold to the swarm of second-hand dealers. As late as midnight of the 12th there was a stream of harlots and their servants, laden with property, leaving the segregated area. During the afternoon the police visited every house and informed the women that they might remain in Storyville, but that they must take down their red lights, and that they would be watched and arrested if they attempted to operate. Gertrude Dix was among the few who remained, and after a few months she reopened her house at No. 209 North Basin Street and ran it surreptitiously until May 13, 1918, when she was arrested by agents of the Department of Justice, who also raided four other places on North Basin, Julia, and North Rampart Streets. Five women were indicted, and on June 20 Gertrude Dix pleaded guilty and was sentenced to the House of Detention for five days.

453

On November 14, 1917, two days after the closing of the red-light district, the *Item* announced that the police planned to round up the male parasites of Storyville and send them into the country to help the farmers. Nothing, however, came of this extraordinary idea. The next day many leading churchwomen, and members of the Louisiana Federation of Women's Clubs, held a meeting and appointed a committee to help the prostitutes. But none applied for succor. Few, in fact, needed it. They had simply moved from Storyville into various business and residential sections of New Orleans and were doing very well.

6

DESPITE the activities of several groups of suppressionists, Storyville was reasonably successful from the beginning, partly because public opinion favored such a district, and partly because the police department increased in efficiency during the successive administrations of Mayors Walter C. Flower (1896–1900), Paul Capdeville (1900–4), and Martin Behrman (1904–20), and enforced the laws relating to prostitution with a severity which must have seemed strange indeed to the shades of departed politicians. The operation of the New Orleans experiment over a period of twenty years proved that segregation with strict police supervision was unquestionably the best method ever devised for the control of vice. The omnipresent streetwalker was frequently encountered in the respectable portions of the city, and occasionally an assignation house was discovered in forbidden territory, but not more than twenty times in as many years were attempts made to operate open brothels outside the prescribed limits. The day when a New Orleans family might awaken any morning to find that the house next door had been transformed into a bordello ended with the adoption of the Story ordinance — and didn't return until Storyville was abolished. Moreover, even within the district the number of brothels and prostitutes steadily decreased. In 1899, when New Orleans had a population of about 285,-000, Mayor Flower and Chief of Police D. S. Gaster reported that there were in Storyville 230 houses, thirty places of assignation, and approximately 2,000 prostitutes. In 1910, when the Federal Census recorded the population at 339,075, the district contained about 175 houses, including cribs, and fewer than 800 women, of whom almost a hundred, employed in nine cabarets, were only part-time prostitutes. Of the inmates of the brothels, about 250 were Negresses. Only seven octoroons remained, three in Lulu White's house at No. 235 North Basin Street, and four at Countess Willie V. Piazza's, at No. 317 North Basin. The decline of Storyville continued, slowly but surely, for the next several years, and when the district was abolished not more than 100 houses and 450 women were affected. Learned sociologists advanced many profound reasons for these phenomena, which were observed in other American cities as well as in New Orleans, but the principal influences were probably a rising public sentiment, and a radical change in the viewpoint from which pre-marital relations were regarded. There was considerable truth in the classic remark of Countess Willie V. Piazza:

"The country club girls are ruining my business!"

BIBLIOGRAPHY

T HE RESEARCH for this book was done in the Howard Library, the City Archives, newspaper offices, and many private collections in New Orleans, and in various libraries in New York, Chicago, and San Francisco. Following are some of the most helpful of the sources consulted:

ALEXANDER, CAPTAIN SIR J. E., 42nd Royal Highlanders, F.R.G.S., M.R.A.S., etc.: *Transatlantic Sketches, Comprising Visits to the Most Interesting Scenes in North and South America.* Two volumes. London, 1833.

Amended Charter of the City of New Orleans, with Ordinances Passed by the Council of the City of New Orleans, The. Anonymous. New Orleans, 1871.

A No. 1, " THE FAMOUS TRAMP ": *Mother Declassee of the Hoboes.* Erie, Pa., 1918.

ANTHONY, IRVIN: *Paddle Wheels and Pistols.* Philadelphia, 1929.

BERNHARD, HIS HIGHNESS, DUKE OF SAXE-WEIMAR EISENACH: *Travels through North America during the Years 1825 and 1826.* Two volumes. Philadelphia, 1828.

BISPHAM, CLARENCE WYATT, S.T.M.: " Fray Antonio de Sedella," Part II; in the *Louisiana Historical Quarterly,* October 1919.

BOUVAIN, FRANCIS: *Louisiana Almanac for 1867.* New Orleans, n.d.

BROWN, ROBERT, M.A., F.R.G.S., Ph.D., F.L.S.: *The Countries of the World.* Chapter on Louisiana. New York, n.d.

BUEL, J. W.: *Metropolitan Life Unveiled, or the Mysteries and Miseries of America's Great Cities.* San Francisco, 1882.

BURNS, FRANCIS P.: " Charles M. Waterman, Mayor of New Orleans "; in the *Louisiana Historical Quarterly,* July 1924.

BYRNES, THOMAS: *Professional Criminals of America*. New York, 1886.

——: *Professional Criminals of America*, New and Revised Edition. New York, 1895.

CABLE, GEORGE W.: *Strange True Stories of Louisiana*. New York, 1889.

CARRADINE, REV. B., D.D.: *The Louisiana State Lottery Company Examined and Exposed*. New Orleans, 1890.

CASTELLANOS, HENRY C., A.M., LL.B.: *New Orleans as It Was*. New Orleans, 1895.

CHAMBERS, HENRY EDWARD: *A History of Louisiana*. New York, 1925.

CHARNLEY, MITCHELL V.: *Jean Lafitte, Gentleman Smuggler*. New York, 1934.

CLAPP, THEODORE: *Autobiographical Sketches and Recollections during a Thirty-five Years' Residence in New Orleans*. Boston, 1857.

COATES, ROBERT M.: *The Outlaw Years, the History of the Land Pirates of the Natchez Trace*. New York, 1930.

COBB, JOSEPH B.: *Mississippi Scenes, or Sketches of Southern and Western Life and Adventure*. Philadelphia, 1851.

COLLENS, T. W., compiler: *Analytic Digest of the Acts of the Legislature Now in Force, Constituting the City Charter of New Orleans*. New Orleans, 1846.

Correspondence between the American and Italian Governments in Relation to the Killing of Prisoners in New Orleans on May 14, 1891. Washington, 1891.

Creole Tourists' Guide and Sketch Book to the City of New Orleans, The. New Orleans, n.d.

CUSACHS, GASPAR: "Lafitte, the Louisiana Pirate and Patriot"; in the *Louisiana Historical Quarterly*, October 1919.

Dark and Terrible Deeds of George Lathrop, Who, after Passing Through the Various Degrees of Crime, was Finally Convicted and Hung in New Orleans June 5, 1848, for the Robbing and Murder of his Father March 8, 1847, The. Anonymous. New Orleans, 1848.

DART, HENRY P.: "The Smuggler St. Michel"; in the *Louisiana Historical Quarterly*, July 1924.

——: "Politics in Louisiana in 1724"; in the *Louisiana Historical Quarterly*, July 1922.

"Description of New Orleans, A"; in the *Liberty Magazine and American Register*, July 1805.

DEVOL, GEORGE H.: *Forty Years a Gambler on the Mississippi*. New York, 1926.

DICKSON, HARRIS: *The Port of Queer Cargoes and Other Articles on New Orleans*. New Orleans, 1931.

————: " Old New Orleans, a Story-Telling Ramble "; excerpt from *Collier's Weekly*, February 13, 1915.

DIDIMUS, H.: *New Orleans as I Found It*. New York, 1845.

DIMITRY, CHARLES: " Zamba's Plot, a Chapter in the History of New Orleans "; in the *Magazine of American History*, December 1884.

DOUGHTY, FRANCIS ALBERT: " The Under Side of New Orleans "; in *Lippincott's Monthly Magazine*, October 1897.

DYER, ISADORE: *The Municipal Control of Prostitution in the United States*. Reprinted from the *New Orleans Medical and Surgical Journal*. New Orleans, 1899.

ELDRIDGE, BENJAMIN P., and WATTS, WM. B.: *Our Rival the Rascal*. Boston, 1897.

ESKEW, GARNETT LAIDLAW: *The Pageant of the Packets*. New York, 1929.

FARLEY, PHIL: *Criminals of America, or, Tales of the Lives of Thieves, Enabling Everyone to be his Own Detective*. New York, 1876.

Fashions and Consequences as Now Found in High Places and Low Places, by a Minister of Many Travels. Louisiana, 1855.

Figaro, The. Issue of 1884.

FLINT, TIMOTHY: *Recollections of the Last Ten Years*. Boston, 1826.

FLUGEL, FELIX, editor: " Pages from a Journal of a Voyage down the Mississippi to New Orleans in 1817 "; in the *Louisiana Historical Quarterly*, July 1924.

FRÉMAUX, LÉON J.: *New Orleans Characters*. New Orleans, 1876.

GAYARRÉ, CHARLES: *History of Louisiana*. Three volumes. New York, 1854.

GOULD, EMERSON W.: *Fifty Years on the Mississippi*. St. Louis, 1889.

GREEN, JONATHAN: *Gambling Exposed, a Full Exposition of All the Various Arts, Mysteries and Miseries of Gambling*. Philadelphia, 1857.

Guide Book to the City of New Orleans. Anonymous. New Orleans, 1895.

HALL, A. OAKEY: *The Manhattaner in New Orleans, or, Phases of Crescent City Life*. New York and New Orleans, 1851.

HARRIS, LAUNCELOT MINOR: " The Creoles of New Orleans "; in *Southern Collegians*, Washington and Lee University, January 1898.

HARRISON, FAIRFAX: " The Virginians on the Ohio and Mississippi in 1742 "; in the *Louisiana Historical Quarterly*, July 1922.

Historical Sketch Book and Guide to New Orleans and Environs, with articles by George W. Cable, Lafcadio Hearn, and Charles Gayarré.

History of the New Orleans Police Department. Anonymous. New Orleans, 1900.

HOLBROOK, J.: *Ten Years among the Mail Bags*. Philadelphia, 1874.

HOWE, WILLIAM: *Municipal History of New Orleans*. Baltimore, 1889.

Illustrated American. Issue of April 4, 1891.

IRWIN, WILL: " The American Saloon "; in *Collier's Weekly*, February 29, 1908.

JEWELL, EDWIN S.: *Jewell's Crescent City.* New Orleans, 1873.

———: *Charter of the City of New Orleans, Annotated and Indexed.* New Orleans, 1882.

JOHNSON, CLIFTON: *Highways and Byways of the Mississippi Valley.* New York, 1906.

KENDALL, JOHN S.: " The Municipal Elections of 1858 "; in the *Louisiana Historical Quarterly*, July, 1922.

———: " Piracy in the Gulf of Mexico, 1816–1823 "; in the *Louisiana Historical Quarterly*, July 1925.

———: *History of New Orleans.* Three volumes. Chicago, 1922.

KERR, LEWIS: *An Exposition of the Criminal Law of the Territory of New Orleans.* New Orleans, 1806.

KING, GRACE: *New Orleans, the Place and the People.* New York, 1896.

———, and FICKLEN, JOHN R., B.Lit.: *Stories from Louisiana History.* New Orleans, 1905.

KNOX, THOMAS W.: *Underground, or Life Below the Surface.* Hartford, 1875.

LAFARGUE, ANDRÉ: " A Reign of Twenty Days "; in the *Louisiana Historical Quarterly*, July 1925.

Lantern, The. Issues from 1886 to 1889.

LEE, OLIVE: " New Orleans Illustrated "; in the *Period*, January 1898. Dallas, Texas.

Louisiana Scrap Book No. 2; Some Celebrities of New Orleans.

Mafia in New Orleans, The. Collection of pamphlets in the Howard Library.

" Mafia Lynching, The "; in the *New Review*, May 1891.

Manual of the City of New Orleans, 1901 and 1903.

Mascot, The. Issues from 1882 to 1895.

McGINTY, J. J., compiler: *A History of the Great Reform Movement in New Orleans, April 21, 1896.* New Orleans, n.d.

McWATTERS, GEORGE S.: *Detectives of Europe and America, or Life in the Secret Service.* Hartford, 1883.

MERRICK, GEORGE BYRON: *Old Times on the Upper Mississippi.*

MOREL, CHRISTOVAL, Esq., and COLLENS, T. W., By Authority: *A Digest of the Ordinances in Force in Municipality No. One on the 13th May, 1846.* New Orleans, 1846.

New Democrat Illustrated Almanac. Anonymous. New Orleans, 1882.

New Orleans Guide, with a Description of the Routes to New Orleans, etc. Anonymous. New Orleans, 1893.

" New Orleans Mafia Case, The "; in the *American Law Review*, May–June, 1891.

OUDARD, GEORGE: *Four Cents an Acre.* Translated by Margery Bianco. New York, 1931.

PARTON, JAMES: *General Butler in New Orleans, a History of the Administration of the Department of the Gulf in the Year 1862.* New York, 1864.

PEDRICK, W.: *New Orleans as It Is, With a Correct Guide to All Places of Interest.* Cleveland, 1885.

PHELPS, ALBERT: *Louisiana, A Record of Expansion.* Boston and New York, 1905.

Picayune's Guide to New Orleans, Revised and Enlarged. Anonymous. New Orleans, 1905.

——: Tenth edition, 1910.

PICKETT, ALBERT J.: *Eight Days in New Orleans in February 1847.* Montgomery, Alabama, 1847.

POWELL, AARON M.: *State Regulation of Vice.* New York, 1878.

QUINN, JOHN PHILIP: *Fools of Fortune, or Gambling and Gamblers.* Chicago, 1892.

Report of the Select Committee on the New Orleans Riots. Washington, 1867.

RICHARDS, ADDISON, editor: *Appleton's Companion Handbook of Travel, etc.* New York, 1860.

RICHEY, EMMA C., and KEAN, EVELINA P.: *The New Orleans Book.* New Orleans, 1915.

RIGHTOR, HENRY, editor: *Standard History of New Orleans, Louisiana.* New Orleans.

RIPLEY, ELIZA: *Social Life in Old New Orleans.* New York and London, 1912.

ROUSSEL, WILLIS J.: *Jottings of Louisiana.* New Orleans, 1905.

RUSSELL, CHARLES EDWARD: *A-Rafting on the Mississip'.* New York and London, 1928.

RUSSELL, WILLIAM HOWARD: *My Diary, North and South, During the Civil War in America.* London, 1862.

SAXON, LYLE: *Fabulous New Orleans.* New York, 1928.

——: *Father Mississippi.* New York, 1927.

SCROGGS, WILLIAM O.: *Filibusters and Financiers, the Story of William Walker and His Associates.* New York, 1916.

461

SOUTHWOOD, MARION: *Beauty and Booty, the Watchword of New Orleans.* New Orleans, 1867.

SPEAR, THOMAS J.: *Ancient and Modern New Orleans.* New Orleans, 1879.

STAHL: *The New Orleans Sketch Book.* Philadelphia, 1843.

STERLING, JAMES: *Letters from the Slave States.* London, 1857.

Strangers' Guide to the City of New Orleans. Anonymous. New Orleans, 1874.

Terrors of the Sea, as Portrayed in Accounts of Fire and Wreck, and Narratives of Poor Wretches Forced to Abandon Their Floating Homes without Food and Water, Thus Compelling Them to Resort to Cannibalism with Its Attendant Horrors. By an Old Salt. New York, n.d.

Tourists' Guide Book to the City of New Orleans. Tenth Edition. New Orleans, 1910.

TWAIN, MARK: *Life on the Mississippi.*

VAN EVERY, EDWARD: *Sins of America, as "Exposed" by the Police Gazette.* New York, 1931.

Visitors' Handbook of New Orleans. Anonymous. New Orleans, 1884.

WARING, GEORGE E., JR., and CABLE, GEORGE W.: *Social Statistics of Cities.* Washington, 1881.

WARMOTH, HENRY CLAY: *War, Politics and Reconstruction.* New York, 1930.

WILLIAMSON, JEFFERSON: *The American Hotel.* New York, 1930.

WILSON, JAMES GRANT, and FISKE, JOHN, editors: *Appleton's Cyclopedia of American Biography.* Six volumes. New York, 1887.

Files of the New Orleans newspapers, including the *Courrier de la Louisiane,* the *Advertiser,* the *Crescent,* the *Gazette,* the *Bee,* the *Delta,* the *True Delta,* the *Republican,* the *Times,* the *Democrat,* the *Picayune,* the *States,* the *Item,* the *Times-Democrat,* and the *Times-Picayune.*

Files of New York newspapers, including the *Sun,* the *World,* the *Tribune,* and the *Times.*

INDEX

Abadie, Sieur d', 45
Abriel, Pedro, 348, 349
Absinthe House, 135–6
Acadians, 48–9
Actors' Benevolent Association, 327
Adam, Jean, 270–3
Adams, D. W., General, 148
Adams, John, 67
Adams, L., Recorder, 305
Adams, Lionel, 236, 326, 413, 415
Ajona, 264
Alabama (revenue cutter), 168
Alexander, Dr. James, 281, 282
Alexander, Sir James Edward, 8
Allard, Louis, 148
Allen, Abbie, 392, 393
Almonaster y Roxas, Don Andres, 51, 60, 116, 117
Almonaster y Roxas, Michaela, *see* Pontalba, Baroness de
A. L. Shotwell (steamboat), 106
Alton, Josie, *see* Arlington, Josie
Alvarez, 139, 140
Améliorations, Café des, 135, 136
American Law Review, 407
American Theater, 114–15
Amsterdam Dance-House, 332, 345, 346–8, 349
Anderson, Crazy Bill, 334, 335–6, 346

Anderson, Thomas C., 433–5, 442, 450, 451
Antoine, Père, *see* Sedella, Antonio de
Ardotta, Giutano, 409
Arlington, Josie, 448–51
Arlington, Lobrano d', *see* Arlington, Josie
Arlington, the, 435, 448–9, 450, 451
Arlington Annex, 433, 434, 450
Arlington Saloon, 434, 435
Arnold, Benedict, 64
Artful Dodger, the, *see* Kelly, Jim
Astoria Club, 435
Atkinson, Ulric, 417
Atlantic (steamboat), 204
Aubri, Charles, 45

Bachemin, Zach, 277
Badger, A. S., General, 405
Bagnetto, Antonio, 413, 418
Baker, Judge, 413, 415
Baker, Newton D., 451
Baltimore dance-house, the, 345
Banker, May, 402
Banks, Nathaniel P., General, 229
Banks, Thomas, 172
Banks' Arcade, 172–3, 175, 179, 183

i

Barrel-houses, 319–20, 328

Barringer, Daniel M., 181

Barton, Leila, 362

Baumann, Emile, 327

Bayonne, Vincent, 348–9

Bazar, John, 274–5

Beares, George, 366

Beares, James D., Senator, 364–5, 366, 367

Beaudoin, Father, 28

Beauregard, Dr., 259

Beauregard, P. G. T., General, 231, 240, 297

Bee, New Orleans, 286–7, 289, 316

Behan, W. J., Mayor, 235

Behrman, Martin, Mayor, 452, 454

Belleisle, 35

Belmont, Frankie, 425

Béluche, René, 159, 164, 165, 166, 167

Benjamin, Judah P., 287

Benrod, Emile, 437

Bernhardt, Sarah, 438

Bertin, Pierre, 324, 325

Bessel, Fred, 412–13, 420–1

Bienville, Jean Baptiste Le Moyne, Sieur d', 4, 5–7, 8, 9, 10–12, 13, 14, 17, 24, 25–6, 27–9, 30–2, 39, 40, 48, 60, 69, 115, 127, 145, 213, 237, 238, 240, 350, 428

Big Nellie, Miss, 393

Bigelow, Big Tom, 401

Biglow, Horatio, 174

Bismarck, the, concert-saloon, 322

Bispham, Clarence Wyatt, 56

Black Code, 24–5, 49, 69, 127, 238, 257

Black Hand Society, 422–3

Blackbeard, 154, 155

Blackbeard II, 170

Blackleg Cavalry, *see* Wilson Rangers

Blanchard, Newton C., Governor, 423

Blue Anchor dance-house, the, 345

Blue Book, New Orleans, 439, 442, 444–8

Blue Light dance-house, the, 345

Boasso, Theodore J., 398

Boats, river, 74–87, 105–13, 197–8, 209

Boland, D., 408, 409

Bolden, Garibaldi, 403, 404

Boré, Étienne de, Mayor, 33, 69, 95

Bossu, F., 16, 246

Boston Club, 220

Boudousquie, Charles, 123, 125

Bowie, James, 175–7

Bowie, John, 175–6

Bowie, Resin, 175–6

Boyd, Isadore, 348

Boylan, Thomas N., Colonel, 408

Bradford, Justice, 308

Bradford, Margaret, 445

Bradley, Andy, 345

Brady, John T., 451

Bras Coupé, 149, 244–7, 265

Bravo (schooner), 168

Brewster, Robert, 397

Bricktop, *see* Jackson, Mary Jane

Bridget Fury, *see* Swift, Delia

Brown (desperado), 169

Brown, Jessie, 442, 445

Brown, Tom, 207

Buchanan, James, 190

Buckley, Mary, *see* Johnson, Molly

Buel, J. W., 261–5

Buffalo Bill House, 323–4, 325

Bunch, Colonel, 179

Bunch, Eugene, Captain, 402
Burke, Billy, 401
Burr, Aaron, 66–7
Burrows, Rube, 402
Bussey, Frank, 437, 438
Bussey, Willie, 437–8
Butler, A. J., 226, 228
Butler, Benjamin F., General, 52, 140, 225–8
Buys, William de, General, 149, 244, 245

Cabell, W. L., General, 231
Cabildo House, the, 14, 60, 68, 70, 115, 213, 246, 267, 286, 299, 300, 302, 312, 313, 351
Cable, George W., 97, 137, 275–6
Cadillac, Lamothe, 4
Cairo, the, 445
Cajun, see Bussey, Willie
Caldwell, James H., 114
Calvé, Julia, 123
Cambre, Antoine, 274
Canada Bill, see Jones, William
Cannon, Jack, 401, 402
Cannon, John W., Captain, 112, 113
Canonge, J. F., Judge, 249
Canton, Oliver, 345
Canton House, 345
Capdeville, Jean, 324, 325
Capdeville, Paul, Mayor, 454
Capuchins, 20, 41, 42–3, 54–9, 60
Caresse, Pierre, 47
Carmelites, 42
Carol, Miss, 392, 393
Carondelet, Baron de, Governor, 59, 60, 61–2, 66, 72, 116, 254
Carroll, Billy, 212
Carroll, Jimmy, 401
Casa-Calvo, Marquis of, 57

Casey, Anna, 451
Casket girls, 12–13, 19, 149, 204
Cassidy, Charles, 221, 222
Cat Island mutiny, 40–1
Cave-in-Rock, 84
Cervantes, 323
Chameau, Le (ship), 12
Chappell, Holly, 207
Charivaris, 116–17
Charnley, Mitchell V., 157, 176
Charton's, 216
Chevalier, the, 136–7
Chevillon, 270–1
Chicago Belle, 393
Chighizola, 159, 166
Chinee, 437, 438
Chiquita, 445
Cholera epidemic, 291–4
Choppin, Dr. Sam, 194, 195
Christine, Mamie, 425
Christmas, Annie, 82–3, 100, 102; 246, 265
Christy, William, Colonel, 308
Citizens' League of Louisiana, 452
Citizens' Protective Association, 327
City Exchange, 134, 138–40; and see St. Louis Hotel
Claffey, Bill, 319
Claiborne, W. C. C., Governor, 57–8, 69, 71, 145, 146, 162, 164, 165–6
Clan, the (Murrel's), 90–2
Clapp, Theodore, 291–4
Clare, Josephine, 428
Clare, Louis, 397, 398
Clark, Daniel, 68, 145
Clark, Martha, 445
Clark, Patrick, 366–7
Clay, Rev. E. A., 428–9
Clay, Henry, 141, 416

Clovis, 128
Club, the (bagnio), 445
Coates, Robert M., 73, 92
Cobez, Joe, 275
Code Noir, see Black Code
Coffee, General, 166
Cohern, Gib, 199
Colby, Mother, 102, 103, 104, 105, 336
Cole, King, *see* Denham, James Cole
Collier's Weekly, 434
Collins, Ellen, 341–2
Collins, Lizzie, 338–9
Comet (steamboat), 106
Compagnie des Indes, 19; *and see* Mississippi Company, the
Concert-saloons, 319, 320–4, 325–7
Concha, Don José Gutierrez de la, 182
Conclave concert-saloon, the, 322, 323
Condé Street Ballroom, 117–20, 121–2, 133
Constitution (steamboat), 111, 198
Contreras, Juan, 103, 104, 105
Contreras, Rafe, 103, 104, 105
Conway Cabal, 64
Correction girls, 12, 13, 149, 204
Corte, Pasquale, 407
Cotton, John B., Judge, 296–7
Count Lorenzo, *see* Lewis, Lorenzo
Cowbellions, 141
Crazy Bill, *see* Krause, Frederick
Creole, defined, 92
Creole (steamboat), 179, 180
Crescent, New Orleans, 186, 313, 344
Crescent City (steamboat), 185
Crescent Hall Saloon, 193, 327

Crittenden, John, Colonel, 182, 184, 185
Crittenden, John Jordan, Attorney-General, 182
Crockett, Davy, 175, 177
Croquère, Bastile, 151
Crozat, Antoine, 4–5, 23, 24
Cummings, Little Dave, 401
Cunningham, Katherine, *see* Townsend, Kate
Curry, Bill, 105
Curry, John, 219
Curtius, 221
Cuvilier, Alexander, 149

Dallas, George M., 288
Daniels, Josephus, 452
Dante, 264
D'Artaguette, Diron, 26, 27–8, 30–1
Dauphin, Marcel, 151
Davis, Jefferson, 181, 227, 288
Davis, Mrs. Jefferson, 193
Davis, John, 122, 123, 125, 126, 216, 220
Davis, Julia, 365
Davis, Lemuel, Captain, 417–18
Davis, Pierre, 123
Davis, Star, 199
Davis, Toto, *see* Davis, Pierre
Dean, Julia, 439
Decker, Fanny, 425
Deckert, Annie, 425
Dédé, Sanité, 260, 261, 262, 265, 266
Deering, Eunice, 442, 445
Delaney, Crooked Neck, 403
Delisle, Anthony, 270–3
Delsa, George, 435
Delsa, Irene, 435–6
Delta, New Orleans, 183, 315, 415

Democrat, Louisville, 179
Denegre, Walter D., 417
Denham, James Cole, Captain, 171
Desfargues, Jean, 168
De Soto Hotel, 322
Deubler, Mary, *see* Arlington, Josie
Deubler, Peter, 449
Devereaux, Jack, 204
Devereaux, Tom, 405
Devol, George, 207, 208–9, 210–12, 222–3, 224, 225, 228
Diamond Tooth, the, *see* Emmette, Queen
Diana (steamboat), 106
Diana and Norma, 445
Dick, John, 165
Dix, Gertrude, 435, 445, 453
Dixie: origin of name, 81
Dog-fighting, 332–4
Dominique, Captain, *see* You, Dominique
Donnelly, Captain, 281
Doran, S. A., Major, 233, 234
Douglas, Stephen A., 204
Doville, Mme, 12
Dreyfus, Louise, 445
Dubreuil, 33
Dueling, 118, 142–53, 192
Duffy, Charley, 345
Duffy, One-Legged, *see* Rich, Mary
Duffy, Yorker, 334
Dumas, 128
Duncan, Johnson Kelly, Captain, 298–9, 302, 303, 304, 306, 307, 308, 312, 313–14
Dunn, Oscar J., 208, 277
Dupuy, 203
Duroux, 40–1
Dutch Jake, 212
Duvergier, 13–14, 15

Early, Jubal A., General, 231
Eden concert-saloon, the, 322
Elkin's, 216
Emerson, Billy, 334
Émigrés, Café des, 137
Emmett, D. D., 81
Emmette, Queen, 442
English Turn, 39–40, 170
Enterprise (steamboat), 106
Esposito, Giuseppi, 407–9, 411
Eugénie, Empress, 125
Evans, May, 441
Exilés, Café des, 137

Farragut, David Glasgow, Admiral, 52, 69, 140, 208, 223, 224, 225, 312, 314, 319
Farrar, Edgar H., 412, 417
Farrell, M. J., 406
Fellowes, C., 303–4, 306, 307
Fifty, Committee of, 412
Fightin' Mary, 390
Filibustering, 172–96, 203
Fink, Mike, 81, 82
Fireproof Coffee-House, 331
Fires, great, in New Orleans, 53–4, 59–60, 101
Firm, the (bagnio), 444–5
Fisher, Clara, 368
Fisher, Thomas F., Colonel, 187–8
Fitzgerald, Jimmy, 199
Flaugeac, de, General, 166
Fleury, Laurent, 342, 343
Flower, Walter C., Mayor, 412, 454, 455
Flugel, J. G., 107–8, 109–10, 198, 244
Fluger, 84–5
Flynn, Bill, 234
Flynn, Frank, 234
Flynn, John, 234

Ford, Patrick, 397
Ford, Thomas J., 397
Forno, Henry, Colonel, 303, 311
Forrester, Billy, 401
Foster, Murphy J., Governor, 399
Foucault, 45
Fozatte, Mary, 392
Frank, Helen, 428
Frank Leslie's Illustrated News-paper, 415
Frank Pargoud (steamboat), 112, 113
Franklin, Bill, 232
Frederico, Lawrence, 422
Freeman, Carrie, 425
French Opera House, 125
French Quarter, the: original bounds, 14
Frénière, Nicolas Chauvin de la, 45, 47
Freret, William, 302
Fresh, Lady, 393
Fulton, Robert, 105–6, 107

Gaëtano, 97–8
Gaines, James, Colonel, 174
Gallus Lu, 390
Gálvez, Bernardo de, Governor, 53, 62–3, 254
Gambi, Vincent, 159, 160, 166, 167
Gambling, 197–223, 228–36
Garbright, Nettie, 442
Garcia, Francisco, 246–7
Gaspar, Nellie, 389–90
Gaster, D. S., 455
Gates, Horatio, 64
Gayarré, Charles, 15–16, 20, 21–3, 25, 27–8, 38, 42–3, 56, 60, 128, 142–3
Gazette, Baton Rouge, 146

Gem concert-saloon, the, 322, 367
Georgina (bark), 179, 180
Gertie, Queen, *see* Livingston, Gertrude
Gertrude, Sister, 12
Gibson, John, 397
Gildemeister, 244
Girod, Nicholas, Mayor, 170
Glapion, Christophe, 266
Globe-Democrat, St. Louis, 421
Glover, Hannah, 387–8
Gonzales, Ambrosio, General, 178–9, 182
Gonzales, Antonia, 442, 444
Gorman, Sam, 324
Gottschalk, Louis Moreau, 243
Gould, Annie, 281
Graithe, Alexander, 149
Grampin, 214–15
Grand Opera House, 438
Gray Sisters, 12
Green, Jonathan, 215
Green Book, or, Gentlemen's Guide to New Orleans, The, 442
Green Tree Dance-House, 336, 345–6, 349
Gregg, Hotel, 402
Gregson, Harry, 437, 438
Grey, Annie, 233
Grymes, John R., Colonel, 162–3, 165, 217
Guerin, Paddy, 401
Guillotte, J. Valsin, Mayor, 235, 398–9, 402
Gutierrez, Bernardo, 173

Haas, Heinrick, 274
Habanero, 185
Habar, Salvador, 332, 334
Hachard, Madeleine, 17–18, 19
Hackett, Johnny, 335

Hagan, Richard, 147
Hale, Edward Everett, 173
Haley, Blue, 404
Haley, Nellie, 392, 439
Haley, Red, 404
Half-Way House, 193, 194, 195
Hall, John M., 356
Hamilton, " Colonel," 365
Hamilton, Edna, 447
Hamilton, Hattie, 364, 365–7, 378, 387, 435
Hanly (owner of dog pit), 332
Happy Charley, 359
Hare, Joseph Thompson, 88
Hargraves, Dick, 202, 203, 204
Harman, Alderman, 429
Harpe, Micajah, 88
Harpe, Wiley, 88–9
Hartman, Maud, 445
Hastings, Solomon, 281
Haunted Saloon, 252
Hayes, Rutherford B., 395
Haymarket dance-hall, the, 438
Hayne, Frank B., 417
Hearn, Lafcadio, 97
Heley, J. J., 362
Henderson, John, Senator, 173, 178–9, 180
Hennessy, David C., 405, 406, 408–9, 410, 411, 412–21
Hennessy, Mike, 405–6, 408–9
Henry, Thomas, 417
Henry, Thomas, Colonel, 191–6, 308
Hewlett, James, 138, 140, 141
Hewlett's Exchange, 138, 139, 216
Hicks, 138
Hines, Mary E., see Reed, Abbie
Hinkley, Abraham M., 382, 386
Hobgood, Carl, Colonel, 402
Hoffmire, Gertrude, 435

Holland, John, Sheriff, 251
Holland, Kendrick, 387–8
Holmes, D. H., 290
Holy Brotherhood, the, see Santa Hermandad, the
Honduras National Lottery, 230
Houlihan, Irish, 402
House of All Nations, 447
House of Rest for Weary Boatmen, 101, 105, 336
Houston, James D., 397, 417, 418
Howell, Joe, Major, 193–5
Howell, Richard, 193
Hoyle, 205
Hueston, 146–7
Hulburt, Stephen A., General, 229
Humble, James, 144–5
Hurley, John, 404

Iberville, Pierre Le Moyne, Sieur d', 4, 5
Icarus (warship), 190
Incardona, Bastion, 413, 415, 418
Indian Father, The, 34
Inquisition, the, 20, 55, 56, 57
Irwin, Lillian, 448
Irwin, Will, 434
Italian Vigilance Committee, 422
Item, New Orleans, 435, 451, 454

Jack, Dr., 258–9
Jackson, Andrew, 14, 52, 70, 135–6, 137, 156, 165–6, 167, 204
Jackson, David, 367
Jackson, Lou, 281, 282
Jackson, Mary Jane, 340–2, 343–4
Jackson, Nina, 441–2
Jacques, John A., Colonel, 311
Jennings, Harry, 332, 333, 334
Jesuits, 41, 42–3

Jesuits and Capuchins, War of the, 41–3
Joe the Whipper, 389
John, Dr., 257, 258
John, Joe, 403
Johnson, Bascom, 452
Johnson, Emma, 392, 394, 447
Johnson, Kitty, 362
Johnson, Molly, 373–4, 377
Johnson, Robert, 168
Jones, William (Canada Bill), 207, 208–10
Jordan, Little Louise, 401
Joseph (Negro counterfeiter), 37
Josephine Icebox, see Clare, Josephine
Jousset, Claude, 28

Kearnaghan, Peter, 368
Keeley, Pat, 403
Kelly, Jim, 401, 402
Kendall, John S., 226, 284, 286, 294
Kent, George, 345
Keppler, 334
Kerlerec, Louis Billouart de, 38, 39, 41, 43–4, 45
Kerlerec, Mme, 39
Keys, Charley, 342–3
Kidney-Foot Jenny, 390
Killeen, Josephine, 364
King, F. D., Judge, 453
King, Grace, 33, 59, 126, 127, 128, 132, 157
King Cole, see Denham, James Cole
Knuckley, Bill, 334, 336, 346
Knuckley, Mike, 334, 336, 346
Krause, Frederick, 105
Kuhn, Ambrose, 399
Kuhn, Mary Catherine, 399

Kuneman, Counters, see Reed, Abbie
Kuneman, Jules, 426

Labouisse, H. R., 417
La Branche, Alcee, 146–7
Labruzzo, Tony, 408, 409
Lac, Perrin du, 16, 246
Lacomb, Emile, 437–8
Lacroix, 128
Lafayette, 248
Lafitte, Jean, 136, 156–68, 169, 170, 172, 174–6, 179, 217, 338
Lafitte, Pierre, 157, 158, 159, 161, 162, 163, 164, 165, 166, 167, 168
La Frénière, see Frénière, Nicolas Chauvin de la
Lagerbeer, Charley, 334
La Harpe, 24
Lahey family, 319
Lalaurie, Delphine, 247–51
Lalaurie, Louis, 247, 249, 250, 251
Lamana, Peter, 422
Lamana, Walter, 422
Lambert, Fanny, 444
Lantern, New Orleans, 388
Larkin, see Cassidy, Charles
Larney, John, 401
Larrimore, Representative, 217
La Salle, 4
La Sère, Emile, 146
Latizar, Ferdinand, 72
Latour, Malvina, 270, 276–7, 278, 280, 282
Lauraine, Augustus, 221, 222
Laussat, Pierre Clément de, Prefect, 68–9, 95, 213, 254
Laveau, Marie, 265–70, 272, 273–4, 275–6, 277, 280, 383
Law, John, 3, 5, 9

Lawler, Johnny, 211
Leary, Red, 401
Leathers, Thomas P., Captain, 112
Lee, Robert E., 181
Lee, William, 336, 346
Lefebvre, Felix, 249
Legendre, Marie, 266
Legoaster, 128
Lehde, George, 403
Lehman, Conrad, 346–7
Leigh, Madge, 425
Le Moyne, Jean Baptiste, see Bienville, Jean Baptiste Le Moyne, Sieur d'
Le Moyne, Pierre, see Iberville, Pierre de Moyne, Sieur d'
Leoni, 407–8
Leoni (lugger), 408
Leslie, Miss, 444
Lester, Madge, 442
Lesueur, Pierre, 27, 28
Levy, Sally, 425
Levy, Sam, 221
Lewis, John L., General, 147, 295, 301, 302–5, 312
Lewis, Lorenzo, 221
Lewis, Micajah, 145–6
Lewis, Tommy, 334
Lillie, Chris, 288, 294
Lincoln (employee of W. G. Stephens), 385, 386
Lindsay, Joseph, 274
Little Annex, the, 447–8
Live Oak Boys, 330–1, 334–6, 340, 346, 347
Livingston, Edward, 162–3, 165
Livingston, Gertrude, 426, 427, 428
Livingston, Robert R., 106, 162
Lloyd, Grace, 447
Lobrano, Josie, see Arlington, Josie

Lobrano, Philip, 449
Lockerby, Albert, 334
Lockerby, Charley, 334
Lodi, Olga, 447
Long, James, General, 174–5
Long Charley, 340
Longfellow, 361
Looney, 324
Lop-Eared Kid, see Wilson, Charley
Lopez, Narciso, General, 177–80. 181–4, 185, 186
Lottery, see Louisiana Lottery
Louis, Jean, 60
Louis XVI, King of France, 62
Louisiana Ballroom, 274
Louisiana Federation of Women's Clubs, 454
Louisiana Gazette, The, 72
Louisiana Historical Society, 6
Louisiana Legion, 169
Louisiana Lottery, 219, 229–31
Louisiana Tigers, 185
Lovell, Mansfield, General, 224
Lowe, Jack, 334, 346
Lozières, Baudry des, 17, 246
Ludlow, N., 122
Lulla, Pépé, 151–2, 186–7
Luzenberg, C. C., 452
Lynch, Barry, 334
Lyons, Frank, 404
Lyons, Jack, 334, 335, 336, 404
Lyons, Ned, 401
Lyons, Sophie, 401

Macheca, Joseph, 413, 415
Mackey, Tom, 199
MacPherson, Edward, 306
Maddox, Dr., 176–7
Madeleine, Sister, see Hachard, Madeleine

Mader, Prussian Charley, 403
Madison, James, 166, 167
Mafia, the, 406–22, 424
Magee, Augustus, 173
Mahogany Hall, 425
Maison Coquet, 68
Maloney, George, 400
Mansfield, Mother, 392
Marchesi, Antonio, 413
Marchesi, Asperi, 413, 415, 418
Mardi Gras, 141, 350, 352, 448
Marie, Sister, 12
Marigny, Bernard, 144–5
Marigny, Mandeville, 149
Marigny family, 172, 217
Maroney, Jim, 403
Marquis, Pierre, 47
Marshall, Mattie, 425
Martin, Joe, 403
Martineau, Harriet, 130–1
Martinez, Ollie, 439–40
Mascot, New Orleans, 365, 367, 378, 388, 392–3, 394, 396, 425, 428, 429, 439–40, 450
Mason, Molly, 347
Mason, Samuel, 88
Maspero, Pierre, 137, 138, 139
Maspero's Exchange, 137–8, 172, 175
Masters, Aleck, 103–4
Matches, Mollie, *see* Larney, John
Mather, Joseph, Mayor, 127
Mather, T. D., 417
Matranga, Charles, 409, 410, 411, 413, 415, 418
Matranga, Tony, 409, 410, 411
Mays, Sam, 88–9
Mazaret, Eugene, Captain, 256–7
McArdle, W. H., Colonel, 146
McBride, Bob, 105
McCarty family, 247

McCarty's Ranch, 387
McCord, Mrs. V. E. W., 189
McDonald, Tom, 403
McDuffie, John, 402
McEnery, Samuel D., Governor, 327, 398, 404
McGittigan, Tommy, 400
McGrath, Price, 220–1, 222
McLane, Jim, 199
McLern, 373, 374
Mealey, Patrick, 396, 397, 398
Merritt, Annie, 425
Merwin, Samuel B., 417
Milhet, Joseph, 47
Miller, Charles P., 233
Miller, John, 342–4
Mills, Clark, 52
Miner, Jim, 206–7
Minnie Haha, 361–2, 436
Miró, Don Estevan de, 20, 53, 54–5, 56, 63, 64, 65, 66, 127, 129, 145
Mississippi Bubble, the, 9–10; *and see* Mississippi Company, the
Mississippi Company, the, 3, 4, 5, 7, 9–10, 11–12, 13, 15, 17, 19, 23, 24, 26, 28, 32, 36, 42, 213
Mochlin, 295
Monasterio, Pietro, 413, 416
Moniteur de la Louisiane, Le, 72
Monk, *see* Bussey, Frank
Monroe, James, 168
Monroe, John T., Mayor, 227, 312, 316, 386
Montegut, Edgar, Mayor, 257–8
Montiro, 221
Mooney, James, 408, 409
Moore, Thomas O., Governor, 224
Morgan (operator of the Green Tree), 345
Morgan, Sir Henry, 154

Moss, 381
Mowry, John, 72
Mullen, James, 274
Mumford, W. B., 226
Murphy, Archie, 338, 339, 340, 341, 345
Murphy, Cap, 397
Murphy, John, 397
Murphy, Louisa, 391
Murphy, Margaret, 403
Murray, Tom, 342–3
Murrel, John A., 89–92
Mutine, La (ship), 12
Mystic Krew of Comus, 141

Napoleon, 159, 170
Napoleon concert-saloon, the, 322
Natchez (steamboat), 112–13
Natchez Trace, 87–92
National Theater, 322
Nelson, Dr. H. L., 327
New El Dorado concert-saloon, the, 322
New Orleans (steamboat), 105–6, 107–10
Newhouse, Tom, 400
Nez Coupé, *see* Chighizola
Nicaraguense, El, 186
Nicholls, Francis T., Governor, 395, 404, 405
Noailles, Sieur de, 31
Nolan, Philip, 173
Norton, M. O. H., 304
Noyan, Jean Baptiste, 45, 46, 47, 48
Nuñez, Don Vincente, 53

Oakey, S. L., Colonel, 147–8
Oaks, the, 148–50, 152
O'Brien, Hugh, 334
O'Brien, Hugh, Jr., 334–5

O'Brien, Jimmy, 330–1, 334
O'Brien, Mary, 425
O'Brien, Matt, 334–5
O'Brien, Monk, 402
O'Brien, Tom, 233
O'Connor, William J., Captain, 411
O'Donnell, Don Leopold, 178
Ogden, H. B., 417
Ogden, R. N., 306
O'Hara, Theodore, Colonel, 178–9, 180
O'Leary, Steve, 295
O'Malley, Dominick C., 413–15, 416
One-Eyed Sal, 390
One Hundred, Committee of, 395, 397–8
O'Neil, Dan, 332, 347–8
O'Reilly, Don Alexander, Governor, 46, 47, 48, 49, 50, 51, 52–3, 60, 127
Orléans, Philippe II, Duke of, 6, 9
Orléans, Théâtre d', 122–5, 126, 133, 135, 216
Orleans Artillery, 169
Orleans Ballroom, 125–6, 133–5, 140, 216
Orleans Gazette, 95
Oster, Phil, 402, 403
Otero, Richard, Judge, 451
Oyster Johnny, 324

Packard, Stephen B., 395
Palmerston, Lord, 227
Pampero (steamer), 183, 184, 185
Paris, Jacques, 266
Parker, John M., 417
Parkerson, William S., 417, 418–20

Parton, James, 225, 226
Patorno, Philip J., 422
Patterson, Commodore, 164–5
Pauger, 14, 17
Paulding, Hiram, Commodore, 190
Pauline (mulatto slave), 257, 258
Pavillon concert-saloon, the, 322
Paydras, Julien, 62
Pedro, Don, 257
Peel, Fanny, 389
Périer, Governor, 21
Perritt, Henry, 220, 222
Perritt Guards, 222
Petrie, Henry, 334
Petrie, Redhead, 334
Petrie, Whitehead, 334
Phelps, Albert, 9–10, 24–5
Phillips, Robert, 366–7
Phillips, Tilly, 365
Philomene, Mary, 374
Phoenix, the, 444
Piazza, Countess Willie V., 447, 455
Picayune, New Orleans, 105, 171, 200, 245, 272, 297, 335–6, 344, 354, 370, 375, 386, 389, 396, 398, 399
Picayune House, 387
Pickett, Emma, 356–7
Pickett, Tom, 346, 349
Pierce, Franklin, 188
Pierson, N. H., 417
Pig-Trough Carrie's, 387
Pinch, *see* Pinchback, Pinckney
Pinchback, Pinckney Benton Stewart, 207–8
Pitot, James, 58
Pizzaro (warship), 180
Pizzini's Café, 374
Plug, Colonel, 84–5, 197

Plume, John J., 365, 367
Plume, Samuel W., 365
Police Gazette, 439
Politz, Manuel, 413, 415, 416, 418
Polk, James K., 288
Pollock, Oliver, 52–3
Pontalba, Baroness de, 51–2
Pontalba, Xavier Delfair, Baron de, 51
Pouilly, J. N., 138
Poulaga, 152
Powell, John, 202, 203–5
Poydras, Julien, 72
Pradat's, 216
Prieur, Dennis, Mayor, 146, 246
Prostitution, 68, 99, 102, 105, 214, 337–40, 344, 347–8, 350–94, 424–37, 439–55
Provenzano, George, 409–10
Provenzano, Joe, 409–10, 411
Provenzano, Peter, 409–10, 411
Putnam, 382

Quadroon, defined, 126–9
Quadroon Balls, 126, 131, 132, 133–5, 142, 242
Quinn, John Philip, 219–20
Quitman, John A., Governor, 173, 178, 180, 182, 183

Radzo, *see* Esposito, Giuseppi
Railly, William, 452
Randella, Snooks, 445
Rassac, Redon de, 36
Razzy Dazzy Spasm Band, the, *see* Spasm Band
Red Light Liz, 389
Red Shoe, 27
Redeck, Peter, 257, 258
Reed, Abbie, 426–7
Reed, Annie, 362

Refugés, Café des, 137
Regulators, 92
Republican, New Orleans, 317, 323, 325
Rice, Harry, 345
Rich, Mary, 345
Richard, Lady, 393
Rider, Jim, 105
Ringrose, W. B., 425
Ripley, Beulah, 449
Rivers, R. J., 142
Rivoire, Emile, 153
Robert E. Lee (steamboat), 106, 112–13
Robin, Abbé Claude C., 212–13
Robinson, Al, 212
Robinson, Gil, 212
Robinson, Jack, 438
Robinson, Mary, *see* Sweet, Fanny
Robinson's Circus, 212
Rochambeau, Count, 212
Rochemore, 39, 45
Roffignac, Count Louis Philippe de, Mayor, 101, 240
Rogers, Jim, 105
Roman, André L., 153
Rosalie (would-be Voodoo queen), 265
Rose, Rev. Mr., 407–8
Rosière, Gilbert, 151, 152
Ross, Etta, 442
Rouvillière, Michel de la, 34–5, 36, 37
Royal, Hotel, 142, 402
Royal Palace Beer Saloon, 322, 327
Russell, Blanche, 362
Russell, Sir William Howard, 316–17
Russell, White Pine, 399
Rynders, Isaiah, Captain, 288

Safety, Committee of, 395–6
St. Charles Hotel, 140, 142, 146, 189, 290, 311, 401
St. Cyr's, 216
Saint-Louis, Sister, 12
St. Louis Cathedral, 14, 55, 60, 118, 126, 148, 267, 268, 270, 272
St. Louis Hotel, 134, 138, 139, 140–2
St. Mary (sloop of war), 188, 189, 193
St. Nicholas concert-saloon, the, 320–2
St. Philip Theater, 122, 133, 152
St. Pierre Theater, 72, 133
Salazar, Joachim, 72
Salcedo, Don Manuel de, Governor, 68, 118–19, 120
Salizar, Ferdinand, 72
Salmon, Norvell, Commander, 190–1
Sans-Regret, La, 12
Santa Anna, General, 177
Santa Hermandad, the, 49–50, 60
Santini, Joseph, 139–40
Sauvinet, 158, 166–7
Saxe-Weimar, Bernhard, Duke of, 122, 132–3, 134, 135
Saxon, Lyle, 55–6, 126–7, 134, 142, 151, 282–3
Scaffedi, Antonio, 413, 416
Schaumberg, Colonel, 149
Schneider, Mme, 390
Schoenhausen, Otto Henry, 327
Schwartz, Emma, 435
Schwarz, *see* Lobrano, Philip
Sedella, Antonio de, 20, 54–5, 56–8
Sedley, Bill, 81–2, 98, 103, 104–5
Seidensahl, Joe, 341–2

Semmes, Thomas J., 413

Sentinel, Vicksburg, 148

Seraphine (schooner), 170

Setton, *see* Harpe, Wiley

Seuzeneau, Recorder, 271

Seventeen, Committee of, 395, 398

Seward, William H., 227

Shakespeare, Joseph, Mayor, 234, 235, 236, 396, 404–5, 406, 412, 421, 426

Shakespeare Plan, 234, 235

Shaw, Jimmy, 333

Shepard, Rash, 403

Shepley, George F., Governor, 228, 344

Sherwood, James, 220, 222

Slidell, John M., 287–8

Smith, C. Pinckney, Justice, 179

Smith, Izzard, 386

Smith, Jack, 346

Smith, Kate, 364

Smith, Lena, 393

Smith, Lieutenant-Colonel, 179

Smith, Lizette, 447–8

Smith, Mary, 448

Smith, Peter, 274

Smith's European Circus, 389

Society for the Prevention of Cruelty to Children, 428

Sol, Dr., 281

Spanish Agnes, 392–3

Spasm Band, 437–8

Spencer, May V., 447

Spiders, the, 402

Spirit of the Times, New York, 221

Squier, *see* Bras Coupé

Stag saloon, 434

Stalebread Charley, *see* Lacomb, Emile

Starr, Charles, Colonel, 200–1

States, New Orleans, 362, 364–5, 369, 374–5, 403

Steadman, Charles, *see* Gorman, Sam

Stein, Charlie, 437

Stephens, William G., 384–6

Stewart, La Belle, 450

Stewart, Virgil, 91

Stewart, Yellow Henry, 402, 403, 404

Stith, Gerard, 297, 309, 310

Stockholm dance-house, the, 345

Stoppagherra Society, 406; *and see* Mafia, the

Story, Sidney, 403, 433, 454

Storyville, 430–55

Strauss, Hattie, 364

Strong, George C., 227

Struve, Billy, 434–5

Studio, the, 392, 447

Summers, H. M., 311, 312, 356

Sunday Sun, New Orleans, 439, 440–2

Sure Enuf Hotel, 102, 103–4, 105, 336

Susan Loud (brig), 179, 180

Swamp, the, 100–5, 159, 328, 336, 350, 390, 403

Swan, Bill, 331, 332, 333, 334–5, 336

Sweet, Fanny, 364, 378–87

Swift, Delia, 341, 344–5

Sykes, Treville Egbert, 372–3, 374–8

Sylvester, George, 403, 404

Tammany Hall, 288

Taney, Gus, 372

Taylor, Zachary, 178

Teetzmann, 244

Theurer, Madeleine, 440

Thimecourt, Captain, 152
Thomas, Jerry, Professor, 140
Thompson, Henry, 330–1, 334
Thompson, Maggie, 368, 369
Thompson, Mary, 391–2
Thornton, Thomas, 332, 333
Tilden, Samuel J., 395
Times, New Orleans, 125, 135, 268–70, 322, 333, 336–8, 344, 347, 349, 358, 360, 361, 362, 364, 366, 406
Times-Democrat, New Orleans, 281, 404
Times-Picayune, New Orleans, 452
Tivoli concert-saloon, the, 322
Tom the Dog, *see* McDonald, Tom
Tomasi, Chevalier, 149–50
Torrence, Cecile, 427–8
Toto, Lady Beulah, 393
Toussaint's, 216
Townsend, Kate, 360–1, 362, 364, 366, 368–78, 387, 435, 436, 448
Trait d'Union, New Orleans, 153
Travis, William Barret, 175, 177
Tribune, New York, 315, 407
Tropic, New Orleans, 146
True Delta, New Orleans, 222, 295, 298, 315–16, 318–19, 378–9, 380, 381–2, 383, 384, 386, 406
Tuckers, John, 168
Tugman, Tom, 332, 333
Turner, Rev. Mr., 276–7
Turpin's Cabaret, 172
Turpo, 404
Twenty-One, 364, 366, 367

Ulloa, Don Antonio de, 45, 46
Umbrella Jim, 206–7
Unión, La, New Orleans, 185

Unzaga, Don Luis de, 52
Ursulines, 17–19

Valdes, Don Geronimo, 178
Valdeterre, Druot de, 19–20
Vanderbilt, Commodore, 188
Vaudreuil, Mme de, 35, 39
Vaudreuil, Pierre Rigaut, Marquis de, 3, 32, 33–6, 37, 38, 39, 40, 127, 213, 238–9
Vesta (brig), 187
Vesuvius (steamboat), 106
Victor, General, 68
Vieux Carré, *see* French Quarter
Vigilance Committee: first, 298–314, 316; second, 395–6
Villeneuve, Le Blanc de, 34
Villere, Gabriel, Sheriff, 417–18
Villeré, Jacques, Governor, 96
Villeré, Joseph, 46, 47
Vinton, Josie, 427–8
Voodoo, 243, 254–83, 378, 383, 386

Wabash (frigate) 190
Wacousta (steamboat), 207
Waddell, Reed, 233
Waggaman, George A., 146
Walker, Joe, 193, 326–7
Walker, William, 184, 186–7, 188–91, 192, 195, 196, 302, 308, 382
Walla, Willie, 402
Wallack's Theater, New York, 189
Walmsley, S. P., 417
Walsh, Billy, 362
Walsh, Father Patrick, 57
Walsh, Recorder, 366
Warm Gravy, 437, 438
Warmoth, H. C., Governor, 208, 275, 325

Warrington House, 252
Washington, *see* Yah Yah, Dr.
Washington (steamboat), 111
Washington, George, 64, 162
Washington Ballroom, 122, 133; *and see* St. Philip Theater
Waterman, Charles M., Mayor, 297, 301, 302, 303–5, 306–8, 309–11, 312, 316, 356
Waters, Molly, 393
Watkins, George, Mayor, 95
Watson, Dutch Freddy, 401
Wayne, Anthony, 66
Web, the, 402
Weinthal, Bertha, 447
Wells, Samuel, 176–7
Welsh, Paddy, 345–6
Wenger's Garden, 323
West End, 438
Wet Grave, the, 8
Wheat, Robert, Colonel, 179, 180, 181–2, 184
Whisky, *see* Benrod, Emile
White, Benny, 200
White, George M., Major, 202–3
White, Jim, 372
White, Jimmy, 200
White, Lulu, 425–6, 455
White, Minnie, 447
White, Napoleon Bonaparte, 199–200
White League, 141–2, 395, 404
Wickliffe, John C., 415, 417, 418, 420

Wickliffe, Robert C., Governor, 296
Wilkinson, James, 64–7, 69
Williams, Alice, 447
Williams, America, 341–2
Williams, Bison, 323, 324, 350
Williams, Molly, 364
Williams, Nellie, 425
Williams, Red Sam, 171
Williams, Sam, 199
Wilson, Bully, 84, 85, 197
Wilson, Charley, 401
Wilson, Red Bill, 330
Wilson, Tug, 400–1
Wilson, William, 346
Wilson Rangers, 222–4, 225
Winterhalter, 125
Woman Order, General Butler's, 226–7
World, New York, 252–3
Wright (English cotton-buyer), 147, 148
Wright, Norris, Major, 177

Yah Yah, Dr., 258
Yellow-fever epidemic, 291, 294
Yellow Henry gang, 402, 403–4
You, Dominique, 159, 164, 165, 166, 167, 169–70
Young Men's Democratic Association, 404–5

Zozo, 262–4